SAINT AUGUSTINE OF HIPPO

Also by Miles Hollingworth

The Pilgrim City: St Augustine of Hippo and his Innovation in Political Thought

Saint Augustine of Hippo

An Intellectual Biography

Miles Hollingworth

BLOOMSBURY
LONDON • NEW DELHI • NEW YORK • SYDNEY

First published in Great Britain 2013

Copyright © Miles Hollingworth, 2013

The moral right of the author has been asserted

No part of this book may be used or reproduced in any manner whatsoever without written permission from the Publisher except in the case of brief quotations embodied in critical articles or reviews. Every reasonable effort has been made to trace copyright holders of material reproduced in this book, but if any have been inadvertently overlooked the Publishers would be glad to hear from them.

A Continuum book

Bloomsbury Publishing Plc
50 Bedford Square
London WC1B 3DP

www.bloomsbury.com

Bloomsbury Publishing, London, New Delhi, New York and Sydney

A CIP record for this book is available from the British Library.

ISBN 978 14411 737 20

10 9 8 7 6 5 4 3 2 1

Typeset by Fakenham Prepress Solutions, Fakenham, Norfolk NR21 8NN

Printed and bound in Great Britain by CPI Group (UK) Ltd, Croydon CR0 4YY

To Dad
– For all the conversations that stayed the course

Contents

	Preface	ix
	Acknowledgements	xiii
	Chronology of the main events in Augustine's life covered in this book	xv
1	Out of Africa	1
2	Augustine's intellectual milieu	11
3	Augustine's remarks on his parents	38
4	Reflections on infancy	58
5	Traumas of initiation into the Earthly City	85
6	Cicero and a sense of purpose	105
7	Manichaeism	127
8	On the singular deportment of death, love and grief	142
9	Christian conversion and reflections on the supernatural	171
10	To write against self-consciousness and its effects	204
11	Last days and reflections on the style of man	241
	Abbreviations of Augustine's writings	255
	Notes	261
	Index	307

Preface

In writing this book I have had the sensation of having written the story of one of the world's great novelists.

To the specialist as much as to the lay reader, Augustine ranks as one of the major sights of Western late antiquity. He is on the itinerary of anyone who wants to understand how the dying fall of the Roman Empire incorporated Christianity, and became out of that the outlook and ethos of the Dark Ages. He trained to become a professional teacher of rhetoric – he very quickly became one of the very best of his generation. But his heart lay with philosophy and the academic study of wisdom. Later, as a Christian, he was quickly promoted to bishop of Hippo Regius: and from that moment his talent with words became called to the defence of Christian orthodoxy in the Church's formative and uncertain age. But the forensic analysis of religious faith interested him little. And his vast production of devotional and apologetic material was put out at an astonishing pace – he averaged nearly two books a year for the 44 years of his adult working life. This does not include his hundreds of sermons and letters, or his monumental exegesis of the Psalms.

What did interest him truly was what has always interested the great novelists. This is the single story that is contained within every human story. The story of how, as high-born creatures of intellect and volition, we battle the indignities of flesh and death. And how out of that battle we keep a foot in either camp, a little in heaven, a little in hell. In other words, we do what the gods cannot do in the traditional constellations of their fixed brilliance. It is this overcoming aspect of the human race that Augustine so persistently identified as the tension – as even the fragility – of beauty and truth whenever we touch these things in writing and art. The gods are lights in the firmament. It is true that they can descend to sport with humans, and often have done so; but when they do, it is by replicating the regular geometries of human nature and attraction. What they cannot do is summon up the wilfulness and irrationality of human love. They are simply too all-seeing for that. As the Presocratic philosopher Xenophanes put it, 'everything of god is without toil'. Augustine knew especially well that each human story is a narrative poised, and tight, between the animal and the sublime. At either end it shares bulk with these destinations, but in that snap-taught middle bit, it expresses the angst and panics of abandonment. Only man must love his Maker out of an exile's understanding. Only an exile's understanding can bring out (somehow and mysteriously) the fairness and rightness of a predestinated universe.

When Augustine had the time and leisure to write at his own bidding he produced his unique autobiography, his *Confessions*. This was instantly taken up as a classic and has remained on the lists of the Western Greats – a book ahead of its time: critical, psychological, and intimating the unconscious. But in saying all of this I am thinking really of his other signature work: his *magnum opus* composed over 13 years: his *City of God*. This book brooked few of the methodological considerations that make for a modern work of theology, or philosophy, or history. It is as wide open to criticism as any of those. But in its own time, and for centuries afterwards, it was simply many people's favourite book – most famously the Emperor Charlemagne's. And they read it like we read Tolstoy's *War and Peace* today; turning page after page, staying up late, wondering how it all comes out. The setting was Rome in the early fifth century; and the backdrop was one of the symbolic military disasters of ancient times: the sacking of the Eternal City by Alaric the Goth in 410. The plot was the claim, by the Romans, that their newly-acquired Christianity had left them helpless to this outrage. Where we see a petty lashing out and a scapegoat, Augustine saw the epic meta-narrative. We are all of us, from the moment of our birth, building eternal cities against the sky. And this instinctive building to save our skins is the quantum of Reason that we hold against God. It is the decision decided for us by conditions of life that none of us asked for. It is neutrality called out of a cardinal unfairness.

I once heard a famous war-correspondent say that when they were first sent up to the action, they quickly decided to accept that there are human experiences just too immediate for perspective. That the only way to depict them in words is to take a side – your side. And that the only proper judgement left at the end of it all is to say that you were there. A great many giant minds are characterized by giant detachment. The books they produce engage impressive but distant problems which we can turn ourselves on and off to. But Augustine's books tend to leave the shelf and follow people around. Wittgenstein thought the *Confessions* to be possibly the most serious book ever written. But above all it is the danger that Augustine puts you into as a reader. It is ever-present because he will always begin in some ground that you share with him and thought was safe – then he'll start pointing out the booby-traps, one by one, until the fear you taste is real, adrenal, metallic. There is a sense of relentlessness that I have not experienced with any similar writer. He just doesn't care to catch his breath.

To me anyway this book has the character of a series of reports written from the frontline of a man's life. I charged with him; I ducked when he ducked. I hunkered down with him. Sometimes there were lulls, blessed lulls; and in those moments quiet and space for unusual clarity and reflection. At those times I tried my best to record the type and significance of the territory we were passing through, as well as any lasting impressions that might be of importance to my readers. In keeping with this, notes to the endless, but remarkable, secondary literature on Augustine have been kept to a limit and representative. I tried as far as possible to see things through the eyes of his original writings and turns of phrase. For one of the surprises for the professional biographer of Augustine is how shallow the wedge has been driven: in splitting open his life and the resources of his thought, scholars have relied on a kind of baton-relay of axiomatic excerpts, handed down through the literature. On the one hand, there is just too much material to be going deeper with; and the other hand, Augustine is just so punchy and quotable – so many of his insights can stand perfectly well on their own. But by no means have all scholars done this: and what is more, this way of working does not misrepresent Augustine and his potential in any significant way. None the less it is only fairly recently that serious attention has turned to some of his unexplored masterpieces – the 'sleepers', so to speak. Chief amongst these is his *Enarrationes in Psalmos*. The constantly varying subject matter of this work really brings across his unbidden eclecticism of mind; and to watch him make the connections that he does is to realize that his infamous rejection of systematization must have been a conscious decision, coming up from the priorities of a writer's sensibility. But most of all, and beyond this, one is left thinking that major work is yet to be done on understanding Augustinianism from the point of view of this man's great gift for making words go into the spaces that doctrine leaves for dead.

I should finally add that, in rendering Augustine's words into English, I have worked primarily from the Latin texts in the *Nuova Biblioteca Agostiniana* (Roma, Città Nuova Editrice, 1965–), or adapted the translations of others where I felt that that was more appropriate. All Biblical quotations are from the King James Version. All quotations from other languages are also in my own translation unless otherwise indicated.

Acknowledgements

Heartfelt thanks must first and foremost go to my publisher at Bloomsbury, Robin Baird-Smith, who commissioned this book from me and then let me go at it with near total freedom. Cynthia Read at Oxford University Press came into the project later on, but was just as good at catching hold of what I was trying to do. Thanks must also go here to my steadfast agent Rachel Calder.

This book would have been impossible to write without the financial support of a number of institutions. First, the Society of Authors awarded me their Elizabeth Longford grant for Historical Biography. Then, the Royal Society of Literature awarded me one of their Jerwood Awards for Non-Fiction. Both these awards allowed me to get up a good head of steam with the book and I am extremely grateful to all who made them possible. Especially, of course, the judges. For the Elizabeth Longford Grant: Simon Brett, Alan Brownjohn, Flora Fraser, Sam Leith, and Julie Myerson. And for the Jerwood Award: Mark Bostridge, Ferdinand Mount, and Claire Tomalin. St. John's College, Durham University, must get a special mention here because they have been faithful and unstinting supporters of my work from the start. The Right Rev'd Professor Stephen Sykes, DD, appointed me to my first post there when he was Principal and strongly encouraged me to write this book. And now the College continues to support me superbly under its current Principal, The Rev'd Professor David Wilkinson. So thank you.

Nicola Rusk at Bloomsbury and Sasha Grossman at Oxford University Press expertly took the book through its production stages and beyond. Everything moved speedily – with the excellent work of Kim Storry and the team at Fakenham Prepress Solutions. Martyn Oliver at Wordspace did a super job of copy-editing the book. And the design team at Oxford University Press created a really beautiful cover.

Miles Hollingworth
Valsolda, Italy, 2012

Chronology of the main events in Augustine's life covered in this book

354 Augustine is born to the pagan Patricius and the Christian Monica at Thagaste, in Roman North Africa. The day is 13 November, a Sunday. On the insistence of his mother, he is signed with the sign of the Cross and seasoned with salt as he leaves her womb.

354–65 Infancy and begins to undergo his first studies in his home town.

ca 365–9 Goes to study in Madauros, a small but relatively well-known intellectual centre, also in Roman North Africa.

369–70 Returns to Thagaste, where he is forced to spend a frustrating year in idleness while Patricius gathers the funds to send him to university at Carthage.

370–1 Patricius is helped to the funds by a rich citizen of Thagaste, Romanianus. This man will go on to become one of Augustine's patrons and friends. Augustine goes up to Carthage and early on meets his lover there – a woman, and a fellow African. He will soon after take her as his mistress and remain faithful to her for 15 years.

371–2 The death of Patricius; around the same time, the birth of Augustine's son, Adeodatus, by his mistress.

373 Reads Cicero's *Hortensius* and is inspired by it to a love of wisdom. Astounds his professors by reading and expounding Aristotle's *Categories* to them. At this time he also comes under the influence of the Manichees, becoming a Hearer in their sect. He will retain this status for nine years, then waver for a further two. In this year Augustine also completes his studies at Carthage and returns to Thagaste to open a school of rhetoric there.

376   The death of a great friend hastens his return to Carthage, where he opens a new school.

380–1   Writes his first work on aesthetics, *De pulchro et apto*, 'On the Beautiful and Fitting'. Unfortunately, this work has not survived.

383   Faustus of Milevis, the famous Manichean teacher, arrives at Carthage to meet Augustine and try to convince him on points of Manichean doctrine in relation to natural philosophy. Augustine likes the man, and esteems his mysticism, but finds his answers on scientific phenomena very naïve and evasive. Later in the same year he departs to teach at Rome, in a move engineered by some prominent Manichaean friends. His departure is the scene for the famous episode in which he deceives his mother to leave her standing in a little chapel dedicated to St Cyprian at the Port of Carthage. Fed up with her pious Christianity, and wearied by her reactions to his Manichaeism, he is determined to set sail without her.

384   In the autumn, under the aegis of the pagan Prefect of Rome, Symmachus, he is appointed Professor of Rhetoric at Milan. Monica had not joined him and his household in Rome and makes no initial attempt to join them now in Milan. Begins to formally dissociate himself from the Manichees and starts to take a professional interest in the sermons of Ambrose, the intellectually charismatic Bishop of Milan. The drift away from Manichaeism will trigger a major reality check and Augustine will be tipped into a depression by facing that he is possibly a genius yet unable to hold a religious faith like other people. He begins to style himself as something of a sceptic after Cicero and the Academics, but starts to read Neoplatonist books in Latin translations by Manlius Victorinus.

385   In the late spring Monica arrives at Milan and begins to exert a matronly influence over his flamboyant household of friends and disciples. Encouraged by Monica, Augustine begins to come under the influence of Ambrose's teaching and personality and takes to him like a spiritual father. Yet a sense that Christianity may yet have something original to say in him becomes something for him not to admit – and an awkwardness when he is around Ambrose.

386: early Reads and studies the letters of St Paul and hears the story of St Anthony and Christian Monasticism from a fellow African, Ponticianus. Is staggered to learn that Christianity could be as romantic as a flight of will into the desert. Begins to understand that his pain of dislocation from everyone else's normal is his anger at God: begins to understand that his anger at God is writing the story of Adam and Eve before his eyes. Does not yet understand that his whole purpose and personality could be to become the man to write that story as the thing of exceeding beauty.

386: spring/summer His conversion to Christianity begins to appear to him like everything that he formerly held against God being held, by God, against him. All the questions that he held as questions of belief have been redressed as questions of aesthetics. Humanity is how God loved us first, so even that and all beauty and fairness has gone across to God's side. In fact, everything and all kudos has gone across to God's side, so that there is only left Augustine, on his own, feeling sorry for himself, and with not one reason to be where he is. He finds that there is nothing left in the equation of Augustine and God but the will to step across.

386: summer/autumn Under the pressure of Monica, his lover is sent away from him and back to Africa. They will never meet again. The boy Adeodatus remains with them in Milan. A promising Christian marriage is arranged instead – again by Monica. But the girl is two years short of the age of consent and Augustine must wait for her hand. In the event, and with the dramatic changes to come, this match will come to nothing. Monica also stamps on a plan of Augustine and 10 of his closest friends and patrons for a detached, and semi-permanent, community of philosophical seekers. She is aided by the wives of the married men, who feel that its communistic plans for life and property are wishful thinking. In private, watched only by his great friend Alypius, and in the garden of his lodgings at Milan, under a tree, Augustine steps across to God – his conversion to Christianity.

386: autumn/winter Decides that he will take baptism from Ambrose, along with Alypius and Adeodatus, in spring 387. Decides to end his career as Professor of Rhetoric forever, by handing in his resignation during the Vintage vacation (August 22–October 15). Takes the country villa of a fellow Rhetorician, Verecundus, at Cassiciacum, with the plan of using it as a soul-searching interim place away from the prying eyes and gossip of Milan. Takes his household with him, including Monica and Adeodatus.

386: winter–387: spring   Begins to know in his heart of hearts that he is a writer; but also that he fears the revelation that all words, and wordplay, suggest their own story; which is the story of what they cannot accomplish on their own. Writes a number of traditional philosophical dialogues in quick succession: *Contra Academicos, De beata vita, De ordine*. But the real discovery of this time is that he cannot be creative and self-conscious at the same time. His *Soliloquiorum*, written during the privacy of his night-time meditations, breaks new literary and philosophical ground by exploring this problem.

387: spring   Returns to Milan and is baptized with Alypius and Adeodatus on 24 April.

387–91   Decides to return home to Africa and found a monastic community at Thagaste, on portions of the family estate. Travels via Rome and Carthage. Experiences a vision of the soul's inability to surmount itself with Monica while staying at Rome's port of Ostia. The death of Monica shortly afterwards, in 387, and then the death of Adeodatus in 389, will close a chapter in his life and begin a new one. Continues to write philosophical dialogues: *De immortalitate animae, De quantitate animae*, and *De libero arbitrio* all composed during this time. But is haunted by the freedoms of the creative, composing spirit inside him – and how they are recollected freedoms. Plots an encyclopaedia of the liberal arts in defiance of this; but only completes two books: *De grammatica* and *De musica*. Starts to write books against the Manichaeans. Forced into ordination by the congregation of Hippo Regius while visiting a friend there in 391.

391–401   Begins his new life in the Church as one of its prize captures and adjusts to life as a public intellectual. Negotiates from his Bishop at Hippo, Valerius, time to read and reread the Bible. Founds a small monastic community at Hippo, and settles on this as his pattern of daily life. Succeeds Valerius as Bishop of Hippo in 395; founds a more structured monastic community for himself and his clergy. Continues in this routine to his death. But still disturbed by his own inner creativity – and how opposed it appears to be to God's. Starts to show his genius as a writer by putting this unresolved quality of himself into his books. Begins to develop the word and argument forms of his mature theology of 'two loves' and their 'two cities'. Begins to develop the purpose and personality that will allow him to use these forms to reproduce the breakdown moment of his conversion for the motif in all his major works. When we are all angry and indignant at God, we are all Augustine, who was the fallen Adam and Eve when he could no longer find a shard of evidence to stand the wrong side of God than his will to be doing it. Writes his pioneering *Confessiones* as the story of this (397–401).

401–29 Continues his autobiographical technique into a series of landmark works of Western thought. *De Trinitate* (399–426); *De Genesi ad litteram* (401–15); *De civitate Dei* (412–26). Writes numerous other works in defence of Christian orthodoxy against the heresies of Manichaeism, Donatism, Pelagianism and Arianism. The tendency of human mental intelligence to subdivide knowledge and predestine itself by historical cause and effect grows to preoccupy Augustine as he grows older. The human body as the spiritual contraflow to this becomes his radical advancement on his age. The body should neither be idolized nor demonized: and the humanity of Christ on the Cross becomes the mystery of what this might mean. He will explore this in two giant works that hearken back to the earthy happinesses of his former life with his lover and son. These will be the works of his most engaging humanism – dealing with the limits of what the Church can sensibly say to us. The Bishop will have his heart wrung further by the fall of Africa, and its perfect expression in the faces of his congregation. The *Enarrationes in Psalmos* (392–418) and *In Iohannis Evangelium Tractatus* (408–420).

430: 28 August Dies of a fever in bed at Hippo.

1

Out of Africa

When I search for Man
in the technique and the style of Europe,
I see only a succession of negations of man,
and an avalanche of murders.

Frantz Fanon

To begin a biography of Augustine is to find oneself at one of the more interesting and accessible points of early Western history. Grand things are afoot: the Roman Empire is beginning to undergo a sustained challenge from the raiding barbarian armies, while civilized men everywhere are being forced to make terms with the longstanding deficiencies of Roman rule. We, of course, have the advantage of knowing how it all turns out. From the ancient world of pagans and priests and cruelty will eventually emerge the new Christian ethic of meekness and equality before God; but hand in hand with this will come a stifling attitude to rational enquiry and, eventually, the Church's monopoly on truth in all things. It is this last development that has traditionally given the medieval period its dark and unfruitful connotations in the popular mind. A succession of brilliant historians have done much since to add detail and life to the glum picture of 'decline and fall', so that we are no longer required to think in the frameworks of the old narratives; but aspects of what might be called the human story of this period remain inconclusive and largely untold.[1] And this is all the more disappointing when this human story is made up of preoccupations that are in the nature of the case timeless and universal. What is more, Augustine is renowned as the figure of antiquity who shows more than any other how we can look inside our own hearts and minds and recover these preoccupations alive and intact from a trove of foundational material – material which the philosopher P. F. Strawson would refer to simply as the 'massive central core of human thinking which has no history.'[2]

It is certainly an odd thing to say that something which persists through all time has no history: but then this is, of course, a statement about what counts as historical evidence. We live in the aftermath of the great age of Criticism which began with the birth of philosophy in classical Greece; and it is well enough known that the really ancient historians wrote poetry and myth and concerned themselves most with the tilts called human nature. What mattered to them greatly was narrative coherency in stories about men – or indeed the supermen as gods. Their accounts contained just as much truth as a modern history of an English village; it was just that it was the truth of the deathless configurations of human behaviour – love, envy, anger, suspicion, mercy, and so on. A great deal has since been invested by the West in the notion that this way of conceiving truth is naive, and that a grown-up and critical history revisions any vestige of this approach and tries to tell simply of fact shaping fact. And yet it is patently the case that not all facts act geologically: some are propelled by a human hand. And whenever this occurs, a space opens up for what Strawson was talking about. The novelist Germaine de Staël was on to this, too:

> ... the morality of history only exists in bulk. History gives constant results by means of the recurrence of a number of chances: its lessons apply to nations not individuals ... the exceptional circumstances consecrated by history leave vast empty spaces into which the miseries and wrongs that make up most private destinies could easily fall.[3]

Late antiquity – Augustine's age – could be considered to be one of the last active theatres of this scenario. It is tantalizingly well known to us in written evidence and the rock-solid of what has been dug out of the ground. And then Augustine and his North Africa are its special sentinels because they represent so signally what has come out of it to dominate us today. This is the whole cast of mind summed up in the idea of Western, that is Latin, Christianity. Late antiquity describes the transitional period between the late Roman Empire and the middle ages: it is a European phenomenon. But before Augustine come the African theologians Tertullian, Cyprian and Lactantius – and Augustine himself is famous proof of the African preoccupation to have a Christianity of the heart as much as of the mind. It could also be said that he is proof of the advantages and disadvantages of having an 'outsider' hold the mirror up to a tradition at its formative stage. As we shall presently see, Augustine's intellectual milieu was characterized by the conservatism of European rationalism. Yet Africa is the cradle of man: and man is flesh and blood: and against this mortality of his, an overcoming wilfulness. Augustine is the African thinker who reacquaints the West with this aspect of itself, lost to the flameproof absolutes of theoretical knowledge. It is the sensual meta-narrative of all humanity in Adam and Eve that interests him most.[4] And this is surely why Augustine and his age continue to fascinate today and challenge the historian's handling of his discipline.

Late antiquity lacks microchips and modern medicine but in all other respects it is still our common European pod; and it is probably true that we have of late been moving even closer to it and the classical world as our root. At the same time, professional history writing takes its deportment from the Enlightenment revelation about ideas and their power when they are hoarded by the ruling classes. It is still braced hard against the name of this fear; it sides with Science on the dogma that facts, like people, deserve equal consideration.

Furthermore, Augustine's age presents us with the first instance of a Christian European state coming to terms with multiculturalism, in the wake of empire and its colonial past. An intellectual biography of Augustine is, therefore, a slightly unusual case. It is of the moment, so that we can come into it with real questions about the human condition and the West's effort to make progress with its leading institutions of happiness and virtue. But Augustine's own preoccupation with human freedom and the philosophy of history means that late antiquity becomes also, through his eyes, a working over of professional history's *modus operandi*. For when one thinks about it, the modern historian must be a diplomat. He must promote the democracy of facts on the principle of equality – and in light of the understanding that social power has historically been wielded in the prejudices of the 'grand narratives'. Man over woman; civilization over barbarism; religion over reason. Yet he must not go so far as to eliminate altogether the space for human agency and the spiritual currencies of the human heart. He must not take his analysis so fine that he writes only of what Charles Morgan called the 'flat statistics of existence'.[5] For if the spirit of enquiry were given its head and free reign to do this, it would show that there is nothing that cannot be explained as cause and effect from the point of view of the proper considerations. This double entendre, in the equation of its modern statement, was first investigated by Pierre Simon Laplace:

> Probability has reference partly to our ignorance, partly to our knowledge. We know that among three or more events, one, and only one, must happen; but there is nothing leading us to believe that any one of them will happen rather than the others. In

this state of indecision, it is impossible for us to pronounce with certainty on their occurrence.[6]

In the humanities, we still give the human will a special immunity – but what is human thought other than electricity and chemicals? How do any of us really act, other than according to these predictable pinging reactions to the geo-logic stimuli of our world? The most pristine history imaginable would explain away all chance and write the book of our mechanical coherency as creatures of instinct. It would preach that the democracy of facts and statistics, in other words the democracy of infinite truths, is just this one gigantic Truth of our utter predestination – or evolution, or however one chooses to define the monism at work.[7] Revulsion at the sheer inhumanity of this eternal perspective (this ready written-out book) would be one most excellent reason not to want to believe in a monotheistic god. And by declension, this has become familiar, too, as the Western liberal argument against the god-like certainties of dictatorship in the State.[8]

Late antiquity didn't exist at all as a respectable period of history until historians began to see it through the filters of critical method. For centuries, Rome had haunted the modern European mind as a kind of myth: and the awesome spectacle of its decline and fall was revered as a kind of scripture. Civilization was its living truth. The Romans had been gifted this precious possession then finally ruined it in shameful neglect of their higher calling. There was a lesson for all! Encouraging this sensation of an heirloom was the addition of Christianity after its nadir as something appointed and magnifying of this. Virgil had died in 19 BC, in time to script his curious foretelling of the age of Christ: 'Now is come the last age of the Cumaean song;/The great line of the centuries begins anew./Now the Virgin returns, the reign of Saturn returns;/Now a new generation descends from heaven on high.'[9] Clearly this reverential attitude could only have a short life expectancy once the refinement of the historical criterion of truth got properly underway. First a general naturalism removed the gloss of determinism and the immemorial lesson. Then the new appreciation of the theoretical observer and his partialities added to the urgency not to take a biased position. Civilization became 'culture': something made. Something made implied the power agenda of those who had made it: 'class'. Class worked for a while but ignored the diversities of lived experience: 'ethnicity'. And ethnicity was fantastic for colouring in the blurred edges of empire where these took in the *Wanderlust* of barbarian nations. But it couldn't trace the movements of the Christian religion: 'identity'. Identity is just about where scholars are with things today. That is to say, late antiquity will continue to open up to us as we learn to see its inhabitants and players as tragic and reacting.

Christianity flourished because it was the universal solace of the individual soul. To be Christian at the dawn of the dark ages was to be identified with an ideology that glorified suffering as proof of redemption and replaced the shards of empire with the completeness of cosmic citizenship. Augustine's legacy is the extent to which he exemplified and accelerated what was in this sense afoot. In a new Epilogue to his classic biography of Augustine, Peter Brown has spelt out the fruits of this approach:

> This powerful sense of momentum was what Augustine passed on directly to the Catholics of Italy and Gaul in the years that immediately followed his death. The writings of an admirer, Prosper of Aquitaine, show that those in Gaul and Italy who rallied to support Augustine's teachings on grace and free will did so because they appreciated men of action cast in a late antique mould. Such men showed that God's grace was still at work in a dangerous world ... This time they were not martyrs. They were bishops: 'strong figures who could tame the unjust powers of the world and protect otherwise helpless communities from the ravages of war.'[10]

This is of course an altogether true and perceptive conclusion, extracted from a singular mastery of the complex resources of today's scholarship – and showing at work the great hinges of ages. But one is left feeling that an Augustine in this way historicized lacks the ambition of the man himself. Practical helps for an age in flux were the stock in trade of his sermons and pastoral activity – and Christianity has always exhibited an intrinsic concern for the vulnerable. But there is another legacy, just as well known, in which he appears as the chronically impractical and unhelpful fan of all things soulful and supernatural.

Augustine was obsessed with the idea that the writing out, and speaking out, of reality – Confession – was the only way that we could grasp something. All autobiography, all history, was to prove identical to him on this point. His *Confessiones* speak for themselves in this regard; but it is not so well known that his historical masterpiece, his *City of God*, was conceived on this same obsession – that the smallest circumstantial grit in any human history can be worked over until it becomes the pearl that shows how all human stories together write the one single story of Adam and Eve. *War and Peace, Crime and Punishment,*

Paradise Lost.[11] This is the idea, shared by some of the great novelists, that what is heartrending and moving in beautiful fiction is its depiction of how men and women must carry themselves between heaven and earth. The tragedy of such a condition is that it has them projecting the most sublime emotions onto transitory goods that will betray the confidence. They can love each other, and life. They are, after the Original Sin, congenital materialists.[12] But this is a spiritual universe, and so they are doomed to be going about things the wrong way. Those we earlier called the really ancient historians probably had a keener sense of this and stuck to poetry and myth. Whatever did not actually happen in these fictions of theirs could at least be dwarfed by the realisms of the sublime emotions they were seeking to portray.[13]

The legacy of Augustine that comes out of all of this and down to us is that he has shown the European sensibility how to feel the utter incongruity of a human life. 'What manner of man is any man, since he is but man?'[14] Other cultures may have a more direct access to this information, and therefore show a more ardent homage to the Nature that tolerates them. But the European experiment with self-knowledge becomes, after Socrates, an adventure of ideas; of the distinctions between ideas; and of the power of ideas to anaesthetize man to the homesickness of his heart.[15] Here we arrive at the great motif of Augustine's mature theology: his idea of Christianity as the universal religion. His idea, that we can freely criticize the happiness that the world purports to provide us with and call to God out of a related sense of loss. His image of the 'unquiet heart'.[16] You have almost to take Augustine out of the Christian context of his popular image to fully appreciate this and bring it up to date. This is because there is a very real and important role for Christian thought in which it contributes positively to the normative adjustments that we must make to life in the world. Brown's assessing of Augustine refers to this. Then there is the wider, mainly secular tradition of marvelling at what a human life can open up to us. This tradition has predominantly been carried on in the disciplines of humanism and letters. What does Augustine contribute to it as the early African intellectual *par excellence*? He contributes his determination to make the West accept the unquiet heart as the Wisdom of God in a fallen world.[17]

> Men go forth to marvel at the mountain heights; at huge waves in the sea they do the same. The same again at the broad expanse of flowing rivers, at the wide reaches of the ocean, and the circuits of the stars. Yet themselves they will pass by.[18]

Why God created man only for so much to go wrong with him is a legitimate question and a long-time *non sequitur* of academic theology. Augustine proves unusual by suggesting an aesthetic rather than a purely intellectual answer to this question. Since the fall, the human heart has been allowed to remain by God like the needle in a compass.[19] It quivers between its poles; and that possibility of its turning shows the effect upon it of what Augustine would call his 'two cities': 'Two cities, then, have been created by two loves: that is, the earthly by love of self extending even to contempt of God, and the Heavenly by love of God extending to contempt of self.'[20] This magnetic possibility of the human heart to decline this way or that is correctly enough called 'freedom': but on the Augustinian analysis, freedom is simply the precondition of 'love' in a rational creature. It makes love actual and meaningful. The Western mind has learnt to understand the concept of freedom on the binary 'either/or' of action and its obstructions. An understanding that supports relativism at the same time as it promotes the absolute right of anyone to be the author of their destiny.[21] When Adam and Eve loved God in Paradise they were not, for Augustine, 'free' to turn away from Him in this sense. Their love of God was entirely secure so long as it was not confronted with a rival – that moral which we find at the climax of Evelyn Waugh's *Brideshead Revisited*, and Julia telling Charles, '... the bad thing I was on the point of doing, that I'm not quite bad enough to do; to set up a rival good to God's.'[22] When this happened, and with pride actuated, freedom became the precondition of something else – of self-consciousness and its discontents.[23] The state in which men are to be seen, '... glorying of the letter, and on their own strength perversely, like men frantic [*phreneticos*], relying ...'[24]

> The first stage of liberty, then, is to be free from crimes [sinful conduct] ... When a man has begun to be free from these (and every Christian man ought to be), he begins to lift his head to liberty. But at this stage it is only liberty begun, not completed ... In part liberty, in part bondage. Not yet entire, not yet pure, not yet full liberty, because not yet eternity.[25]

The 'utter incongruity of a human life' is therefore this. That we can love God from inside a predestinated world – and that this fact can be aesthetically relevant to Him and to us alike. Augustine does not generally go into this in any more detail than we are doing here; his concern is to cradle an intuition, and not to bring it too far into the harsh light of understanding. This intuition is that human pride has made it that freedom is our infernal distraction and wasting away: 'For if you do not have Him to sit on you, you may lift up your neck, may strike out your heels. But woe to you without a ruler, for this liberty sends you among the wild beasts to be devoured!'[26]

It is 'wholeness' that is drawing us on in our best moments – wholeness as it touches us when life declares beauty; and then when beauty flashes the blinding coordination of each to its own.[27] As human beings we, deep down, wish to collapse into this spiritual truth and love it – and love God. But the indignity of this whenever it proposes itself to our hearts keeps us instead in our quivering, indeterminate place.[28] As Friedrich Schleiermacher lamented, '*In stiller Ruhe, in wechselloser Einfalt führ ich ununterbrochen das Bewusstseyn der ganzen Menschheit in mir.*' 'In a still rest, and a changeless simplicity, I bear within me, and uninterrupted, the consciousness of all humanity.'[29] In the original aesthetic of Eden, Adam and Eve lived as though humanity were God's seeing of His own Goodness. Humanity, that piercing vale of sympathies, was God predicating something of Himself, though tantalizingly mysteriously. Augustine would see it of even greater moment still that Christ had been made man. Humanity, for him, was *pluvia occultis*, 'hidden rain'.

> Collected together from hidden sources, it flows on. At death it returns to where it is hidden. This intermediate state called life sounds and passes away. Of this brook He drinks: He has not disdained to drink of this brook: for to drink of this brook was to Him to be born and to die. What this brook has, is birth and death. Christ assumed this, He was born, He died.[30]

The present situation is a counterfeit aesthetic in which we charge an inhuman God for the ravages and calamities of Time. We no longer love Him, but ourselves instead. Our eyes have been opened; and the first thing they have seen is Freedom, couched in all the difficulties of its present-day usage. Freedom is how we pat ourselves on the back for having exchanged one perfect love for another – God for ourselves. We cannot be creative or original in the way that God can; in the sense in which he creates *ex nihilo*: and so we find that we have become free only to be made depraved and determined by the materially existing – our new point of reference. The incongruity of any human life is how we lash out at God for the error of our judgement. 'You do not say to God, I am just, and You are unjust: but you say, I am unjust, but You are more unjust.'[31] And what we have discovered of the laws of history and biography shows us only the magnitude of the way back. As Tolstoy was to put it in the final words of his great historical novel of human life: we must '... renounce a freedom that does not exist and ... recognize a dependence of which we are not personally conscious.'[32]

Augustine's preference for painting in the broad brushstrokes of the novelist has made him the most evocative of the early Church fathers; but the lamentation of the heart when it is written so exceptionally well is difficult to follow out into the world as a practical code of conduct. What is more, despite his sensitivity to the human predicament he was chronicling, Augustine could all too easily show the irritation of the artist on points of detail or explanation. At the height of his powers this becomes nearly indistinguishable from the kindred frustration of the genius that others are not being moved to act on the clear black and white of his seeing: 'Why then do we seek out the mountain as though it were absent? Why do we not ascend to it as a thing present? Why do we not do this so that the Lord may be in us "great, and greatly to be praised?" [Ps. 47.1]'[33]

It is often the case that the flow of a mind like Augustine's flows only because it refuses to be bidden to the microsecond adjustments that we are all the time making to be on reasonable terms with the world. By the time that he had found his mature voice in his idea of the 'two cities', his outlook and style had become almost perfectly adapted to seeing all human activity in terms of the category of 'love'. It was here that he most successfully transferred his classical training as rhetor to the new demands of Christian apologetics. 'Irony' – the rhetor's armour-piercing shell – became his special tool for showing that there is no middle ground between the love of self and the love of God. It is one of the standout images of his work. It prompted Benjamin Jowett to call him a '... strictly polemical or controversial writer who makes the best of everything on one side and the worst of everything on the other.'[34]

To continue our earlier metaphor, all human endeavours give off a definite magnetic declination. In fact Augustine's elaboration and attack on the concept of the 'middle ground' to make this point is one of the more underappreciated aspects of his thought. Soon after his death his doctrine of the 'two cities' was taken up into papal power politics as the authoritative argument for the total supremacy of the Church in all matters. It was celebrated as a purist Christianization of the Platonic promotion of idealism over matter. It was not until the middle ages rediscovered Aristotle in the twelfth century that a sophisticated rendering of the middle ground of human life could begin to be contrasted with Augustine's neglect of it. It is important to emphasize again, though, that if Augustine could disappoint by not laying down blueprints for the business of human flourishing on earth, it was for his peculiarities of temperament and vision. Moreover, it was because he had felt so devastatingly in his own person the commitments of human life that he pitched everything at the breaking free from habit and death: '... there is need of much loud remonstrating to raise up those who have grown hard by habit. Yet at the voice of the Lord's cry, the bands of necessity are burst asunder.'[35]

One of the really striking early examples of how this has caused him to be handled is Dante's *Divine Comedy*. This iconic work is itself a great re-visioning of pagan and Christian wisdom in light of (what was then) the emerging 'third city' and *via media* of civic virtue. Dante's age was still on the way to the confident posturing of the 'republicanism' of early modern Italy's city politics; but the recent influence of Aristotle, and his ennobling as *the* philosopher by St. Thomas Aquinas, had none the less fostered a sense of the dignity and exemplary rationality of social and political association. What is so really striking in this example is simply the fact that Augustine hardly features in Dante's masterpiece at all – a strange omission indeed given the form and subject of the work. Peter S. Hawkins, Professor of Religion and Literature at Yale University, has argued convincingly for a 'political' reason – that Dante chose to ignore what he did not like of Augustine's critique of Roman civilization and brought out what he did like by putting those sentiments into the voice of Virgil. This mischief allowed Dante to '... correct Virgil's Jovian prophecy of an earthly empire without end; but he does not echo Augustine's refusal of empire's providential aims.' If this were true, then Dante should be figured among the many down the years who have been forced into creative measures by the sheer altitude and aspirations of Augustine's words and ideas. According to Hawkins, Dante is forced to make himself '[s]eer of the earthly city and visionary of the City of God, he reconciles the opposition between his authorities by transcending them in himself – Christian Virgil and *alter Augustinus*.'[36] This references, too, our earlier comment about Augustine the African and outsider 'holding up the mirror' to the Western tradition. Augustine certainly has a way with thinkers like Dante. It is tempting to say that the adamant of his rhetoric simply out-stares them: so that they are forced, in the end, to blink. What the mirror then shows is them to themselves, but in a new configuration that has reached to the heart of the matter.

2

Augustine's intellectual milieu

Be near me when the sensuous frame
Is rack'd with pangs that conquer trust;
And Time, a maniac scattering dust,
And Life, a Fury slinging flame.

Tennyson

In respect of the large questions of human life, Augustine's age looked out upon a world of intensity.

On the one hand, there was the human quest for happiness, given dignity and poise by the philosophies of classical Greece, and thereafter incorporated into the theoretical universe of Rome. And on the other hand, there were the problems generated by pluralism – by the sense of dislocation and uncertainty that had come to plague antique society in the age of Empire. Where once there had been only small, parochial city-states, and when citizenship had meant kinship and custom and an infallible method of life, there was now the whole Roman Empire, with its myriad different peoples, and its myriad different customs. But above all, with its citizenship based on the rarefied category of rights.[1]

Today it is far easier to see the advantages of this scheme, now that large aspects of modern societies and cultures in the West have been shaped by it. Back then, however, it was liable to seem an impersonal and cynical contrivance for (world) rule. It was eminently suited to international feats of administration and organization; and that seemed to put it dangerously out of alignment with the basic requirements of the human soul. Before Rome, Mediterranean civilizations had flourished in a more unquestioning and unquestioned way – in what John Burnett called their 'charmed circle[s] of law and custom'.[2] But Rome threw them together into a disorienting multiculturalism of ethics and divinities. They could no longer presume on the old languages of perfection.

And the certainties that they had brewed within their city walls were apt to be mocked to scorn in the cosmopolitan atmosphere of Empire. We can recreate the force of this today by considering how often it is that the idea of 'pluralism', or 'negative' freedom, is leaned upon as a general prop whenever we need to make terms with the bewildering democracy of values in the globalized world. The historian Polybius wrote even of Greek communities who, at the outset of the change, were nerved to commit appalling acts of race suicide.[3]

From the theoretical point of view, Christianity was doing something to help the situation by its unprecedented monotheism: its idea that the Christian God can be worshipped by any people, anywhere, and that His worship *in peculiam* is sufficient for salvation. This was not the relief of cosmic citizenship, or even the idea of the cathedral of reason – these had been current in Greek thought for some 600 years; it was the doctrine of the shocking relevancy of each human life to God and history. And of Christ sent down in human form to prove that.

From at least one very dominant public perspective this doctrine could seem seriously deficient. From its inception, Christianity had always had to negotiate the ancient expectation that religion and politics should form a single piece.[4] In the Roman Empire this had caused many to look upon the Christians as subversives, holding back their allegiance from the Emperor to give it instead to the God in Heaven. This was not so much looked upon as an abnegation of piety but as an issue of practical urgency. The general concern was that a Christian citizen, with his otherworldly prerogatives, would not feel the normal compulsion to serve his Emperor and his State – say in times of battle. The modern idea of a religious institution, intrinsic to the political authority but independent of its supervision and control, was just too revolutionary for the times. We stand the other side of the well-known problem of 'Church and State', which had its beginning in these problems, and which would go on to characterize so much of the history of Europe.

By the time that Augustine had become an established Church figure and public intellectual, the Roman Empire had been 'Christian' for nearly a century. His *De civitate Dei* was begun 90 years after the conversion of the Roman Emperor Constantine (323) in 413. In the eyes of many Christian intellectuals this event, coming just a decade after Constantine's decisive Edict of Milan (313) (which declared an official policy of religious tolerance and equality), implied a clear imputation. Christianity, which had hitherto been persecuted, was now the personal religion of the supreme ruler of the civilized world. What is more, it contained just the equipment to fortify and sustain theories of world government. A happy union. For instance, it gave human history and even time itself a beginning and an end, *ex nihilo*, something that had not been attempted in the wisdom of pagan antiquity. In addition to this, it referred all happenings to the march of a providential plan for the good – history was the outworking of the will of a single benign King, piloting, in tandem, with His king on the ground. It did not take long for some to realize that these facts could be combined with Rome's longstanding view of herself as the leaven of civilization to give an unprecedented force to the actions of Constantine. In the words of one who was to become one of the more outspoken exponents of this view, Eusebius (ca. 260–341), bishop of Caesarea in Palestine:

> The One Saviour of the universe, like a good shepherd keeping wild beasts from His flock, drives away by His Divine and invincible might the rebellious powers which used to fly about in the air above the earth and harass the souls of men. So too the one dear to Him is adorned by Him from on high with the trophies of victory over his enemies; by the rule of war he masters the open enemies of the truth and brings them to a right mind ... He himself directs and guides from on high with the reins of an inspired harmony and concord. At one and the same time he traverses the whole world under the sun; he himself is present to all; he himself oversees all. The kingdom with which he is invested is an image of the heavenly one. He looks up to see the archetypal pattern and guides those whom he rules below in accordance with that pattern.[5]

Augustine would himself do a great deal to amplify this view that the optimum condition for a people is to be ruled by a Christian king. He would also use the fact of Christianity's unlikely rise to worldwide status as a telling proof. The Church, he would remind people, is '... a place both truthful and sanctioned by usage.'[6] However, he would also take the innovative step of writing and ministering from the 'ground up'. He felt that there was something unsatisfactory – perhaps just plain impractical – in offering people the huge theory that explains everything as the help for their particular puzzle. Far better to point out that the Christian dogmas of Grace through Christ are not unqualified, in the sense that so many people and heresies would say. The happiness that is intimated in our hearts, and which agitates us to seek it in the world, is not our memory of a particular state of affairs but rather the memory of what it once was to know God. It is not so much the intellectual question of apologetics as the earthy question of human descent in its line from Adam. 'It is', as he would put it, 'the special wretchedness of man to be now without God, without Whom he cannot *be*.'[7]

This approach, which was so central to Augustine's conversion to Christianity, and which was to anchor the whole of his subsequent career, gives an immediate point of contact between what is called 'Augustinianism' and the longstanding foundations of Western thought.

The laws of nature that have featured so prominently as Western foundations are not, says Augustine, to be taken automatically for the same thing by the Christian. That is to say, the Garden of Eden is not to become famous as their historical explanation. Golden beginnings and utopias are popular features of Western thinking on man and society. They show that it is an ethical, directional tradition. However, the paradise and fulfilment of Eden was to know and to love God, not to understand His will in any ethical or moral sense; as first principles in a book-wisdom. To imagine that history since the fall of man has been waiting to be redeemed after the method of, say, a Hegel or a Marx, was the thought that he was taking special care to guard against. There is no doubt that the modern theory of historicism which states that history has an intelligent purpose is clearly implied in the Christian teachings on God's omniscience.[8] But the more profound lesson that Augustine was teaching was that the attempt to intrigue with God's eternal vision succeeds only in putting man into a box which does him no justice at all, and from which he cannot escape.

> I confess not to be able to know what particular things lie concealed in the counsels of God. I am but a man. Though I will say this: whatever that counsel be, it stands most sure, and excels in equity and wisdom, and incomparably, all that can be conceived by the minds of men. It is with truth that it is said in our books, '*There are* many devices in a man's heart; nevertheless the counsel of the Lord, that shall stand' [Prov. 19.21].[9]

One is reminded of C. S. Lewis, who took a similar view:

> ... every attempt to see the shape of eternity except through the lens of Time destroys your knowledge of Freedom. Witness the doctrine of Predestination which shows (truly enough) that eternal reality is not waiting for a future in which to be real; but at the price of removing Freedom which is the deeper truth of the two.[10]

If Nietzsche was able to call Plato a Christian before Christ it was because the history of Christian writing was so marked by a self-conscious debt to Platonism.[11] The traditional example of this, of course, is Augustine; but there are many other compelling examples to be found in the writings of the Church Fathers who precede him.[12] Others could be struck by the situation too. Numenius, a Platonist philosopher of the second century, could put it that Plato was essentially a Moses speaking Attic![13] In each case the point of comparison was the same. Christianity affirms there to be foundational moral and purely intellectual ideas whose existence can only be accounted for by the principle of anamnesis. In other words, these ideas are such that they could never have been induced from any observations of plain human behaviour, or, for that matter, of the behaviour of the world. We say that they are entirely foreign to the utilitarian sentiments that might be produced in us were the world to run exclusively on its own logic.

In the first instance they invite us to love ourselves less – or maybe even last. And in this sense, they represent the present means to doubt and enquiry, when the world is otherwise a sure-footed place, confident in its gritty realisms. But the idea is for this doubt and enquiry to lead out into the elevating thought that happiness could consist in the non-material pleasure of conforming to a standard of right. It is here, on this question of a supernatural and world-defying morality, that Christianity and Platonism are traditionally said to converge. Impulses that are located in the conscience allow us to judge behaviour. From this, and by declension, we construct the schemes of the 'good life' – the positive alternatives to the status quo.

It is a well-documented fact that the classical Greeks were the first to go about this in a systematic and theoretical way; so in what follows we turn to them for the narrative. However, our eye will be always on the degree to which their philosophy was innovative on previous modes of critical thought. We are looking to fit Augustine into the general human spirit of enquiry as it came down to him.

The first philosophers

The distinguishing feature of the first philosophers was their determination to explain phenomena on a principle, with a view to prediction. This fact alone can make them seem familiar though they lived as long ago as the sixth century BC. Bertrand Russell has a lucid way of explaining how the step of laying mere opinion alongside instances of fact in the world could have pointed the way to what we take to be reliable in our modern criteria of truth:

> ... minds do not *create* truth or falsehood. They create beliefs, but when once the beliefs are created, the mind cannot make them true or false, except in the special case where they concern future things which are in the power of the person believing, such as catching trains. What makes a belief true is a *fact*, and this fact does not (except in exceptional cases) in any way involve the mind of the person who has the belief.[14]

Before the birth of Western philosophy men were not discerning in quite this same way.[15] They were just as concerned to explain phenomena; and, like today, they were most concerned to explain the phenomena that lay outside their control, such as the processes of the physical world. But the difference was that they did not as yet see the advantage in regarding the world as inanimate and bound to patterns of action and reaction.

The reason why may be largely circumstantial. The great majority in the ancient world lived on the margins of existence and had neither the time nor the motivation to question the mythical explanations that were then customary. Those who did, namely the ruling elite and the priests of the state religions, were often as not led into a kind of enlightened cynicism that they did well not to exploit. There is a line from Thomas More's *Utopia* where he recommends religious awe as, '... the strongest, if not the only incentive to good behaviour.'[16]

Notwithstanding this mercenary good sense, it was widely accepted among the ancients that religion should serve the moral and political needs of the state. The idea that the spiritual aspect of life is by definition separate from the secular is very much a Christian invention. So much so, that it would be in retaliation to it, and piqued, that the Roman Empire would bring out its most belligerent and contrived civic religions. As A. N. Whitehead described them:

> The cult of the Empire was the sort of religion which might be constructed to-day by the Law School of a University, laudably impressed by the notion that mere penal repression is not the way to avert a crime wave[!].[17]

The ancients were liable to be most struck by the capriciousness of the physical world; as such, the first philosophers concerned themselves solely with this aspect of life. Their speculations had for their subject the main concerns of modern science. To some this makes it seem odd that they should be counted among the philosophers at all. But in the way they went about things and their spirit, they were philosophers. They were determined not to acquiesce in the settled order of things but to have reasons for their thoughts and actions. They wanted to be intellectually critical.

This preoccupation with the physical world also explains their customary designation as 'pre-Socratic'. Socrates, the inspirational hero of many of Plato's dialogues, is credited with turning Greek speculative thought from the physical world to the human – to the concerns that we associate with ethics. In performing this service he was actually resolving the problem that had come to beset Greece in his time: this was the relativism that had been unleashed by the methods of the pre-Socratics (the first philosophers), made worse by the difficulty of the old schemes of right conduct to stand against it. This relativism was chiefly promoted by the itinerant philosophical teachers called Sophists, who earned out of it their opprobrium and reputation as subversives. Certainly Socrates was anxious to know whether the traditional Greek conception of the good life could be defended as something of value in itself.

The first philosophers could not have anticipated this crisis in life that their discoveries would bring about. They shared a common method; this was to regard the physical world as a rational system of cause and effect, of action and retribution. Their leading idea was of a harmony of parts, or of a just differentiation between things based upon their functions. And the kindred concept that some things must simply be beyond the pale. One of their most outspoken protagonists, Heracleitus, reckoned, for example, that, 'Sun will not overstep his measures; otherwise the Erinyes, ministers of Justice, will find him out.'[18] It may even have been that this method was partly subliminal, based more on the traditional encounter with the life of the city-state than on any outright discovery.[19] Or perhaps it was, as Lucretius speculated, 'a certain vital habit of the body – which the Greeks call harmony – which causes us to live with a capacity for sense'.[20] In any case, and however it might have been, the overall effect was of a signal moment in Western history. It came rapidly to be accepted, as a new and higher rung of common sense, that '... this orderliness in Nature, and this intelligence in Man, seemed to have been specially created to play partners in a kind of cosmic cotillion of *rationality*. Mind made laws of reason: Nature obeyed them.'[21]

What essentially can it mean to 'liken the world to a human mind'? Thales of Miletus, the first of the first philosophers, is alleged to have said that '... the mind of the world is god, and that the sum of things is besouled, and full of daimons; right through the elemental moisture there penetrates a divine power that moves it.'[22] This fragment of his thought is unabashedly full of the happy mixture of science and myth that is typical of the pre-Socratics; but at the same time it has a clear meaning which resonates with contemporary instincts about truth in science, and of the relationship of the latter to the religious forms of thought.

For to say, as Thales did, that the world is possessed of a mind is really the same thing as to say that it is logically and historically determinate – that its processes do not occur arbitrarily but can in fact be estimated from the point of view of their end results. To say, moreover, that 'the mind of the world is god' is to suggest in addition that God is limited by human categories of understanding – that His omniscience (if this is a quality one wishes to ascribe to Him) must consist in something other than His freedom to act in a way unopposed by human conceptions of what is right and good. There is on top of this the iconic question of whether the inductive method of science is logically defensible at all. David Hume was the first philosopher to investigate the status and provenance of our willingness to trust the constancy of events in the way that the pre-Socratics were hoping to. His so-called 'problem of induction' has never been solved on its own bleak terms. It takes a backwards look from the future in which all experimental knowledge waits to be made true. It asks what we can certainly know about that future, if anything at all: and from that it concludes that the basis of scientific reasoning is a psychological impulse, explicable only in relation to the menace of time, and what it keeps from us.[23] The biologist Julian Huxley's anxiousness about the notion of 'purpose' in evolution makes a good comparison:

> Purpose is a psychological term; and to ascribe purpose to a process merely because its results are somewhat similar to those of a true purposeful process is completely unjustified, and a mere projection of our own ideas into the economy of nature.[24]

As far as we know, Thales's defining belief was that all matter, and therefore life itself, was derived from water. Water had a foundational presence and rôle in his outlook: it was the basic component in all things, remaining constant through their various changes and developments. Aristotle would summarize this tendency of the pre-Socratics by saying that '[m]ost of those who first philosophized thought that in the materials of things would be found their only beginnings or principles.'[25]

Now, in the first instance, this would seem to suggest the very un-Christian idea of a material point of reference, antedating the shaping forces and the most meaningful expression of eternality – more meaningful, that is, than any theistic living will or creation *ex nihilo*.[26] And this would be true. The pre-Socratics are the preeminent example of the ancients' preference for maintaining their gods within the same logics that govern human behaviour. These deities abound in magic and glamour but act out the vicissitudes of men: their picaresque dealings are so definitely a projection of human feelings that the impersonal explanations of science seem, by comparison, to be totally unrelated. But when once you have retrieved your scepticism from the scenario it is possible to find, as L. S. Stebbing did, an abiding trajectory that links both these aspects of the ancient mind to the modern. It is a common commitment to certitude. If you can but keep the gods and all the heavens within the same great city of the universe that man inhabits; if you can bind them to the same broad laws that man obeys; well then you can have your constant, your basis for prediction. It is just one dream that is all the time making common cause of myth and science, religion and rationalism:

> There seems to be a deep-rooted tendency in the human mind to seek ... something that persists through change. Consequently the desire for explanation seems to be satisfied only by the discovery that what appears to be new and different was there all the time. Hence the search for an *underlying* identity, a persistent stuff, a substance that is conserved in spite of qualitative changes and in terms of which these changes can be explained.[27]

An unchanging material substrate of the sort of Thales's 'water' evidently offers classic possibilities for prediction. If its presence in all things could be identified, and if its properties were at the same time known, then there is no reason why it would not furnish the basis for inductive conclusions of the sort: 'if A under these conditions then A again under these same conditions in the future'. Yet again we find that we are covering ground that, in its familiarity, reveals the magnitude of our debt to these first philosophers. On the one hand, it is possible to draw a straight line from Thales to contemporary physicists; and on the other hand, we recognize in the pattern of his thinking the general human method for accumulating knowledge in all things. How we tend to move from the particular to the general, to recognize like cases according to their properties, and to act on this information.[28] Perhaps a brief examination of one other example of a pre-Socratic substrate will reinforce this.

Anaximander was Thales's pupil and successor at Miletus. He is credited with being the first to signify the concept of the primordial material with the Greek word *arché*, from which is of course derived the English word 'archetype'. Too few of his writings have survived for there to be any certainty about the composition of his *arché*; but certain secondhand accounts give the full measure of its intended explanatory power. The following account by Simplicius (*Physica Ascultatio*, XXIV, 13) includes an original quotation from Anaximander's writings:

> Of those who say that it is one, moving, and infinite, Anaximander, son of Praxiades, a Milesian, the successor and pupil of Thales, said that the principle element of existing things was the *apeiron* [indefinite, or infinite], being the first to introduce this name of the material principle. He says that it is neither water nor any other of the so-called elements, but some other *apeiron* nature, from which come into being all the heavens and the worlds in them. And the source of coming-to-be for existing things is that into which destruction, too, happens 'according to necessity; for they pay penalty and retribution to each other for their injustice according to the assessment of Time', as he describes it in these rather poetical terms.[29]

Although it would be better to have more in the way of material detail, the conceptual clarity of this account is striking. The symbolism that is the feature of the older mythological accounts of nature is abandoned and replaced with the straightforwardness of a foundational scheme of order. Anaximander is saying that nature is constituted by a process of declension from the first principles located in the *apeiron*. This substance is apprehended in a kind of thought experiment. It appears from its singling out as the dominant fact of our condition from the point of view of knowledge. Things are changing continuously as they are through time, yet we can have an understanding of their essential natures that does not. So the *apeiron* is stable in relation to temporality; it is eternal; but it is also rational in so far as it explains the beginning and destruction of things on a principle of just retribution. It is, in fact, eternal reason.

What, briefly, are Augustine's thoughts at this moment in the narrative which seems so triumphant? Only a note of warning: we should reflect that there may be a hazard in conceiving the higher things in such a way, from our limited outlook in time. The hazard would be a kind of subjectivism – difficult to notice because pride has got in the way once we are taken up into the idea of an eternal reason that is also indigenous to us. It is not that the pre-Socratic instincts are altogether cosmologically wrong, but that nothing should erode the human responsibility for evil. That responsibility should prompt and direct the search for the truth of the matter. We shall in time see that when he was a Manichee, Augustine spent considerable energy learning to convince himself that the presence of human evil, troublesome as it is to the grand systems of enlightenment, should be explained on the Gnostic principle of 'two natures' in man – one materially bad, and one materially good; the materially good being what we gladly share with divinity at large. He would eventually reject this as depleting and betraying the final potential of man, and what we can all experience as wisdom. 'Reality', said G. K. Chesterton, 'is a thing in which we can all repose, even if it hardly seems related to anything else. The thing is there; and that is enough for most of us.' But,

> ... if we do indeed want to know how it could conceivably have come there ... if we do insist on seeing it evolved before our very eyes from an environment nearer to its own nature, then assuredly it is to very different things that we must go.[30]

The human experience of reality is always, for Augustine, a tangible goodness of God's bestowing. For it seems to exceed the pessimistic conceptions of human nature that history delivers in wars and discord; and in the same way it survives the great harshness and cruelty it meets in the natural world of volcanoes and earthquakes and lives snuffed out. Over and above these things we manage to conceive a benign intelligence, and prove it by the apparent correspondences between processes in the world and the human mind. In this sense the pre-Socratics accelerated into history something inevitable. But the question why there have to be these correspondences in the first place remains a real question that is not solved by multiplying out the examples of their existence. This defines the hazard of subjectivism that Augustine thinks will become a complete disaster if it is ever forgotten. For the time being, however, it remains protected and kindled in more Spartan fields like mathematical logic, where the question of truth is in the nature of the business. Take, for example the following reflection from Alfred Tarski:

> The notion of a true sentence functions thus as an ideal limit which can never be reached but which we try to approximate by gradually widening the set of provable sentences. (It seems likely, although for different reasons, that the notion of truth plays an analogous role in the realm of empirical knowledge.)[31]

The effect of Socrates

Socrates has a specific importance in the history of philosophy. He takes the old and familiar idea of a special justice between humanity and the world and articulates it in the theoretical style of the pre-Socratics. He births ethics out of his conviction that the traditional forms of right conduct are the most meaningful expression of human excellence, and that a reasoning philosophy can be used to defend them as well as to debunk them. In his time, the debunking of traditional morality had become very popular. In his dialogue *The Republic*, Plato gives an indication of the type of philosophical argument against ordinary morality that Socrates was coming up against.

> ... people censure injustice only because they fear to be its victims and not because they have scruples about being unjust themselves. So it is, Socrates, that injustice, when practiced on a large enough scale, is stronger and freer and more successful than justice. What I said at the outset, then, remains true. Justice is whatever serves the interest of the stronger; injustice, on the other hand, is whatever serves the personal advantage of any man.[32]

Variations on this argument are heard very often; together they can be said to represent the realist point of view. This is the idea that it is more natural for us to follow our appetites than their consciences. The realist says that the basis for a proper ethics should be the human condition as it really *is*, not the human condition as we may think it ought to be. For what we think it ought to be may never in fact attain the existence it would require to be counted as evidence; whereas pride and greed and the selfish use of force have been endemic features since the beginning of time. They and power should prescribe the parameters of excellence and efficacy. It is really into this intuitive and evolutionary style of thinking that Socrates disturbs with the thought that ideas, and most especially moral ideas, may possess qualities that make them more real than the material things they signify. What we think the human condition *ought* to be may by reason and logic turn out to be the superior basis for action.

So Socrates' thought makes appeal to the same fact of the human condition as the pre-Socratics. In their case, flux and chaos suggested that knowledge would be with whatever was discovered to be resisting beneath it all. What Socrates did was to inherit this staple of Greek thought but to look for the resistant among the ideas associated with individual goodness and virtue. In much the same way that the pre-Socratics sought to decline diverse reality from the single *arché*, Socrates envisages a scheme of knowledge in which truth is expressed perfectly in principal ideas. These ideas hold the meaning that is only ever encountered in its diluted form in the lower-order ideas of everyday expression. Socrates' method of apprehending the principal ideas, and therefore the knowledge required to act virtuously, was to challenge his fellow citizens to clarify their thoughts dialectically in the direction of their source. The following example comes from Plato's dialogue *Euthyphro*. The entire dialogue is a conversation between Socrates and Euthyphro.

> *Soc.* … just at present I would rather hear from you a more precise answer, which you have not yet given, my friend, to the question, What is 'piety'? When asked, you only replied, Doing as you do, charging your father with murder.
> *Euth.* And what I said was true, Socrates.
> *Soc.* No doubt, Euthyphro; but you would admit that there are many pious acts?
> *Euth.* There are.
> *Soc.* Remember that I did not ask you to give me two or three examples of piety, but to explain the general idea which makes all pious things to be pious. Do you not recollect that there was one idea which made the impious impious, and the pious pious?
> *Euth.* I remember.
> *Soc.* Tell me what is the nature of this idea, and then I shall have a standard to which I may look, and by which I may measure actions, whether yours or those of any one else, and then I shall be able to say that such and such an action is pious, such another impious.[33]

Today we are far less inclined than Socrates was to take the step of believing that the abstraction of these principal ideas – their stability of meaning – must place them in a kind of independent reality. For reasons of technology and modernization, we are not so immediately faced (as the ancients were) with the impermanent and transitory character of life. The contrast between the calm and the certainty of the world of ideas and the fickleness of life on earth cannot now do so easily to us what it once did to Socrates. And then it may also be that we do not want it to. We may feel that Augustine's note of caution about anticipating the highest things from this lowly altitude should apply as much to Socratic idealism as it does to pre-Socratic science. However, in the case of Socrates and the history of philosophy there is an element in his thought that remains untouched by this criticism because it is really different to everything that goes before it. This is his rational ethics. By suggesting that, as a species, the human race is marked by a compulsion to call things right and wrong and to act on the right, he puts into theory the truth that had only been hinted at in myth. After Socrates, men will be far more likely to question the orthodox categories of right and wrong and find themselves wanting by a standard they discover in their consciences.[34] And it would famously be this reproving quality of his thought that would ultimately cause him to be put to death by his city, Athens.[35]

Plato and Platonism

If it is true that Socrates nearly single-handedly gave the good life a universal rather than a civic connotation, it was his pupil Plato who fully developed his doctrine that the knowledge of what we should do to be happy is freely available to all who seek it. And this is arguably Plato's chief contribution to the European mind. We stand squarely in his debt if we feel today that freedom is a personal matter, depending chiefly upon our desire to think for ourselves. There is a quotation from W. E. H. Lecky that explains how from this comes the European idea of enlightenment as 'independence' – independence from the mere instinct for survival that we share with the beasts:

> He who has realized, on the one hand, his power of acting according to his will, and, on the other hand, the power of his will to emancipate itself from the empire of pain and pleasure, and to modify and control the current of the emotions, has probably touched the limits of his freedom.[36]

Now how to reconcile this independence, this individualism, with the communal life that we do clearly also need is the question for social and political philosophy. And social and political philosophy as the science of the good life is what Plato would pass on as his signature contribution. But it should now be possible to see that he could not have done so without Socrates' insistence that unencumbered reason brings a man into communion with what is true.

It is very difficult to come fully to terms with the main lines of Plato's thought unless one is prepared to moderate them, as he was, with the premiss that philosophy should show itself in the improvement of mankind. To make every effort to pursue ideas for their own sake, and alone, may well be the first conviction of the thinker who has touched their tranquillity of being; and there are, of course, philosophies and religions that encourage this course; but Plato's reputation is chiefly derived from his very Greek conviction that knowledge should be measured against its usefulness in the world. If pure ideas are otherworldly, Plato is firmly in the line of the pre-Socratics. His instincts tell him to trust that the best parts in man are essentially the same as the best parts in the universe. And this decouples him from Augustine's warning – we should really say Augustine's Christology – that a mediator is called for to bring humanity across from this world into the next. In one of Plato's later works called the *Laws*, he will, for example, be able to state it as matter of fact that:

> ... if the whole path and movement of heaven and all its contents are of like nature with the motion, revolution, and calculations of wisdom, and proceed after that kind ... we must say it is the supremely good soul that takes forethought for the universe and guides it along that path.[37]

Plato's philosophy, then, is one of the truly outstanding attempts to extract a concrete method of virtue from the abstract idea of the 'good' as it is delineated in the ordinary advance of life. This means that, while there is Plato and Platonism (as well as the later derivatives called Neoplatonism), there is no original worked-up structure to call 'Plato's system'. For Plato's philosophy was intended (much like Augustine's Christianity) to be the midwife of what stands to reason in the world:

> There does not exist, and there never shall, any treatise by myself on these matters. The subject does not admit, as the sciences in general do, of exposition. It is only after long association in the great business itself and a shared life that a light breaks out in the soul, kindled, so to say, by a leaping flame, and thereafter feeds itself.[38]

This helps to explain the next important thing about Platonist philosophy. It is temperamentally conservative. It encourages that wisdom once apprehended is sufficient to be its own vindication because it is everywhere the same, and has never changed. It is practical and beneficial because it speaks of the just and rational character of the universe. The revolutionary spasms of human energy are unhelpful: the energy should go into clearing away what puts us far from the truth:

... he who provides for the world has disposed all things with a view to the preservation and perfection of the whole, wherefore each several thing also, so far as may be, does and has done to it what is meet ... Thine own being also ... is one such fragment, and so, for all its littleness, all its striving is ever directed towards the whole ... [and] the purpose of all that happens is what we have said, to win bliss for the life of the whole; it is not made for thee, but thou for it.[39]

The theologian Ernst Troeltsch wrote in 1912 that the quality of conservatism in Western institutions and attitudes to human intelligence was, for its pervasiveness, a kind of proof that '[t]he whole of European philosophy and science stands essentially under the influence of Platonic rationalism.' As he would continue:

This in turn presupposes, to be sure, the subjectivism and relativism of the Sophists, and in so far has its roots in empiricism; but at the same time its consistent aim is to transcend the merely actual through the demonstration that, seething and developing within it, is a rationally necessary conceptual element.[40]

We have established that the sentiment of the Platonist philosopher who would not only apprehend wisdom but actually apply it to do good in the world is for something static and inflexible. For if the greatest benefit to society and the state is that some straight line be established between those who can apprehend wisdom and those who cannot – so that it works to the perfection of everyone – then the traditional conception of the good life is a matter of differentiation. That is to say, one should first set down grounds for differentiating between the philosophers and the non-philosophers in the state; then set up an architecture that makes it possible for the former to rule in accordance with wisdom, and for the latter to acquiesce in what is appointed to them. If we only now agree to call this architecture that admits each to his natural station 'justice', and conclude that its entire success must depend upon a system of education that eradicates envy and suspicion in the lower classes, we will have sketched the main, and infamous, argument of Plato's *Republic*. A passage from the *Republic* that shows all of this is the following:

My friend, you have forgotten that the law is concerned not with the happiness of any particular class in the city but with the happiness of the city as a whole. Its method is to create harmony among the citizens by persuasion and compulsion, making them share the benefits that each is able to bestow upon the community. The law itself produces [philosophers] in the city, not in order to let them do as they please but with the intention of using them to bind the city together ... Because [they] have seen the reality of beauty, justice, and goodness, [they] will be able to know idols and shadows for what they are. Together and wide awake, [they] will govern our city, far differently from most other cities today whose inhabitants are ruled darkly as in a dream by men who will fight with each other over shadows ...[41]

This prototype benign dictatorship was to encounter, in theory at least, all the standard problems that we now associate with these instruments for rule. On the one hand, there was the problem of human nature (the problem why anyone who is not a philosopher-king should flawlessly accept their mandate to rule), which Plato circumnavigated with an ideological system of education that in the event looked far too much like propaganda. And on the other hand, there was the problem of consistently identifying and nurturing the few who are born to the philosophic caste. This was solved very logically – in a sincere scheme of eugenics that looks very unsavoury today.[42] However, these measures, though they continue to earn Plato opprobrium, do at least underscore how tricky it is to accommodate in a single conception the ideas of 'wisdom, or rule of the wisest' and 'pride, or human nature'. We mentioned a little earlier that Augustine always resolved this item of his intellectual inheritance into the general-case problem of human evil. The familiar shapes that states take when they are hierarchic or meritocratic; the question of who should rule, and how; the relationship of these enterprises to the 'perfect' society – in the Western tradition and his education, Augustine witnessed how all aberration is interpreted, in the end, as some failure to muster one's personal organizing principle. In his own broad age, and in the case of, say, a Plotinus, this remained a matter for religion:

> ... so long as any part of his conduct is unwilled, Man is a god doubled with a daemon, or rather, with a second god having his own lesser excellence. But with the vanishing of the unwilled, there is only deity – a god among those that walk with the First God. For the self of the Man is that which came from Yonder; and by his own nature, were he but again as at his first coming, he is even now in the Divine.[43]

More famous still is St Paul's formula:

> For I know that in me (that is, in my flesh,) dwelleth no good thing: for to will is present

with me; but *how* to perform that which is good I find not. For the good that I would I do not: but the evil which I would not, that I do.[44]

Today one's 'personal organizing principle' is likely to be interpreted not as a god, or a divine spark, but as a properly balanced psychology. But not a great deal else has changed.

Stoicism and the idea of a universal natural order

The idea of the natural order that, in Ernest Barker's words, '… includes the Divine and the *daimones* and all humanity in its wide embrace,'[45] would reach its classic form in the philosophy called Stoicism. This philosophy was directly in the line of the so-called post-Aristotelian philosophies that came to prominence as the traditional city-states of classical Greece went into decline in the fourth century BC.[46] These philosophies are also known to historians of ideas by the rôle they played in furnishing the ancient world with its first meaningful alternative to the 'positive' freedom of the city-state.[47] We have said something already about how these institutions, the city-states, had in their maverick prime been able to form their citizens for all they needed – giving them the apparatus of life entire from laws to his gods. And also about how this state of affairs which depended so much on insularity was unlikely to be replicated by the expanse and diversity of the Roman Empire. This great change would contribute significantly to the popularity of the intellectual movements promising individual self-sufficiency – whether through the religious methods of asceticism and mysticism or the philosophical method of personal calibration to a universal morality.[48] To some scholars the utility of these movements compares directly to the existential aims of modern psychological therapy.[49] And certainly today, in the Western world, and accelerated by social media, there are many parallels in the ambivalence shown to national politics, and the increasing relevance of local and spontaneous solidarities.

We might only add that the triumph of the original Greek philosophy of goodness – the homogenous society governed by knowledge – is remarkable for having taken place as events in the 'real world' were moving in the opposite direction. The Peloponnesian war, the Macedonian Empire, and the conquest by Rome – the Greek genius achieved what it did in the hands of a few thinkers largely by ignoring the imputations of these events. Ever since, the Western intellectual has had to bear the suspicion that he is 'behind the times' if his ideas do not show proper respect to the 'facts'. In times of revolutionary zeal, the facts have a way of swapping places with his ideas, so that they become the ardent, utopian dreams of the regime, and his conservatism (now seen for what it is) can be extinguished as the obstacle to progress.

As Christianity hovered over the Roman Empire in the years before Christ, it was possible to see what had happened in the European mind as a fitting out for the personal experience of sin. Calvinism and the Protestant work ethic have come so far now as to be social theories of general explanation, and parodies. But sinfulness experienced as a dreadful reckoning with the flesh, the combing of one's conduct, the sensation of having done something wrong and earned it: the grim vitality of working towards an ever-receding shore. These had not been the hallmarks of the ancient societies. Things could go terribly wrong with them; a famine, or a war. But when the wrath of the gods was felt the blame lay corporately, over the whole community. Any individual might be singled out for blame or sacrifice. A miserable end, but, from his point of view, just sheer bad luck. The Christian message of personal redemption and a personal Saviour actually needed the boon of philosophical individualism to run its course into sin. The prevailing atmosphere in which it was to do so well was categorized by Gilbert Murray as one in which

> ... the aim of the good man is not so much to live justly, to help the society to which he belongs and enjoy the esteem of his fellow creatures; but rather, by means of a burning faith, by contempt for the world and its standards, by ecstasy, suffering, and martyrdom, to be granted pardon for his unspeakable unworthiness, his immeasurable sins.[50]

The call of Hellenism, as the Greek influence came generally to be known in Rome and the wider world, was to an essential parity with the gods on the level of mind. Now it is true that, before this, a related thing had occurred. The ancient religions of Greece and Rome had to one extent or another humanized the gods; but when they had done this it had been by emphasizing their freedom of action: their capriciousness. These gods were not, for instance, bound to any sort of continuing ethic; nor were they particularly interested in coinciding with the final purpose of mankind. They were believed to have their own lives, as well as their own reassuringly ordinary and sordid preoccupations. Altogether, this tended to ensure that their interventions in human life were limited to providing good luck and fortune in exchange for the proper sacrifice or formula – or indeed to withhold these things with disastrous consequences should the due observance not occur. And the gods, like a modern mafia, were everywhere – in fields and doorjambs and rivers, so that even the most sensible men considered it foolishness to refuse to pay for their protection.

In the event, and as it went along, this prolific scheme was able to bring simplicity and regularity to the impulse to have a token of certainty, however superstitious. But, by and by, this also made it liable to become a cynical tool of manipulation in the hands of an unscrupulous ruler or priest; for naturally a vast power to influence was vested with whoever had sovereignty to interpret the sacred rites.[51] In the Roman Empire a number of priesthoods would for this reason become important offices of state, the focus of political ambition as well as greed. They simply offered too many unchallenged opportunities for the accumulation of wealth.[52]

Up to the coming of Christianity this mercenary attitude would play a rôle in insulating an increasingly cosmopolitan Empire from the problem that it should by all rights have been negotiating: the (modern) problem of religion and politics: the problem of where final power in life and law should reside. Rome simply conceded, with martial good sense, that a thousand different peoples should, by rights, have a thousand different gods. What mattered was the correct and continuing cataloguing of this diversity – the right god, to the right need, in the right moment. It may have been contrived, but it was entirely satisfactory. And in any case, modern scholarship has stopped being judgemental about these schemes when it finds them in the world and studies them for social science.

Unfortunately, this happy compartmentalization of religion and politics and philosophy was to be shown up badly by the innovations of Christianity. Philosophy had been left to flutter about as the general *savoir faire*. It was how the urbane man conducted his wisdom. It was not expected to seriously attack or jeopardize the status quo. That would be unpatriotic. So we see that, when Christianity arrived on the scene, there was a great deal for it to upset simply by highlighting some essential inconsistencies at play. For one thing, the idea that the gods should flaunt every regrettable discomposure of human life while men below should be aspiring to conquer these things through reason had always been queried by serious schoolboys like Augustine.[53] But it could also be welcomed as an acquisition by the connoisseur. It was Semitic, it was exotic, it was sensual. In time it would possess Scriptures, organized and written through with prophecies and hidden meanings. By Augustine's age of late antiquity, it had come through its persecution as something suspect and potentially (politically) destabilizing and was profiting from a kind of theistic common sense made up of all the things we have been talking about. It appealed to those in the sophisticated circles, who in every age feel that they must be a little above and supervising the main ideas. And it turned out that God had always been on Rome's side. Consider, for example, the following, spoken by Symmachus, one of Augustine's contemporaries and Prefect of Rome: 'Everyone has his own customs, his own religious practices; the Divine mind has assigned to different cities different religions to be their guardians ...'[54]

But of course this party line from an imperial official reflects only the charming aspect of cosmopolitanism – late antiquity's 'celebration of diversity'.[55] To those more troubled in heart and mind by the demise of the old municipal patterns of life, it would effectively be two classic Stoic ideas that would provide the real relief – so much so that we still encounter them today all over the European mind, and forget that they had their start in history. These were the ideas of the individual's identity *qua* the cosmos, and its correlative: his kinship *qua* the human race. We all want a home; and homesickness is one of the most primal of all afflictions; and when it strikes the adult heart as a criticism of life it is very difficult to turn back. Perhaps no two ideas evoke so well what the post-Aristotelian philosophies were trying to achieve as a whole. Why should lost souls not seek solace as citizens of the world?

There is a famous lecture by St Paul to the 'people at Athens'. Many of them were Epicurean and Stoic philosophers. The Epicureans had chosen the other route to the Stoics. A sort of 'catch me if you can hedonism' shaking an angry fist at life. Anyway, Paul noticed how these people at Athens had set up an altar to the 'unknown God' – a prudent thing to do if you have been brought up in a culture where religious piety means leaving no god out and having all their addresses on file. But he does something totally new and unexpected. Like a man releasing pent-up water into swift channels that show by their running what all the build-up was about in the first place, he questions their superstition. Why the unknown God? Why deceive yourselves? Either you have a name for Him, or you are still searching. If you are searching, then it is for the same reason that all the philosophers have ever searched. Come, I declare to you that I know Who this God is. Now see if you recognize Him in what I say.

> Then Paul stood in the midst of Mars' Hill, and said, *Ye* men of Athens, I perceive that in all things *ye* are too superstitious. For as I passed by, and beheld your devotions, I

found an altar with this inscription, TO THE UNKNOWN GOD. Whom therefore ye ignorantly worship, Him declare I unto you. God that made the world and all things therein, seeing that He is Lord of heaven and earth, dwelleth not in temples made with hands; Neither is worshipped with men's hands, as though He needed any thing, seeing He giveth to all life, and breath, and all things; And hath made of one blood all nations of men for to dwell on all the faces of the earth, and hath determined the times before appointed, and the bounds of their habitation; That they should seek the Lord if haply they might feel after Him, and find Him, though He be not far from every one of us: For in Him we live, and move, and have our being; as certain also of your own poets have said, For we are also His offspring.[56]

By passing from this straight to the first stanza of the Stoic Cleanthes' (ca 331–232 BC) *Hymn to Zeus*, we will really get the sense of how Paul could feel that he was communicating in the line of a single tradition – that, as T. R. Glover thought, 'He slid, as we also do, into using the speech of our day, where it coincides with what we know to be true.'[57]

> Most exalted of the immortals, with many names, always ruling all,
> Zeus, prime mover of nature, you who govern all things according to law,
> all hail! For it is fitting for all mortals to call on you.
> For it is from you that we have our origin, we alone – among
> everything mortal that lives and moves on earth –
> have attained the likeness of the god.
> Therefore I will praise you and always sing of your power.[58]

Law, and the laws of nature, was another classic Stoic idea, related to the two that we have already mentioned. Paul would have been intrinsically aware of it as part of his common language with the people of Athens. It is, when you think about it, the only purely intellectual means of getting across from the cosmos to the human race and then back down again to your ethical needs on the ground. Nothing else unites these spheres like law making them subsets of each other. In the first century, the Jewish philosopher Philo would refer to Adam before his fall as a 'citizen of the world', operating according to the 'constitution of right reason' – the same constitution 'as that by which the whole world operated'.[59] In sum, it was an aspirational mood that St Paul spoke to. Henry Drummond's description of it in the laws of nature, though now old-fashioned, is still the best for capturing it.

The Natural laws then are great lines running not only through the world, but ... through the universe, reducing it like parallels of latitude to intelligent order. In themselves ... they may have no more absolute existence than parallels of latitude. But they exist for us. They are drawn for us to understand the part by some Hand that drew the whole; so drawn, perhaps, that, understanding the part, we too in time may learn to understand the whole.[60]

We have been explaining Augustine's intellectual milieu as the story of Western philosophy and science. Of its analytical sensibility. It had in the end to make a rapprochement with Christianity; but we have shown that it only had to do this after social and political realisms had gone ahead of it to carve the 'God-shaped hole'.

How Augustine would react to his situation in history is really the story of all that follows in the pages of this book. But we may give some indication here of where the emphasis fell. We have in any case covered some of this ground in the previous Chapter.

The Stoic Emperor Marcus Aurelius wrote that '[t]he man who does not know that there is an orderly universe does not know where he is ...', and continued:

> ... one who does not know the purpose to which the universe is by nature directed does not know his own nature or that of the universe. He who is without knowledge of any of these things does not know for what purpose he himself was born.[61]

One of Augustine's enduring collateral achievements was to be the conduit of safe passage for a whole range of classical learning that would have been burnt and trodden to dust by the barbarians had it not turned up all over his writings. He wrapped it up in Christian papers and it shone a light into the dark ages until Aristotle was rediscovered and things picked up again and the universities of Europe had something to base themselves on. One of the pieces of learning which he transmitted wholesale and wholeheartedly was this whole idea that reality is susceptible to rational interrogation – and that it gives itself up for knowledge as laws. Laws of processes of atoms banging together. Laws of the fundamental joys and outrages of human behaviour. These laws attenuate the freedom of the rational creature. We obey or disobey them; they prove free choice of the will.

> Whoever has been alongside you is your fellow; it stands to reason – unless, that is, you have worn out on earthly desires what puts you in the image of God ... For you judge rightly that there is evil in whatever you do not wish to suffer; and what holds you to this is an inward law written into your heart.[62]
>
> Let me briefly remind you of something that bears on the question. You certainly know it. All laws and all means of discipline; all commendations, censures, exhortations, threats, rewards and punishments; indeed all the things by which mankind is managed and ruled. These are all utterly subverted and overthrown and found to be absolutely devoid of justice unless the will is the root cause of the sins which a man commits.[63]

Augustine was not just the Christian intellectual and bishop who wrote a library. He was a man who had achieved equal success either side of the curtain. A man of letters appointed to one of the great public chairs of learning by an Emperor. Then a convert, and a monk – an ascetic and reclusive man. With lives such as these we are given an unparalleled opportunity, not available with the hard cases who were always for or against a cause. We are given the opportunity to trace what does not change over the years. And that turns out always to be the real story of the *life*. We are all of us humans before we become the ideas we had and the books we wrote.

With Augustine we find that he never gives up on what C. S. Lewis called the 'madness of knowledge'.[64] It is something that he never becomes censorious about. There are things about the world that will always submit to the human mind because that is what they are there to do. To the unreasoning animals they are hidden. Where he did, however, come to concentrate his effort once a Christian thinker, was on the ready sprung-up shapes of the human mind. But on one overriding shape in particular. Because, after all, no one assumes anymore that knowledge flutters into our nets like untouched butterflies. Things intervene along the way – partialities and subjectivities and then those we don't control. The overriding shape that he took his special interest in as a Christian was the value judgement that seems to dart behind the big intellectual visions like a secret premiss.

The summit of all wisdom and understanding is more often than not portrayed in terms of the passions and prejudices that must be overcome to reach it. In Augustine's day this was the image of the philosopher, alone in his retreat. Or the Christian hermit, following St Anthony's example into the desert. Nowadays we have an even more striking image that we call by a rather telling name: 'artificial intelligence'. We have accepted the superiority of the machine on the principle that there is an event horizon across which the totality of all there is to know will eventually push us – as by its critical mass. Machines and computers neither tire nor complain. Augustine's interest became to ask what this 'event horizon' signifies. For when you think about it, it is strange that it exists at all as the conclusion to such an austere discipline of the mind – or the machine. It would be more fitting, surely, if we just evaporated with no regrets. But apparently that stage has not yet been reached; and we know this because scientists and religionists are still arguing over *who* will arrive first at the great emotion and discomposure of final *happiness*. Or the event horizon.

Seneca, the 'humanist saint' of the first century, and a Stoic philosopher, would have been known to Augustine as one of the great examples of this shape of the mind. A shape that makes it that knowledge turns up in it, and takes it, as from some clear and present future. As evidence of certain goodness.

> The maker is God; matter is the material; the form is the general character and lay-out of the universe as we see it; the model naturally enough is the pattern which God adopted for the creation of this stupendous work in all its beauty; the end is what God had in view when he created it, and that – in case you are asking what is the end God has in view – is goodness. That at any rate is what Plato says: 'What was the cause of God's creating the universe? He is good, and whoever is good can never be grudging with anything good; so he made it as good a world as it was in his power to make it.'[65]

Of course Augustine never went on to challenge what he had noticed *per se*. These statements about the intrinsic goodness of creation were key articles of Christian faith, and major truths for him personally. He would spend some bleak years as a Manichee, perplexed by evil and doubting the goodness of all things and God's power to bring them home to the end. His writings against this heresy in particular, once he had moved on, would provide the Church with some of its classic and most resounding versions of these articles. He is typical of Latin Christendom with its special regard for law, both eternal and human, and its promotion of the Church as the appointed interpreter and administrator of this instrument.

What he did do, though, was question the meeting place it left open for mankind and God. Happiness, the dream of the philosophers, the Unknown God – Christianity was the religion that prospered on a special regard for this trajectory. You were a Christian if you were an exile and homesick. Christianity had the story of a Paradise lost, and a way of showing how pride was the fuel that kept one away, and on the move. Redemption was as simple as coming home. So it worked on Augustine that at times this beautiful simplicity of a Father and a prodigal son should be lost in a scheme for enlightenment – a scheme keeping things too much in the abstract. What he meant was that the orthodoxy of calling God good, and a life with Him a happy life, is correct, but not at all immune from the relativism inherent in these descriptions.

Western thought has over its history become almost totally habituated to knowing and noticing this relativism. Its tolerant modern society is the fruit of this awareness. But Augustine worried that this could create problems for his Christian readers. To say that we are all moved towards goodness and happiness and that God is the true version of these things is an obvious and effective argument. To say in extension of it that all is well with the world (despite how it may look) is the additional comfort that this argument provides. Yet goodness and happiness are known to us far more intimately than the terms of propositions which can never be decisive because they are taught to be emotive and opinionative. Augustine in fact says that they are derivatives of the careless freedom that Adam and Eve enjoyed in the Garden of Eden. We only have them as part of our vocabulary because we recall this freedom in a process like anamnesis. Believing this allowed him to be original in two important ways.

First, the philosophical puzzle of emotive language in relation to truth became his most sophisticated argument for God. Augustine was not one of the Church Fathers who tried especially hard to prove God; however, whenever he did break out into what is manifest, it was invariably that our lives bring news of our one time knowing God – and all in a way that Adam and Eve and our descent from them are the only possible explanation of it.

Second, he was able to supplement the *imago Dei* dogma with the insight that whenever a lost soul is reunited ecstatically with its God, the freedom of that place is enjoyed equally by both. This freedom, and its memory on earth as goodness and happiness, was what he worried could be lost in the intellectualist depictions of the distance between man and God. These depictions which we have explained here in terms of a short history of some aspects of Western philosophy up to Christ; well, Augustine thought that they could be a little patronizing of man and God; though he knew that they did not set out to be so.

'The Holy Ghost', he would write in this mood, '"bloweth where He listeth" [John 3.8]. He does not follow men's merits, but actually produces them Himself. For the Grace of God is extinct unless it is totally free.'[66] In effect, this was his way of saying, too, that the whole of man is implicated in what Christianity calls sin. Pride, which we are all said to exhibit, is self-love. And self-love is the deficient way of being happy. Oh yes – it is possible to be happy in the natural earthly way of, say, Dante's *Limbo*. In such situations happiness is looked to and enjoyed as the quality of a discrete activity. The philosophers in Dante's *Limbo* – men like Seneca – had chosen the activity of studiously contemplating God at large in the things of His doing. They had come so close, but they had not done what Augustine had in his early contemplations – '… and we turned back again to the sounds of our mouths, of words beginning and also ending.'[67] Augustine's point was that this turning back was a defeat for the human mind versus eternity and the omniscient God; no question about it; but surely such a losing battle was not what God had intended for salvation. Why else did He send His Son? We do not have to turn ourselves inside out to be saved. The human mind, exalted and lording it over its human form, is ultimately a cruel, self-harming form of love. All that is required is the example of humility in Christ – the humility before which 'all pride bends, breaks, and dies.'[68]

3

Augustine's remarks on his parents

> Not utterly unworthy to endure
> Was the supremacy of crafty Rome;
> Age after age to the arch of Christendom
> Aerial keystone haughtily secure
>
> Wordsworth

The previous chapter was helpful to show that, when Augustine uses punching phrases like 'the single conspiracy of the society of the unfaithful',[1] or 'the stormy society of human life',[2] or even 'the rebellious community of human affections',[3] he is not being recriminatory. It shows rather the extent to which he is trying to make this present state look like the ideology. This is his technique, and it is a clever one: at any rate, it was certainly able to bring the best out of a clever man. It strikes, at first, as a slightly disorienting technique, because it removes the burden of proof from Christianity and its revealed articles of faith, and places it instead on the world and its lust for self-vindication. We are used to religions being the ideological schemes. But Augustine is saying that this conditioning is cheating us out of an authentic bearing up to the world – and death.

> Believe me, there is great need to withdraw from the tumult of the things which are passing away. By this means, there may be formed in man the capacity to say 'I fear not' – though in a way superior to insensibility, or presumption, or vainglory, or just plain superstitious blindness.[4]

In Augustine's day, one issue in particular was always likely to bring this 'technique' to bear. This was the problem of how to handle the confluence of Roman historical achievement and Christian revelation: of man's leavening through self-knowledge and intellectual advancement and Christianity's challenge to these things in Christ.

The Lord Jesus knew whereby the soul of man, that is, the rational mind made after the image of God, could be satisfied. Only by Himself. This He knew; and he knew also that man waited in fulfilment of this fullness. He knew that He was manifest; and yet He knew that He was in some way hidden. He knew what in Him was exhibited, and what was effectively concealed. He knew all this.[5]

We have already said how Christian intellectuals in the Roman Empire could be enthused by the eschatological feature of Christianity to see a new historicism. Eusebius was the example. In the opinion of these thinkers, God had with great cunning used the Romans (and their Empire's dimensions) to marshal all men to the equality of the universal law in just the same way that He had used the Greeks to fit them with the idea of the universal mind. And the conversion of the Roman Emperor Constantine had been one of those rare but spectacular glimpses of this. Like the sighting of a great comet, the dispensation of God had emerged from the pandemonium of human affairs to trace a clear line across the sky. It was the sudden brilliance of a sign: the most potent conviction that the ancient mind could have: and Augustine wanted to sound the note of circumspection. A point that we must clear up immediately is the question of his engagement with what Oscar Cullmann first called *Heilsgeschichte* – 'salvation history'.[6]

Augustine was convinced that the Christianization of the Empire was a miracle – brought through against considerable odds, and proof of God's sovereignty. It was happy history-in-the-making for the Christian, but it was also a solemn reminder of what could not be expected to change. The what-cannot-be-expected-to-change would of course become one of his specialist subjects. His fabled *realpolitik*. Christianity, though it promotes doctrines of Divine foreknowledge and makes use of the languages of kingship and government, is actually manifested in discrete acts of rebirth and salvation; but in a way that while these may on occasion combine to achieve positive historical change, they are not to be estimated in terms of it, in ways that pre-empt God's freedom of movement.

> Therefore that God, the author and giver of felicity, because He alone is the true God, Himself gives earthly kingdoms both to good and bad. Neither does He do this rashly, and, as it were, fortuitously, – because He is God not fortune – but according to the order of things and times, which is hidden from us, but thoroughly known to Himself; which same order of times, however, He does not serve as subject to it, but Himself rules as lord and appoints as governor.[7]

Augustine's note of circumspection was to remind his readers of one important consequence of God making man. God might just as easily have made perfect statues of the human forms of man and woman. His majesty would have remained the same: they would have been just as 'good' creations as living men and women. But that is not what He chose to do. He chose for there to be left a history of His dealings with the human race. Here is what was significant for Augustine: what history is uniquely able to make happen. As it goes along it builds the framework that creates the spaces for little episodes here and there – or big episodes, as in a suddenly Christian Rome. A lot of it is boring and repetitive because everything has to touch everything else and be connected; so the key lies with how it is interpreted. It can be left just to be all cause and effect if you grind it fine enough – we called this interpretation 'geological' in the opening chapter. Or certain moments might be shown to have an independence of meaning, over and above the facts. Prophetic. Or two different people might be struck by two different truths in the one thing. Multi-layered. The historian R. A. Markus was the first to theorize a distinction in Augustine's thought between '"history" as what has happened ("the past") and "history" as the record of what has happened.' History as the 'record of what has happened' is the subjective activity of interpreting facts; here Markus brings up the term 'Sacred History' to describe the divinely inspired insights that the canonical Christian writers, the writers of the Scriptures, were able to bring to bear on the history of their times.[8]

All these possibilities of interpretation, when he considered them, left Augustine sure that history itself was perfectly capable of meeting man's needs and God's as it was. It did not, as we put it in the previous chapter, need to be redeemed or even Christianized. And as he thought on this more and more, he came to see, too, how it was a kind of liberating doctrine all of its own. But so easy to miss in the triumphant Christianity of his day.

> For in this most righteous government, whose ways are strange and inscrutable, there is, by means of unknowable connections established in the creatures subject to it, both a severity of punishment and a mercifulness of salvation.[9]

This could mean predestination, and in the example that we have been following, an irrepressible Christian Europe. Or it could mean having a great burden lifted from one. To Augustine this was the burden of having to maintain a corroborating history. The burden, in effect, of having to do God's work for

Him. The burden of having to use history as the remedial device when really it should be something left running as a fundamental condition of life – as fundamental as breathing.

> Entrust to the truth whatever you have gained from the truth and you will suffer no loss.[10]

This message was meant by Augustine as a relief from having to squint into the far distance of historical meaning.

> The simple truth of the explanation which we adduce ought to be like the gold which binds together a row of gems, and yet does not interfere with the choice symmetry of the ornament by any undue intrusion of itself.[11]

This 'choice symmetry' may, when it is seen, be something that is not entirely to our liking. Realism has a way of showing us the consistencies of human nature that depress rather than uplift. But the temptation to dabble and speak in the languages of great normative change can be the real danger. Nationalism is a poor fit for human history and its individual testimonies. No one seriously doubts that today. It is based in the real truth that we prefer to have homelands and identities, and to be partisan for them. But that makes it also monolithic and belligerent in relation to the whole host of human experiences that can hardly be expressed in words; because they are so many shades in meaning. Augustine feared very much the invention of a Christian nationalism over his preferred concept of 'two cities'.[12] Later in his life, he would actually have to face down such a movement in the Donatist Church of Africa.

His antidote, which he put into all his writings, was to remind his readers constantly of the ceaseless activity of God – abroad in every life, everywhere. This was not a call to apathy. They should work harder than ever for the good that they might do. And Augustine was one of the most practically active bishops of late antiquity. It was a call to remain vigilant: to beware of crossing a line into the private and mysterious domains of human feeling. For these domains are God's special theatres of operation. And there is no excuse for trespassing on them because He has gifted the human race empathy. Without knowing precisely what is going on in each other's hearts, we can none the less respect the force of feeling we see in the face. Predestination, like nationalism, is an invention designed to circumvent these protections and produce colour charts for knowing ahead of eternity the good and the bad. Augustine's portrayal of how God saves a life is the polar opposite:

> For dismissed by You from Paradise, and having taken my journey into a far country [Cf. Luke 15.13], I cannot hope to return unless You meet me, the wanderer. For in truth my return has been sustained by Your mercy throughout all the tract of this age's time.[13]

When Augustine said things like 'if you have understood Him, he is not God', we see that he really meant it.[14] And he said these things a lot. He really meant it to protect the untold good that an unbidden God can do in a life. It doesn't always make for clear and satisfying theology when we want to know exactly what God is all about all of the time, and how Grace works, but it is the reason why he has always been instinctively cherished as the Doctor of the heart. Probably the classic assessment along these lines is still Eugène Portalié's.

> He belongs indisputably to all ages because he is in touch with all souls, but he is preeminently modern because his doctrine is not the cold light of the School; he is living and penetrated with personal sentiment. Religion is not a simple theory, Christianity is not a series of dogmas; it is also a life, as they say nowadays, or, more accurately, a source of life. However, let us not be deceived. Augustine is not a sentimentalist, a pure mystic, and heart alone does not account for his power. If in him the hard, cold intellectuality of the metaphysicians gives place to an impassioned vision of truth, that truth is the basis of it all. He never knew the vaporous mysticism of our day, that allows itself to be lulled by a vague, aimless sentimentalism. His emotion is deep, true, engrossing, precisely because it is born of a strong, secure, accurate dogmatism that wishes to know what it loves and why it loves. Christianity is life, but life in the eternal, unchangeable truth. And if none of the Fathers has put so much of his heart into his writings, neither has any turned upon truth the searchlight of a stronger, clearer intellect.[15]

We say that he had a flair for illuminating this universe of right and wrong with the sheer possibility of what God might say. And that he did this chiefly by stressing the human obsession with history; with philosophies of history; and with the belief that in the improvement of history we recover our self-esteem. What if all this sincerity and good intention could be replaced with the plain unblinking vision of how things merely are? That was his seditious, counter-cultural thought. 'It is true that we were made by the hands of Truth. However, because of sin we have been cast forth upon days of vanity.'[16]

> Animals both great and small see it, but they cannot question it. In them, reason has not been placed in judgement over the senses and their reports. But men can ask questions, and this makes them able to see the invisible things of God ... However, in loving such things as they see, they become subject to them; and in subjection they can no longer pass judgement on them. Nor do things submit to those who ask unless they are men of judgement. They do not change their voice, their beauty, when one man merely looks at them but another both looks and questions. It is this that is responsible for how they can appear one thing to this man, another to that man. They are essentially the same to both. What makes the difference is the silence of their beauty to one, but its enjoyment by the other. We say that reality speaks to all: but only those understand who compare its voice taken in from outside with the truth within them.[17]

To achieve this 'plain vision' – to be disabused of the Earthly City's rhetoric and to call to God out of a real sense of His absence – was, on the face of it, a free and unaided act of will; but at the same time it carried such severe penalties of isolation and dislocation that Augustine always suspected it must reflect the through and through practical work of Grace. To make the final choice to change one's citizenship and live as a Christian pilgrim was to die to the world and become an exile. Only Grace working to replace the whole of the old heart could bring anyone through such a deadly, counterintuitive decision:

> He operates without us, to make it conceivable that we may will. But when we do actually will, and follow it up in action, He also co-operates with us in the venture. We can therefore do nothing to effect good works of piety without Him either working that we may will, or co-working when we will. Now, concerning His working that we may will, it is said: 'For it is God which worketh in you both to will and to do of *His* good pleasure.' [Phil. 2.13] While of His co-working with us, when we will and act by willing, the apostle says, 'we know that all things work together for good to them that love God.' [Rom. 8.28] What does this phrase, 'all things', mean, but the terrible and cruel sufferings which affect our condition? This tribulation makes it that the prospect of Christ can seem a burden too great; but that is only while we are not loving Him. While we love Him, it becomes at once light. For to such did the Lord say that His burden was light [Cf. Matt. 11.30], as Peter was when he suffered for Christ, not as he was when he denied Him.[18]

In short, no one could be expected to wish upon themselves the obvious social and psychological difficulties of living as though the world were a *locus ruinosus*, a 'doomed place', a veil of tears.[19] In Augustine's age, the age of duty and patronage and honour, this was an especially awkward outlook to adopt. So much of one's success could rest on not rocking the boat.[20] But on this point he believed that all ages would essentially remain the same – that this was always going to be the world from which escape would never seem viable on its own merits: 'Such is the strength of onerous habit! Here I can abide, although I would not; there I wish to be, but cannot; in both ways am I wretched.'[21]

> All men ask counsel about what they wish, but they do not all hear what they wish. Your best servant is he who looks not so much to hear from You what he wants to hear, but rather to want what he hears from You.[22]

'Confession' is one of the ideas that is indelibly associated with Augustine. The title of his revolutionary autobiography; the theme of countless sermons. Like Degas's dancers, it was the image that his art responded to most. So clearly it meant more than owning up to things like a naughty child. More even than a sacred ritual meant to remind adults of a great truth. It was an ongoing means of catching hold of fragile little testimonies, too sublime for the nets of historical explanation – or for that matter, of any kind of analysis at all. There are some things that are designed to be caught by the human mind: but the understanding of them has nothing to do with the catching: but consists rather of handing them back, intact, to their Maker.

However, he was not just thinking of the circumstantial, case-by-case nature of each life – liable to be ridden roughshod over by the historical narratives. He was thinking also of the hopeful side of human life. There are moments in which pure thought imagines itself to be above hope, to have conquered it by the steely mind. But you find that even in its irreproachable dignity it wants to bend itself, still, to some sort of compassionate ending. Confession is, for Augustine, a whole rational theory of knowledge – better than the rest because it accounts completely for this oddity of life. We are not animals or machines, though we can admire the guiltless predator and the insatiable calculator. Our social life as a species is glued together by the unseen soulfulness of faith, hope and charity. Even the simplest transaction between two humans involves mutuality: a level of trust and understanding in what lies hidden within.

If faith is taken away from human affairs, who will not conclude that disorder and awful confusion must follow? For how can anyone love another out of mutual charity when loving itself is of the order of things unseen, and if we choose not to believe what we cannot see? In this way will the whole scheme of friendship perish insofar as it is premised in our belief in mutual love … To this degree are human affairs thrown into disorder, if we choose not to believe in what we cannot see. In fact, they would in this case be altogether and utterly overthrown if we did not believe in the unseen good intentions of men towards one another … If, then, we choose not to believe those things which we cannot see, the first victim will be human society, which is sprung from a concord of men's wills.[23]

I know not whether we could find any place on earth in which we could live if we could not trust the oaths on which men swear. For not only on the frontier, but throughout all the provinces, the security of peace rests on the oaths of barbarians. And from this it would follow, that not only the crops which are guarded by men who have sworn fidelity in the name of their false gods, but all things which enjoy the protection secured by the peace which a similar oath has ratified, are defiled.[24]

Observe this whole world, ordered, as it were, in a single human commonwealth. Observe its administrations, its degrees of power, its conditions of citizenship, its laws and manners and arts! All of this has been brought about through the soul, yet this power of the soul is not visible.[25]

Confession, while it lasts, is like entering a sort of solitary confinement from the world to see it better. Not that solitary confinement would be something you would enter into willingly, or be able to sustain for any considerable length of time. Augustine is realistic that it can be no world-changing theory. But it is the well that we can be going back to when we thirst. It has no agenda than truth, so it puts reality and God into a single piece: 'I have poured forth my soul above myself, and there remains no longer any being for me to attain to, save my God.'[26]

Time and again, drawn to a detail that it was natural for a rhetorician and philosopher to notice, he will refer to the exquisite irony of our having to broach the things of eternity in syllables and words that must give up their meaning in time – syllables and words that he returns to describe in the final book of his *Confessiones* as simply the *abyssus saeculi et caecitas carnis*, the 'abyss of this age and the blindness of our flesh'.[27] The life of the mind has a tragicomic destiny, which he tried to keep abreast of as a theme running through all his books. On the one hand, it must stand aloof and upright, the bearer and instigator of the critical functions that check the headlong of life. But on the other hand, it cannot exist apart from what it analyzes, and the imputation of what it analyzes, as God. This, its parasitic aspect, means that it can never approach to the beating source of real originality and creativity – which it must spy and envy from afar.

> Who can comprehend the abiding Word? All our words sound, and pass away. So who can comprehend the abiding Word, save he who abides in Him? Would you comprehend the abiding Word? Do not follow the current of the flesh. For this flesh is certainly a current; it has nothing about it that abides. Men are born from what would appear to be a kind of secret fount of nature. They live, they die; but all in a manner that keeps hidden their coming or going. Theirs is indeed a hidden water. It shows itself only as it leaves its source; it flows on, and is seen by its course; but then finally it goes hidden again into the sea. Let us remember these characteristics of this stream – flowing on, running, disappearing – let us not forget them.[28]
>
> For their eyes, that is their mind, is beaten back by the light of truth, because of the darkness of their sins; by the habitual practice of which they are not able to sustain the brightness of right understanding. Therefore even they who see sometimes, they who understand the truth, are yet unrighteous still. They cannot abide in their brightness because they come too quickly to love those things they understand – and they are turned aside from the truth. In this sense they carry about with them their night; which is not only the habit, but even the love, of sinning. But if this night shall pass away and they shall cease to sin, and this love and habit be put to flight, the morning will dawn, so that they not only understand, but also cleave to the truth.[29]

As Michel de Montaigne would write of death: 'I dominate it in the mass; in detail it harasses me.'[30]

Augustine's handling of his parents has aroused considerable interest. He has been careful to say comparatively little about them; but what he has said has generally been considered to be too generous to his mother and too cool to his father. Almost all his significant remarks occur in his *Confessiones*. There are inevitably some indirect and oblique references deposited in his other writings, but these mainly supply fact and variation to the picture already established in that book. In short, the modern biographer of Augustine must contend with the following tendency: that when a man develops a highly original and influential critique of human society and then depicts his parents in a noteworthy way, it is very easy to take the wrong sort of encouragement from the fact.[31]

To the majority of scholars, Augustine's father Patricius remains the most high-profile victim of Augustine's discretion. There seems little doubt that Patricius was rather an unremarkable father for so a brilliant a son as Augustine to have had. Where he rose above the average, such as in his generous attitude to financing his son's education, there will be a kind remark in the *Confessiones*.[32] But in most other respects he seems to have conformed to a stereotype in his son's mind, and by that means to have merged with the scenery. On the other hand, Augustine's mother Monica was considered by her son to have played a decisive, God-given rôle in his life. Unlike her husband she was a committed, confessing Christian as well as a relentless mother.[33] It distressed her greatly when her son scorned Christianity as a young man, and she had no qualms about dealing with him sternly afterwards. However, she continued throughout to support his career in the world, consoling herself with premonitions of his salvation.[34]

Augustine's father, though a pagan by birth and image, seems to have tolerated his wife's Christianity well. At any rate, he allowed her to bring up their children as Christians. As he grew older and more morbid, he wavered, eventually making a full confession and baptism on his deathbed, as was then common. So close to death it was said that one had less time for a sinful relapse to occur. Augustine retained a distinct impression of his family arrangement as it appeared to him when he was still young:

> I already believed, as did also my mother and the whole household [this would have included the slaves]; excepting my father alone. Still he did not overthrow in me the authority of my mother's devotion, so that I would not believe in Christ, even as he did not believe in Him. For she strove in every way that You, my God, would be my father rather than he. In this You aided her, so that she overcame her husband, to whom she, the better partner, was subject. For in this she assuredly was serving You who order her to do so.[35]

To a sensitive child making terms with the world, Roman North Africa in the fourth century could be discouraging. All about was the sag and surge of history and in between a heightened sense of the fragility of life. The province and its cities were fitted, often splendidly, to portray the eternal pretensions of Rome; but this was border country, and beyond lurked the burgeoning menace of barbarism.[36]

It is now obligatory to note at these junctures that Augustine lived through the dying fall of the Roman Empire. Born in 354 he died in 430 – just months into the siege of Hippo and in the midst of the total capitulation of the province to the Vandals. In a late and consoling sermon to his parishioners he will refer explicitly to the dramatic visible decline of the province: 'However, we do admit that some things are happening more frequently; that through lack of materials and a deteriorating state of affairs, those buildings that were previously constructed with great magnificence are now falling and collapsing into ruins.'[37]

This coincidence of a famous life and a formative period is a happy one indeed for the historian. The details of Africa's decline add piquancy to Augustine's own preoccupation with temporality and the booms and busts of human empires that you could set your watch by. But at the same time, this preoccupation demanded an eye for what lies beneath history – as well as the nerve to discount the sensationalism of any passing moment. Augustine the boy as much as Augustine the man would find the stuff of life in the inexorable descent from the particular to the general. It is, for instance, no accident that in his *Confessiones* the thoughtless theft of pears from a neighbour's tree when he was a teenager will lead down to a lengthy speculation on man's predilection for evil. This could be taken as a model for the whole book, which is written to show how the singularities of one life veil over what is common to all. Human consciousness, its navigation of time and form, and the indefatigable impulse to religion.

But if this is the general direction in which knowledge works, there is inertia in the sensuous and intellectual delights of life. One of the reasons for Augustine's fascination today is that he became a Christian late and experienced many of these firsthand. There is a corresponding authenticity in his accounts of human temptation and the plain joys of living that is missing from other, more dogmatic authors. His youthful prayer, 'Give me chastity and continence, but not yet!' is legendary.[38] Yet there is more still. In Augustine's thought these things are often left to be surprisingly neutral. Women, the beauty of art and music, literature and even sport: any of these might have aroused suspicion and censure in a fifth-century Catholic bishop, yet Augustine chooses to treat each according to the dictates of common sense. These things have 'no small sweetness of their own' – he does not doubt that; he remembers it.[39] However, when you think about it, none of them is capable, either, of being anything final in itself. That quality of value is given them in the degree to which they are used by freely-choosing humans. Reaching, perhaps, a little too far to make his point, Augustine will explain it thus:

> But why, you could say that even to have sons is an evil thing; for after all, when their head is in pain, Non-Christian, unbelieving, mothers will seek furiously for impious charms and incantations! These point to the sins of humanity, not of the sons or the things put over them.[40]

This is in any case grounded firmly in the dogma of Genesis that 'God saw every thing that he had made, and, behold, *it was* very good.'[41] Where Augustine is a little unusual is in how he develops this into his interpretation of the *imago Dei* doctrine.

In his opinion, our intellectual and psychological equipment is perfectly adapted to notice those moments when we are briefly in concert with the Divine creation: those pauses between apprehending and understanding that the artists and mystics know so well. 'The beautiful things transmitted through the artists' souls into their hands all come from that beauty which is above their souls …'[42] At these times we may feel that we are like receiving sets tuned into the frequency of the Divine Mind; but the whispers of a phrenological order of truth and beauty are an illusion, and the real message is that God could have chosen to bring about any other creation with just the same effect.

> Even though we have some way or other dispersed the clouds, by walking as longing leads us on, and for a brief while have come within reach of that sound, so that by an effort we may catch something from that house of God (yet through the burden, so to speak, of our infirmity), we sink back to our usual level, and relapse to our ordinary state.[43]

If we could but take away our drive to become God-like by reverse engineering His creation, we would, Augustine thinks, be close to the original peace of Adam and Eve who neither 'looked before and after' nor 'pined for what is not'.[44] As it is, we remain highborn creatures of intellect and volition, capable of hearing and obeying God and therefore also of reproducing the complexity of His pleasure in the fitting and the right – of worshipping Him *ingenua voluntate* 'by ingenuous inclination'.[45] We cannot, as Augustine relentlessly stresses, be 'formed' apart from this direct, supernatural inspiration;[46] and so it is that until this happens we inhabit our fallen world of whispers and glimpses and (in place of God) our own method for making sense out of these things. 'This,' explains Augustine in a sermon to catechumens on the Creed, 'is the reason why the mind cannot be comprehended even by itself, because in it is the image of God.'[47]

As a child, Augustine did not have the advantage of this insight. In its absence, certain features of his family and their situation would have made a deep impression on him.[48]

Most abiding may have been the tenacity of his family's Latinity. It can be imagined how the strident and coherent identity of Latinity might have appeared to a self-conscious and enquiring boy, much given to analysis and with the child's gift for noticing irony. And as this is done it should be remembered also that to be a Latin in a far-off province of the Empire was to feel that one was part of the vanguard of an entire culture and civilization; and that one of the chief practical effects of this was a continuing sense of sacrifice and duty. Augustine's family were, in his own estimation, poor – and not the least cause of this was his father's status as *Decurio* 'Decurion'.[49] Decurions held a similar position in their towns to the Senators at Rome, but in the smaller scale of their world this was often to mean trouble and grief.[50] For as the Empire had grown it had become increasingly prudent to leave the administration of towns and cities to the local upper classes. On the whole they were happy enough to take this power and the opportunity to exploit. But over time, and inevitably, the costs of administration and the expectations of patronage could become a real burden.[51] They were expected to be munificent, in buildings, in statues and in games; yet the larger part of the taxes they collected were for Rome; so they were endlessly having to dig into their own pockets.

It seems that Augustine's father was in this position – and that his character and temperament were much described by it. These men felt status and civic honour as a double-edged sword.[52] In watching this pressure play out as a dynamic between his parents, Augustine may have had his first unfavourable introduction to the idea of worldly ambition and advancement. Certainly his assessment of his early years is remarkable (remarkable, that is, for a man of antiquity) for being set within a framework made out of his parents' competing agendas. On the one hand he gives us his father, slavishly pursuing the conceits of his age and being diminished by them. And on the other hand he gives us his mother. She is presented in the more expansive and kinder terms of spiritual destiny. Like her husband she harbours hopes of a brilliant career for her gifted son, but these are superseded by the care that she shows for his soul. In a letter written to Proculeianus, a Donatist predecessor of his in the see of Hippo, Augustine will give a picture of how these impressions had stayed with him down the years: 'Children have the same home with their parents, but not the same house of God. They desire to be secure of the earthly inheritance of those with whom they wrangle concerning the inheritance of Christ.'[53]

Augustine seems to have noticed in his mother many of the preoccupations that it was the business of the day to scorn. She stood for realism, but not the bourgeois realism of her husband. In her Christianity she had found an alternative to the martial certainty of the Latin as well as a way of referring her thoughts and actions to the gentle, quiet things that should ultimately matter more in the world. For example, when her husband was filled with the obvious joys at the signs of his son growing into puberty, she worried over the greater question of her son's salvation and became troubled in heart:

> You had already begun to build Your temple within my mother's breast and to lay there the foundations of Your holy dwelling place ... she was moved by a holy fear and trembling, and although I was not yet baptized [with time yet to err and return to cleanliness] she feared the crooked ways on which walk those who turn their back on You and not their face towards You.[54]

Notwithstanding why a boy like Augustine might have inclined towards his mother, it is necessary today to make some comment about it – if only to reassure that it was not for reasons of sentimentalism or to compensate for some unusual relationship. Modern psychological analysis will continue to see a promising case in Augustine: and the radicalism of many of his later ideas suggests to many this kind of an explanation. In a fascinating psychoanalytic study of the biographical foundations of Augustine's thought, Professor James E. Dittes couldn't help remarking that, '[i]f Augustine's neo-Platonic understanding of God and the world is monistic, it may not be too facetious to say that it is also mom-istic[!]'[55] Probably the most ordinary explanation is his genuine thanks to her for being the unstinting Christian voice in his life, and a guilt complex. As we shall see in coming chapters, Augustine tended to endure his father but lash out at his mother. He became more like him as he excelled in his studies and licked his lips at success. But he hated himself for selling out: and in proportion to this he became then very dismissive of his mother and her moralizing. On occasions he would be downright rude to her. Her glowing portrait in his *Confessiones* may be just a son making good.[56]

Scholars mostly agree that Augustine and his family were of indigenous African stock – Berber – though very much Romanized and speaking only Latin at home as a matter of some pride and dignity.[57] John K. Ryan speculates that if they had shared the typical features of their race (called *Afri* by the Romans) they would have been '... fair-skinned, with brown or yellow hair, and blue eyes.'[58] Clearly the more telling consideration is the question of self-identity. In his writings, Augustine leaves information to how conscious he was of his African heritage; and to standing out as one. He refers to Apuleius as 'the most notorious of us Africans.'[59] To Ponticianus as 'a countryman of ours, insofar as being African.'[60] To Maximinian of Madaura as 'an African man writing of Africa, or at any rate, with that flat nose that you see in Africans.'[61] And to Faustus of Milevis as 'an African Gentleman.'[62] Moreover, he will pick Cyprian out as the African in a line-up of bishops: 'Cyprian the African, Ilarius the Gaul, Ambrose the Italian, Gregory the Greek.'[63] Finally, when Julian of Eclanum meant to slight him by calling him Punic in one of their heated exchanges over Pelagianism, Augustine effectively played the race card. He reminded him that Cyprian of sacred memory had been Punic, and accused him of making an *argumentum ad hominem*. Julian was an Italian, the son of a bishop from Apulia.[64]

On a more humorous note, Augustine mentions that when he went up to Milan as Professor of Rhetoric his African accent was immediately picked up on as provincial, and made to feel embarrassing. He fought back, of course, and with the African Latin's weapon of choice: their fierce defence of the tradition: 'Nevertheless, the Italians still mock my pronunciation of many words, and in exchange they are always reprimanded by me over questions of pronunciation!'[65]

Embarrassment and its corollary, exasperation, were to feature heavily in Augustine's memories of his early years. The Latin culture of the Empire had tended, in the name of practical success, towards eclecticism rather than originality; what is more, it held to the general maxim of antiquity that wisdom was a finite quantity of infinite future applicability. The aim of the Roman schoolmaster was to locate it in the great books and then empty it whole into the minds of his pupils. The general-use concept of wisdom was also linked to practical success – far more even than it had been in classical Greece. And the measure of practical success, and therefore also the key to its influence over education, was (in the absence of our modern statistics and information) the ability to apply the static, enduring conceptions of wisdom to life in ways that were beautiful, elegant and, ultimately, persuasive. Rome's most celebrated teacher, Quintilian, would sum up the general ethos in the following way:

> If we constantly have occasion to speak of justice, fortitude, temperance, and other

similar topics, so that a cause can scarcely be found in which some such discussion does not occur, and if all such subjects are to be illustrated by invention and elocution, can it be doubted that, wherever power of intellect and copiousness of language are required, the art of the orator is to be there pre-eminently exerted?[66]

It was always the intention of Augustine's parents that their son should master this education and then proceed to a career in one of the great centres of Empire. The general pragmatism of the age made this a viable and proven aspiration for parents in their position and with an exceptional child. However, to its object the boy, the mercenary bent of it could also bring on cynicism and a despairing kind of hauteur. Augustine leaves no doubt as to his early delight in knowledge and understanding – and this notwithstanding the regular, institutionalized beatings which were the crucial part of an education that turned on memory and the faultless reproduction of archetypes. But it is the speed with which he passed through this stage and on to a reflective frustration that he wants us to consider of account in his life.

When he writes about these things it is usually in a way to make his readers ponder what true motives lay behind his education and his parents' full-bore attitude to it. His teenage years in particular are recounted under a sense of anger and disillusionment that so many of the critical parts of his personality have been left untouched and undeveloped.[67] He had a conscience and a sense that its demands were a vision of something great; in a sermon he will talk of how certain things are intuited *oculis cordis*, 'by the eyes of the heart';[68] yet it seemed as though his world did not reward interest in such things. It is probably not insignificant, then, that the first book to really 'change his life' – Cicero's *Hortensius* – will be picked up by accident, as an interlude from the regular tedium of university studies.

> In cahoots with those of my shallow [*inbecilla*] youth I studied the treatises on eloquence, in which I desired to shine, but for a damnable and inflated purpose. All directed towards empty, human joys. In the ordinary course of study I came upon a book by a certain Cicero, whose tongue almost all men admire in their ambition; but not his heart.[69]

To add to his general ire, he was to master the pattern of excellence demanded of him very young, in a way that invited him to consider himself the *de facto* superior of his parents and milieu. And we say additionally that the anecdotal style of his autobiography which excites us so much in a man of antiquity is perfectly adapted to convey this sense of the forlorn irony of life. A great part of its design must have been occasioned to bring this feature out into the open of its narrative. However, it is generally in his sermons to his parishioners – fellow Africans – that we see the ripened fruit of these early observations:

> They say that it is a great duty of natural affection for a father to lay up for his sons. We say that it is a great vanity. For, on the face of it, one who must soon die is only laying up for those who must soon die also. But let us forget the question of inheritance for a second and ask, 'Why do you even accumulate things for yourself in life, seeing that you must leave all behind you when you die?' This will of course be equally true for your children: they will certainly be succeeding you, but not to remain here long: and when they do eventually pass on, it will be like you, empty-handed. I haven't even begun to talk about what sort of children they may be – whether a happy debauchery will not simply waste what your care and covetousness has amassed. It may end up that they, by sheer dissoluteness, squander what you put together by so much sweat. But perhaps I am being excessively morbid? I will move on. It may just as well be that they are good children. That is true. Not being dissolute, but keeping what you have left them. Increasing what you have kept, and not dissipating what you have heaped together. But what conclusion can we still make from this happier scenario? Only that your children will then have been just vain as you if they did all of this well by your reckoning. By imitating you their father, they imitated only your vanity![70]

An emerging picture of the world as a place in which comfort and peace of mind are bought at the expense of unquiet hearts would not have been helped by the colonial traits of life in Roman North Africa: Augustine's early sense of misalignment will mature into a sense of his distance from the complacencies and assurances of Christian civilization – in fact a profound mistrust of the logics that human reason can impose on Christian revelation will remain a feature of his thought to its end. In later chapters we will see that his depictions of the traumas surrounding his conversion were chosen to show that sanity is not necessarily an ordinate response to our treatment by the world; that Christianity may often (to those who are fully conscious of it) be chosen over a profound kind of madness. There is a kind of morbid promotion of 'life' that gets at minds like Augustine's. Not the promotion of life as a spiritual phenomenon, as we associate it with thinkers like Tolstoy. But the kind of jolliness that turns, in the end, on those that cherish the consolation of sadness in what they see.

And how much human nature loves the knowledge of its existence, and how it shrinks from being deceived, will be sufficiently understood from this fact alone: that every man prefers to grieve in a sane mind, rather than to be glad in madness. And this grand and wonderful instinct belongs to men alone of all animals; for, though some of them have keener eyesight than ourselves for this world's light, cannot attain to that spiritual light with which our mind is somehow irradiated, so that we can form right judgments of all things.[71]

What it meant to be a provincial, and especially, as in the case of Augustine's family, a member of the curial class, was to have the Emperor's will hang over your head like the Sword of Damocles. This had not always been the case; but developments in the Roman world since 'the Golden Age' of the first and second centuries had led to a more personal and intervening style of imperial government.[72] Writing in his Enarrationes in Psalmos, Augustine will be able to talk meaningfully and fluently of the looming reality of the Emperor's will.

Just as in all things which you see done throughout the provinces, whatever the Emperor wills goes forth from the inner part of his palace throughout the whole Roman Empire. How great commotion is caused at one bidding by the Emperor as he sits in his palace! He but has to move his lips, when he speaks: then the whole province is moved, at what he has spoken being executed.[73]

This Machiavellian combination of fear and love that Augustine would have detected in his father's daily anxieties seems to have left its clear mark on him. In his most ostensibly political work, *De civitate Dei*, he will, for instance, cite with relish and approval the story of Alexander and the pirate. It was probably known to him through Cicero's *De re publica*. When asked by Alexander what he meant by infesting the seas, this brave pirate apparently answered: 'the same thing as you mean by infesting the world; but because you do it with a great fleet, you are called an emperor, and because I do it with a small ship, I am called a pirate!'[74] It would be by just such applications of a healthy sense of the ridiculous that Augustine would build on the learning of antiquity, showing how Christ breaks the circle by allowing us to encounter true otherness in Him for the first time: 'Hence Christ Himself also departs into the mountain from the men whose habit is to seek for His kingdom with earthly conceptions of it.'[75] But as we have already said, the child did not have the insight of the man. Patricius' entrapment in this vast web was to meet with a time-honoured response in his clever son: he became a figure of fun and assumption – along too with the general bombast of African Latinity.

As, perhaps, with colonial life anywhere, the overriding quality that Augustine was reacting to here was that of magnification. His family owed their status vis-à-vis the indigenous tribes of the province to a distant city that they had been born apart from and never even journeyed to. It was a tenuous situation that, in the right circumstances, might collapse under the weight of its superficial aspects; so the idea was to be always assertive and belligerent. It was a reputation for feistiness: Juvenal could despair of a Rome bedevilled by patronage and sluggish to real talent, and advise the best to leave, instead, for 'Africa' – *nutricula causidicorum*, 'nurse of advocates'.[76] Augustine will later be able to speak of how, '... city-bred men, even when illiterate, seize upon the faults of rustics.'[77] In the opinion of the wider Empire, the *Afri* were guilty of overworking their cultural inheritance – even if they had, for their part, contributed so much to the quality and vitality of the culture of the later Empire. Johann Gottfried Herder, a devastating critic of provincialism as a general tendency in any age, described a 'closed-in Pandaemonium of good taste [that] might blossom forth to the honour and slight advantage of [its] little corner of the world.'[78]

In essence, the *Afri's* use of Latin was deemed self-conscious and pointed; and that was because it had, on the whole, to do too much. The ordinary processes of intellectual cross-fertilization that might keep the Latin of the greater Empire modern and in step could not have their effect in the majority of the towns of Africa. It was left instead for Latin there to become a kind of relic, paraded about and fought over by schoolteachers, lawyers and men of education. Augustine will later have to censure a fellow African and man of letters, Maximus of Madauros, for facetiously ridiculing the Punic language in an exchange about religion: '... you ought even to be ashamed of having been born in the country in which the cradle of this language is still warm.'[79] Brown would call the whole effect 'Baroque'.[80] And one thinks also of Robert Graves's *Count Belisarius*: and the opinion of his Greek narrator on late antique Latin: 'The falsetto of a female impersonator[!]'[81] Augustine would of course go on to become the most well known and skilled exponent of the visual and energetic 'African Latin'. But it is not so often noticed that (after his childhood) he would link its idiosyncrasies, through his education, to the maddening perversity of earthly priorities.

Men suffer themselves to be cut and burnt, that the pains not of eternity, but merely some more lasting sore than usual be bought off at the price of an even severer pain. To win a languid and uncertain period of short repose, and that too at the decrepit end of his life, the soldier is worn down by all the hard trials of war. More restless in his labours than he will ever have rest to enjoy his prize at ease. To what storms and tempests, to what a fearful and tremendous raging of sky and sea, do the busy merchantmen expose themselves, that they may acquire riches inconstant as the very wind. Riches full of their own perils and tempests – greater even than those by which they were acquired! What heats, and colds, what perils, from horses, from ditches, from precipices, from rivers, from wild beasts, do huntsmen undergo. What pains of hunger and thirst, what straitened victuals of the cheapest and meanest meat and drink, that they may catch a beast! And sometimes, after all of that, the flesh of the beast for which they have endured turns out to be of no use for the table. And although a boar or a stag is finally caught, we know it to be sweeter to the hunter's mind because it has been caught, than it is to the eater's palate because it has been dressed. By what sharp corrections of almost daily stripes is the tender age of boys brought under! By what great pains even of watching and abstinence in the schools are they exercised, not to learn true wisdom, but for the sake of riches, and the honours of an empty show, that they may learn arithmetic, and other literature, and the deceits of eloquence![82]

4

Reflections on infancy

Begin, baby boy, to recognize your mother with a smile:
Ten months have brought her long travail.

Virgil

Six chapters into the first book of his *Confessiones*, Augustine offers a sustained series of remarks on infancy. He begins, naturally enough, with his own infancy; or at any rate, of what he was later told of it by his parents and nurses. He also lets it be known that he is drawing on his own observations of infants through the years – mainly, one assumes, of his son, Adeodatus; but he chooses not to mention this explicitly. These remarks are often remarked upon in turn by readers touched and surprised at their presence in a mind of such antiquity, as if the ability to be candid is a reflection on modern times. And yet it would be fatal if they were to be sentimentalized here.

Infancy was a condition of deadly seriousness to Augustine. Each new infant carried with it the hopes of mankind – could, in its growth and development, prove or disprove the human capacity for good, around which Christianity had staked the greater part of its intellectual respectability. 'Of our toil that is to come, the infant's very cry is witness. From this cup of sorrow no one may be excused. The cup that Adam has pledged, must be drunk.'[1] Pre-Christian thought had never faltered in its assumption that we have at least a portion of our destiny entirely in our power. In the very worst scenario, we have free will. That is to say, we can at least choose whether to go kicking or quietly with the Fates. Then Christianity dropped all of a sudden into this pleasant scheme that offered benign if awesome visions of the Heavens, and a responsible rôle for man beneath them. Like a disturbing ripple that goes to every corner of a surface, Christianity dropped the question of the innocence of the human condition – what Vladimir Nabokov called the 'dark dews of its unhallowed origin'.[2]

This subversive idea of innocence was always going to be the most serious disturbance to the pagan theories of moral action and their requirement of a clean slate for reason to work upon. Innocence introduced a pristine condition, sufficient only to be lost; and never to be recovered quite the same again. And so it came to pass that some of the highest philosophy and theology was made to hang breathless over the thrashing limbs of babes. Some of Augustine's most bitter and protracted polemic would be spent on the Pelagian heresy and its insistence that infants bring nothing of this new anthropology of sinfulness into the world: that the Christian dogma of Grace and new birth is a needless and cruel imposition, badly out of alignment with the esteem in which we would prefer to hold the all-good God.

Today the pinch is more likely to be felt in the psychological point of view. Innocence is the suppressed premiss to many psychological techniques of enlightenment and liberation that associate human ills with fundamental maladjustments of one sort or another. The psychoanalytical school of Sigmund Freud is the outstanding example and historical first. It has entered the popular mind as the idea that a human life is a chronological sequence of reactions – some conscious, but by far the greater number, unconscious, and therefore more decisive overall. The cause of these reactions is society in its moral guise as civilization. For whenever a child arrives into the world it finds more in civilization to inhibit its natural inclinations than to encourage them. And it is the oftentimes arbitrary basis of these inhibitions that makes the eventual effects of repression appear irrational. As Freud would put it:

> With irresistible might it will be impressed on you by what processes of development, of repression, and of sublimation and reaction there arises out of the child, with its peculiar gifts and tendencies, the so-called normal man, the bearer and partly the victim of our painfully acquired civilization.[3]

It goes without saying that the depth of this kind of analysis exceeds anything that was available in Augustine's day because it incorporates the unconscious. However, the requirement of innocence is there to allow a straight line of sorts to be drawn. The idea that we can recover our pristine selves from the archaeology of our psychological formation turns out to be as potent a myth as the ancient idea that we can capitalize on our intellectual consanguinity with the Divine. For in both myths, reason labours to remove the tarnishing effects of the world and restore us to the idealized versions of ourselves. And yet some might say that the inspiration for these idealized versions comes from another place; so that it is unrelated, *post hoc, ergo propter hoc*, to the actual human capacity for self-improvement. It turns out, of course, that Augustine was one of these. In his writings against Donatism, he would deploy one of his trustiest insights to make this point.[4] Against the Donatist preoccupation with purity – the purity, in this case, of the Christian sacrament of baptism, and its dependence for this on the purity of those who administer it – he would set the Christian portrayal of the world as a place in which all secular narratives of enlightenment and progress are parasitic upon the good that God has chosen to inject into history. The human need to administer God turns out to be incidental to His final plans; it may or may not be used by Him to further them. In a sermon, Augustine will, for example, talk of how the traditional lights of conscience are *de furtis fecerunt*, 'stolen', and passed off as *peculia sibi*, 'private property', by those eager to have their benefits reflect well upon them.[5]

It was this wilfulness, congenitally passed from generation to generation, that Augustine was to remind the Donatists of. It is the possessive side to fallen human understanding that causes it to hang, at times, as by a thread. In a better world it would be trumped and superseded. For now God tolerates it is the impetus, as even the ornament, of civilized life; but the Christian imputation is that the final happiness that it intimates is a Person, rather than a belief, or even a special degree of understanding. Moreover, in the exciting projects of life and careers, of success, we are liable to forget that there must be some serious wound left for God to tend. Otherwise He simply passes out of all range of relevancy and existence.

> You don't seek out a physician in order to wound yourself; but you do seek one out when you have been wounded and need to be tended. This shows that, even though we are evil, we know how to give good things to our children after the present time – temporal good things, such as concern the body and flesh. This is a true logic of care and a true giving. For who would doubt that these are good things? A fish, an egg, bread, fruit, wheat, the light we see, the air we breathe, all these are good. We can go on to include the very riches by which men are lifted up, and which make them loathe to acknowledge other men as their equals. Riches which cause men to be lifted up rather in love of their dazzling clothing, than with any thought of their common nature. Yes, even these riches, I repeat, are good. But here comes the point: all these goods which I have now mentioned may be possessed by good and bad alike; and though they be good themselves, yet have no power in themselves to make their owners good.[6]

Whenever Augustine expressed the hope that 'God's good that they love, may be the God Himself Whom they love',[7] he was therefore triumphantly declaring the importance of the 'life' – of the human life. Of any human life. For lives do need a Saviour, after all; rather than salvations that can be written out like prescriptions. This is proved, in any case, by how the grateful patient will go behind the prescription to the reality, or even just the idea, of whomever wrote it. To give thanks. The even-keeled handling of the good things of the world is a very difficult neutrality for anyone to keep up. It requires a God Who is trusted implicitly. Augustine thinks that this is unlikely to happen this side of eternity. It is just too difficult for us not to keep beginning at the end of the story, where happiness goes. We forget, so easily, once words get going, that human lives are not for planning in advance – though that is how we are forced to conduct them so much of the time. A Personal Saviour, interacting and piloting in the present, is really the optimum on any considered reflection. This is not, however, an entirely abandoned theme. It still bursts out in some literature, such as Alexander Solzhenitsyn's *Cancer Ward*:

> 'Happiness is a mirage.' Shulubin was emphatic, straining his strength to the utmost … As for the so-called 'happiness of future generations', it's even more of a mirage. Who knows anything about it? Who has spoken with these future generations? Who knows what idols they will worship? Ideas of what happiness is have changed so much through the ages. No one should have the effrontery to try to plan it in advance. When we have enough loaves of white bread to crush them under our heels, when we have enough milk to choke us, we still won't be in the least happy. But if we share things we don't have enough of, we can be happy today! If we care only about "happiness" and about reproducing our species, we shall merely crowd the earth senselessly and create a terrifying society …[8]

It was through thoughts such as these that Augustine reacted to Donatism – setting up its partisanship as a prime example of how the mysterious Christian process of Grace and new birth discredits these boastful visions.

> For it is the Church that gives birth to all, either within her pale, of her own womb; or beyond it, of the seed of her bridegroom – (either of herself, or of her handmaid.) But Esau, even though born of the lawful wife, was separated from the people of God because he quarrelled with his brother [Cf. Gen. 25.23]. And Asher, born indeed by the authority of a wife, but yet of a handmaid, was admitted to the land of promise

on account of his brotherly good-will [see Gen. 30.13]. It was also not the cause of being born of a handmaid, but his quarrelling with his brother, that stood in the way of Ishmael, to cause his separation from the people of God. And he received no benefit from the power of the wife, whose son he rather was – for after all, it was in virtue of her conjugal rights that he was both conceived in and born of the womb of the handmaid [see Gen. 16.11; 17.20]. In the case of the Donatists it is the same. It is the right of the Church (which exists in baptism) that whosoever is born receives his birth; but unless they agree with their Catholic brethren in a unity of peace, they will not come to the land of promise – from there never to be again cast out from the bosom of their true mother, but to be acknowledged in the seed of their father. If they persevere in discord, they will have none of this and belong to the line of Ishmael. For Ishmael was first, and then Isaac. And Esau was the elder, Jacob the younger. Not that this should imply that heresy 'gives birth' before the Church, or that the Church herself gives birth first to those who are carnal or animal, and afterwards to those who are spiritual [by a necessity of rebaptism]. The question goes rather to the actual lot of our mortality, in which we are clearly born of the seed of Adam, of which, '... that *was* not first which is spiritual, but that which is natural; and afterward that which is spiritual.' [1 Cor. 15.46]. All dissensions and schisms are based in some level of heedlessness of this. There can be no baptizing or re-baptizing according to the mere animal sensation [*animali sensu*] of man, because, '... the natural man receiveth not the things of the Spirit of God ...' [1 Cor. 2.14] And the apostle says that all who persevere in this animal sensation belong to the old covenant [see Gal. 4.24].[9]

As we might expect of a man concerned with the final good of humankind, Augustine introduces his reflections on infancy with a dilemma of perspective. He addresses a prayer to God in which he ponders '... whence I came into what I may call a mortal life or a living death.'[10] It is relatively well-known which perspective he did eventually take for his own: his *Soliloquiorum* contain this infamous and divisive question: 'What death would not be preferable if the soul so lived as we see it in a boy newly-born?'[11] Elsewhere, in his *De civitate Dei*, he asks again, 'If anyone were offered the choice of suffering death and becoming a child again, who would not recoil from the second alternative and choose to die?'[12]

Questions like these are liable to be very shocking, especially to those with children of their own; but Augustine's purpose in making them was only partly to inquire into our need to associate infancy and childhood with the innocence and hope of a clean slate. His main purpose was rather to invite reflection on the realities of these conditions – on how, for instance, childhood does actually appear to the child with its different priorities, and before it has been too heavily compromised by its involvement in life. For he fervently believed that the shock that arises from any blunt questioning of the myth of human innocence has behind it a kind of mawkishness; and that it is correspondingly open to anyone to journey into their memory and find there an early and complex episode that resonates with the Christian analysis of the human condition. The telling episode that Augustine would find in his memory would come from his teenage years and the bathhouse at Thagaste. It is recorded in his *Confessiones* and is considered in some detail in the next chapter.

But Augustine quickly moves from here to a very technical philosophical speculation that he admits in advance is a little gratuitous:

> What does it matter to me if someone does not understand this? May he also rejoice and say, 'What is this?' [Cf. Exod. 13.14] May he rejoice even at this, and may he love to find You while not understanding, rather than, while understanding, not finding You.[13]

It involves him making a distinction between *vivere*, 'life', and *esse*, 'being'.

Life is the mysterious vitality that holds us all in thrall and whose sway is even today only imperfectly understood. It is one of the major objects of natural wonder for Augustine; and speculations on it therefore feature throughout his writings. This examples is from his *De Trinitate*:

> We ourselves, *i.e.* our minds, are not sensible things, or bodies, but intelligible things, since we are *life*. And yet, as I said, we are so familiarly occupied with bodies, and our thought has projected itself outwardly with such a wonderful proclivity towards bodies, that when it has been withdrawn from the uncertainty of things corporeal, it flies back at once to those bodies, and seeks rest there in that same place from which it has drawn the very weakness of uncertainty. This in spite of knowing full well that it could be fixed with a much more certain and stable knowledge in that which is spirit [14]

Now the key point in these speculations in relation to infancy is as follows. When Augustine puts such standard rhetorical questions as 'Where except from You, O Lord, could such a living being come? Who has the art and power to make himself?',[15] he actually has in mind a specific and perplexing detail that is responsible for much of the sense of unfairness and injustice in the world. It is the detail that none of us chooses to be born. In fact, such a choice is a logical impossibility. Yet the sense of luck and arbitrariness associated with the circumstances of a birth is something that has to be dealt with very seriously, and after the fact, by moral and social philosophy. Or, perhaps, in times to come, by medical engineering.[16]

> God made the poor and the rich of one clay; so the same earth supports alike the poor and the rich. By dint of human right, however, one says, 'This estate is mine, this house is mine, this servant is mine.' We see therefore that 'by human right', is meant the 'right of the emperors'. Why so? Because God has distributed to mankind these very human rights through the emperors and kings of this world.[17]

By the same token death is for the time being unavoidable. One can choose when to die, and how; but the choice not to die is out of one's control. But Augustine's purpose in beginning with these things is not pure gloom. It is the interesting one of undercutting, by repeated suggestion, the venerable imagery of the limbo of infancy. It is often enough marvelled at that many animals give birth to competent youngsters – kicking and fighting and soon on their own feet. The newborn human is said, by comparison, to be hopelessly helpless. This is true enough in terms of the physicality of survival. But Augustine thinks that to see the matter only in these terms is to cut short a whole host of insights. There is so much that can be learnt by considering first the extent to which the newborn child is already, irreparably, underway; sparked from nowhere in the miracle of generation, but nevertheless, and tragically, underway.

> In the daily casualties of life we are each of us so beset by the possibilities and threats of numberless deaths that I would ask whether it is not better to suffer one straight off, and die, than to live in fear and uncertainty of them all? I am not unaware of the mean-spirited fear which prompts us to 'choose life', and to persist in what we could call the cruel suspense of living. But the weak and cowardly shrinking of the flesh is one thing, and the well-considered and reasonable persuasion of the soul quite another.[18]

Being is the psychological condition that life puts us into. Being implicates all human resources for survival, up to and including the rational apprehension of knowledge. Being is therefore something that we do not share in common with God. It is of the order of the negative developments that came out of the fall of Adam and Eve. It is really another term for self-consciousness. Like self-consciousness, it seems to have had the significance to Augustine of a parable. Meditating on it he was able to get himself into a full flow of material that resonated with the humanism of the day, and that also allowed him to feel the classical antecedents of what he was doing. For classical authors tended to reset to the thought experiment of an original position when drawing out the common sense of what reason had to contend with. So Augustine could feel in good company and genuinely encouraged that what he was picking out was an unbroken line, tracing a single contour. Just this one example from Cicero shows it well:

> There is one special difference between men and brutes. The latter are governed by nothing but their senses, never looking any farther than to what is striking and affecting them in the present. They have very little, if any concern, for what is past or to come. But men are creatures endowed with reason, which gives them a power to carry their thoughts to the consequences of things, and to discover causes before they have yet produced their effects. They see through to the whole progress of things, from their first seeds, and the first appearances of them. They compare like occurrences with like: and by joining what is past and what is to come, they are able to make a just estimate of the one from the other. They see their lives in this whole view of them, and accordingly make provision for the necessities of them.[19]

For Augustine, then, being is profoundly related to the perception of it. In the Garden of Eden it might not have been distinguished from life at all had Adam and Eve not wilfully dissociated themselves from the eternal perspective of God's decisions for them. But now that that divorce has taken place, it must bear the full burden of this present condition in which the future monopolizes what is not known, the past determines what *is*, and the present is set in stark but elusive relief by both.

> And the whole of this life is without question a tribulation to the understanding. For the soul has two tormentors, that do not set to torturing it at once, but keep up a sadistic alternation. These two tormentors' names are, Fear and Sorrow. When it is well with you, you are in fear; when it is ill, you are in sorrow.[20]
>
> What then is man's life, even that which is called a long one? They call that a long life, which relative to this world's course, is minuscule; and what is more, groans abound even before the decrepitude of old age. What they call a human life is but brief, and of short duration; yet how eagerly is it sought. With how great diligence, with how great toil, with how great carefulness, with how great watchfulness, with how great labour do

men seek to live here for a long time, and to grow old? And yet what is this very 'living long', but running to the end? You had yesterday, and you wish also to have tomorrow. But when this day and tomorrow are passed, they are both lost to you. We say, therefore, that you wish for the day to break, that that may draw near to you what you in truth have no wish to come! You make some annual festival with your friends, and hear it there said to you by your well-wishers, 'May you live many years!' And of course you wish that what they have said may come to pass. But hang on a second. You mean you wish that years and years may come, but that the end of these years may not? That is exactly what you mean: but see now how your wishes are contrary to one another. You wish to walk on, yet do not wish to reach the end.[21]

Augustine's approach to infancy, and the question of what gets underway at birth, prompted him to develop advanced interests in 'time' – or what is called the philosophical problem of time; the difficulty we have when separating it out from life-on-the-move by the ordinary methods of perception. The problem of time became a kind of shorthand for what he meant for 'temporality'. And his kindred interest in the rhythmical requirements of words, sounds and music led to him giving it a very full and fluent treatment across his writings; though nearly everything that he had to say is included in his famous set-piece treatment of it in the 11th Book of his *Confessiones*. It has always been admired. Bertrand Russell thought it was the aspect of his thought that worked best as a standalone item of secular philosophy.[22] It is subjectivist, even solipsistic: but it begins in the importance of proving, against various sceptics and the classical tradition, the viability of the staple of creation *ex nihilo*.

To say, as the Christian must, that God created the universe from nothing, was to come up sharply against the longstanding classical dogma that eternity is represented in some or other primordial matter – some *urstoff*. For this *urstoff* was said to continue, unperturbed, beneath the flux of life, so that all Divine creative activity could be explained, in the first instance, as this material's submission to the demands of form, purpose and reason. We have already examined in Chapter 2 how this general idea attracted the classical mind. And it is not much of a stretch, either, to see that this role for God was in fact very similar to the thin role that a scientist today might assign Him for the explanation of the start of the universe – as the Aristotelian 'unmoved mover' of an otherwise inexplicable first event.

Given these facts, it was always going to be likely that educated pagans would see holes in the traditional Christian language of Divine immutability and omniscience – language in any case borrowed from the idealist imagery of Platonism and Neo-Platonism. This discourse took it for granted that God is the final, logical counterpart of all human brooding and indecision: therefore Augustine faced critics primed to point out that a God Who decides to create the universe at some arbitrary moment cannot be the same God Whom we wish to envisage when we apply the logics of impassability. He cannot be the same God because to undergo the internal changes we associate with volition would make Him irredeemably, psychologically human. If He had to come into His own mind on the question of creating the universe then He must be subject to that same moral reasoning by which we punctuate and parse our time-bound experience. And this, of course, is intolerable to Christian orthodoxy. If a man had existed serenely in some fixed and eternal perfection of behaviour, then suddenly created the universe from nothing, we would say that he had changed the terms of his existence. We would also probably say that, in acting without any conceivable precedent, he had acted irrationally. Even if we allow that God could have decided to create the universe and be unchanged by that decision, we face the question of why He acted when He did. Moreover, if, as Christianity teaches, He acted to create something that was good and pleasing to Him, why did He not act sooner to produce this effect?

Overall, then, these pagan arguments achieved their effect by drawing attention to the special difficulties created by the Christian insistence on a monotheistic, personal God. This insistence asks us to conceive of God as a being – albeit a very special being – Who is living out a narrative, much as we are. However, in God's case, it is a narrative which, by its very nature, must be higher than, better than, and in fact the negation of, all that we would predicate of Him. The problem is that of the Divine being, living and acting and occupying time Himself. To the pagan mind it is natural to assume that this is what the Christian means – that time, and the possibility of a narrative through it, is anterior to God as much as it is anterior to man. And having made this assumption, it is only natural for him to point out that you cannot have this *and* the language of impassability for your God.

Against this, Augustine fell back on the plainest dogma. The Christian has been misunderstood. He does not wish to see his God in this way as a kind of superman in time. What he means by eternity and the residence there of God is not the endless extension of time forwards and backwards. Time, like everything else, was actually a creation of God *ex nihilo*.

There simply was no time when there was only God, and nothing else. In Augustine's words:

> Time would not have existed without a creation. It took something to be made, which, involving motion, could bring it about through change ... Since the various parts of change and motion cannot all happen at once, time is what occurs when one passes away and another succeeds it in longer or shorter intervals of duration.[23]
>
> There is no doubt that the world was not made in time, but with time ... When it was created, change came into existence.[24]

Differentiation, and all that depends upon it intellectually and materially, requires that reality actually pass us by; and this is tantamount to saying that were all the things that make up reality suddenly to vanish, we would not be able to talk of time in any sensible way. In fact, we would not be able to talk at all on the terms of the theory. In a favourite expression of Augustine's, syllables and words become the most acute descriptors of our temporal restrictions and cancel this outlet altogether.

> They rise and set; and by rising, they begin as it were to be; and they grow, that they may become perfect; and when perfect, they wax old and perish; and all wax not old, but all perish. Therefore when they rise and tend to be, the more rapidly they grow that they may be, so much the more they hasten not to be. This is the way of them. Thus much have You given them, because they are parts of things, which exist not all at the same time, but by departing and succeeding they together make up the universe, of which they are parts. And even thus is our speech accomplished by signs emitting a sound; but this, again, is not perfected unless one word pass away when it has sounded its part, in order that another may succeed it.[25]

If eternity does indeed underwrite temporality, it is not because it outpaces it in any of the continuing, passive senses of the classical imagination. We are not so much *here* because it is *there*. Augustine has something different in mind to the assurances of Newtonian absolute time. We are here because from here we must escape to there: to God. As he puts it:

> Who will hold the heart of man, that it may stand still, and see how the still-standing eternity (itself neither future nor past) utters the times future and past? Can my hand accomplish this, or the hand of my mouth by persuasion bring about a thing so great?[26]

Of course this is not yet Augustine's subjectivist, solipsistic theory of time. It is still very much what is technically termed an 'internal-relational' theory; the belief that time is satisfactorily accounted for by the motions of bodies. What links this to the purely mental activity of the contemplation of time is a new difficulty, which shows itself as we accept time as a concrete structure of creation. What Augustine means is the age-old question of the measurement and definition of time:

> For what is time? Who can easily and briefly explain this? Who even in thought can comprehend it, or set out a single word that truly concerns it? Yet when we speak we refer to nothing more familiarly and knowingly than time. And thus certainly we understand something when we speak of it; and we understand also when we hear it spoken of by another. What, then, is time? If no one puts the question to me, I feel I know the answer. But if the question is put, and I begin to explain, I enter upon unknowing. But yet I am able to say with confidence, that if nothing were passing, there would be no past time; and if nothing were coming, there would be no future time; and if nothing *were*, there would be no present time. These two (sandwiching) times, past and future, beg the question of their existence: for what can they possibly *be* when the past is no longer, and the future is not as yet? And yet again, if the present were always present, and did not travel into past, time truly could not exist – but an eternity. This leaves it that if time present only comes into existence because it travels into time past, can we really say that it exists at all? That is to say, if its very cause of being is that it shall not be, we are left with the conclusion that time is something real enough to be worded but defined by perpetual migration.[27]

This passage makes it clear to see what a modern like Russell could so admire in Augustine's analysis of time. He constructs the whole problem around the seditiousness of the present – but more to the point, around how that seditiousness relates to our psychology as ethical beings. Time is always making us think of her twin-sister Eternity. She is always slipping into her clothes. We know that the two of them look identical; but we have given them these different names and separate identities. So it is all about us; and what naming and differentiating mean to us; and how these activities describe us. 'O human soul,' Augustine will put it, 'to you it has been given to perceive and to measure periods of time.'[28] Perhaps he means that the whole traditional problem of time is that it simply runs us too close to our equipment of soul. Perhaps time is all of itself a language of meaning rather than one of the discrete phenomena that a language of meaning would confidently set out to describe. All spoken human languages are languages of meaning: they are all related to accomplishing the task of meaning. But when you think about it, one such language of meaning cannot actually be used to describe another in the deconstructive, analytical sense. You can use one language of meaning as the signpost to another. You can point at German to make a general statement of class about English. And seeing them both as examples of the same thing will tell you something real about language. You might take this further, and dissect them side by side into their grammars. This you can do. But you cannot talk about talking, or write about writing, without invoking psychology, theology and God.

Time is something that we feel in its passage through our soul, the special instrument of its perception. For Augustine, this means that it is intimately related to our deportment as rational decision-makers: 'Time does not take "time off"; nor for that matter, does it turn without a purpose through our senses. In fact it works wondrous effects in our minds.'[29] It is on this basis that he is able to give an entirely authentic account of the seditious present – what the psychologist William James was to call a 'saddle-back'.

> In short, the practically cognized present is no knife-edge, but a saddle-back, with a certain breadth of its own on which we sit perched, and from which we look in two directions into time. The unit of composition of our perception of time is a *duration*, with a bow and a stern, as it were – a rearward and a forward-looking end.[30]

The actual present of our consciousness must clearly have some duration, or even occupy some space. In the 11th book of his *Confessiones* Augustine opts for the convention of saying that it must have 'length'. But this much that seems obvious becomes immediately problematic when we try to specify the actual present quantitatively. The effort launches us on the frustration of an infinite regress; it can be snipped smaller and smaller; and soon it becomes clear that the difficulty of isolating the actual present is in direct proportion to the dilemma we would be in if it were not there.

> Let us imagine that the present time which alone we found could be called long is abridged to the space of a single day. But even this requires qualification. For no one day is present to us as a whole. It is made up of at least 24 hours of night and day. Of these, the first hour looks to all the others as its future; the last looks back to them as its past; while any in between look forwards and backwards to hours past and hours to

come. And of course, any one hour passes away in fleeting particles (of minutes and seconds). Whatever of it has flown away is past, whatever remains is future. The present is therefore properly speaking that particle of time of which no further diminution can be conceived. Continuing this logic, we say also that the present is that particle whose flight from future to past is so rapid that it could not conceivably be increased or extended in its size by any delay of this movement.[31]

The Augustinian present is given to us in his writings so as to appear as an intellectual conceit. It reminds us of his character and technique as a Christian apologist. He is not seeking our judgement on an explanation of God's status in human affairs that he can give. He is more in the cast of the interrogator, patient and unstinting, who develops in rapport and common ground the real table that can be turned. Time came to him as a good example of something that we can be cavalier with in the everyday; yet under close analysis it can undo us. And undone, and under its interrogation, we will say things we meant to keep hidden. Everything that is real is possible of doing this to us. Any reality looked on for meaning will (if we can keep up the gaze of *meaningfulness*) take us into self-knowledge; then out of that to God. Time is outstanding and traditional as one of the classic cases of this.

Augustine's whole analysis of time is based upon his assumption that it enjoys some kind of substantial existence. Not, as we pointed out earlier, the kind of indifferent existence of Newtonian absolute time; Augustine has in mind rather the kind of existence enjoyed by all God's creations. As something sprung up from nothing and being sustained. This assumption drives him further into the idea that only the present can be real to us if by 'real' we mean a sensation directly consonant with its instant of perception. So we might say that the past is real only in terms of the memories of it that we invoke in the present of our consciousness, while the future is real only as a projection of our present fancies and fears.

This latter point is particularly striking. Augustine does not adopt the convention of saying that the future is like a train, setting off from some distant station and certain to arrive. He says something very different and destabilizing. He says that the future cannot bear any of the timetabled familiarity of the arriving train save in the mental confections of it that we are compelled to make. Inductive reasoning in the present gives us the future, as a calculation of probabilities based upon our memory of the characteristics of the past.

But here Augustine has a question. He wants to be able to know how God has been able to convey things future to his prophets. Now if the future were a fruit that God could pluck and hand back to man, or a train that he could cause him to meet ahead of schedule, this question would seem theologically straightforward and admit of a simple answer. But the problem, for Augustine, is more profound than this; and in any case, he means by his question to imply something very bold. How does God pluck what does not exist to be plucked? On the modern Newtonian view we think of the future as a country that we have not yet journeyed to, but a country none the less. It has fruit trees and trains. The question of future uncertainty is a question of probabilities; that is, of the exact coordination of properties already known. God holds a perspective on this which science may one day have for its own. We say in this event that the future will always remain as the thing approaching, but, by supercomputing all the known causes of its effect, we might one day no longer have to live in the thrall of what might be.

However, the question that Augustine has to ask about how God teaches the prophets takes for its raison d'être that none of this can be. In Augustine's mind is the future as something that must assume all the traits of God's personality. So the future is something that is truly and utterly unknowable. And being unknowable it confounds the swagger that we create upon knowledge. The future is the standoff between what God is doing *ex nihilo* and what we are doing when we say that it will be Monday or Tuesday or Wednesday. These names, and others like them, are pylons that we string through with the ancient mind's dream of the unbroken, eternal primordial matter. God may do what He likes, but we can tug on this cable, and somewhere the future feels it. It is this idea of time travel along the stood-up line that Augustine wants to question:

> How is it, Ruler of all, that You teach to certain souls the things of the future? I mean, of course, the manner in which You have taught Your prophets. How is it that You to Whom nothing is future are able to teach these men future things? Or as I should really express it, how do You teach as the presently knowable what stands already in the future? For what stands in the future does not exist. And what does not exist we know cannot be taught.[32]

Augustine may be the first Western thinker to launch this idea that time is what the infant breaks out into as into its first language of meaning. Strictly speaking, of course, this happens at that indeterminable moment of its first life in conception. But we can pass over that question here. To think requires a starting point and a space for logic to unfold; to speak, more emphatically so still in the sounding out of words. As we grow older, we graduate into the sophistications of vocabularies and grammars. But no such sophistication overcomes and eradicates the infant trauma of being catapulted into existence. All language bleats 'I am here' before it makes up into propositions about things.[33] This latter, predicating function of language would seem to suggest that we can attain to a respectful distance from life and stand in judgement over it. But what it really shows – what all of it shows – is how we were underway from our very first breath. Driven into our minds the better to perform the sacrament of measurement over a world that it would seem implausible to grasp by any other means than such self-consciousness.

> In you, O my mind, I measure times … In you, I say, I measure times. I do this by noting the impression which things make on you as they pass you by. A certain something remains to linger in my memory once they have passed: it is this lingering thing that I measure as time present: and not the ceaseless movement of future into past. This I measure when I measure times; and in such wise that if these are not times (as we customarily call them), then I don't know what I measure, and what are! But wait. Am I saying, then, that we could measure a silence – and say that such and such a silence has lasted as long as such and such a voice? I assuredly am. Why not? – it leaves its impression all the same. For example, do we not extend our thought to the measurement of a fictitious voice as if it had sounded, whenever we wish to say something about the intervals of silence in a given space of time? With both the voice and tongue still, we go over in thought poems and verses, and any discourse, or dimensions of motions; and we do this in order to settle concerning the spaces of times, how much one may be in respect of another; and we do this in silent mental calculation as if we were speaking it out loud. Another example. A man wishes to utter a lengthened sound, and determines with forethought how long it should be. We see how in silence he passes through a space of time in order to procure this mental determination. Then we see how, so determined, he commits that determination to memory. When finally he produces his lengthened sound and speech, it will be from memory that his determination will have issued. These examples show us that human intentionality (as it were) consumes the future. Furthermore, intentionality would be inconceivable without memory. It is in the memory that present time exists as the kind of backdating of the future which we wish to reconcile with the past of our intention.[34]

In sum, Augustine thinks that advanced speculation on time can be fruitful and revealing, but that these benefits accrue when it is realized that it is a tautologous activity. Only God can look out on time as from a distant shore and not be changed by what He sees; this is because 'He knows all times with a knowledge that time cannot turn back upon to measure.'[35] In the case of man, the smallest movement of his thoughts turns out to be as meaningful a measure of time as the revolutions of the planets, and so he is left hopelessly implicated from the start.[36] Augustine is often prompted by this thought to move seamlessly between time and the idea of 'vanity': '"Man is like to vanity: his days *are* as a shadow that passes away." [Ps. 144.4] Like to what vanity? We mean time, which passes on, and flows by. For this vanity is said in comparison of the Truth, which ever abides, and never fails.'[37] And yet Augustine knows that you cannot round on this level of embroilment with the directness of antivenin. For time must in some sense at least be a part always of a plan of creation in which rational intelligence figures as the opposite of instinct – as the gift, in other words, of being able to be intentioned towards God in the free act of loving Him. And of being able to choose to obey Him over all the alternative routes to foreknowledge.

> In You, being and life cannot be different things, because supreme being and supreme life are one and the same. You are supreme and You are not changed [Cf. Mal. 3.6]. Nor is this present day spent in You – and yet it is spent in You, for in You are all times everywhere [Cf. Rom. 11.36]. Unless You contained them as their Orchestrator, they would have no way of passing on [Cf. Lam. 1.12]. And because Your years do not fail, Your years are the same thing as the single day of every day [Cf. Ps. 102.27; Heb. 1.12]. No matter how many days we have already spent in our lives, and then the days of our fathers – these *all* have passed through this single present day of Yours. From it they have taken their measures and their manner of being: and others still shall pass away and receive their measures and their manner of being in the same way. 'But Thou *art* the same' [Ps. 102.27], and all things of tomorrow and all beyond, and all things of yesterday and all things before, You shall make into today. And in fact You have already made them into today.[38]

Reflecting on infancy also allows Augustine an insight into the doctrine that all true good in the world can be shown to be attributable to God alone.

He begins by considering that most earnest and untrammelled goodness of all in the case of the infant: he means the milk that he received from his mother and various wet nurses:

> Through them You gave me the infant's natural food, meted out to me in accordance with Your law, and reflecting the riches that You have distributed down to the lowest levels of things. You gave me to want no more than You were prepared to give; but You gave also to those who nursed me the very will to give me what You had given them. By an affection that is its own explanation they gave me willingly what they possessed so abundantly from You. It was not merely good for them (spiritually) that my good should flow from their free gift; it was sacramental that something passed, not from them, but *through* them.[39]

Our mastery of nature has done a good deal to ruin this effect. But Augustine clearly intends to imply the sense in which we can be struck dumb by our meticulous calibration to the whole of the universe; the calibration that it has historically been the business of natural theology to investigate as evidence of God's generosity and majesty.[40] Things here were once upon a time made for our enjoyment and delight. You can see that in a wildflower or a waterfall. The difficulty of sustaining this sensation into a viable way of life is this whole wretched business of being, and its survivalist imperatives. It is no wonder, then, that Augustine moves his narrative quickly on to something that we touched on a little earlier. A subject that was of great importance to him as a man of letters and former Neo-Platonist philosopher: the human acquisition of language. To any idealist thinker, words are honoured with being the interface between mere human thoughts in time and the stable regions of truth that are said to exist outside this dimension. Augustine will call them *vasa electa atque pretiosa*, 'precious cups of meaning', and go on to exemplify this practice.[41] In another place he will put it as follows:

> If we closely consider the purpose we hold in mind when we are speaking … what else are we trying to do but to bring our mind (as far as this can be done) into touching distance of the mind listening to us. And, moreover, in such a way that this very tactility creates the broadcast of our knowledge and understanding. In a sense, then, we remain in ourselves and take no step outside ourselves, yet we produce a 'token' whereby there may be the comprehension of us in another. We might even say that this process, as it were, propagates the other mind to indicate its meaning.[42]

This emphasis has generally caused the idealist outlook to give rise to what are called 'picture theories of language', in which words are sensible only in relation to realities that they can signify. Today these theories are regarded after Ludwig

Wittgenstein to be rather naive, unable to account for the fact that the pictures behind words – their sense – are open to infinite manipulation by communities of speakers sharing a set of rules about their use. What is more, there are a great many words that we use relatively and relationally, to impart logical sequence to language. And these, as Wittgenstein would point out, do not have their obvious corresponding pictures.

> Augustine, in describing his learning of language, says that he was taught to speak by learning the names of things. It is clear that whoever says this has in mind the way in which a child learns such words as 'man', 'sugar', 'table', etc. He does not primarily think of such words as 'today', 'not', 'but', 'perhaps'.[43]

Now the passage from Augustine that Wittgenstein had in mind when he made this observation was his description of how he first learnt to speak as an infant child. Let us look at it now:

> I was unable to express all that I wished; nor was I able to express it to all whom I wished. And I pondered over this in memory: so, when they named a certain thing, and, at its name, made a gesture towards it, I observed the object and recognized that it corresponded to the name they uttered when they wished to show it to me. This procedure evolved before me in their bodily gestures, in a manner natural to all men. I was taught by their changes of countenance, nods, movements of the eyes and other bodily members; and of course the sounds of their voices, which indicate the affections of the mind in seeking, possessing, rejecting, or avoiding things. So little by little I came into the logic that the words set in their proper places, in various sentences, heard by me frequently, were signs of things. And when my mouth had become adept at these signs, I began to express by the means of them, my own wishes.[44]

However, we have already seen enough to know that when Augustine thinks of the infant's negotiation of being, he has in mind more than discrete examples. As we began this chapter by observing, the infant – his infancy – was his special muse for all things most deadly serious. The infant makes us think of life and being, time, goodness and evil, and now, language. The infant makes us think of ourselves as the little test-cases that we once were. Was it innocence that got us from there to here? God's wisdom is always a wordless quantity for Augustine – a phenomenon that he tries to convey in phrases like the *ineffabilia penetralia veritatis*, the 'unspeakable recesses of truth'.[45]

For the Word does not advance or increase as those increase who know It. Quite the opposite. It is entire if you abide by it: entire if you depart from it: entire when you return to it. It abides alongside itself, renewing all things. It is the very form of all things. It is the unfashioned Form – quite utterly unlike you, as I have said, and thus also without space. For whatsoever is contained in space is circumscribed. Every normal form is circumscribed by its bounds; it has limits, and an excellence it reaches to and fills. Again, we say that whatever can be contained in its particular place, must be less in each of its parts than in its whole. God grant that you may understand the import of this.[46]

Language struck Augustine as being of the order of human equipment that was originally created to make it possible for Adam and Eve to be drawn into the full security and happiness of God's Will. Its present function of articulating human volition in distinction from God he therefore took to be a telling aberration, and the perverse use of a paramount faculty. On the Augustinian analysis, language is, for this reason, part innate, part acquired; factory-fitted to the chassis, but driven on to a breakneck agenda. We might note also that, having made this distinction, Augustine did not then go on to what modern linguists and philosophers do, and investigate where exactly the balance should lie. This is probably why he has always had a place in the history of the study of language, yet has never been numbered among its great original contributors. The latter can come as a surprise; and it has been noted as an item of scholarship.[47] His overriding concern was rather to distinguish between bare rational intelligence, that is to say, the stripped machinery of it, and true wisdom, which he understood to be a function of the will to love and obey God. 'Believe the commandments of God, and do them, and He will give you understanding as your strength. Do not put (as it were) the last first, and prefer knowledge to the commandments of God.'[48]

At this thought we arrive at one of the great dichotomies of Augustine's thought. This is the difference between the human mind turned in upon itself and thrilled by what it sees, and innocence, a stranger to this proud self-sufficiency. When we have perfect peace in Heaven, he thinks that it will be signified by the fact that we have *nihil nobis repugnabit ex nobis*, 'nothing of ourselves opposed to ourselves'.[49] That Christ will have taken away *fluctuationem mentis de cordibus*, 'the fluctuation of mind from our hearts'.[50] The real tragedy of the human condition, the tragedy of pride and arrogance and self-love, is really the complete inability of the human being to be creative on its own initiative:

> For which reason the Apostle says, 'For our rejoicing is this, the testimony of our conscience.' [2 Cor. 1.12] See, there is the oil, the precious oil; this oil is of the gift of God. Men can put oil into their vessels, but what they will never do is create the olive.[51]

The problem is that a postlapsarian human intelligence must always rank true acts of creation and inspiration as arbitrary. Into this ranking, too, must go the Will of God. To the human animal everything is arbitrary until it has found some use for it. The pride of the race is the question 'Why?' – shorthand for the question 'To what purpose?' Wonder is said to point towards reason and the magnificence of the species. This is probably also why human wisdom is traditionally written up in books. Books can have a beginning, a middle, and an end: a purpose. Against this static and tame wisdom Augustine saw immediately how fearful the Face of God must really be. A Face with lips actually moving to create commands (that no amount of books could keep pace with). The dislocated human intelligence could analyze and debunk, classify and relate, but it could not do this – it could not reproduce the inspiration of God's Voice as it creates the emotions of love and longing that alone do bring about right experience of the world. In his philosophical dialogue *De libero arbitrio*, an early work begun in 388, just a year after his baptism, he would separate wisdom from the forensic possibilities of language, and the science of meaning.

> It is one thing to be rational, and another to be wise: for it is by reason that anyone is capable of receiving [and comprehending] a command, but obedience is a matter of faith. Just as it is the nature of reason to comprehend a command, it is wisdom which counsels obedience. This is the same thing as to say that it is in the nature of a rational creature to receive and comprehend commands, but wisdom is a function of something else, namely, the will.[52]

For Augustine this meant, too, that all instances of true insight, everywhere, occurring in the minds of Christians or non-Christians, had to be attributed to God's direct intervening. On his premises it was technically not possible for it to be otherwise. Unaided human reason may be able to heap up knowledge about the world; but knowledge about the world is knowledge about the world as it *is* – a genial cross-section of it. Wisdom (he meant the traditional 'highest' wisdom of the philosophers) was instead to do with what it might on the whim of God become. Here he struck a categorical difference between the world as it is capable of being understood by human reason and the world as it is moving to its final, preordained conclusion.

> That statement, therefore, which occurs in the gospel, '*That* was the true Light, which lighteth every man that cometh into the world' [John 1.9] has this meaning, that no man is illuminated but by that Light of the truth, which is God; so that it follows that no person should think that he is enlightened by his human teacher, even though that instructor may happen to be – I will not say, any great man – but even an angel himself. For the word of truth is applied to any man externally by the ministry of a bodily voice, but yet, '… neither is he that planteth any thing, neither he that watereth; but God that giveth the increase.' [1 Cor. 3.7]. Man indeed hears the speaker, be he man or angel, but in order that he may perceive and know that what is said is true, his mind is internally besprinkled with that light which remains forever, and which shines even in darkness. But just as the sun is not seen by the blind, though they are clothed as it were with its rays, so is the light of truth not understood by the darkness of folly [see John 1.5].[53]

To the modern mind convinced that the Christian guilt about sin has been a retarding force in the West, Augustine is the villain of the piece – the man who allowed his personal anxieties and tensions to give such a regrettable shape to so much of Christian thought. For, after all, if sin is to be something tangible, something that science might prove or disprove – a stain, perhaps, or a consistent behaviour – then the human capacity for goodness would seem to have the upper hand. Augustine is consistent and famous for warnings such as this: 'Bilge-water neglected in the hold does the same thing, in the end, as a rushing wave. Gradually it leaks in through the hold; and by long leaking in and no pumping out, it sinks the ship.'[54] But while history would back him up in its production of bad people, and bad episodes, it has also produced enough people of remarkable and instructive goodness. And then there is, more importantly still, the way that we have all had the personal experience of weighing ourselves against our moral consciences. We have all done bad things at one time or another; but in recording them as bad we prove that they were chosen over the good; and chosen freely, no less, in a way that makes the good seem just as plausible as the bad.[55] An American pastor writing during the Great War in 1918 was prompted to put the general difficulty in the following terms:

> … here we come upon the paradox that man is both impotent and free. He cannot change his heart at will any more than the leopard can change his spots; yet the

assumption which underlies all religious and ethical theory of any consequence is that he has to accept responsibility for his actions.[56]

In Augustine's reflections on infancy we may, however, have seen something at work that immunizes him from these criticisms. For the full force of his analysis falls on the infant will. It is the prized human freedom to act, rather than a nebulous concept of sin, that is his watershed between damnation and redemption. He says that the infant is not born innocent because he is born in full self-consciousness: and that this was not the state that Adam and Eve were created in but is the state that they had wilfully to fall into. 'For who was not born blind? Blind, that is, in heart.'[57] 'For if that infant could speak to you, it would say, "Why do you heed my infant cries and demands? It is impossible for you to see why from my pathetic actions of body: but I have been conceived in iniquity."'[58] As a result of this, the infant finds himself just the wrong side of eternity, and through no conceivable fault of his own. And of course it is around this cardinal unfairness that the Christian case has traditionally seemed to wilt.[59] But Augustine sees the situation somewhat originally, from the point of view only of the absence or the presence of God.[60] The outstanding feature of infancy is actually the infant's capacity to 'live within itself', in a state that 'escapes all cognizance and human perception'. We can, he continues, 'arrive at no date, or facts, to sustain controversy on the subject.'[61] The allowances that are made for infant behaviour are rooted in this feature – in the adult understanding that the infant has not yet situated itself in the wider world of other beings with equal and competing interests, and the rules that signify these things.

> I did reprehensible things at that time, but because I could not yet understand why anyone should blame me, there was nothing of custom or reason that was allowed to hold me to account. As we grow up, we root out such things and cast them off.[62]
>
> Consider what we see when nurses and mothers descend to babes, and although perfectly capable of speaking Latin, choose instead to shorten their words, and waggle their tongues about in a certain manner we know so well. They do this in order to frame childish endearments from a methodical language; and all of this because if they speak according to rule and rote, the infant will simply not understand and profit. And of course this gets taken to an even more extreme degree if we are talking of a father, well skilled in speaking – even such an orator that the forum resounds with his eloquence and the judgment-seats shake. If such a father has a little son, he returns home to him putting aside at once all that forensic eloquence to which he had ascended. And there,

in child's language specially adapted to the purpose of his love, he descends to his little one.[63]

What, then, is to be said of the mind of an infant, which is still so small, and buried in such profound ignorance of things? The mind of a grown man which knows anything at all shrinks from the sheer darkness of it ... In the case, too, of the other bodily senses, we find that the souls of infants hone in upon these faculties with staggering myopic intensity. In fact they are so bent upon them, that they either vehemently detest or vehemently desire only those things which offend or allure through the flesh. They do not think of their own inward self, nor can be made to do so by admonition; this is because they do not yet know the signs that express admonition (of which the chief of these are words). As with so many other things, they are wholly ignorant of them.[64]

What the infant is gifted at birth, then, is not innocence, but a short-lived concession from the grown-up pandemonium of preferences and rights – and, in the absence of God's Voice, no clear-cut way of reconciling these things. And this is why Augustine ends the story of how he acquired his language by referring it, through the theme of infant wilfulness, to the Earthly City: 'To those of my household I communicated the signs of what I wished to express. Through this means I entered more deeply and surely into the stormy society of human life; although still dependent on my parents' authority and the will of my elders.'[65]

Infants are true little unripe humans. Their ability to be so uselessly helpless and flapping about yet draw out the most unconditional resources of care and patience from their parents is one of those unquantifiable mysteries that grows. But in venerating it as we should, we can become muddled until we miss the bigger picture which it is always the purpose of Augustine's writing to give. Adam and Eve and what happened to them are always there as the central characters in Augustine's thinking – even when he does not explicitly introduce them. They are the centre of gravity of his mind. And this in turn accounts for something that happens very often with him in the really advanced scholarship. We can take his 'theory of language' as the example because we have ended with it here and it is convenient. If you try to pin any of his ideas down to another point than this centre of gravity of his in Adam and Eve, the effort often disappoints. To those wanting a compartmentalized theory of language for its own sake, Augustine's begins well, in an intuitive and vivid place; but it ends up by lacking detail and comprehensiveness. We might take Christopher Kirwan's disappointment at it as a classic reaction – a reaction that could just as easily work for other, similarly isolated aspects of his thought – politics being a well-documented example, but equally his psychology or ethics. From Kirwan, then: '[His] characterization of language ... is neither original nor profound nor correct. Nevertheless it is appealing, it is bold, and it has had – partly through the wide currency of Augustine's writings – a lasting influence.'[66]

For a long time, assessments such as Kirwan's have been deemed to show the appropriate level of generosity and respect to Augustine now that so much water has passed under the bridge. They contain the vital truth that Augustine's writings have enjoyed the most remarkable and sustained *wirkungsgeschichte*. This has been partly due to the comparative intellectual freedoms that Augustine enjoyed in his day – not yet working under the constructions that we must contend with when we think, say, of historical Christianity in its European context. His ideas could freewheel between classical humanism and the exciting new access that Christian ideas like sin and self-deception granted to the dark and unatoned places of the soul. Tragedy and misfortune had been well-chronicled by the earliest poets as the clockwork destinations of human nature. But to make human nature itself the destination for intriguing inner battles of psychology and the will was the Christian change. In this respect, Augustine is one of the giant interdisciplinarians of the post-Christian West; and his recognition as such is one of the burgeoning discoveries of scholarship.[67] His sheer output with it (and range) has meant, too, that he is now being allowed to take on the kind of prestige that Plato has enjoyed: the writer-philosopher, never subordinating words and their melodies together to reason: and therefore often unable to give any greater coherence than the beauty of the big vision. The City of God. He had to brook precious few of the intellectual proprieties and subject boundaries that have defined scholarship since. He could be unabashedly creative to this end. And if he was not always being accepted as the last word, he was increasingly being taken as the fashionable first word, and starting place, for various schools of thought. Professor Karla Pollmann has recently brought to completion the first international project that traces the whole of this reception history to the present day: *The Oxford Guide to the Historical Reception of Augustine*. Its remarkable breadth and detail will be the best argument for this legacy of his for years to come.[68]

This leads us finally to one important, parting consideration. Augustine's reflections on infancy could be said to exemplify what is sometimes called his 'anti-intellectualism'.

The infant enters the world in a state of shock and is then broken-in. Its inborn wilfulness and pride are educated, step by step, into the dignities of the self-sufficient human being. To be the thoughtful adult after such a start as this is to have to contend with the suicide-prospect of giving up self-sufficiency when it is the most tried and tested life skill. This made it that traditional philosophical wonder was not, for Augustine, taboo; it was just that the questions it set, and the answers it gave, had a way of reinforcing the vacuum-state mind that pride develops. He had noticed how preoccupied the self-sufficient outlook has to be with 'evidence' – and how it can only admit into its consideration things that cross its chosen thresholds of 'truth'. This would not matter at all were God (and most especially the reality of the Father, Son and Holy Spirit) not the total opposite of the vacuum-state mind. If we determine ahead of time what will count as our seeing, if we lay down premises, we will not see at all in the way that God sees. We will certainly not see God. If we only look for evidence of reality, we shall see only the evidence for it, not what in fact may be real – or most real of all as Spirit. It is this cancelling-out effect that creates the vacuum-state, and allows Augustine to take it as axiomatic that only God is truly *real*.[69]

> There is here something ineffable which cannot be explained in words. A situation in which there should both be, and yet also not be, *number*. Allow that there should appear a definite kind of number in the Trinity: Father, and Son, and Holy Ghost. The number 'three'. But three of what? It is here that number now fails us. God seems neither to keep apart from number, nor to be comprehended by number. Most strange. That we are orienting on number (as evidence) is clear because there are three entities. And yet if you ask of what three, number ceases to prove anything ... You can only begin to reflect on the Trinity by numbering; but when once you have finished numbering, you cannot tell what you have numbered. The Father is Father, the Son is Son, the Holy Spirit is the Holy Spirit. What are these three, the Father, the Son, and the Holy Spirit? Are they not three Gods? No. Are they not three Almighties? No. Not three Creators of the world? No. Is the Father then almighty? Manifestly almighty. And is the Son then not almighty? Clearly the Son is also almighty. And is the Holy Spirit then not almighty? He, too, is almighty. Are there then three Almighties? No – only one Almighty. We are left to conclude that it is only in their evidencing of each other that they suggest number. And that this cannot carry us across [beyond self-sufficiency] to what we wish to comprehend when we think of their essential existence.[70]

The charge of 'anti-intellectualism' is therefore unfair to Augustine. Close inspection reveals him to be writing always of the cooption of reason rather than of its poverty.[71] For when a man is saved, it is by Grace working with reason that he notices the ideology of his fallen heart: it is by truth having its claim on his mind that he comes into all the emotional equipment of a sojourner in a hostile land: 'In this world there is not a man who is not a stranger; though all do not desire to return to their own country.'[72] In a letter to the young pagan Senator, Volusianus, Augustine will try to explain this. Reason is not the magic stuff of Divinity. It is merely the currency of Divine instruction and obedience. While it is true as far as it goes to say that God has His reasons for doing things, the deeper truth is that these reasons are in the service of His omniscience – as much, indeed, as fallen reason can be said to be in the service of damnation. The Divinity of God is Who He is, not what is on His mind. The Christian correspondingly aspires to have the singular quality of His Will imparted to his own actions on earth. This is wisdom.

> Here, if the reason of the event were to be sought out and found, it would no longer be a miracle. If an example of a precisely similar event were to be demanded, it would no longer be unique. Let us grant that God can do something which we must admit to be beyond our comprehension. In such wonders the whole explanation of the work is the power of Him by whom it is wrought [not some counterpart correspondence].[73]

5

Traumas of initiation into the Earthly City

In ancient shadows and twilights
Where childhood has strayed,
The world's great sorrows were born
And its heroes were made.
In the lost boyhood of Judas
Christ was betrayed.

George William Russell

During his 16th year Augustine experienced one of those disorienting events of utter clarity. The special productions of youth on the cusp of adulthood, in which the world is revealed to be a grinning and uncaring place. His father noticed him one day at the baths – noticed, in fact, how he was *vidit pubescentem et inquieta indutum adulescentia*, 'growing into manhood, and clothed with an unbiddable youth'.[1] Roman society was famously matter-of-fact about sex and nudity. It had not passed through the modern conservatism about these things, then the triumphant return to them as display items of the victory over repression and inequality.

And you really have to bear this in mind when comparing the Western societies of today with 'uninhibited Rome'. This typical teenage event would have passed with less comment and analysis then that it could ever now. There was, for example, no literature of pastoral care for the embarrassment of Augustine to be taken up into; no psychological theories to accommodate his state of inner motivation and conflict. Only Patricius, his father, the über-Roman, to see it. And only Patricius to announce the über-Roman, uber-practical conclusion. Augustine is kind to it when remembering it – and puts it gently: 'From this, as it were, he already took pride in his grandchildren, and found joy in telling it to my mother'.[2]

It is events like these that pierce and punctuate a life; that retain their vividness over time; that are turned to again and again for explanation, or the final nail in the coffin. It seems that this was one of Augustine's. As he sat down to write his autobiography some 25 years later it was still fresh in his mind as a classic example of issues now preoccupying him as a bishop and Christian intellectual. Human life can be seen as remarkable for the collective loss of control that it exhibits; in the sense that our most acute discomforts are more often than not being met by an even greater degree of panic in the weird and dominating shapes of the intellectual systems of understanding. And so one form of panic is only ever handed on into another form, and something is never resolved. And Augustine says that sexual lust is the exemplary loss of control. It has a real sweetness of its own that suggests it should be the pinnacle of something, but none of the earthly contrivances for regulating it can properly be said to achieve this: 'Sadness now tortures itself over the lost things in which desire once took delight.'[3] In fact all of Augustine's mature remarks on sexuality are essentially from this point of view: the point of view of the practitioner turned ascetic: the point of view of one who has put away a pleasure because its validity is too fine a thing for the thumbs of human hands.

> This connubial embrace ... which marriage-contracts point to as intended for the procreation of children, if we considered it simply in itself, that is, without any reference to fornication, would appear as a thing good and right. And it would, because: though it is by reason of this body of death (which is unrenewed as yet by the resurrection) a thing inconceivable without a certain amount of bestial motion (which puts human nature to the blush), the actual idea and emotion of the embrace is without sin. The idea of the embrace draws reason on to the idea of children; and the idea of creating a child from love is one of those ideas beyond the cynicisms of mere sex. It overmasters evil.[4]
>
> Thus the soul commits symbolic fornication when it is turned away from You [Cf. Ps. 73.27]: and when apart from You it seeks the pure, clean things it will not find except when it returns to You. In a perverse way, all men are in fact imitators of You, who put themselves far from You, rising up in rebellion against You. Even by such imitation of You they prove that You are the creator of all nature, and that there is no place where they can depart entirely from You [as from the logics of ultimate love and desire].[5]

But this was only an aspect of the episode at the bathhouse. Far more serious was how it seemed to set before Augustine the insuperable vision of his future. As something drawing him on by the constant evolution of hope into despair. It appeared to him as a future in which a son would be made ingeniously to follow in the footprints of his father. A future in which the still distant hypocrisies of adulthood would be brought closer by the very sincerity of that father's love. And a future in which Augustine would one day find himself just as compromised, and just as unable to break free from the wheel of mortality. Every evolution of hope into despair is a revolution that only needs that turn to its beginning to be able to start all over again. Here is real panic – and something truly to be feared.

> The man who goes in a straight line begins from some point, and ends at some point. However, the man who goes in a circle, never ends. Such is the toil of the wicked … Indeed every proud man is false, and every false man is a liar. Just think of how men toil in speaking falsehood; when in the confidence of truth they are able to speak with entire facility and pleasure. This is because it is toil to have to make what you say. When you speak the truth, however, it is impossible to be toiling, for truth herself is speaking, not you.[6]
>
> Think now about a wheel and how it completes its purpose in revolution. It is first lifted up on the part of what is behind, then is thrown down on the part of what is in front. Is this not what happens to all the enemies of the people of God?[7]

Overall, Augustine thinks that his puberty – that time when the awkward rush to adult form heightens the sense of dislocation from God – was met with the gaucheness of an exceptionally unexceptional father. It is a very even-keeled assessment. Dominating it is the process of the turning of the wheel. Patricius and Augustine are doing nothing other than being totally sincere, but from their separated perspectives. The lesson here concerns youth – the institution of youth, as something constructed from the convergence of two kinds of panic, or hysteria. The father is hysterical about controlling the son's freedom to swerve from the established narrative of children, and grandchildren, and the world-wise yardsticks of accomplishment. The son is hysterical about having to experience his first great taste of the first great mysteries as guilt. The real victim is God, Who sits like the Emperor in the Coliseum, in all the power of life and death (and the possibility of intervening); but Who watches them fight it out. In outrageous looking-on.

> How else was I to know this delight than to desire to love and be loved? …Clouds arose from the slimy desires of the flesh and from youth's seething spring. They clouded over

> and darkened my soul, so that I could not distinguish the calm light of chaste love from the fug and guilt of lust. Both kinds of affection burned confusedly within me and swept my feeble youth over the crags of desire and plunged me into a whirlpool of what are called shameful deeds.[8]
>
> In this youth of mine I burned to get my fill of hellish things. I dared to run wild in different darksome ways of love. My comeliness wasted way in the diffusion of it, and I stank in Your eyes. But something in the achievement of it pleased me; and likewise, I actually desired in this way to be pleasing to the eyes and expectations of men.[9]

The situation was evidently fraught enough for Augustine to retrospectively censure his parents for not having pushed him into marriage at an early age. As modern readers we are apt to be a little dismayed by this idea; but of course it would not have been unusual then, when lives were considerably shorter and infidelities with married women could become enormous headaches of honour and retribution. So Augustine puts it like this: 'My parents took no care to save me by marriage from plunging into ruin. In fact their only care seems to have been that I should learn to make the finest orations and become a persuasive speaker.'[10] Now, of course, persuasive speaking was to go on to become the hallmark of Augustine's later careers as rhetorician and then Catholic preacher. So it is natural that we find in one of these sermons a homily on the wider and more general moral to be drawn from all of this.

> The human race is characterized by such perversity that sometimes I'm afraid that a chaste man will feel ashamed in lewd company. That's why I never stop making you alive to this feature. Just take these examples. If any one of you were to commit murder, he would be driven at once from the country. If any one of you were to steal, he would be hated and scorned. If any one of you were to give false evidence, he would be abominated and regarded as scarcely human. If any one of you were to covet someone else's property, he would be considered unjust and rapacious. But now consider this. If anyone of you has tumbled in the hay with his maids, he is rather admired: he is given a friendly welcome, any injuries he has suffered from their self-defences are turned into jokes. And moreover, if a man now comes along who says he is chaste, so does not commit adultery, and is also known not to do so, then he is made ashamed to join the company of those others who are not like him. For he knows that they will insult him and laugh at him because he is not in their image of a man. So this is what human perversity has come to, that someone conquered by lust is considered a man, and someone who has conquered lust is not considered a 'man'. What upside down

madness. The winners are celebrating and they are not men; the losers lie flat on their faces, and they are men! Let us finally say this: If you were a spectator in the amphitheater, would you be the sort who thought the man cowering before the wild animal was braver than the man who killed the wild animal?'[11]

If the episode at the bathhouse is portrayed by Augustine as the *de facto* parting between father and son, it was grouped in his mind with other partings, just as serious. We have talked already of his early impressions of home and country. Just as decisive, and more extensively recorded by him, were his reactions to his schooling.

The episode at the bathhouse occurred during a year in which Augustine was disastrously underemployed at home. A year in which, as he puts it, '... the briars of unclean desires crowded over and about my head, and there was no hand to root them out.'[12] The problem was that his father had run short of the funds to complete his education, and had therefore recalled him from Madauros, the city and intellectual centre where Augustine was educated from about his 11th year.

Madauros would have been a natural choice for this – just 25 kilometres from Augustine's home town of Thagaste and famous for having produced the great African writer Apuleius. Before leaving for this city, Augustine seems to have undergone the typical course of schooling, largely unchanged since the early days of the Empire.

The first part of this was taken at home; and we have described some of its characteristics in the previous chapter. He imbibed from his nurses and parents the basics of speech and grammar, reading and writing. Then at some stage, probably around the age of 6 or 7, he began to attend a local elementary school, where the serious business of absorbing the classical authors would have begun in earnest – 'for the masters of Roman eloquence themselves did not shrink from saying that any one who cannot learn this art quickly can never thoroughly learn it at all.'[13] This was also the time when Augustine would have been introduced to the harsh realities of the Roman school. The long hours, often stretching from dawn till dusk, and the almost total power of the teacher.

There was, of course, another whole side to the business which Augustine does not ignore, but which he sidelines in order to be able to keep up his critique of the processes by which children are prepared for life. This is the timeless theme of parents, with a bright son and a tantalizing future but the agonizing choices and sacrifices that that brings – the question of the right school, and how to secure it. In Roman late antiquity, plotting this safe passage was made especially difficult by the uncoordinated and unregulated nature of public education. Teachers could become formative influences and lifelong friends, but indolence and exploitation for profit could just as easily govern their relationships to their pupils – and only the more so as parents were often prepared to send their sons far from home and into the care of strangers. Patricius evidently made an outstanding effort for his son's education, and was unstinting in his single-minded promotion of it. In his *Confessiones*, Augustine leaves us in no doubt that this performance was vital to the chance that took him from obscurity to Empire-wide fame.

> Who did not at that time praise and extol my father because, quite beyond the resources of his own estate, he furnished his son with everything needed for his long journey to be made for the purpose of study? There were many far richer citizens, but none made the same provision for their sons.[14]

But never far behind is the counterpoint.

> O God, my God, what great misery and deception I met with when it was impressed upon me that, if I were to behave properly as a boy, I must obey my teachers. This was all in support of the idea that I might succeed in this world and excel in the arts of speech which bring honour among men – to gain, then, deceitful riches. So I was sent to school to acquire learning, the utility of which (wretched child that I was) I did not know. Yet if I was slow at this learning, I was simply beaten. This method was praised by our forebears, many of whom had passed through this life before us and had laid out the hard paths that we were being forced to follow. In this way are toil and sorrow multiplied for the sons of Adam[15]

Now this time-honoured depiction of the rigours of school was not Augustine's manifesto for a revolutionary change. In fact a little further on he will grudgingly accept that, short of corporal punishment – short of some sort of compulsion – the child can hardly be expected to embrace the rigid constructions of formalized education. He admits that even he himself '… would have learned nothing unless forced to it.'[16] But notwithstanding this, he shows himself also to be some way ahead of his time in his insistence, too, that the ground that the rod makes up is artificial and contrived. That is to say, education then, and surely also now, is nearly totally adapted to a world in which power and honour and wealth are equated with success. A material world. 'Hence it is plain enough that for learning a language free interest has greater power than frightening constraint.'[17] The child has, of course, the freedom of thought to understand his punishment at the time as the last resort it invariably is. But to hold onto the wisdom of this wider view is desperately difficult when you must at the same time feel profoundly obligated to the parents who nurtured you and the teachers who invested in you, and so on – and not even considering how well or badly all of this was done. The problem (or the trick) is that the very justice of the punishment is inflicted against the principle that would go against it – or whatever the child is able to grasp about the perversity of being beaten in order to become a 'good' citizen of a broken-down city. In this sense it is not really a punishment at all but an initiation. For the rod is not the neutral extension of an abstract office called 'justice' but a culpable signal of the way things are (and have to be) in a fallen world. It will itself one day be held to account by the True Justice.[18] For Augustine, initiation is everywhere once you have learned how to identify it. Just look for the precious pause for thought; children are so good at it.[19] Then watch what superior realism leaps out to ridicule it.

> Every man finds himself born into a place; and he goes on to learn his tongue, and to become habituated to the manners and life of that same land or region or city. What should a boy do, then, if born among Heathens and told to worship a stone, inasmuch as his parents have suggested that worship? From them he has heard the first words of this: that error he has sucked in with his very milk. And here is the real conditioning: because they that spoke were elders, and the boy who was learning to speak an infant, what could he do but follow the authority of them, and deem that to be good which they recommended?[20]
>
> What wonder was it that I was thus carried away into vain practices and went far from You, my God? For the very men set up for my models [as teachers] were utterly dejected if caught in a barbarism or solecism while telling about some of their own acts – and even if the acts turned out, in this case, to be not actually bad. But here is the thing. If they would instead be describing some of their lustful deeds, but in detail and good order, and with correct and well-placed words, would they not on the latter account happily glory in the praise they got? ... Regard, O Lord my God, patiently regard as is Your wont, how carefully the sons of men observe the proprieties of letters and syllables handed down to them as the received wisdom of former speakers, and how they neglect everlasting covenants of eternal salvation which they have received from You ... Certainly no knowledge of letters is more interior to us than that written

in the conscience [Cf. Rom. 2.15]: that one does not to another what he himself does not want to suffer [Cf. Matt. 7.12; Luke 6.31].[21]

Augustine was to feel that a truly universal and insurgent critique of the human condition would always be kept down by pride and the real cost of speaking out. It seems that God has chosen other and more mysterious ways to work. So between parents loving their children to death in ambition and vainglory, and the child's more circumspect approach, can stretch the whole method of life in the Earthly City.[22] Children seem able to roam with a grief that doesn't seem otherwise to happen if you are older and having to work for a living. The novelist F. Scott Fitzgerald was to call this grief a 'gesture older than history'.

> ... for a hundred generations of men, intolerable and persistent grief has offered that gesture, of denial, of protest, of bewilderment, to something more profound, more powerful than the God made in the image of man, and before which that God, did he exist, would be equally impotent. It is a truth set at the heart of tragedy that this force never explains, never answers – this force intangible as air, more definite than death.[23]

This, at any rate, had been Augustine's experience. It was supported by a series of standard conclusions. He had been born and kept safe by nothing more secure than the (ordinate) affections that his new-born state could inspire in his family and those around him. From this helplessness he had grown into independence of mind and the freedom to question things. But what could he gain by questioning anything if God was absent and silent and he was really on his own? Augustine's recollections of this time in his life are remarkable for being punctuated by thoughts such as this. We encounter in him, not the ancient orientation on tradition and acquiescence, but something approaching modern individualism. 'Tear off the disguise of wild delusion [*obstaculis insanae opinionis*], and look at the naked deeds: weigh them naked, judge them naked.'[24]

But where was God when he was being made to suffer so much?

> While still a boy, I began to pray to You, my help and my refuge [Cf. Ps. 18.2]. And in so praying to You I broke the knots that had tied my tongue in this matter. A little one, but with no little feeling, I prayed to You not to be beaten at school. When You did not hear me – and it was not to be reputed folly in me [Cf. Ps. 22.5] – my punishments, which were then a huge and heavy evil to me, were laughed at by older men. More grievous still by my own parents, who wished no harm to befall me.[25]

The answer (as he would later come to appreciate it) was that God *was* there, in everything; but in a way that human cognisance is liable to misconstrue. That is to say, He was there in two seemingly antagonistic senses. In His secure foreknowledge of how Augustine's life was to proceed, He was there; yet in a chronologically real and meaningful wait 'in time' for the boy to reject his initiation and call to Him out of all the desolation of an exile – yes, He was there too. As always, we are more metaphysically capable than we realize. The human will is a truly, mighty, time-shattering weapon. But so taken up are we with the body of this death that we hardly notice this at all.

> Lord, You Who are long-suffering, most merciful, and most truthful [see Ps. 103.8; 86.15]: You see these things, and yet You remain silent [Cf. Is. 42.14]. But will You keep silent forever? Even now will You draw out of this most terrible pit the soul that seeks You and thirsts for Your delights [Ps. 86.13; 63.2; 42.3; 16.11], and whose heart says to You, 'Thy Face, Lord, will I seek' [Ps. 27.8].[26]

Augustine's thesis is that self-sufficiency is a total blindness – and that being a total blindness it is heightening our ethical sensibility to the point where we have to interpret the supernatural as Grace. In exactly the same way, in fact, that we have to interpret freedom as time. In both cases, our intellectualizing leaves us woefully short of what our full capacities could be; and indeed once were, before the fall, in the fully human Adam and Eve. The doctrinal achievement of making Grace make sense to human dignity is one of those deadly excursions into pride. The doctrine of prevenient Grace which Augustine came eventually to accept is only as radical as the Christian truism that God supports all life and reality in the manner of a vital source, which, if it were for one second to be unplugged, would plunge all of this into instant non-existence. 'How hidden are You who dwell on high in silence, You the sole great God [Cf. Is. 33.5]! By unwearying law You impose the penalty of blindness upon unlawful desires.'[27] The real difficulty of Grace going along is the question of self-love – pride – and its relationship to the silence of God; the silence which makes self-love seem like such a good idea and the only sane alternative in any case. What we get from the autobiography of Augustine's early life is the valuable insight of his actual, true-life struggle with this question. And this struggle is an important source for his later theological promotions of prevenient Grace – for example, in one of his last works, *De praedestinatione sanctorum*, written in 428/9, in response to questions from the so-called 'semi-Pelagians' of Southern Gaul:

men like John Cassian and Vincent Lérins.[28] As a clever and misunderstood teenager he seems to have suffered under something very much like his very own 'death of God' thesis.[29]

The silence, or death, of God is a thesis that you have to build up to. This is because it is a cynical, knowing kind of thesis whose whole logic of appreciation is the sound of the house collapsing. And to learn to appreciate the sound of anything collapsing requires a certain little hardening of the heart. For natural, unadulterated joy does not work like this; it builds things, and people, up. This makes this thesis one that is probably also worked out ahead of time, in unanswered questions that children learn to keep entirely to themselves. It is possibly the gravest of the untested assumptions that deliver us into adulthood with nothing left to say, but only this to know. That we never abandoned God like He did us. Ours was the slow hardening against hope that must now share regret with its triumph. 'Receive me fleeing from these, as though Your house-born servant; for did not these receive me, though another Master's, when I was fleeing from You?'[30]

The teenage Augustine was already offending against traditional Christian morality with impunity; so much so, indeed, that his mother's warnings against fornication were beginning to sound like a craven morality, quite unattached to any higher truth and with their own designs against fun and normality.

> Ah, woe to me! Do I now dare to say that You, my God, remained silent when I departed still farther from You? Did You really remain silent to me at that time? For whose words but Yours were those that You sang in my ears by means of my mother, Your faithful servant? And yet none of them sank deep into my heart, so that I would fulfil them. It was her wish, and privately [that is, out of earshot of her husband] she reminded me and warned me with great solicitude, that I should keep from fornication – and most of all from adultery with any man's wife. Of course such words seemed to be only a 'woman's warnings', which I should be ashamed to bother with. But they were Your warnings; and I knew it not. I thought that You kept silent and that only she was speaking: but of course, she was the living proof that You were not silent to me [Cf. Isa. 42.14].[31]

In fact Augustine was coming to wonder how it is that men can freely disobey the various normative laws laid down for their benefit yet not disturb the higher, eternal law of God's sovereign Will. If the various normative laws are moral, that is to say, if they stand to reason, what, then, is the eternal law? Is it moral in any intelligible sense, or does it represent something else altogether? Indeed, does it have any positive existence at all, or does it merely express the magnanimous conviction that God will mysteriously work all things to a good and just end?

> But I, poor wretch, was working myself into a real lather: I followed after the sweeping tide of passions and I departed from You. I broke all Your laws [Cf. Lev. 10.11], but I did not escape Your scourges. For what mortal man can do that? I mean that You were always present to aid me, merciful in Your anger, and charging with the greatest bitterness and regret all my unlawful pleasures. This was done so that I might still retain the capacity [however weakened] to seek after pleasure that is free from disgust, to the end that, if I could find it, it would be in none but You, Lord. In none but You … Where was I in that sixteenth year of my body's age, and how long was I exiled from the joys of Your house? We know this place. It is framed by the discovery that the madness of lust is licensed by human shamelessness but forbidden by Your laws. I was completely under its sceptre, and I clutched it with both hands.[32]

The shock (and it seems to have come as a terrible shock to Augustine) that the Christian God of his mother and upbringing was so alloyed to human belief in Him that rudimentary teenage experimentation could bring the whole edifice of His apologetic crashing down was the amulet that he would carry around in his heart, unbeknownst, from this time forth. God was indeed working in mysterious ways.

On the one hand, '… every disordered mind is its own punishment.'[33] God has allowed it that His constant presence and activity in the world will continue to be unseen by those with eyes only for themselves – eyes that, unaccustomed to the sharp light of truth, squint into the near distance of things credible, or things brought nearer to credibility by reliable instruments of telescoping. The decisive role for Christian belief which some would say he is notorious for promoting turns out to be nothing to do with any romanticism or detachment in God's evangelical strategy and all to do with His extraordinary position vis-à-vis man.

> For in human things reasoning is employed, not because it is of greater certainty, but because it is easier to use. But when we come to divine things, this faculty turns away; it cannot behold; it pants, and gasps, and burns with desire; it falls back from the

light of truth, and turns again to its familiar obscurities – not from choice, but from exhaustion.³⁴

The patronizing thought that God waits patiently to be put into the day's idiom of reasonableness and proper expectation is really the fruit of the seed of doubt planted in the Garden of Eden by the rhetorical question, '[H]ath God said, Ye shall not eat of every tree of the garden?'.³⁵ Augustine calls it a thought prompted *vano timore*, 'by vain fear'.³⁶ He seems genuinely to have thought that his early forays into the intellectual credibility of Christianity were to prove an important antidote to this kind of wishful thinking about God – the kind of wishful thinking that he would later encounter at university and beyond.

> There are those who think that the Christian religion is what we should smile at rather than hold fast, for this reason, that, in it, not what may be seen, is shown, but men are commanded faith of things which are not seen.³⁷

On the other hand, the 'information of the heart' – the intuitions of conscience – are capable of conspiring with free will to bring about a glimpse of something of Adam and Eve's original need for God's total judgement over their lives. This is the sense in which he will insist in sermons that …

> It is not with stones, or clubs, or fists, or heels, that we knock upon the Lord. It is with our whole life which we knock; and therefore it is also to the joy of our whole life that it is opened. The seeking is with the heart, the asking is with the heart, the knocking is with the heart, the opening is to the heart.³⁸

The difficulty is that these conspiracies of conscience and free will are apt to grow weaker over time as the heart is hardened – or in the image that Augustine prefers, 'hurried along' – by the school of the world. For instance, the question, 'For who is there that keeps the commandments of God, or who is there that preserves chastity?' is a valid question that it is open to anyone to ask. But the cunning is that, '… while he thinks that no one does keep these commandments, he himself becomes that no one.' It is as such that Augustine thinks that initiation (in all its myriad forms, and on whatever scale it is perpetrated) works against the mercy of truth by replicating the exact process by which innocence was first lost in the Garden of Eden. It is why he calls it *agit diabolus*, 'the devil's art'.³⁹ Questions of this sort are infamous, in any case, by the sparks and arcing processes of reasoning and self-vindication that they set off across the potential difference of pride. Augustine's later experience as a polemicist was to show him that these sparks, and all that follows them, are the only requirement if the aim is simply to turn men and women from God and into consciousness of themselves – as he will, for example, put it in a swipe at the followers of the Arian bishop Maximianus:

> … it only remains that they should learn how to blush to their soul's health. For it is by this shame that they will be able to seek the name of the Lord, from which they are now turned away to their utter destruction, while they exalt their own name in the place of that of Christ.[40]

These insights give the clue also to Augustine's inclusion of the 'pear tree' story in this period of autobiography in his *Confessiones*. There are many to say that this agonized analysis of his teenage theft of pears is emblematic of an unhelpful gift for popularizing and amplifying the Christian neurosis about sin.[41] But perhaps now it might be seen that there is evidence here, too, of a sincere and heartfelt desire to document some small part of the psychology, and meta-psychology, of initiation – as well as initiation's post-traumatic legacies of self-deception, and the urge to perpetuate the right of passage on new generations, wide-eyed and impolitic. This is actually the human predilection for evil in a new and more sympathetic light. Augustine's approach is not the hellfire and brimstone of affirming or denying evil, but to show instead the quality of these insights that have come down to help us 'as dew from the mists of human frailty'.[42]

> In a garden close to our vineyard there was a pear tree, loaded with fruit; though I must say that it was unripe, desirable neither in appearance nor in taste. Late one night – for we would keep up our street games to these dark hours – we set out to shake down and rob this tree. We took great loads of fruit from it, and not for our own eating, but rather to throw to the pigs. Such was the shape of this crime, which, though we did eat a little of the fruit, was done for the sheer pleasure of that fact that it was a thing forbidden.[43]
>
> I must ask, then, what I loved in that theft of mine? That is to say, in what way did it allow me to think that I was perversely or viciously imitating my Lord? Did it please me by some sensation it afforded of going against Your law – at least by trickery, for I could not go against it by sheer might? Or did it please me as it pleases a captive to ape a deformed liberty by doing with impunity things illicit? Did I think it gave to me a

shadowy bearing of the likeness of Your omnipotence? Behold, Your servant flees from his Lord and follows after a shadow [Cf. Job 7.2]!⁴⁴

The thing is that I would never have done it by myself – such, I remember, was my state of mind at that time. Yes, alone I would definitely never have done it. So this means that I loved also in it my association with the others with whom I did the deed … If I had, say, merely liked the pears that I stole, and merely wished to eat them, I could have done so by myself, were doing that wrong deed enough to lead me to my pleasure. I would not have needed to arouse the itch of my desires by a rubbing together of guilty minds. But my pleasure, it seems, lay not in the pears as objects of conquest: it lay in the evil deed itself, which a group of us joined in sin to do.⁴⁵

Behold, the living record lies before You, my God. By myself I would not have committed that theft in which what pleased me was not what I stole, but the plain fact that I stole. This would not have pleased me at all if I had done it alone; nor by myself would I have done it at all. O friendship too unfriendly! Unfathomable seducer of the mind. What took me up was the greed to harm for fun and sport; some horrid desire for another's injury. And what sparked me to it was not any desire for my own gain or for vengeance, but merely the moment of someone saying, 'Let's go! Let's do it!' Why do we go, and why do we do it. Because it is shameful not to be shameless!⁴⁶

By the time that he had finished his primary and secondary schooling Augustine was by his own admission a *tortuosissimus et implicatissimus nodosus*, a 'most twisted and intricate mass of knots'.⁴⁷ He had serious academic talent of the sort that quickly gets noticed by teachers; but in his battles with the Greek language and his less than total dedication to his studies lay something of the relentless pragmatism of the Augustine to come.⁴⁸ Here was a mind and a disposition that was waiting to flourish in the service of something real. Anything less was a horse that was simply not going to run. 'No one has an abiding grasp of anything unless he loves it.'⁴⁹

The twin forces that shaped a Roman education were discipline and the promise of praise and honour. Perhaps it had to be this way for a basically martial people who had, in Juvenal's words, 'mastered the art of forging deadly steel on an impious anvil.'⁵⁰ We have seen that Augustine had his own reasons for detesting both. Yet now enters into the equation his growing mortification at having been unable to act decisively on this information.⁵¹ And this, he was later to realize, is not a unique conundrum. In fact it is rather more than that. The philosophical puzzle of a free will battling with itself was the human emblem that St Paul chose specially to address. In Augustine's case, he was to look upon himself as having symbolically sided with the father whom he was secretly scorning, while rejecting openly the mother in whom he should by all rights have sheltered. She was by no means perfect, but she did at least represent to him something that neither the rod nor vainglory could completely extinguish in the Roman education; one of its enduring benefits and lessons. In the words of Tacitus: to approach the ancient authors with a view to 'unrolling the pages of the past and learning therein the branches of knowledge, of human nature, and real events.'[52] It seems that in the rare moments when Augustine was enjoying his education for its own sake it was just this play of truth in history that he was enjoying. And one of the great reassurances of his later life will be to have it proved in his work that Christianity need fear nothing from privatization, and the throwing open of truth to the public conscience. 'Behold where He is, it is wherever truth is known.'[53]

> For it is through God that men come to know (and even in those studies which are termed liberal by those who have not been called to the true liberty) anything in them which deserves the name. For these studies have nothing which is consonant with liberty, except that which in them is consonant with truth ... The freedom which is our privilege therefore has nothing in common with the innumerable and impious fables with which the verses of silly poets are full; nor with the fulsome and highly-polished falsehoods of their orators; nor, finally, with the rambling subtleties of philosophers themselves – who, either did not know anything of God, or when they knew God, did not glorify Him as God ... Historical works, on the other hand, whose writers strive only to be accurate in narrating *events*, may perhaps, I grant, contain things worthy of being known by free men. Since the truth of the narration is regardless of whether the subject described in it be the divine or the profane in human experience.[54]

This grounding of Augustine's thought in the standout experiences of his life goes a long way to explaining the political language that he took to using when describing the transformational effects of Christianity on the soul. His language of citizenships, rights and obligations; his two cities, and distinctions between earthly and heavenly kingship. To the incoming citizens of the City of God, there is, as he puts it, 'the army of an emperor seated within their mind'. It is not so much a question of becoming a better person in relation to virtue and its performance. It is that one is released from the burden of personality formation. Modern psychology and psychopathology have worked hard to show how this burden is in many respects the explanation behind our common conceptions of normality and abnormality. This Augustinian idea of Christian freedom is therefore interesting if it does indeed refer to the freedom from endless self-construction. The image of the person of Christ as the ruler and guarantor of our innermost triggers is a powerful but threatening image. Augustine talks of it as though 'the cedars of Lebanon [see Ps. 92.12; Ezek. 31.3], levelled to the ground, and fashioned by the skilful craft of love into the form of the Ark, cleave the waves of this world, fearless of decay.'[55]

> For as it is by his army that an emperor does what he will, so the Lord Jesus Christ, once beginning to dwell in our inner man, (*i.e.* in the mind through faith [Cf. Eph. 3.17]), uses the virtues as His ministers. And by these virtues which cannot be seen with eyes, and yet when they are named are praised (and they would not be praised except they were loved, and not loved except they were seen; which leaves it that if not loved except seen, they must be seen with another eye, that is, with the inward beholding eye of the heart), the members of the human body are visibly put in motion. So the feet of the Christian are now walking in Christ, but whither? Whither they are moved by the good will, of course, which as a soldier serves the good Emperor Christ. So the hands are now also working, but to what end? To the end which is instructed by charity – to the end which is inspired within by the Holy Ghost. We can finish by saying that the members are seen when they are put in motion. But He that orders them within is not seen. But most important of all is this final conclusion: that this vital connection between Christ the Emperor and each obedient human will is enacted secretly, in the deeps and motivations of the heart of hearts.[56]

Augustine was to learn early that history is accomplished on the rack of individual fear. In the first instance, this works out to be the fear of disappointing one's parents. Then, it graduates to teachers, friends, the general loss of face, bankruptcy, starvation, and so on. 'You have saved my soul from the necessities of fear [*necessitatibus timoris*], that with a free love it may serve You.'[57] We might say that fear is the work ethic of history.

Now this is not to say that everyone is fearful all of the time and acting from that place; but rather to point out how, when general theories of action are sought, we tend to prefer to frame them with reference to things we would not wish to suffer. To frame them negatively rather than positively – as per the 'golden rule' of doing unto others as you would have them do unto you. And perhaps we do this because self-evidence seems to sit more automatically with this negative way of handling things. Aiding and abetting medical research is an automatic good because we take it as given that everyone desires good health and long life. We could go on and give further obvious examples of how the model society of today creates whole discourses of right and wrong from a handful of key assumptions about things to be avoided – things 'beyond the pale'. What is interesting to note here is that the refinements of the human sciences that take us deeper into this project produce, inevitably, their own telling outbursts and reactions against it. As more and more mental energy is diverted from the traditional, positive projects of the good life and into the describing and archiving of humanity, the arch-question of 'what to do' is flooded over with data and metadata. The problem is that the increasing accuracy of factual knowledge will never cease. We can always learn something new of this sort by the simple act of bothering to go out and learn something new. Yet no base of knowledge – yes, not even the venerable self-knowledge of Socrates – can ever on its own be the same thing as the answer we seek when we frame the philosophical 'ought' of the question 'what ought I to do now?' Augustine often is criticized for putting it as bluntly as this: 'God's Grace is apart by itself, the nature of man apart by itself.'[58] Others like C. S. Lewis have concentrated on arguing that this limitation prevents us from ever truly crossing the bar into socio-political creativity:

> There has never been, and never will be, a radically new judgement of value in the history of the world. What purport to be new systems or (as they now call them) 'ideologies', all consist of fragments from the *Tao* [he means the laws of nature] itself, arbitrarily wrenched from their context in the whole and then swollen to madness in their isolation, yet still owing to the *Tao* and to it alone such validity as they possess.[59]

But a better example that really goes to the heart of the point we are making is Karl Popper and his two-volume *The Open Society and its Enemies*. This excellent historical argument for the pluralistic Western society shows how the effort to bring ourselves out at the happy ending which we can all embrace as a society turns out too often to be exhausting, depleting and violent. There is an innermost adversary to it inside each one of us. In its positive aspect it is very frightening: it suggests a highly particularized source of inspiration: Augustine's image of Christ the Emperor. It is difficult to know how one would practically arrange such a society of such privately mandated individuals. So Popper is drawn instead to its negative aspect as the idea that '... there is no one man more important than any other.'⁶⁰ This offers a way to arrange a society in which at least the space for private inspiration is given to each member equally. But it is even more interesting how he finds that he has out of all of this a statement to make to the missing, unaccounted-for history of the human soul in its relationship to God:

> To maintain that God reveals Himself in what is usually called 'history', in the history of international crime and mass murder, is indeed blasphemy; for what really happens within the realm of human lives is hardly ever touched upon by this cruel and at the same time childish affair ... If that could be told by history, then I should certainly not say that it is blasphemy to see the finger of God in it.⁶¹

The fact that the censure of blasphemy should enter like this into the conclusions of a study of free thought and its struggles is surprising, but instructive. For, if it is not God Whom we are thinking of when we lament the great cycles of war and peace, then it is some idealized Justice. But either case proves that we can sustain a sentiment against the imputation that human freedom is an illusion – an illusion in relation to the overwhelming movements of higher freedoms, and higher purposes, which cannot be resisted. Popper shows how we still want instinctively to associate the idea of God with the personalized care of our souls – and how the history of these happenings, if it could be written out, would be the morally superior history and the true education. It would trump the Machiavellian lessons of social and political realism; it would spare us some of the pre-emptive strikes of the foresight that bases itself on this principle. Augustine talks of mere *sapientia verbi*, 'word-wisdom', as this God-shaped situation which the pluralist society becomes so adept at bringing about. It makes it that 'the cross of Christ is made of no effect. [See 1 Cor. 1.17]'⁶² For what outbursts like Popper's express is the need of Personality in human history. Not the concept of the giant personality of an all-presiding God. Not that kind of reassurance that all will be well. But rather the dynamic reassurance that all the billions of personalities of lives will not be ironed flat by the new pragmatisms of the vast, fluid world societies. Of the language of freedom as a space: the human being as a prickly skin of rights: and initiative as the prepossessing originality of the foregone conclusion.

The arrow of human intelligence tells us that we are after the ability to know all things: so one day it really will deliver us, finally, into the power of being able to predict ourselves out of all possibility of wonder and surprise. Where, then, will be the God of arbitrary instruction and command, Who throws open doors on unimagined scenes and grants us personalities from our experiences of those places? Augustine wants to know, how else can personality truly be?

In Augustine's portrayal of the traumas of his initiation into the Earthly City we encounter this outburst – as he saw it then, at his pivotal age. This life is a *domum somni*, 'house of sleep'.[63] The vanity of the human condition is a supine vanity. The idea that we grow wiser and more able to be free and spontaneous with age is a fantasy that, literally, is put to bed each night – as we arrange ourselves gladly into what Freud called the 'premundane state of our existence in the womb'.[64] This motif of our inveterate sleepfulness is one of Augustine's favourites; you find it everywhere.[65] He seems to have thought that sleep was something that we needed like a mercy; for in the imaginary condition of unceasing wakefulness we would come all too quickly upon the truth of the race of humans as a single organism, entirely consistent to pride, and would have no means to depart from the waking nightmare. Yes, it is sleepfulness that makes us blink and fall back from the brilliance of Light: and this is something that philosophers like Plato have always maintained: and Augustine's use of the metaphor covers this sense of it, too. But when we include his conviction that the totality of all truly knowable things must be the same thing as God's single vision of a condemned mankind, then sleepfulness must also be one of the paramount practical inventions that keeps the Earthly City from imploding on itself. Instead of being burnt raw and shrivelled in God's single-day we have the cool of refreshing mornings to keep waking up to – and Hope. But the hope that works childlike, for Humility's chance.

> And so I found myself on the threshold of the world's customs and contrivances. I felt myself to be standing fearfully, as though on a stage and arena. At the top of the catalogue of high sins was to commit a barbarism of language. This pinnacle of my dread entombed me: for those who did not commit these barbarisms became my competitors – and envy [rather than love] became our interconnectedness. I say these things in confession to You, my God, because to be further entombed in this way was precisely what earned me praise from men – and to earn their praise was, for me, to lead a live of honour, and glow ... Who says that anywhere in this is the outlook of boyish innocence? It is not, O Lord, it is not: and I pray leave to say it, my God. For

this same hysteria is acquired from tutors and teachers; and from nuts and balls and birds it passes to governors and kings. In time, then, it comes to bear upon money and estates and slaves. This outlook persists, then – and makes it that as we grow older more severe punishments succeed the birch rod. It was therefore the symbol of humility that You recommended in the child's estate when You said, 'for of such is the Kingdom of Heaven. [Matt. 19.14]'[66]

6

Cicero and a sense of purpose

I long for scenes where man has never trod;
A place where woman never smil'd or wept;
There to abide with my creator, God,
And sleep as I in childhood sweetly slept:
Untroubling and untroubled where I lie;
The grass below – above the vaulted sky.

John Clare

Finally, in 371, Augustine's enforced year at home ended. His father had found the money to bring his education to its final stage at Carthage, one of the major centres of Empire, the capital of the province of Africa Proconsularis – and therefore also a significant intellectual centre with an established university. Given Augustine's essential relationship to higher education as a student and then one of its celebrated professors, we should say something briefly about it here.

In Augustine's day, Carthage could claim to be second only to Rome as a seat of learning in the Western Empire. And notwithstanding how loosely organized the system of education then was, the essential idea of the ancient 'university', or tertiary school, was broadly similar to what it is today. Though we should point out that the term 'university' is strictly speaking an anachronism. Before the thirteenth century, and the universities of medieval Europe, the term *universitas* had no special attachment to the idea of a seat of learning. It stood broadly for the idea of a corporation of common purpose – along, for example, with words like *corpus*, *societas* and *consortium*. Likewise Augustine never speaks in terms of modern, chartered institutions when describing his removal to Carthage for study, or, later, his appointment to the public Chair of Rhetoric at Milan. In the latter case, he says only that they advertised for a *rhetoricae magister*, a 'master of rhetoric'.[1] We should think of cities like Carthage in the ancient world as generating reputations for scholarship. These were places that the great minds and teachers were attracted to. They would set up schools around their names and charge fees; and so one of the great questions of ancient education became the question of quality and accountability. In time this was met by the practice of towns and cities buying in certain prominent teachers and supporting them at public expense. Augustine mentions that he was tested for his Milan job *dictione proposita*, 'by public discourse'.[2] Arrangements of this sort would create the formality and continuity that we today associate with the 'university city'.

We know that from at least the time of the Emperor Vespasian (70–9), notable rhetoricians at Rome were being funded by the State. The Emperor Hadrian (117–38) is credited with taking the next step of putting up a dedicated building, complete with lecture halls and the capacity to take in a large number of students. He also added to the number of professors on the State payroll. The whole institution was actually known then as the *Athenaeum*. By the time that Augustine arrived to study at Carthage, the whole arrangement had undergone further refinements and been transported with great success throughout the provinces. Public professors were now in a privileged and protected class – exempt from many tax and military duties as well as the strains and responsibilities of municipal office. To become one of these men was to enter a recognized elite of the Empire, with all the promise of wealth and potential high office that that held. In some European countries this signification of the Professor as an officer of the State is still retained.

These few details show that it is perfectly permissible to imagine the freshman Augustine going up to a big-city university experience that in broad essentials has remained unchanged: those twin thrills of lodging in the thick of it, far from the supervision of parents, and then of finally finding oneself right on the intellectual cutting edge – and all that that might prove or disprove of one's dreams.

Getting together the money for Augustine's further education had been a real labour; and in fact Patricius had only managed it with the help of one of Thagaste's really substantial citizens and patrons, Romanianus, quite possibly a relation of his. This was a man whose sway Augustine would later allude to in his first work, *Contra Academicos*, written against the sceptical philosophy of the so-called New Academy.[3]

Let us now imagine the following scenario. You give to your citizens bear fights and spectacles such as have never been seen by them before, and are always received with the most enthusiastic applause of the whole gathering. You are praised to the skies by the unanimous and united cries of foolish men – and there are a great many of these. In fact, no one ever dares to risk your displeasure. There are municipal records that signal in bronze how you are a patron not only of the citizens, but also of the neighbouring peoples. Statues of you are erected, honours heaped upon you. You are even invested with powers greater than is customary in municipal appointments. Now to your table, which is sumptuously laden for banquets every day. We say that a man might confidently ask of you and be assured of receiving whatever he needed, or whatever his fastidiousness desired; and even many who do not so ask will be lavished with these benefits… What a fine picture! And we only need to complete it with the throngs of people pronouncing you as a most kind person, most generous, most elegant, and most fortunate, and so on. Now let me be daring and put to you this: Is there any, Romanianus, I ask you, who would take in all of this only to speak to you of another happiness – a happiness which alone is happiness?[4]

This dedication to Romanianus also gives up a further insight. The Roman instrument of patronage is often stereotyped like its later counterpart, feudalism. It certainly had its cynical, political component. But in the case of a Romanianus and an Augustine, it had also a higher purpose that is not so readily appreciated today. At a time when truth was not the vexed question of meaning that it would later become; at a time when it was broadly understood what was meant by wisdom and the wise man; a Romanianus could buy into the personal brilliance of an Augustine in a perfectly serious transaction of money in exchange for future hope and happiness.[5]

The paradigm of enlightenment in the ancient world was intrinsically involved with the dream of freeing oneself from the daily grind and attaching oneself to some teacher of truth. It was therefore something that required both wealth and leisure. For the rest, a basic acquiescence in the unbending customs of the civic religions was there to provide a different, more superstitious sort of peace of mind. Peter Brown has arguably done most to show how these conditions made it possible for Augustine to exert an astonishing influence over his contemporaries.[6] In that fluid world a gifted and talked about man could easily, and at the very least, set up his own school. It would be *him* and not some curriculum that his pupils would clamour to engage with. And in time these pupils might become his friends and perhaps even his disciples (if they were not already those things). So it was not primarily with a view to a worldly payback that Romanianus supported his young countryman; it was certainly more with the intention of hanging on to his coattails as he blazed up to the outer atmospheres. We might note how Augustine will choose similarly to seek out the guidance of experts at the decisive points of his life. His decision to give up Manichaeism will be prompted by a long-awaited but disappointing meeting with Faustus – one of that religion's celebrated teachers. And it will be Bishop Ambrose of Milan who will finally call the bluff on his stylized scepticism and call forth his instincts about the relationship between Christianity and the idealist theories of knowledge.

However, as flattering and inevitable as all of this may have been, it was not necessarily what Augustine welcomed. Carthage was without doubt his ticket away from the frustrations of home; but at the same time, these new expectations and obligations had a nasty way of drawing you yet further into the mire of life. Like a man struggling in quicksand, he was to discover that every attempt to leave the world behind on the power of your own struggling limbs actually draws you deeper into it. It is some mighty exquisite logic that creates this effect and holds us fast by things as beautiful and touching as the very bonds of sociability and interdependence. The sins of the fathers are visited upon the sons – but in incremental ways that keep perfect pace with our growing up so that we hardly notice them at the time.

Like so many others before and after him, Augustine was to go up to university in a way already initiated; for a series of standard calibrations had already taken place within the interior mechanism of his heart. Out of infancy had arisen his will, the bearer and also the victim of his congenital self-consciousness; and out of his will had arisen that peculiarly human relationship to the sceptre of judgement. That is to say to love – and to love's ability to make us orbit things in tighter and tighter circles of agitation.

> 'Thy throne, O God, *is* for ever and ever: the sceptre of Thy kingdom is a right sceptre. [Ps. 45.6]' The right sceptre is that which directs mankind. They were before crooked, distorted; they sought to reign for themselves. In fact, they loved themselves; loved their own evil deeds. They submitted not their own will to God, but would even have bent God's will to conformity with their own lusts. For this is the typical attitude of the sinner and the unrighteous man: he is generally angry with God if it does not rain! yet will not stand God to be angry with him if he is profligate.[7]

> We all certainly desire to live happily; indeed there is no human who does not assent to this statement almost before it is made. But the title happy cannot, in my opinion, properly belong to him who has not what he loves (whatever it may be), or to him who has what he loves if it is hurtful to him, or to him who does not love what he has, although it is a thing good in perfection. For one who seeks what he cannot obtain suffers torture, and one who has got what is not desirable is cheated, and one who does not seek for what is worth seeking for is diseased.[8]
>
> And the supreme good is said to exist at that point beyond which it could not conceivably extend itself to anything higher – or to which it is related. In it is the resting-place of desire; in it is assured fruition; in it the most tranquil satisfaction of a will morally perfect.[9]

And like so many before and after him, Augustine was to feel love as a monstrous state of agitation. Oh not to be borne along by it but have what the philosophers dream of in the imagination of their hearts! Perhaps a place of stillness and quiet that time does not harry: some gentle and pleasant meeting-place with truth and God. For this is always the problem of the contemplative: the problem of how to choreograph stillness.[10]

> Even prayers are often hindered by vain thoughts, so that the heart scarcely remains fixed on God. To remain so fixed is its deepest wish – yet how often does it somehow flee from itself, and find no frames in which it can enclose itself? No bars by which it may keep in its flights and wandering movements, and stand still to be made glad by its God? Scarcely does one such prayer occur among many.[11]

Yes, Augustine would remember it as love that was stalking him in those early episodes with guilt and sin. There was its shadowy presence: a glimpse of it behind each impulse to happiness. Rolling and tussling with its omnipresence. The events themselves are mundane, sordid – demeaning even. But the emotions are out of all proportion huge and devastating. Nothing could be more trivial and nothing could be more serious. Adolescence and the awkward lurch into adulthood could never have grown into its accepted infamy if it did not unfold beneath this cosmic presence of Adam and Eve. First loves are so vivid and vital – and adults may smile and call it the effect of the first taste; and that is all. But Augustine wants to focus on those little pangs that stab the way across to the world of Earthly citizenship. All those doings which did not pass easily into our conscience; and which we had to help across the gap by learning to convince our minds, that those were not our moral decisions to make. Of course, without the haunting presence of Adam and Eve there would be no gap. But that again is precisely Augustine's point. Three short quotations taken from different spheres of his writing (a letter, a sermon, and his *De civitate Dei*) will illustrate the extent and depth of his conviction on this matter.

> For the violence with which present things acquire sway over our weakness is exactly proportioned to the superior value by which future things command our love. And we must wish that those who have learned to observe and bewail this may succeed in overcoming and escaping from this power of terrestrial things![12]
>
> But he who is so turned aside from what he was, as to say in his heart, 'God does not see me: for He does not think of me, nor care whether I sin' has turned the helm to be borne away by the storm. He has been driven back to the point he came from. For there are many thoughts in the hearts of men; and when Christ is absent, the ship of these is tossed by the waves of this world, and by tempests borne.[13]
>
> The right will is, therefore, well-directed love, and the wrong will is ill-directed love. Love, then, yearning to have what is loved, is desire; and having and enjoying it, is joy; fleeing what is opposed to it, it is fear; and feeling what is opposed to it, when it has befallen it, it is sadness. Now these motions are evil if the love is evil; good if the love is good.[14]

Augustine's youthful self-analysis (and then his return to it as a mature writer of the human condition) provides also the evidence for the view of him as a neurotic or obsessive personality type. Such honesty, written out so engagingly, has a way of implicating the rest of us in its conclusions. We are all human after all. So, on the whole, Augustine's going up to Carthage has been treated as a kind of diversion in accounts of his life. A chance for the reader to breathe out and relax and find some common ground with the 'sinner-saint'. This is always a reassuring thing to do. Carthage offered all the age-old delights of the big city: so there is much in addition to theorize about concerning his sexual life.[15] However, his own conviction that these times were exemplary beyond raw sin and its cataloguing is difficult to take on board unless we treat his words of autobiography very carefully – and allow them to take us into the real clue. 'I came to Carthage,' is his legendary proclamation, 'where a cauldron of shameful loves seethed and sounded about me on every side.'[16] Yet this Babylonian detail which leads us into the image of the 'sinner-saint' is not it. In any case, it is a turn that he has passed off with only a minor flourish – a middling play on the words *Karthago*, 'Carthage', and *sartago*, 'cauldron'. Perhaps he had in his sights, too, the more enthusiastic declaration of his countryman Apuleius, made some five centuries earlier. 'Carthage,' Apuleius had waxed, 'venerable teacher of our province ... celestial muse of Africa.'[17] What we are looking for is contained in Augustine's unusual choice of words for what he wants to say next. 'I was not yet in love,' he begins, 'but I was in love with love [*et amare amabam*], and by a more hidden want I hated myself for wanting little.[18]

To be 'in love with love' when love has no concrete existence in itself was a grave accusation for Augustine to have made of himself. Love is the quickening of the whole being: it is the magical moment when all the disparate elements of the human psyche can be felt to pull together, in one direction. Love, like sexual desire, is of the special order of high sensations left intact after the original sin; probably it is altogether the highest. Augustine certainly gives it the eternal significance in all his writings. *It* hovers before the will. *It* discloses the final citizenships of all mankind. So to be 'in love with love' was to be taken up with the idea of the great persuader, the whisperer. To be nostalgic and sentimental and forgetful of all these eternal prospects and dooms.

> For I know that I do not love love, except I love a lover: for there is simply no love possible where nothing is loved. Therefore in this business there are three things – he who loves, and that which is loved, and love.[19]

It is a classic snare. We become lost to the mere sensation of love that is only in reality a part of the scheme. But pride contributes the myopia, which engages us to the beautiful idea, which blinds us to the realization that as we love we are joining ourselves to the ends for which we will finally be judged. There can be nothing about this that is idle, or passing, or fanciful. Augustine's last word on this time in his life will be correspondingly unequivocal.

> And so such things are done when You are forsaken, O fountain of life, Who are the sole and true creator and ruler of the universe. And when as the consequence of this, a false unity is loved in the part, by a personal pride.[20]

With such a choice of words Augustine could pluck an important string. It was Neoplatonist common sense of his day to say that the supreme deity alone is sufficient to reconcile all the parts of the universe into their single meaning of purpose. So this bleak picture of a jealous humanity, fingering the shards of Paradise lost, sinking from the bigger picture, carried with it the serious charge of a crime against aesthetics. And crimes against aesthetics are always taken up with gusto because they put us in the judge's seat before we realize that it is also us in the dock. Augustine describes himself in this dock by the phrase 'I hated myself for wanting little'.[21] But yes, such self-hatred was going to be a difficult thing to sustain in a city like Carthage! Augustine was there to work hard and repay the faith and kindness of his parents and patrons, but he was also going to stretch out his legs and reclaim the ground that he felt had been taken from him at home. It is at Carthage, then, that he will indulge the most damaging vice of all. Not sexual desire, but the affectation of innocence. This, he will later reflect, is the chief sense in which 'Man's iniquity lies to itself [*mentitur iniquitas sibi*].'[22]

Clever university students of the right persuasion can affect a meticulous languor whose sole pleasure is noticing itself in grand poses of disinterest – what Evelyn Waugh called 'the relaxation of yet unwearied sinews, the mind sequestered and self-regarding'.[23] But you can't cheat life like this; your character will continue to hound you. The emerging picture is of Augustine as a tense young man, with the blood really pounding in his ears. He will make every attempt to repose in the normal and acceptable life of his new city; yet he will feel unable to enjoy it with the same ease that he will observe in those around him. He will feel that he is being permitted to live only a *fugitivam libertatem*, a 'fugitive's freedom'.[24] It is one of the particular consequences of individuality and the first-person perspective that you will always assume that you are the only one going through these things. And if God has been a part of your upbringing, then this is the moment when God usually gets it in the neck – as the spiteful architect of it all. Why should we be obliged to call Him good and make up the shortfall in a disingenuous belief? One is reminded of Martin Luther before his discovery of the doctrine of Justification by Faith:

> Though I lived as a monk without reproach, I felt that I was a sinner before God with an extremely disturbed conscience. I could not believe that He was placated by my satisfaction. I did not love, yes, I hated the righteous God Who punishes sinners, and secretly, if not blasphemously, certainly murmuring greatly, I was angry with God, and said, 'As if, indeed, it is not enough, that miserable sinners, eternally lost through original sin, are crushed by every kind of calamity by the law of the Decalogue, without having God add pain to pain by the Gospel and also by the Gospel threatening us with His righteousness and wrath!'[25]

Augustine's contribution to the psychology of adolescence seems to be to suggest that the stock intensities of this time arise within a complex about God; about parents (and particularly the father) as the earthly stand-ins for God; and about how the sensation of betrayal by these deities creates those hair-trigger responses to the world. 'For just as vinegar corrodes a vessel if it remains long in it, so anger corrodes the heart if it is cherished till the morrow.'[26] Those who newly enter the world as children are permitted a certain measure of goodwill about it all that the enemy of this has only to destroy by cultivating scenarios in which anger must be carried for long distances. For, by the laws of action and reaction, anger develops in complex and elongated ways into sets of rights – which are those negative assurances held so passionately against all-comers. And from the anger of children forced to compromise comes the adult triumph of the rights-based civilization of the Earthly City, holding its sharpest edge to the neck of God.

Augustine's betrayal by his father will slip all too easily into a hatred of God – or at any rate, into a hatred of the concept of the Christian God Who jealously demands total obedience and worship but Whose substance can evaporate before a clever boy's gaze.

> We must watch lest hatred of any one gain a hold upon the heart, because 'closing the door of our closet' in this way will not only hinder us from praying to God [see Matt. 6.6], but also shut the door against God Himself. For as hatred of another insidiously creeps upon us, and seems to have that single object as its intention, no one who is angry considers his anger to be unjust. [And this implicates God.] Anger habitually cherished against any one becomes hatred, since the sweetness which is mingled with what appears to be righteous anger makes us detain it longer than we ought in the vessel. And one day too late we realize that the whole is soured, and the vessel itself is spoiled.[27]

But if this state of mind was putting its complexion on everything Augustine did, God was not letting go: 'Your faithful mercy hovered above me, but from afar.'[28] For of course this whole problem created by the 'death of God' and the relegation of his parents was a tragedy to Augustine, not to God. God would bring him round by more subtle and mysterious means: and true enough, Augustine was later to hold it deeply important that he was allowed to go through this formative time of not being able to 'believe' his God into material existence before his eyes. For it kept him from vanquishing the unquiet of his heart (and all the otherworldly ambition that it represents) with resolutions for or against (it does not matter) the problem of pain (when God could intervene). In the words of G. A. Studdert Kennedy: 'For it isn't steel and iron/That men use to kill their God,/But the poison of a smooth and slimy tongue.'[29] Instead he passed a great deal of time in Carthage's excellent theatre, immersing himself in the tragedies on the stage. Pawing at them: reduced to the stalls and looking on. Moved by them: yet never deep enough. Because at work inside him, stoking his inner grief, was what always has to be there – pride. If you really hold something *contra mundum, contra Deum* in the way that Augustine did, you are prone to becoming impervious to the searching reach of art and emotional truth. The certainty of your right to feel as you do – your special knowledge – will block the path of those things to your heart. Even if you are touched and cracked open for a moment you will hurry back to an insight you do not want to lose. Thus are we preyed upon by self-knowledge, which, showing us how things are, shows us also how they can never change. The show goes on.

> What wonder was it that I should be infested with loathsome sores – an unhappy sheep, straying from Your flock and impatient of Your protection? And so came my love for such sorrows as I witnessed them on the stage. These did not pierce me deep down; for in truth I had no wish to be so affected, but only to look upon them – and as they were heard and performed, to be scratched lightly, as it were. Enough to feel the finger nails, the strafing of my soul. A proof made out of a burning tumour and a horrid pus and a wasting away.[30]

The saving Grace is always that there are some things more perfect, more honest than truth. For, on the Augustinian analysis, the best truth, the best science, the best philosophy, the best theology – all equally would show for their very best work the irretrievable machine of parents and children. And there would be no hope left for anyone to have, were it not for the possibility of unquiet hearts and troubled souls. And Christianity is the religion that gathers up all of this that never normally finds a home, and says: 'The nations are Christ's inheritance, and the ends of the earth are His possession.'[31] This is the religion of the cry outwards from the earth to a humane Saviour. For if He were not there, the words would simply spend themselves on unheeding planets of rock and dust and the emptiness of space. Just as they spend themselves now on the same materials of the earth, and all its mildewing book-knowledge. In a polemical exchange with the Donatist bishop Petilian, Augustine will make this point.

Christianity is not the static religion of the library.[32] Its erudition is the wordless appeal of Christ; its strength is that it evangelizes from this ready-set need.

> We do not ransack ancient archives, or attempt to bring to light the contents of time honoured libraries. We do not publish our 'proofs' to distant lands. But what we do instead is to bring in, as arbiters between us, all the testimony derived from our ancestors: we spread abroad the witness that cries aloud throughout the world.[33]

When you are rapt by an underlying agenda like Augustine's at Carthage, you are not at liberty to make any easy engagement with the world. Until you have come to terms with yourself you are simply too prone to be envious of any who can transparently give themselves to a course of action. The normal human state of being pierced through by a conviction escapes you; you become rudderless and prone to your internal contradictions. The simple pleasures and beauties of life appear in inflated form to mock you: and the basic human instinct to be seen to side with the dominant elements in society becomes a desperately important but debasing thing. The whole effect can swell to a kind of unqualified romanticism – perfectly coherent on its own terms, but not something that a talent like Augustine should ever really have been aspiring to. Like the poet A. E. Housman, you nurture a wistful regard for those unlike you, with 'flint in the bosom and guts in the head'.[34]

Augustine tells us that he was quickly the 'leading student in the school of rhetoric' and that he was essentially something of a swot: 'I was much more reserved than others, as You know, O Lord.'[35] Yet to his mortification he observed how he was ingratiating himself with the fashionable crowd. These were the *eversores*. This name, their badge of honour, meant 'those who overturn, or wreck'. New naive students seem to have been their special prey, so we can assume that their stock in trade was the shock and awe of freshman initiation. But there was clearly a little more to it than that. Augustine calls their name their *insignis urbanitatis*, their 'emblem of sophistication'.[36]

From this we can infer that they played the part that must be played in all university cities. That is, the part of the smug debunkers of conventional propriety. Their assuredness their understanding that no one who pauses for thought will come off well against their sophistic certainty; their swagger their knowledge that, in the final reckoning, theirs will prove to have been the true evangelism of the world. In the case of Augustine's *eversores*, we can be sure that we are talking of mere affected dilettantes; but he writes in such a way as to alert us to the powers that these groups may or may not realize they are exploiting; and his purpose seems to have been to highlight this general feature as much as the ambivalent nature of his character at the time. When among the *eversores*, he will exhibit what he calls a kind of *pudore impudentia*, 'shameless shame'. The lesser part of him will want their notoriety for his own; the better part of him will flinch at such a low thought; and altogether he will be reft of any remaining doubt about evil's genius for harnessing the whole of human insecurity to its task. 'It grieves [us] more to own a bad house than a bad life, as if it were man's greatest good to have everything good but himself.'[37]

We are here talking especially of ground covered in Chapter 4. There we noticed that, in Augustine's mature opinion, the soft underbelly that we habitually expose to the talons of the world is always self-consciousness rather than innocence. For if it were innocence, then evil might well appear as something of substance – as something that we might pick up in the headlights of our understanding and swerve to avoid. And the idea of evil having anything other than a purely negative existence would be treacherous to Augustine's determination to depict the world as a place in which we are ever being harried or jollied along for not being able to avoid it. 'The whole of this age is roaring by; and roaring by it is seeking whom it may drag along.'[38] The different and more homely idea that evil has some sort of dialectical role to play we associate, now, with those schemes in which we are encouraged to imagine ourselves returning (at any chosen moment) to the path of right conduct; as if awakening from some slap on the head. We have already mentioned Augustine's youthful prayer, 'Give me chastity and continence, but not yet!' And we could flesh this out further to the whole familiar commonsense that good and evil can have a fruitful and intellectually stimulating co-existence – and if handled properly can teach us real things about this life, which seems, in any case, to have grown in cellular fashion from their original dividing. The key thing to understand is that when Augustine talks of evil negatively, according to his privation theory of it – as the wilful turn away from God and His goodness – he has in mind an existential scenario that supersedes the possible benefits of this evolution into a multicellular world of myriad polarities.[39] It is in fact very close to a thesis that Erich Fromm forged to explain the mass psychology behind the twentieth-century totalitarianisms, a thesis which he called the 'fear of freedom'.

To Fromm, the Biblical narrative of the fall of man was a fiction; but notwithstanding that, an important thought experiment – perfectly constructed to isolate the real and contradictory results of intellectual self-determination.

Acting against God's orders means freeing himself from coercion, emerging from the unconscious existence of prehuman life to the level of man. Acting against the command of authority, committing a sin, is in its positive human aspect the first act of freedom, that is, the first *human* act. In the myth the sin in its formal aspect is the acting against God's command; in its material aspect it is the eating of the Tree of Knowledge. The act of disobedience as an act of freedom is the beginning of reason ... The myth emphasizes the suffering resulting from this act. To transcend nature, to be alienated from nature and from another human being, finds man naked, ashamed. He is alone and free, yet powerless and afraid.[40]

We can set alongside this for clarification Ernst Cassirer's approach to the same problem of freedom and its unravelling.

Freedom is not a natural inheritance of man. In order to possess it we have create it. If man were simply to follow his natural instincts he would not strive for freedom; he would rather choose dependence. Obviously it is much easier to depend upon others than to think, to judge, and to decide for himself. That accounts for the fact that both in individual and political life freedom is so often regarded much more as a burden than a privilege. Under extremely difficult conditions man tries to cast off this burden. Here the totalitarian state and the political myths step in.[41]

Augustine arrives at his version of this conclusion by challenging the platitude that evil preys on innocence. This, he says, is in itself an ideological conceit! You simply cannot prey on what was lost with the fall of man and has never been there since. What evil actually preys on is our endless capacity (not shared with the animals) to reason ourselves into the vacuum left by that event. He means that our highest capacity for intellectual construction is forced always into the low-pressure areas of imagined knowledge – that is to say, knowledge imagined wilfully, in privation from what is already known. In his major work, *De Trinitate*, he will put this exceptionally clearly:

We see from all cases carefully considered that the love of a studious and enquiring mind, that is, of the mind that wishes to know what it does not know, is not actually the love of that thing which it does not know, but of that which it still knows. It is always from something still known in this way that it conceives the desire of enquiring into what must lie beyond these certainties.[42]

In this, for Augustine, is the final proof of Christianity's credentials as a religion of truly universal scope. We are all unique, yet counted out as numbers in every *status quo* that comes along; in every settled way of being that argues its wisdom from human essentials, and the characteristics that deny our specialness before God. And His personal care. It is at this exact location that Augustine stands back to unveil his 'final proof'. And it is very ingenious because it brings us along an intellectually respectable route into realizing that God, the personal Christian God, may be the only proof of our sanity we have left. For otherwise we follow freedom into its ironic places of totalitarian submission for no other reason than that we have done it and must do it again, because the underlying psychology can never change. At present we exist, in the West, in one of the decelerating phases called liberalism. But the worry is that history teaches that we must accelerate again, once too much freedom has spooked us. This is the point at which Augustine still has an interesting, and unusual, contribution to make. His suggestion is that freedom – the negative, Western concept of freedom identified by Fromm and Cassirer as being too indulgent – shares little to none of its DNA with the human animal. It is of a different, ultimately incompatible species. It shows the shape of our ambition now that we are no longer innocent, but it begs vast questions about our ability to recreate and administer the care of God to ourselves.

Society has to make decisions based on utility. It has to seek out the greatest good of the greatest number; or alternatively, it has to leave the greatest number to the greatest degree of freedom from interference. We no longer question these parameters. They are a realism that we have come to accept. But this kind of rationality – this kind of secular good sense – is positively inhuman when compared to the manifesto of the City of God: 'You are good and all-powerful, caring for each one of us as though the only one in Your care, and yet for all as though for each individual.'[43] Here is a caring of the human heart that it may be impossible for philosophy ever to achieve on the terms of its own success. If God achieves it, then Augustine says that it is as a miraculous and spiritual achievement.

> For no sin is committed save by that desire or will by which we desire that it be well with us, and shrink from it being ill with us ... And why is this, but because the source of man's happiness lies only in God, Whom he abandons when he sins, and not in himself.[44]

When Augustine recalls his time among the *eversores* he will therefore write of their evil preying on shyness and modesty (*verecundia*) rather than innocence. He would like us to think especially of our own deceiving at the hands of this kind of trickery (every life is full of examples), whereby sport was had by abusing our basic self-consciousness: our basic uncertainty about how, and indeed who, to be. The basic uncertainty that flourishes in the classic situations of 'newness', where we don't yet know the ropes and everyone around us has that advantage on us. He means that trickery, then, which can only be peddled by those who have been tricked in turn. For there is a kind of inborn horror that haunts with the persistence of a nightmare: it places us in the midst of a circle of others, the initiated – arranged around us and looking on. So much of human life is explained by the need to get across and become a part of that circle: and to have someone else pushed into the middle in our place. It is the force of a prevailing current; and from the moral point of view, washes us into the strait of Scylla and Charybdis. And this tsunami-like imagery of futile resistance turns out to be one of Augustine's favourites.[45]

> I associated with them and sometimes took pleasure in their friendship. But I always abhorred their deeds, that is, their acts of wreckage, by which they wantonly mocked at the natural shyness and propriety of the new students. By their coarse tricks they overturned this modesty, and satisfied their own perverted fun. Nothing is more like the acts of demons than the conduct of these ... For they themselves have been altogether overturned and perverted by devils who laughed at them first, and through trickery secretly seduced them in the very way in which they now love to deride and trick others.[46]

In fact, when you make the effort to follow Augustine's narrative and see it all through his eyes like this, the only respite that there can be is the vigorous and ideological promotion of human innocence as a kind of possible ground zero; and human laws and customs as their own criterion of truth; and wilfulness our freedom to write any notion of interloping disquiet out of our histories.

> In this sense, avarice, ambition, luxury, and the delights of all sorts of games and shows – the whole lot are presented to us as harmless fun and innocence; unless it is that they involve some blatantly wicked deed or outrage which is prohibited by human laws. But the encouragement to them is in truth given even more positively than this. Take the example of the man who, without doing wrong to any, has taken great labours and pains

towards any of the following ends: the getting or increasing of money, the obtaining or keeping of honours; even contending in the match, or in hunting, or in exhibiting with applause some theatrical spectacle. It is not enough that popular vanity leaves it that he will checked by no reproofs. He is actually extolled with praises!⁴⁷

Because certain official positions in society cause us to be both loved and feared by men, we see that in this we are hounded by the adversary of our true happiness. He sets his snares everywhere, breathing the words, 'Well done! Well done!' [Cf. Ps. 35.21; 40.15; 70.3] And he does this in the hope of catching us off-guard: in the hope that as we greedily gather up his words we may begin to seek our joy in the deceits of men rather than in the truth. This we would do for the pleasure of being loved and feared, not on account of You, but in place of You. By this means he would have for himself those who have become like himself; that is, not in a freely-chosen union but for company in punishment. This is he who has aspired to put his throne in the sides of the north, in order that men may serve him in darkness and cold who in perverse and distorted ways seek to imitate You [Cf. Isa. 14.13–14].⁴⁸

For Augustine, then, all the recurring questions of life – the traditional questions of philosophy – are sensible only in relation to the Christian God and the particular kind of personal Hope that attaches to His promise of personal care. The human brain is perfectly capable of sitting down on its own and working out the extent to which human nature is fallen, and repetitive, and the world of wars, temptation, and abuse unlikely to change for the radical better. Yet Hope and the scholarly subject of metaphysics endure; and have in fact dictated most of the course of the history of philosophy. That history, which has been so much the history of the effort to dispense with metaphysics as with a superstition, draws its support from our righteous anger at the silence of God. But most interestingly, and as we saw with Popper in the previous chapter, the vision of the new secular history, for all its Godlessness and reform, is not able to dispense altogether with God. God remains in the language of the highest praise of God that the new history would want for its own. The Gospel of good news that will fairly damn all evil in the end is that, for all the brave talk of Godlessness, it is never Godlessness that we are really striving for – but to be Godlike. Augustine saw this very clearly. Like true criminals, we need Him there for that moment of triumph at the end where we stand before Him and gloat and recount how we did it all. 'Therefore, not even Catiline himself loved his crimes, but something else, for sake of which he committed them.'⁴⁹ Or take this pungent example from Dostoyevsky, who understood these things too; in which the humanity of Christ is used to shame the God Whose Church preaches the doctrine of Original Sin before He even begins to explains His Hope.

> Take a soldier and put him in front of a cannon in battle and fire at him and he will still hope, but read the same soldier his death sentence *for certain*, and he will go mad or burst out crying. Who says that human nature is capable of bearing this without madness? Why this cruel, hideous, unnecessary, and useless mockery? ... It was of agony like this and of such horror that Christ spoke. No, you can't treat a man like that![50]

The silence of God matters for Augustine, not just because it provokes the angers and panics of abandonment and survival, but because it reminds us that there are freer forms of seeing and understanding than words and their rules of engagement. In the words of John McTaggart: 'No dogma – at any rate, no dogma of religion – is asserted which is not also denied by able students.'[51] The rules make that possible. Augustine responds by saying that God will speak directly to individuals who seek Him out; but His silence otherwise – His inaction as dramas of bloodshed and wars play out – does also become the inception of an apt and beautiful critique of the human condition. The artistic forms of expression that do not rely upon words but that do try to arouse this spirit are an instance of this. As Augustine puts it, '... there is not the silence, but the words of the silence [*verba silentii*], that is, the meaning of that silence set forth and manifested.'[52]

It was during the course of his studies in eloquence at university that something happened to bring Augustine out of his melancholy and into an unexpected new state of mind. He was prompted to read Cicero's *Hortensius*, a work that has since been lost to us, and that was intended to be a kind of exhortation to philosophy along the lines of Aristotle's lost dialogue *Protrepticus*.[53] Augustine was probably 18 at the time, which would have made the year 373.

> This book changed my affections: it turned my prayers to You, Lord, and by that means gave an altogether different purpose to my life. At once my vain hopes lost their value to me, and in their place I desired unchanging wisdom. I desired it with an incredible warmth of heart; and so I began to rise up, in order better to return to You [Cf. Luke

15.18] ... I did not, then, use this book to sharpen my tongue, for it had not impressed me by its style but rather by the substance of what it spoke.[54]

The emphatic character of this statement stamps it as the uncomplicated first step in Augustine's conversion to Christianity proper.[55] It certainly seems that, without this dialogue and its ardent promotion of wisdom for wisdom's sake, he would have gone further into taking on what he would later call the 'sordid livery of a craven-hearted bondage'.[56] But we should not rush to draw too straight a line from this intellectual uprising to his eventual facing of God. We have been saying a lot about the status of 'belief' in the schema of his thought; and this requires some further working out at this point in his narrative.

We have seen that Augustine consistently divorces belief from its power to give life to the concept of God. This is something that should pique our interest today when 'faith' and 'faiths' can still be respected but 'belief' speaks of the bellicosity of religious thought. That is to say, what is respected in someone's faith is the fact that they are holding it as an attitude of mind. It is their property. And so we have as little right to attack it as we have to burst through their front door and into their living room. Augustine is out of touch with this possessive definition of faith that brings it under the aegis of human rights. However, he is as much against religious belief as we are; if what it refers to is an automaton response to situations in the world. We should all be free enough to move our own minds to a conclusion; and religious truth, when it is found, will correspondingly prove to have been the phenomenon of all minds moving independently to a single conclusion. 'For truth ought to be dear to me not merely because it was not unknown to Anaxagoras, but because, even though none of these philosophers had known it, it is the truth.'[57]

Now of course faith and belief mean much the same thing – and we have made a separation of them here simply to make our comparison of Augustine to the present state of things easier. However, we have seen that Augustine relates belief to two different orders of truth. On the one hand, and it has featured heavily recently, there is the truth of the human condition, sinful and discouraging. Belief relates to this order of truth in the sense that it makes us heavy-hearted to accept it. Why should the world not be changed into a happier place? Realism and realpolitik are another form of positive response that has been mentioned. Then, on the other hand, there is the truth of the spiritual and the supernatural. This the truth most true of all for Augustine; yet to accept it we must swallow so much of our pride, and this only happens with great difficulty and concentration. In both cases, belief is a statement about us and our scruples rather than about truth. What is true, and what is real, takes care of itself. And in fact, Augustine is one of the few Western thinkers to wholeheartedly embrace this manifesto for the other side of things, and chaos, and the vicinity of things beyond all imagining of logic. In fact he may be one of the very few Western thinkers to call this the prefiguring of the Great Comfort, and to summit that Great Comfort in Christ. Whenever Augustine talks of belief on its own being insufficient for salvation apart from 'love' or 'works', he has in mind *this* rather than any Lutheran formulation of the idea of Justification by Faith. The orthodoxy that he is defending is the promise that somewhere, somehow, all the seeking and the climbing will have to end. You could walk right by Christ and not recognize Him for your furrowed brow and head to the ground. But, more to the point, what Christianity calls the 'works', the obedience to His Voice, is the real beginning of the real knowing of Him. This kind of justifying has the effect of bending time back on itself. The devils know Christ as one of the sure things of their universe and their great enemy. There is no ethical component to their knowing; they never slipped, as we did, into using the unfairness of damnation to call into question the existence of Christ. Their hatred is based in desiring His sovereignty for their own – and you can only desire what you believe to exist. We are not so far gone; but see things very unclearly; and do not appreciate the power of our will to bend time by obeying Christ – and making it, decision by decision, that we knew Him all along. For otherwise there is no hope conceivable of this kind of salvation, in which the end as Christ is unrecognizable (and unsearchable) as from a map and a set of personality traits.

Augustine wants to be taken most seriously of all when he says that the appeal of Christ is consonant with the dim intuition we harbour that self-control may be the real defeating death of us and its opposite the entrance into the real point of life – if only we can stop being afraid and take it. As, indeed, Democritus spat out: 'Wretched mind, do you, who get your evidence from us, yet try to overthrow us? Our overthrow will be your downfall.'[58]

> And look: you have before you Christ as your end: you do not need to be seeking anymore. When once you have believed this, you have recognized it too; however, this is not to say that it is merely a matter of faith, but of faith and works. Each is necessary. For, as you heard the Apostle say, 'the devils also believe, and tremble; [Jam. 2.19]' but their believing brings forth nothing. Faith on its own is not enough; it must be joined

to works [and therefore to acts of will]: 'faith which worketh by love, [Gal. 5.6]' as the Apostle put it.[59]

> You have heard in the Psalm, 'I have seen the end of all perfection.' He has said, I have seen the end of all perfection. What, then, had he seen? Do we for instance think he had ascended to the peak of some very high and pointed mountain, and looked out from it and seen the compass of the earth, and the circles of the round world, and said in result of it, 'I have seen the end of all perfection?' For if this is the thing to be praised, let us ask of the Lord eyes of the flesh so sharp-sighted, that we shall but require some exceeding high mountain on earth – from its summit to see the end of all perfection. I say to you, 'Do not go so far in your imagination!' I say to you, everything you desire, is here. Ascend the mountain, and see the end. Christ is the Mountain; so come to Christ: you will see in Him the end of all perfection.[60]

The classical pursuit of wisdom as promoted by a Cicero contains a signal truth: this is that we are haunted by a language of perfection and virtue that clearly could not have arisen in response to facts in this world. Those facts would produce a less uplifting language. So this realization that we are touching something otherworldly and mystical is the thrill of wisdom. Like entering an ancient tomb. But just like breaking and entering an ancient tomb, the archaeological methods that allow you to do it lay down a criterion of truth which is the robbery of the mystery of it. For Augustine, the mystery is the arbitrary and unpredictable nature of Christ's voice. The final paradigm of wisdom and happiness is resurrection into life. Philosophy can take you so far: but only so far.

> This hope the heathen do not possess, because they do not know the Scriptures or the power of God [Cf. Matt. 22.29], Who is able to restore what was lost, to quicken what was dead, to renew what has been subjected to corruption, to re-unite things which have been severed from each other, and to preserve thenceforward, and for evermore, what was originally corruptible and short lived.[61]

This quotation also gives the insight into what Augustine did next after his discovery of Cicero and philosophy. He did something he was bound to do given his upbringing and how the name of Christ had been instilled in him by his mother. He turned in earnest to the Christian Scriptures, hoping, as so many have, that they would continue the momentum of his intellectual awakening. But he found them to be, quite simply, unbelievable.

> And behold, I saw something within [the Scriptures]; something that was neither revealed to the proud nor made plain to children; something that was lowly on one's entrance but lofty on further advance; and that was veiled over in mysteries... In truth it was of its nature that its meaning would increase together with your little ones. I, however, disdained to be as a little child; and puffed up with pride, I considered myself to be a great fellow.[62]

Part of the reason for this reaction of Augustine's was the Scriptures' relative simplicity of form and style. The Latin version that he encountered would have been of individual books, and groups of books, such as the Psalms or the Gospels. There was in his time a recognized canon of these books that corresponds closely with the modern arrangement of the Old and New Testaments; but the problem was that there was no coherent Latin translation of the whole of Scripture, made according to a single conception. This would have to wait for Cassiodorus' translation in the mid-sixth century.[63] Augustine therefore encountered books that could not give up their full meaning to him on their own; and in the case of those belonging to the canon of the Old Testament, he was also to come up against the surprising fact of the moral inconsistencies of the Patriarchs as well as the sweeping and unscientific accounts of the universe's creation and advance. But greater than these factors seems to have been the disappointment of the Scriptures as 'philosophy' and 'salvation literature'.

For we should not forget that what his heart had been quickened to by Cicero was the instant, visual promise of a pristine reality – in every detail the obverse of this world:

> The intellectual apprehension diffuses itself throughout the mind with something like an explosive flash, whereas the utterance of it is slow, and occupies time, and is of a vastly different nature. The effect of this is that, while this latter is moving on, the intellectual apprehension has already withdrawn itself within its secret abodes.[64]

To follow and support this explosive flash in a lifestyle was the call to wisdom that he read into Cicero's *Hortensius*. He was thrilling to an imagined future spent playing with the aesthetic and intellectual possibilities of this. And it is actually in another work by Cicero – his *De officiis* – that we find further confirmation of why this would be so, in the plain fact of how we tend to 'esteem the knowledge of things secret and wonderful as a necessary ingredient of the happy life.'[65] What if the flash of this mere idea of truth is reflected in the face of God rather than in the form and leisure of the studied life of wisdom?

Augustine regularly deploys St Paul's imagery at 1 Cor. 12.13 to write of how we see 'through a glass, darkly'.[66] And now we can see that, on these occasions, his purpose seems to have been to draw attention to something that has received a great deal of attention in recent times. If Edmund Husserl could write of Phenomenology that it is the 'secret longing of the whole philosophy of modern times',[67] then Augustine steps in to supply his addendum. What the flash-truth defends, in the first instance, is the memory of our lost eternity. '[Men] attempt to grasp eternal things, but their heart flutters [*volitat*] among changing things of past and future, and it is still vain [Cf. Ps. 4.4].'[68]

It is a rule, and a wise one, that one should approach these comparisons between the ancient and modern worlds with caution. But it seems true as far as it goes to say that Augustine's appeal to the eidetic data of the human heart is at the very least a foreshadowing of modern Phenomenology's concern to transcend the boundaries of empiricism. The phenomenologist says that the delimitation of science and truth to 'experience' is a poor reflection on the human capacity for snap judgements and intuitions – and quite possibly a prejudice; and Augustine adds that pure, unqualified knowledge (the touchstone of the phenomenologist's dream of a 'genuine' science) is something that is only available to us in what memory we have been permitted of the Garden of Eden. The authenticity of all experiences is the authenticity of this one experience, reverberating through them all.[69] His designation of Christianity as the 'one true religion' follows from his conviction that it alone of all the religions and philosophies makes good in Christ this otherworldly vector of sudden, drastic insight.

> No one discerns the truth of that which he reads from anything which is in the mere manuscript, or in the writer, but rather by something within himself, if the light of truth, shining with a clearness beyond what is men's common lot [*quoddam non vulgariter candidum*], and very far removed from the darkening influence of the body, has penetrated his own mind.[70]

For it remains that, in this fallen world, we are encumbered with the sickly-sweet inertia of our sinfulness; and evil is all about us – as the blameless state of mind into which we may retire with ease. As Augustine will put it to his patron Romanianus in a letter, 'The bee does not the less need its wings when it has gathered an abundant store; for if it lets up for just a second and sinks in the honey, it dies.'[71]

7

Manichaeism

O God, I am not like you
In your vacuous black,
Stars stuck all over, bright stupid confetti.
Eternity bores me,
I never wanted it.

Sylvia Plath

After his promising start with Cicero and philosophy, Augustine did something that on the face of it appears surprising. He fell in with one of the stranger and more esoteric religions of late antiquity: the religion of the Persian mystic called Mani (ca 216–76): Manichaeism. This episode in Augustine's life invariably strikes the reader as a cumbersome addition to his story; in the late fourth century, Manichaeism was considered to be something of an obtuse and even risqué religion. Peter Brown has called the Manichees the 'Bolsheviks' of their day, '… a "fifth-column" of foreign origin bent on infiltrating the Christian Church, the bearers of a uniquely radical solution to the religious problems of their age.'[1] To Gerald Bonner it was simply '… among the strangest and most bizarre of the many strange and bizarre fantasies which the human mind has conceived.'[2] But it was the philosopher David Hume who entertained the idea of the religion as at least a solution to the intractable problem of pain:

> Look round this universe. What an immense profusion of beings, animated and organized, sensible and active! You admire this prodigious variety and fecundity. But inspect a little more narrowly these living existences, the only beings worth regarding. How hostile and destructive to each other! How insufficient all of them for their own happiness! How contemptible or odious to the spectator! The whole presents nothing but the idea of a blind nature, impregnated by a great vivifying principle, and pouring forth from her lap, without discernment or parental care, her maimed and abortive

children! Here the Manichaean system occurs as a proper hypothesis to solve the difficulty.³

The Manichaeism that Augustine came to know was syncretic, mixing various elements of Gnosticism, mysticism, and asceticism with the language and broad message of Christianity. It also contained core elements from the ancient Babylonian, or Persian, religion. It had come to prosper on an old question that had assumed a new significance in the Christian Roman Empire: the question of the predominance of evil. Christianity had encouraged many to confront evil's career in human affairs in a way that the classical philosophies of enlightenment simply had not. These had focused on the corporate expressions of right and wrong in society and the state; and the corporate statements of atonement in public sacrifices and the like. The Christian approach harnessed the sense of evil to human psychology and opened the way for it to run and run through the hardwiring of anxiousness, heartache, regret and doubt. The result has ever after stood as a genuine sea-change of Western history. And there are those who would say that the damage has been of the irreparable order of a Pandora's Box.

You could say that Manichaeism was in a sense 'designed' to take the sting out of this by making evil an elemental substance and principle, rather than a congenital orientation of the will – though 'designed' is unfair to its founder, who ended up dying for his religion under brutal incarceration in his native Persia. He had great initial successes with it, coming under the royal patronage of King Shapur I and being granted the freedom to travel and preach his message throughout the Persian Empire. Shapur I's reign lasted from 241 to 272; and unfortunately, from its end, Mani's royal influence began to wane and the Zoroastrian priesthood became more active in their dislike of him. Under King Bahram I (r. 273–6), the Zoroastrian high priest Karter was finally able to get his way and have Mani imprisoned and tortured.

Mani had taught a fantastic cosmological tale of the arrival of good and evil in the world; and, perhaps more importantly, he had followed it with a strict but achievable code of conduct for those wishing to prosper in its wisdom. What really distinguished Manichaeism was that it derived its authority from a vast and intricate dualism. Good and Evil were both material realities, though poles apart in character. This was, for example, in utter contrast to the privation theory of evil that Augustine would come to hold. If you were a Manichee, you did not believe that evil spread its work through human wills, tricked and turned to its purpose. You did not believe, either, that all created matter is intrinsically good (for being fashioned by a loving God). Two cardinal articles of the Christian faith. You believed that what you were seeing all around you all the time was an admixture of the two substances Good and Evil. And this meant that the primary question for you was the question of how this had come to pass – and then, in relation to that, how the Good could be prioritized and released from its compounding with Evil.

The Manichaeism that Augustine first came into contact with while a student at Carthage had moved west there (as well as to Rome and Egypt) near the end of the third century. After the death of Mani, it had become almost everywhere a suspected and persecuted religion, and took on the characteristics of such an organization: a strong network of agents and supporters, sometimes gone underground, and an esoteric promise to those on the outside looking in. In Persia, it had simply become an unwelcome challenger to the state Magian religion. In the Roman Empire, it was tainted for being an import from one of Rome's great historical enemies – Persia. It did not help, in addition, that it claimed to be the completion of some of the other major revealed religions. For Mani had been born into a family of Elchasaites in Persian-controlled Babylonia. This group held to a form of Jewish Christianity. In two major revelations, at the ages of 12 and 24, Mani claimed to have been shown that the revelations of Jesus, Buddha and Zoroaster were as genuine as his but were only the anticipations of the full truth he had been appointed to proclaim. Augustine will remember the effect well.

> And so this was how I fell in with the Manichees, inflated in their confidence, too fluent altogether in their simple carnal-mindedness, and in whose mouths were the snares of the devil and a kind of birdlime made up of mixing together the syllables of Your name, and more vitally, the name of our Lord Jesus Christ, and the name of the Paraclete, our comforter, the Holy Spirit. These names were never absent from their mouths, but were only the tongue's sound chatter; and their hearts were absent of truth.[4]

Augustine's writings against Manichaeism are, in fact, one of our major and most reliable sources for its late antique form. And of course he would go on to become one of the religion's most energetic and celebrated enemies, pouring out a number of treatises against it and ridiculing its literature as a crude kind of science fiction. 'They spoke untruthfully, not just of You, Who are the one truth, but even of the elements of this world … In respect of these matters … I should have given over even those philosophers, who can speak the technical truth of them.'[5] But for all the effect that this lasting judgement of his has gone on to have, we should never forget that something in the religion *did* manage to conquer him and earn his respect. Manichaeism was not a subtle religion; and it went too far in its claims against established fact. It could be refuted quickly by holding it up to some basic principles of science.[6] But it was also a *suaviloquentia*, a 'smooth language'[7] – at any rate, on its chosen terms of discourse. And its story of a resident Good and Evil and their arch-showdowns was a classic tale, impulsively satisfying. There is no question that Mani wrote well and imaginatively: it is quite possible that his was the fantasy literature of its day. And in this respect, at least, it was an international success. We know that it moved west from Persia into Carthage, Rome and Egypt. It also moved east, into China, Siberia and Manchuria.

Mani produced a canon of seven known writings: the *Shapurakan, Book of the Giants, Great (or Living) Gospel, Treasure, Pragmateia, Mysteries,* and finally, *Letters*. And it is not impossible to imagine that the creative side of Augustine was attracted to its flair and Eastern origins – as indeed so many other artists and movements have looked back to more ancient civilizations for inspiration. Perhaps he even contemplated producing writings of his own in its style. We can never know. What we should do, though, in light of these thoughts, is take an example, and a snapshot, of its overall flavour and promise. Here, then, is one such from Augustine's *Contra epistulam Manichaei quam vocant fundamenti* – his vigorous refutation of the so-called *Letter of the Foundation* by Mani. This document is also known as the *Great Letter to Pattik*, and is alleged to be the same in the canon as the *Pragmateia*. In what follows, Augustine is quoting extensively from Mani's original.

> Hear first, if you please, what happened before the constitution of the world, and how the battle was carried on, that you may be able to distinguish the nature of light from that of darkness ... In the beginning, these two substances were divided. The empire of light was held by God the Father, who is perpetual in holy origin, magnificent in virtue, true in His very nature, ever rejoicing in His own eternity, possessing in Himself wisdom and the vital senses, by which He also includes the twelve members of His light, which are the plentiful resources of His kingdom. Also in each of His members are stored thousands of untold and priceless treasures. But the Father Himself, chief in praise, incomprehensible in greatness, has united to Himself happy and glorious worlds, incalculable in number and duration, along with which this holy and illustrious Father and Progenitor resides; no poverty or infirmity being admitted in His magnificent realms.

And these matchless realms are so founded on the region of light and bliss that no one can ever move or disturb them ... [On the other hand, in the Empire of Darkness] was boundless darkness, flowing from the same source in immeasurable abundance, with the productions properly belonging to it. Beyond this were muddy turbid waters, with their inhabitants; and inside of them winds terrible and violent, with their prince and their progenitors. Then, again, a fiery region of destruction, with its chiefs and peoples. And, similarly, inside of this a race full of smoke and gloom, where resided the dreadful prince and chief of it all, having around him innumerable princes – and himself the mind and source of them all. Such are the five natures of the pestiferous region.[8]

This passage from Mani's *Letter of the Foundation* indicates, in the first instance, how Manichaeism shares one of the main features common to all Gnostic schemes of salvation. This is the belief that the creation of the material world of human habitation is a declension from a higher possibility – rather, that is, than a purposeful act of good *ex nihilo*. The material world is not presented as a doctrinal statement against the human condition and where it would lead us to conclude. Where the Christian is forced to uphold the categorical goodness of God's material creation in the midst of any kind of evidence to the contrary, the Manichee is not. And this puts him often at a distinct advantage. Indeed, Augustine has preserved a classic little example of the style of persuasion that Manichees would have used on many a less-educated and unsuspecting Christian. It goes as follows:

Even if it is only with flies that you are afflicted, let no one steal in and deceive you. For some have been mocked by the devil in this way, and purposefully taken with flies. Just as fowlers will put flies in their traps to deceive hungry birds, so these have been deceived with flies by the devil. Take this case of what can happen next. Someone or other was suffering annoyance from flies; and a Manichaean found him in his trouble; and when he heard that this poor man could no longer bear flies, and hated them exceedingly, immediately he got to work on him. 'Who made them?' said this Manichee to him. And since he was suffering from grievous annoyance, and hated them, and a Catholic, he dared not say, 'God made them'. For that would of course contravene what he had heard in Church. So the Manichee was able to add at once: 'If God did not make them, who made them?' Seeing an opening for apparent truth, the poor Catholic replied, 'I believe the devil must have made them.' And the other was able to say, of course, 'If the devil made the fly, as I see you allow, because you understand the matter well, who made the bee – which you see is only a little larger than the fly?' The Catholic was now in a real fix because he could not logically say that the God Who had not now made the fly had gone on and made the bee. From the bee, the Manichee was able to lead him to the locust; from the locust to the lizard; from the lizard to the bird; from the bird to the sheep; from the sheep to the cow; from that to the elephant; and so at last, to man – as to the coup de grace. By this means he was able to triumph in the unlikely challenge of persuading a man that man was not made by God! And this miserable man, being troubled with the flies, became even himself a fly, and utterly diminished, and the property of the devil. In fact, Beelzebub, they say, means 'Prince of flies;' and of these it is written, 'Dead flies cause the ointment of the apothecary to send forth a stinking savour.' [Eccl. 10.1][9]

Something that Mani believed specifically was that our world represented a kind of overlapping between the two co-eternal realms of Light and Darkness. Its coming into being had been the result of the Darkness's desire to possess the Light; and its continuation into its present state was the result of Light's willingness to fight back in a sort of self-defence. The human race, he preached, stood for the last front in the great battle between these two forces. Initially, Light had been invaded by the Darkness along its outer fringes, and had produced the 'Mother of Life' as its active principle of defence. This had not been enough, and the Mother of Life had produced in a greater effort the 'Primeval Human'. But the Darkness was able to capture this Primeval Human and trap some of its light as particles, and and spread these about among the dark matter. Further efforts were now made by the Light to retrieve its 'lost sparks of divinity': and out of these efforts came the sun, moon and stars – as well as plant life. To Mani these features were devices, charged with the special property of collecting light and releasing it back to its original realm from out of the intermediate region of overlap in which it was mired – our world. In retaliation, Darkness came up with the idea of having two demons mate to produce the Biblical Adam. Two more demons then mated to produce Eve. The plan behind these beings was that they could be an ingenious continuation of the wider situation in miniature. For is humankind not after all a mixture of Light and Dark, Soul and Matter? What is more, by being able to reproduce their kind, they could continue to trap Light within Darkness in this cunning new dimension of a populating earth. The Light's striking back at this was to provide a means whereby the new human race could undergo revelation of the truth of their situation – another main feature of Gnostic schemes; the necessity of saving knowledge, or *Gnosis*. Here Mani committed to his most contentious idea: the idea that a saviour called 'Jesus' had been sent by the Light to deliver this saving knowledge to men and women; but that the 'Jesus' of Christian orthodoxy had been in fact a devil, only masquerading as Christ. For surely no true saviour from the Light could so completely inhabit the Darkness of body as to be crucified and actually die in it? If we turn now to the essence of this saving message as given in the *Letter of the Foundation*, we can see the sheer cheek of it that a Christian would have taken umbrage at.

> These are wholesome words from the perennial and living fountain; and whoever shall have heard them, and shall have first believed them, and then shall have observed the truths they set forth, shall never suffer death, but shall enjoy eternal life in glory. For he is to be judged truly blessed who has been instructed in this divine and saving knowledge, by which he is made free and shall abide in everlasting life.[10]

This much shows the points at which Manichaeism parted ways with Christianity, and radically so. It was one thing to say that the creation of this world and us in it was a regrettable necessity. It was quite another thing altogether to claim that Jesus Christ, and his putting on of humanity, was a sham episode. There were, then, clear ways to deal with the religion from the point of view of it either as a Christian heresy, or schism, or simply as a non-critical fantasy cosmology. In his anti-Manichaean writings Augustine would deploy both. But we should at the same time remember that this religion that seems so naive and easy to ridicule had real success, and captured the attention of Augustine for nine years. In addition, the history of opposition to Manichaeism is a predominantly Christian history, with Augustine as its highpoint. The non-Christian perspective simply has to be taken into account; in which the religion could be considered no better or worse than Christianity – with the latter's doctrines of creation *ex nihilo* and the resurrection of the dead. And if we proceed a little further with this thought, and allow this aspect in each religion to cancel the other out, we arrive at some interesting considerations. First, let us have a look at a quick instance of Augustine 'defending' the religion. It comes from his *De utilitate credendi*. Augustine is reinstating the usefulness of belief: not as the blindest form of faith, but as the only bridge across to truth that we have in certain situations where the restrictions of time and space put it far from our presence.

> How many men are prepared to jump all over our Scriptures as though the only truth they should correspond with is what little puny portion of it we deal with in our day?

> In this they seem to me to be like that weak woman (being as she was simple-minded and of a religions spirit), whom these same men are wont to mock at, who, enraged at the sun being extolled to her, and recommended as an object of worship by a certain female Manichee, leapt at once to her feet, and began to jump up and down on that spot on which the sun was casting its light through the window. And as she was doing it, cried, 'Lo, I trample on the sun and your God! and what do you? Who denies that this is an altogether foolish way in which to go about a serious matter?'[11]

Manichaeism was not to be jumped up and down on in this way. Nor was Christianity. Nor was any heartfelt religion worth its salt. Why? Because all religions – let us say rather, all examples of 'the impulse to religion' – draw from the deepest deeps of the human experience. They are not hobby pastimes, chosen for their ability to distract our minds in idle hours. They are some of the most beguiling expressions of our abiding interest in the big questions of life. In their tendency to produce fanatics, they are the supreme expression of the underlying ardour of that interest. If religion and science were trains, they would run on the same single track in the same direction trying to reach the same conclusion. What Augustine's example of the foolish woman shows is that you cannot for this reason use science to disprove religion out-of-hand. You can show (as he did to Manichaeism) that bad religion is the same thing as bad science, but you cannot use science to stamp on religion. That would be like trying to use tea to disprove water from the point of view of thirst. The sun-god that the foolish woman jumped up and down on was as credible an example of the general hunger for truth as the material foot she used to assert her doctrine of natural positivism. As John William Dunne put it,

> [The universe is] rational in everything save the ultimate observer who makes the picture. He, with his self-consciousness and his will and his dualism of psycho-physical outlook, is irrational; but, no matter how far you may pursue him, you can never discover this. ... [For] all of us hate, with a hatred too deep for expression, the notion of the whole of Nature being, to Life, no more than 'an indifferently gilded execution chamber', 'replenished continually with new victims'.[12]

No, jumping up and down will not resolve anything, because the way of truth 'is a way which is traversed not in any regions of the earth, but in the affections of the heart.'[13] What Manichaeism does not deserve is to be treated as anything less than a concerted attempt at this. If we wish to stand at a distance and criticize it from the neutral point of view, then we should do as Augustine did when he found a window to do just this in his *Confessiones*. We should criticize it in terms of what it reveals about its founder Mani's character. For the religious zeal and vision is, after all, a human phenomenon. It takes hold in a man like Mani and produces these 'affectations of the heart' that drive it on until it overtakes itself and becomes the wild, proclaiming voice that can be ridiculed. Because science happens to be limited to certain subjects, and exerts its pride in the strictness and dispassion of its methods, it seldom if ever reaches this point and has fallen into seeing itself as a class apart. But all it really lacks is the humility to take the supernatural as the only evidence of the natural that we really have. So Augustine says that Christianity is the one true religion – and therefore, also, the one true science. 'Say on whom does My Spirit rest? "even to him that is poor and of a contrite spirit, and trembleth at my word." [Is. 66.2] At these words Peter trembled; Plato trembled not. Let the fisherman hold fast what that most famous philosopher has lost.'[14]

In the case of Mani, the man was intent on presenting himself to the waiting world as a singular, saintly character. He called himself the 'apostle of Jesus Christ'; and his followers were encouraged to see the Paraclete in him. The insight that Augustine developed from this was that it must have meant more to Mani to be regarded as the intense and obscure conduit of final truth than to be proved as a great natural philosopher. For he could not be both and create the same mystical effect. He could not wear the white lab coat and levitate. So what he did instead was really rather clever: Augustine uses the word *devius* 'devious'. He produced his fantastic cosmology, took the hit for it, but asserted his superiority in his chosen field:

> And so this devious [*devius*] character spoke at length on natural philosophy with only this thing in mind: that at the same time as he was being readily refuted by those who had learned the truth concerning these things, he was introducing to their minds the idea of him as master of the sort of knowledge that we associate with the most difficult and hidden subjects of high religion. He simply did not want to be thought of as anything less, and therefore set out to convince men that the Holy Spirit, the consoler and enricher of Your faithful, was personally present in him in full authority. In effect, then, he turned the situation round so that his false pronouncements about the heavens and on the movements of the sun and the moon took on the dignity of sacrosanct assumptions – quite immune from ordinary criticism and things to be taken with wonder.[15]

The answer to what Augustine was doing to get involved with Manichaeism, and why he stuck at it for so long, is now not so far off. We have done something to rehabilitate the religion vis-à-vis the outlooks that write it off too easily. We just need to remember the kind of student that Augustine was at Carthage once he had had the experience of Cicero's *Hortensius*. Some people, having had such an epiphany, would feel youthful again and rejuvenated; would find themselves returning to the library and the literature as the only place to go; would look forward to the best professors and the best opinions. But we have seen just how old Augustine had grown already in his awareness and analysis of his own ontogenesis. Older even than many of his professors. The civilized life of the mind, the proprieties of intellectual debate and discussion: these things he claims not to have regarded once truth was a living possibility for him. His own account of this in his *Confessiones* is in fact so strident that it suggests, yes, the supernova impact of his epiphany – but also now this, his almost insensitive attitude to his genius and its effect on others. The curriculum set before him was just a series of things to understand and be congratulated for; and he had already turned his heart from understanding and set it on something altogether different. The exchange economy of praise for understanding (ubiquitous; hardly ever questioned) was as small-minded to him, then, as a presidential cavalcade would be to an anarchist. And when you are as intellectually coordinated as Augustine, and distracted by your aggression from the pressures that normally make university work hard, your ability to understand actually accelerates. So it becomes a vicious circle – and you become increasingly desperate.

> What did it profit me that when I was scarcely twenty years old certain writings of Aristotle called The Ten Categories fell into my hands? I had gaped at the very name, as if in anticipation of a thing somehow magnificent and divine; for whenever my teacher, a rhetorician at Carthage (along with others who were considered learned men) had praised the work, his cheeks burst and boomed with pride. So what did it profit me that I read and understood these writings by myself alone? ... What did it profit me that I should read and understand all the books on the liberal arts, as they are called – whatever of such books I could get to read? ... In fact, whatever concerned the arts of speaking and reasoning, whatever there was on the dimensions of figures and on music and numbers, I proved that I was able to understand without much difficulty, and without instruction from men ... I did not realize that those sciences are understood with great difficulty even by the most studious and the intelligent; that is, until it came

to me to try to expound them to such men, when I discovered that he was best among them who followed me the least slowly as I explained the subjects through.[16]

Many years later, Augustine would be able to put his finger on what it was that he had been reacting to at this time. It was actually an insight that would come home to him as he reflected on his career as a Catholic bishop and *Difensor fidei*. There is an incarceration and solitary confinement that is only seen for what it is if you have the inclination to notice its walls and bars so close around you. There are whole regions of the soulful and spiritual where we could go in good faith and clear conscience: but walls and bars make us worry what people would think: and worse still, to journey like that is not what anybody really means anymore when they talk about 'originality'. Originality is something that has to reflect well on everyone else. All the great new original paintings have first to be declared so by art criticism; whose very definition as an activity apart is that it could not have dreamt them up and painted them. Does this in the end really matter? Only if you are like Augustine, it does. Because if you are like him, you can be truly terrorized and kept awake at night by this thought – by this whole grubby little way of thinking ourselves clever because we refuse to be moved by what we cannot touch. It was this that would sadden Augustine as he look back upon his activities in polemics. It was something that he felt called to do from his position in the Church, but it was distressing to consider how much of argument is shaped by the criterion of having to come out always at some tactile conclusion that one can drop into an opponent's lap.

> From this there therefore frequently arises a necessity of speaking more fully on those points which are already quite clear – that we may, as it were, present them not to the eye, but even to the touch, so that they may be felt even by those who close their eyes against them. And yet to what end shall we ever bring our discussions, or what bounds can ever be set to our discourse, if we proceed on the principle that we must always reply to those who reply to us?[17]

When Augustine first came upon the Manichees and the books of Mani he was coming upon stirring, imaginative stuff that he had never encountered before. Not the pseudo-history of the poems and epics that he had learnt to be so cynical about. Not the Christian Scriptures, which he had turned to after Cicero as puzzling, inconsistent pseudo-philosophy. Mani could take you on an adventure. His worlds were fantastic, but you could enter into the spirit of them yourself once you had accepted his terms of reference. We have said that it was bad religion and bad science: today it would probably be called pseudo-science: but to Augustine it was also a form of literature that he had not seen before. We earlier called it the 'fantasy literature' of its day to make this point. And this was all it needed to be to a 19-year-old Augustine to grab his attention and offer him a relief from that other world of study which he could excel in but not escape from. But he tells us quite plainly that it was more than that; and in telling us this he tells us something fundamental about himself. He had a conviction, like a wild desire to throw himself from a cliff, that there is more truth in fiction than there is in the certainty of death from such a fall.

> O Truth, Truth, how intimately did even the very marrow [*medullae*] of my mind sigh for you: and these men were bellowing forth your name at me so many times, and in so many ways, by the voice alone – but also by books many and huge![18]

Even Aristotle, who had been presented to him as an arch-example of the latter, had vented the same intuition going along. In his *Poetics*, he had identified the 'irrational' as the 'largest single source of astonishment'. And in turn 'astonishment' as a 'consistent form of pleasure'. And 'an indication of this is that we all tend to add something to a story when we repeat it, assuming that that will be appreciated.'[19]

Before moving on, we should say something briefly about why Manichaeism should appear as a pseudo-science on today's view. The claim to have monopolized all truth in a single system was a perfectly viable ambition in Augustine's day. We should think of the last great attempt to perform this kind of uninhibited rationalism: the ambitious *Encyclopédie* of the eighteenth-century French *Philosophes*. What has been eroded since then is the trust that could once be placed in these exponential growths from pure reason. This has only been happening comparatively recently, as Western societies have come through the 'age of ideology', in which the pathological exploration of humanity flourished, but incited the wholesale treatments of the twentieth century. One of the best working definitions of pseudo-science, therefore, still comes from Karl Popper, whom we mentioned in Chapter 5 in connection with his opposition to these tendencies there.

> I found that those of my friends who were admirers of Marx, Freud, and Adler, were impressed by a number of points common to these theories, and especially by their

apparent *explanatory power*. These theories appeared to be able to explain practically everything that happened within the fields to which they referred. The study of them seemed to have the effect of an intellectual conversion or revelation, opening your eyes to a new truth hidden from those not yet initiated. Once your eyes were thus opened you saw confirming instances everywhere: the world was full of *verifications* of the theory. Whatever happened always confirmed it. Thus its truth appeared manifest; and unbelievers were clearly people who did not want to see the manifest truth; who refused to see it, either because it was against their class interest, or because of the repressions which were still "un-analysed" and crying aloud for treatment.[20]

Manichaeism was not just its cosmology. It had a developed ascetic component that flowed swiftly from the former. This was also a major attraction to a young man like Augustine with his intensity and severe inner disciplines.

The Manichaean way of life took its form directly from the priority of releasing trapped Light from the world. Everything was to be organized around facilitating this. All active Manichees fell into two grades. The Elect were the most important. They actually contained the capacity in their bodies to release the Light from those special plants in which it was being kept. They did this by digestion. The sun and the moon were responsible for reclaiming other portions of Light. So the Elect were the Manichaean priesthood; but their calling was not so much pastoral as instrumental. They were to live as ascetically as possible, according to a discipline of the 'five commandments' and the 'three seals'. Its overall object was to allow them to observe their special Light-releasing diet, but to do so in a way that involved them in as little direct contact with matter and humanity as possible. The five commandments were: 1) no lying; 2) no killing; 3) no eating of meat; 4) no sexual relations; and 5) no owning of property. The three seals were elaborations on this theme – and holy reminders. There was the 'seal of the mouth', which concerned the attention required of the senses. Then the 'seal of the hands', which dealt with actions – especially against killing. And finally the 'seal of thought'. This referred to banishing any undue thoughts against the doctrine of the Light and the sacred process of bringing about its freedom. This brings us to the second grade of Manichee, the Hearers. Augustine was one of these. The Hearers were like ordinary parishioners, expected to attend at Manichaean ceremonies and rites. However, they also had to make up the networks that practically supported the Hearers; for these could have neither a hands-on role in their procurement of food nor a permanent home and family life. The Manichaeans were a religion that looked after their own; and with a jealous zeal. This was another reason why they came to be so largely suspected and whispered about.

We have a first-hand account from Augustine of this side of life as a Manichee.

> Incrementally I was led on to such beliefs as that a fig actually weeps when it is plucked, and that the mother tree sheds its tears of milk. And that if some saint of the Elect were to eat this fig (though of course picked for him by another's sinful hand) then he would digest it in his stomach and somehow breathe forth angels from that process! I was taught that by groaning and retching in prayer, he was breathing out little bits of God! And that these little bits of God would have been eternally doomed had they not had the good fortune to be freed by the teeth and belly of an Elect! My wretchedness at the time was to believe that greater mercy should be shown to the fruits of the earth than to men, for whose sake they are grown. Even if some poor starving beggar who was not a Manichee had asked me for a mouthful I should have piously refused him – for such was the inversion that I should have been more loathe to commit the fruit to capital punishment in his non-Manichee mouth than fill that mouth to save his pain of want.[21]

Augustine has written on Manichaeism in a way that shows that he would not like us to underestimate it. His Manichaean episode could just as easily be our Manichaean episode next time round. And this is because he thinks that we have never really wanted eternity. At least not the kind of deathless, breathless eternity of traditional, philosophical wisdom. And this is not his blasphemy, but his way of saying that we have never really wanted the God of that kind of eternity, but the God our Father in Heaven above. We all want a father so much that we measure our fathers by that standard of the Father above, and divide ourselves against ourselves, and make the family and its authority issues the microcosm of all societies and states.

> In that state when eternity delights us from above and the pleasures found in temporal goods hold us from below, there is only one soul at work. It wavers between this or that course, dividing its will between them [at one time loving one, at another time loving the other]. So long as this continues, that is, so long as eternity is delighted in because of its truth and temporality is preferred because it is familiar and out of habit, the soul is torn apart and badly hurt.[22]

So Manichaeism offered Augustine what so many like Augustine crave at these formative times of their life. It offered a father-figure. An authority. A law to follow. A gyroscopic certainty amidst the myriad uncertainties of life. A raft to float on in this *circuitum temporum*, this 'circuit of time'.[23] You have to consider Blaise Pascal's famous thought, which goes like this: 'It is odd, when one thinks of it, that there are people in the world who, having renounced all the laws of God and nature, have themselves made laws which they rigorously obey.'[24] It is actually not very odd at all, when you think about it. Because it would be a real miracle and work of Grace to be able to step with confidence out of our universe of right and wrong and into eternity's confusing beauty, where everything is what it is, rather than what we label it as.

> But in all things, whatever are small are called by contrary names in comparison with the things greater than they. A perfect example is the form of a man, whose beauty being greater than the ape, is the cause of the ape's being called a deformity in comparison with it. And the imprudent are deceived and jump immediately into labelling the former as good, and the latter as evil. Nor do they trouble to regard the body of the ape in its own fashion – the equality of its members on both sides, the agreement of its parts, its protection of safety, and other things which it would be tedious to enumerate.[25]

> For the period of 9 years, from the nineteenth year of my age to the twenty-eighth, we were seduced and we seduced others, deceived and deceiving by various desires. On the one hand, openly, by the so-called liberal arts; and on the other hand, secretly, in the name of a false religion. We were proud in the one, superstitious in the other. But everywhere vain.[26]

8

On the singular deportment of death, love and grief

Great wits are sure to madness near allied,
And thin partitions do their bounds divide.

Dryden

Augustine ended his time at University by returning to teach in his home town of Thagaste. This was in 373, in the same year that he became Manichee; when he was still only 19. It is worth halting, momentarily, on this fact: for the job of teaching was something that Augustine had private reasons for doubting – not, of course, as a profession, but as an emblem of the way in which the world makes it that, that things beautiful and intimating be taught mercenarily, with a view to what is expedient in life. Augustine is the hero of all students like him, across all ages, when he bemoans how the delights of education consist in little pinpricks of light shining through the matt, arbitrary expanses of curricula.

> In this matter they stand accused of wasting their time and their busy disputes in investigating and measuring, merely, 'the creature'. Yes they sought out the courses of the stars, and the intervals of the planets, and the movements of the heavenly bodies. By this knowledge they arrived at certain calculations that allowed them to foretell the eclipses of the sun and moon. And down to such detail that they were able to foretell that the event would be on such and such a day, at such and such an hour – and also the exact portion of the bodies which would be eclipsed. Great industry, great activity of mind. But the Creator was not to be found in any of these things by the same methods. He was not far off from them, and yet they did not find Him.[1]

Something that may have hastened Augustine's decision to teach at Thagaste (rather than, say, to begin to establish himself in the law) was his father's death somewhere in the years 371–2. We do know that it occurred about a year into his studies at Carthage. It would have had significant financial repercussions for his mother and siblings; there would at the very least have been the matter of reorganizing the administration of the family estate. It is not thought that Augustine was the eldest of Monica's children. He had a brother, Navigius, who likely had that status. But of course he had the education and the prospects to be expected to take a leading role in such a business. It would have been a relatively straightforward decision for him to return to Thagaste under this new impetus; then, once there, to rent a simple teaching room in the town centre, or even to teach from home. Thus established, he could expect to begin selling his learning and sophistication immediately – for after all, he had spent nearly three years at Carthage, and had been sponsored there by Romanianus as one of Thagaste's most promising sons. He would be in high demand – not least because he brought with him also a mysterious new religion.

But if Manichaeism would confirm Augustine's kudos among friends and contemporaries, it could only alienate him from his Christian and conservative mother. The religion was not by its nature outward-looking and generous; its morality, though admirable and for the most part conventional, did not engage with the good life and charity. We have seen how Manichaeism's code was exemplified in the Elect, and their special needs. This was a religion that had to pull people in more than it needed to reach out to the world. It more than adequately fulfilled the stereotype of the 'secret society'. Then there was the rumour (which Augustine would himself encourage later on as propaganda against the religion) that the Manichaean contempt for human procreation as Light-entrapping had in certain instances justified sexually perverse extremes of ritual purification.[2]

It is likely that Monica, a self-respecting woman from a self-respecting household, felt scandalized by her son's public support for Manichaeism; and that she was also maddened that he should fritter away his time in it when his prospects lay with promotion through the *Christian* Empire. Augustine writes that she would not even have him stay in the family home. In fact it was only on the prompting of dreams and after consultation with a Manichee turned Catholic bishop that she mellowed. Something of her anguished state of mind is recorded in this bishop's final, rather tetchy, recommendation to her: 'Go away from me now. As you live, it is inconceivable that the son of such tears should perish.'[3]

At the point in his *Confessiones* where Augustine chooses specially to deal with the singular deportment of death, love and grief – Book 4 – it is not in relation to the death of his father. We are treated instead to a lengthy and impassioned discussion of the death of a great boyhood friend. A man. Augustine does not reveal his name: only that they renewed their friendship after his return to Thagaste to teach: and that they delighted in shared interests in philosophy and religion. This man would be one of those whom Augustine would turn from Christianity to Manichaeism. The picture that Augustine paints is of two big fish in a very small pond. The initiate character of Manichaeism seems to have heightened their sense of closeness. We must assume that so good a friend of Augustine's must have shared his creative aspirations. We should probably think of them as like two eighteenth-century romantic poets. They had chosen each other to share what others did not have. 'This man was now wandering with me in spirit – and truly my heart could not endure to be without him.'[4] But there was a nasty surprise in store. They had scorned Christianity while together; and after his friend had fallen seriously ill with a vicious fever, and was presumed to be at death's door, he was baptized as a last resort, while still unconscious. Augustine was there and thought nothing of it, yet things were to turn out differently.

> Tormented by his fever, he lay for a long time still, in his deadly sweat. And when it came to be that his life was genuinely despaired of, he was baptized while still unconscious. Nothing of this baptism disturbed me. I was certain that his soul would take with it only what I had endeavoured to put into it, not what had been done to it in this last-minute fashion over his senseless body. But how differently it turned out! He came round, and even began to regain his former strength. I was there all along by his bedside, since we could not do without each other. So I was immediately on hand to try to joke with him and lighten his mood. I especially wanted him to laugh with me about that deathbed baptism he had received. I needed him to do that for my own sake. But he started at me as if I were an enemy. And he demanded that I should desist from all such talk or leave his friendship. I confess that I was completely and utterly dumbstruck at this transformation. But I kept this to myself; and moreover, I consoled myself with the belief that he would come round to me, and our old ways of thinking, once he had fully recovered. But this time never came. He was suddenly, and finally, snatched away from my madness and taken up to You for my consolation. I had finally left him for a few days, and in that time he fell ill again, and shortly died.[5]

Love has already entered Augustine's story as the love of his concubine – just two chapters prior to his recollection of his great friend. But whereas his friend will receive altogether six chapters of direct and indirect testimony, Augustine's lover will receive, at this stage, just a brief paragraph.

> In those years I had a woman companion; though not one made to me in lawful wedlock, but one whom my wandering passion, empty of prudence, had picked up. But she was the only woman that I had; and moreover, I was entirely faithful to her bed. With her I learned what a great difference lies between the restraint of a conjugal covenant (mutually made for the sake of begetting offspring) and the bargain of a lustful love, in which a child comes to be born against our will, though once he is born, we cannot but love him dearly.[6]

This is the woman whom he would famously meet while at Carthage for university, and remain faithful to for 15 years. An African like him. Their relationship has been by turns a delicate and a notorious matter for scholars and commentators. That he had a concubine at all, and for so long, has been an embarrassment for the Church and his more orthodox champions, notwithstanding that this was during his pre-Christian life. The taint always remains. The other side of it – that he was to give her up on the insistence of his mother in order to clear the way to an advantageous, society marriage – has earned him the opprobrium of nearly everyone else. We will come to this episode in the next chapter. But over and above this, his determined silence on this woman and the detail of their life together has kept it as one of the great mysteries of his life. We do not even know this woman's name. We know only that she remained Augustine's sole companion and lover for the duration of their relationship. A child was mentioned in the passage from his *Confessiones*; this was the son she bore him, Adeodatus, in what seems to have been around the same time as Patricius' death, in the years 371–2. Adeodatus means, literally, 'the gift of God'. Years later, in Milan, when Augustine could no longer hold out against the pressure to end their union and seek his career-marriage, she would leave their teenage son with him and return to her native Africa, vowing never to be with another man. Augustine's attempt to give a compressed and even description of their parting, works only to stoke the reader's suspicions about the injustice and superficiality of what was going on. Perhaps that was the intention of so deliberate a master of words.

> In the meantime my sins were multiplied. The woman with whom I had been so lovingly sharing my bed was torn from my side as an impediment to my marriage. My heart still clung to her: it was pierced and wounded within me, and the wound drew real blood from it. She returned to Africa, vowing that she would never know another man, and leaving with me our natural son.[7]

There is no question that Augustine comes off very badly in this story within a story. But neither does he make the slightest effort to defend the social and religious proprieties that drove him, through his mother, to his choice. He mentions this all-important relationship only twice, and his words are careful and spare on each occasion. The effect, rhetorically speaking, is of two abrupt and discordant notes that linger; and so lingering, they are there to prompt us to imagine what rich vastness of feeling could drive so gifted and passionate a writer to such a barren peninsula of expression. There is, for example, a well-known book by Jostein Gaarder that attempts to explore these regions of Augustine's silence by purporting to be the translation of a recently discovered letter to him from his bereft and abandoned lover.[8] One should probably write as Edith Wharton wrote of her character Selden in *The House of Mirth*: 'It was pitiable that he, who knew the mixed motives on which social judgements depend, should still feel himself so swayed by them.'[9] Yet maybe he is expecting more of us. Perhaps he never imagined an analysis derived from anything but the tears that would flow from his readers into the empty spaces that he had left for them in his writing. Some women are never forgotten by some men – who are far more the victims of the judgements of society than the giant female power of life that has transfixed them to the end. In any case, 'no man perceives in another the mental act by which divine things are apprehended.'[10]

This mood of being shamed by the deep lingering notes into all the coloratura of life in society is how Augustine chooses to characterize this whole period, from University to his first professional position in Thagaste. These 'deep notes' he will refer to in another place as the *magnam rerum constantiam*, the 'mighty constancy of things'.[11] His Manichaean phase is definitely not an embarrassment – that is to say, if his reasons for grasping it were largely emotional and psychological, his sincerity in clinging to it for so long was a far more substantial thing. At any rate, he is very sure about wanting us to halt over the fact of how one life always contains the elements that mean that it could have been another life, in a different time and place. The only distance that it is impossible to make up altogether is the distance across from Man to Woman. 'Let proud men, who have not yet for their good been cast down and broken by You, my God, laugh me to scorn. But in Your praise let me confess my shame to You.'[12] What would seem to trouble him most are the anaesthetic qualities that spring from the act of judgement: and that allow us to diagnose a life such as his but not be prompted to make the inward turn into our own. 'But how can you ascend when you have set yourselves up high and have placed your mouth against Heaven [Cf. Ps. 73.9]? Descend, so that you may ascend; so that you may ascend to God.'[13] In another place, he puts it in this way:

> There who will triumphantly endeavour to seek out their iniquity, yet secretly fear to ever find it. This is because, if they should find it, there is levelled at their conscience the injunction: 'Depart from it!' However, we see that because there is deceit in the very search after iniquity, in the finding it there comes this sudden defence of it.[14]

Grief is not, therefore, what we think it is. The tunnels into our despondency are begun from faraway places that we struggle to credit. This is the 'perverse subtlety of the human heart'.[15] Grief is not in any way related to naturalism; which teaches now in every school in nearly every land that death and sexual generation are as commonplace as water flowing from its source. There is nothing to be disported about there: only interesting things to study and understand. So how do these commonplaces elicit the inordinate ranges of feeling from us that they do? For Augustine it is because we have not turned to naturalism to be rid of these feelings, but to be rid of God. And this much is not denied. But what we generally find extremely difficult to credit is that a God in the Heavens is the only possible explanation for these feelings that there can be. And so continues the perverse subtlety of the human heart. We don't want a Saviour if it turns out that we can manage just fine on our own. But we do not want to dispense with the language of salvation, if that means that we will have no means left of congratulating ourselves. Death should mean nothing at all. Neither should sexual love. Yet there is no way of abandoning yourself to either without being damaged. When we try to laugh at these things (as Augustine did with his friend), it is only with the hollow laugh of recklessness – as 'with the disposition of gladiators destined to the sword.'[16]

> Let it be said to one when set in some affliction, 'There is a great man, by whom you may be set free;' he smiles, he rejoices, he is lifted up. But if it is said to him, 'God frees you,' he is chilled, so to speak, by despair. The aid of a mortal is promised, and you rejoice, the aid of the Immortal is promised, and are you sad? It is promised you that you shall be freed by one who needs to be freed with you, and you exult, as at some great aid: you are promised that Liberator, who needs none to free Him, and you despair, as though it were but a fable. Woe to such thoughts: they wander far; truly there is sad and great death in them.[17]

Fair is Heaven, but fairer is the Maker of Heaven. But I see the Heavens, Him I see not. Because you have eyes to see the Heavens: a heart you have not yet to see the Maker of Heaven: therefore came He from Heaven to earth, to cleanse the heart, that He may be seen who made Heaven and earth ... You will be cured, says the physician: you will be cured, if I cut. It is a man who speaks, and to a man that he speaks: neither is he sure who speaks, nor he who hears, for he who is speaking to the man has not made man, and knows not perfectly what is passing in man: yet at the words of a man who knows not what is passing in man, man sooner believes, submits his limbs, suffers himself to be bound, often without being bound is cut or burned; and receives perhaps health for a few days, even when just healed not knowing when he may die: perhaps, while being healed, dies; perhaps cannot be healed. But to whom has God promised anything, and deceived him?[18]

Augustine's time of teaching at Thagaste lasted little more than a year. In 376 he returned to Carthage and set up a new school there. The reason that he gives in his *Confessiones* is that it became unbearable for him to remain any longer among the places and memories of his dear friend. But though on its own level that may have been true, the real narrative of this time in his autobiography follows the story of his subtle analyses of his emotions – and his correspondingly striking silences. One insight in particular has been left there by him to take us into the heart of this:

> For You were to me then not what You are to me now. You were but an empty phantom, and my error was my real god. And whenever I attempted to put my burden there, on my error my god, so that it might rest, it hurtled back upon me through the void; and so I myself remained an unhappy place, where I could not abide and from which I could not depart. For where could my heart fly to, as it were, away from my heart? Where could I fly to, apart from my own self? [Cf. Horace, *Carmina*, II, 16, 9] Where would I not pursue myself? But still I fled from my native town. Less often would my eyes seek him where they were not used to seeing him. And from Thagaste I came to Carthage.[19]

And:

> Why could that sorrow penetrate so easily into my deepest being, unless it was because I had poured out my soul upon the sand by loving a man soon to die as though he were one who would never die. And it only continued, because the very solace of other

well-meaning friends restored and revived me, so that together with them I kept up loving what I was loving in place of You. This was a huge fable and a long-drawn-out lie [*ingens fabula et longum mendacium*].[20]

This 'huge fable and a long-drawn-out lie' is Augustine closing to a point of interpretation something that had been opening itself out over the whole of his life. Left in the inadequacy of thoughts that are our own, we reach for law, for what legislation can betray to us of the future, and for what Augustine calls the 'deadliness' of belief.[21] 'For what, after all, is pain but a certain feeling that cannot bear division and corruption?'[22] This had been Manichaeism to him. It had allowed him to laze into zealousness when unquiet would have been the more wakeful response to the truth of his circumstances.[23] But this rough husk which is the known story of this time in his life hides a more meaningful and sweeter-tasting inner core. This is his relationship to his lover and concubine. For this woman, and for the great love that he had with her, he has left silence – but also the testament of a remarkable series of reflections on 'what men inflict on themselves'.[24] These bring together and exemplify the skein of methods and approaches let loose throughout his autobiographical book. They make sense of its unusual combinations of factual recollection and abstract speculation. And you have to say that if he had done the other thing, and tried to right the wrong of her abandonment by a positive discrimination, then he would have been not nearly so successful and beguiling.

In his lover, Augustine had been able to embrace an immaculate item of knowledge: this is that 'human nature itself ... is complete only in both sexes.'[25] That 'unity is the condition essential to beauty in every form.'[26] Now, on the one hand, there is in this the basic logic to what is becoming and meet in all things, when they have to be arranged in order of the traditional structures and hierarchies of association.

> For by a secret law of nature, things that stand chief love to be singular. So that it follows that what are set under, and subject (not only one under one, but, if the system of nature or society allow, even several under one), are set there with a kind of appropriateness and becoming beauty.[27]

But on the other hand, there is also the suggestion of what two lovers really desire when they desire each other.

The very deportment of sexual love is made up of numerous acts in which the profoundest vulnerabilities of manhood and womanhood become arranged so that they release their latent energies as profoundest strengths. Its unity is a metaphysical quantity that is hardly touched by the orthodoxy that children are the end and purpose of marriage.[28] The American novelist William Styron called this quantity a 'strange sorcery', in the sense that, from the male perspective at least, a massive and disintegrating energy is marshalled by something that is 'obscurely, seductively maternal'.[29] Likewise the rational equality of man and woman which is so often at stake in thinking on this subject is always a given for Augustine: it is rather this union of parts unable to be sufficient to themselves that really excites his mind.

> The woman was made from the side of the man – indeed, while he was asleep. And she was made strong through him, being strengthened by his bone, but he was made weak for her sake, because in place of his rib it was flesh, not another rib, that was substituted.[30]

But this reading is pursued only on condition of his conviction – unusual for the time – that the traditional Christian allegories of creation and order, male and female, are counterproductive if they are interpreted to support an unqualified vision of dominant manhood. In the same sense that he would court outrage by choosing to make the hangman[31] and torturer[32] the symbols of the necessity of (social and political) power in a fallen world, he saw a *camera obscura* in the assumption that 'man created first meant man created better'. In fact he comforted himself by thinking that only a fallen world could read such alarm and complication into the idea that woman was created *for* man. For after all, was man not himself created *for* God; and for the straight reason that the virtue of obedience should be given this life and breath as the optimum ornament of Goodness? As created rationality returning freely to its source? The mischief that envy and pride can make with this idea is the product of the human will acting alone. It lashes out at the thought that Right could run this way, back to front, so it seems: an upside down image.

> For they have heard or read that which is written, 'For as many of you as have been baptized into Christ have put on Christ. There is neither Jew nor Greek, there is neither bond nor free, there is neither male nor female.' [Gal. 3.27–8] And they do not understand that it is in reference to concupiscence of carnal sex that this is said, because in

the inner man, wherein we are renewed in newness of our mind, no sex of this kind exists.[33]

The stigma of cause and effect that can be imputed to the Biblical narrative of the creation of Adam and Eve can make it seem that the otherness of the Divine is something that has to be handed down, patronizingly, until it ends up diminished in woman's lap. A view that sees men emerge to become, in Mary Wollstonecraft's phrase, the 'privileged first-born of reason'.[34] But Augustine understands something categorically different. Here is a great and worthy mystery that can only be downgraded if we insist on relating it to an intellectualized Divine otherness. His idea of the equality of men and women is related instead to the one God who created them both. They do not need to compete for the same finite air or space. 'They shall shine diversely, but all shall be there. The brilliancy unequal, the Heaven the same.'[35] It is a question of beauty and the wider universe; not the allocation of resources in a prison camp. It is an approach that brooks none of the artful distinctions of human life.

> But love is a greater gift than knowledge; for whenever a man has the gift of knowledge, love is necessary by the side of it, as its moderator, ensuring that he is not puffed up in it. 'Charity envieth not; charity vaunteth not itself, is not puffed up.' [1 Cor. 13.4][36]

Divine beauty and order operate on a principle quite distinct from that which governs beauty and order in the human world. When a human artisan creates something, he imposes his will and the materials 'obey' him and take on the form of his vision for them. This has led to the convention that beauty and order are the growing out and exaggeration of things seminal and designed in advance.

Like many Christian thinkers, Augustine was to speak on occasions of the mind of God as containing the pristine ideas of all things (those made and those still unmade) like so many packets of seeds. But he always kept this useful picture separate from the sensations that have been shot clean through some of the great minds when they have stared, fully, at the recurring heart of the world.

For Christianity has always been able to profit from the argument that runs from the intricate majesty of Nature to evidence of its Divine inspiration: but proportion, differentiation, adaptation, symbiosis, number: these visible and analyzable features of it do not decode these shooting sensations that can be had. Augustine says that they cannot. They cannot because the mystical component of being drawn on by beauty and order is the call to the edge of a cliff, and to all the reasons that are hardly reasons at all for letting go and jumping. It is only poorly and inadequately served by the interpretation that unfolds in the opposite direction; the idea that God has furnished us with an elaborate system of signposts that will all point back to His existence, and safety. Augustine's instincts tell him that the provenance of our rooted to the spot awe has nothing whatsoever to do with this latter style of argument.

> But that swiftness, with which He has chosen especially to reveal the essence of His incomprehensibility, is above the power of souls. But it is there for them as wings upon which they might raise themselves from earthly fears into the air of liberty.[37]

To ascribe wonder to Nature is commonsense leaning towards magnanimity. Yet the onward-rushing vision that beauty and order provokes demands, by contrast, a brutal satisfaction. That we cannot possibly survive it is the very ecstasy we anticipate. Augustine puts it that we become, in these moments, 'teachable by no man, but by God Himself.'[38] This disconnecting connection with what was always wanted you find only in those writers who have personally put themselves through it – such as D. H. Lawrence:

> The fountain-head was incorruptible and unsearchable. It had no limits. It could bring forth miracles, create utterly new races and species in its own hour, new forms of consciousness, new forms of body, new units of being. To be man was as nothing compared to the possibilities of the creative mystery. To have one's pulse beating direct from the mystery, this was perfection, unutterable satisfaction.[39]

> For among men it is necessity which is the mother of all employments. Just run your mind through any occupations, and see yourself if it is not necessity alone which produces them. Take the most eminent arts, which are so because they seem so powerful in giving help to others: I mean the art of speaking in their defence, or of medicine in healing them. So be it. But if we now take away litigants, who is there for the advocate to help? If we take away wounds and diseases, what is there for the physician to cure? And for all those employments of ours which are required and done for survival in our daily life. To plough, to sow, to clear fallow ground, to sail – what is it which produces all these works, but necessity and want? What stranger is there to take in, where all live in their own country? What sick person to visit, where they

enjoy perpetual health? What litigants to reconcile, where there is everlasting peace? What dead to bury, where there is eternal life? None of those honourable actions which are common to all men will be your employment; nor any of these good works, when necessity has flown like the young swallows from their nest. What then? For I see nothing that will be there to induce me to action. Even what I am saying now and arguing springs from a need. Will there be any such speech and argument when there are no ignorant to teach, or forgetful to remind? Or, for that matter, will the Gospel even be read in that country where the Word of God Itself shall be contemplated? We have to consider, like this, the old paradigm in order to approach to the new paradigm. In that new state they shall be always praising You. And this shall be their whole duty, an unceasing Hallelujah.[40]

There is, on this gaping Augustinian view, nothing to understand in manhood other than the fact of *primus*. This is because the first woman was the first mirror in which the first man saw eternity coming back to him, as from a futurity of endless other unimagined beings, each one the qualification of the last. 'For the past tense is used to express the future. And prophecy constantly speaks in this way.'[41] And therefore none of it the evolution of life into death and the pungent sense that comes from seeing things in that way; but all of it the game-changing thunder of Judgement, rolling on in form and design and what appears before our eyes; calling out faith as the only present conclusion to its truth: 'But faith in things that are true, passes, as one should wish it to pass, into the things themselves.'[42]

> What after all should we expect to see but all those things which we do not presently, but believe in – and of which the ideas we form, according to our feeble capacity, are incomparably less than the reality?[43]

Man can initiate magnificently and spontaneously; and it seems to be true that the historical institutions of life have been designed to glorify this fact in belligerent repetition of the male first claim. But the business and final meaning of life takes place in the long swinging arc and aftermath of Man's pride.

> Was not His resurrection announced by women to the men, in such a way that the serpent should by a sort of counterplot be overcome? For by this means the fact that the serpent used the woman to first announce death to the man would be redeemed by the use of the same logic in the women announcing life to the men.[44]

This logic may also stand behind the reason why the Presocratic Alcmaeon thought that '... men die for this reason, that they cannot join the beginning to the end.'[45] Or as Augustine puts it even more directly still, with a view to that most anxious of all Christian distinctions between 'Grace and works'. Woman was created for man not because he had earned her by any intrinsic precedence of spirit or eligibility, but because she would show him things that he could not have seen for himself because they had been true all along.

> Fire is not hot in order that it may burn, but because it burns. A wheel does not run nicely in order that it may be round, but because it is round. So no one does good works in order that he may receive Grace, but because he has received Grace.[46]

All of this is proved, in any case, by the bare fact that lovers are first attracted to something in each other, rather than to the whole Darwinian project of human generation: 'For it is not only by touch that a woman awakens in any man or cherishes towards him such desire, this may be done by inward feelings and by looks.'[47] 'And in bodily contact sympathy is powerful, and each other sense has his proper adaptation of body.'[48]

The Christian view most prevalent in Augustine's day (and much caricatured) was that sex is one of the paramount temptations to be regulated by suspicion and self-control. It was vectored on the vital truth that the highest goods will always be abused by evil in the gravest ways; and that the development of social practices that limit the opportunities of this must be the priority – over and above anything else. It was based in the historical reality of a time when slavery and the ownership of humans of all ages gave temptation one of its freest hands and licences. Though now you of course have to add that that this present, globalized world is offering its own conditions for renewed human trafficking; and that the internet has created the marketplace – as private and as shameless as your own home – in which sexual exploitation can be taken to its new grotesque heights of unaccountability. In his formal works on Christian marriage and consecrated virginity, Augustine tried to provide the voice of moderation for the historical reality of his age. Late antique Christians could deplore the abuses of sex in their world; but their responses could go too far and tend towards zealousness. He was all too aware that pride might make a pious nonsense of consecrated virginity, or guilt and shame strip sexual love of its sacred symbolism and mystery. So this send-off to Christian virgins is absolutely characteristic:

'you have been able, not to shun marriage, as forbidden, but to fly past it, as allowed.'⁴⁹

So these formal treatments dealt with the postlapsarian experience of sex as one of our exemplary losses of self-control. And that meant that they could not so much deal with the purely aesthetic delights of love, and of sexual pleasure and desire. For these phenomena radiate outwards, away from the remedial controls of human life as it is now. They cannot be handled defensively, to make some point or other: 'You looked for a commandment as a defence: and by that very commandment the enemy has found an occasion of entering in.'⁵⁰ Neither can they be cramped down by any preconception about religion and what fits with its image. When Augustine took on the classical philosophical staple that every truly felt human joy is joy itself – but wanting to flutter back across its ocean like a butterfly – he meant it and stuck with it to the end. Joy and happiness are the ends of all human determination, but only true religion removes the letters and words and meanings and releases the butterfly to where it needs to go. His only warning is therefore against those who, 'with more audacity than religion, bring a very dull heart (*crassum cor*) [Cf. Is. 6.9–10; Matt. 13.15; Acts 28.26–7] to the inquiry into divine things.'⁵¹ We are to be encouraged to use our imagination in these things. Like the first philosophers did. Men like Empedocles. As recently as 1994 a new fragment of his was discovered that shows what progress into wonder a bright heart can make.

> But when Strife reaches transgressively the depths of the vortex, and Love comes to be at the middle of the whirlpool, then under her [i.e. Love] do all these things [i.e. elements] come together to be only one. Exert yourself – so that the account reach not only your ears – and as you listen look upon the unerring evidences that are around you. I will show your eyes, too, where things [i.e. elements] find a larger body: first the coming together and unfolding [i.e. proliferation] that breeding consists in, and all the variety that is now still left in this phase of generation, whether among the wild species of mountain roaming beasts, or with the twin offspring of humans [i.e. the two sexes], or with the progeny of root-bearing fields and the cluster of grapes mounting upon the vine. From these accounts convey to your mind undeceitful proofs: for you will *see* the coming together and unfolding that breeding consists in.⁵²

Then there is that marvellous passage from Thomas Hobbes's Leviathan, in which a gauche interloper at a court is likened to what we become if we try to turn on this wonder and strike out on an analytic understanding from the glimpses of His majesty that God allows us. It enters us into an infinite regress.

> But they that venture to reason of [God's] nature, from these Attributes of Honour, losing their understanding in the very first attempt, fall from one Inconvenience into another, without end, and without number; in the same manner, as when a man ignorant of the Ceremonies of Court, coming into the presence of a greater Person than he is used to speak to, and stumbling at his entrance, to save himselfe from falling, lets slip his Cloake; and to recover his Cloake, lets fall his Hat; and with one disorder after another, discovers his astonishment and rusticity.[53]

All the deep, lingering notes in any life sound from a place which Augustine follows the Psalmist in calling the *cor altum*, 'deep heart'. This, as far as he is concerned, is the meta-place of storytelling. It is deeper than the outward gestures and recordable events that are normally summoned to tell on a narrative. It is brighter than all understanding that does not begin from it. It exalts us. It puts what is human in history immediately in touch with God. When Augustine came to tell the story of his first serious encounters with death, love and grief as a young adult in Book 4 of his *Confessiones*, he therefore sought to find a way to bring this sense across. He played with silences where we might have expected sounds; and the sounds that he did choose to write with were the sounds that these giant emotions make when they harmonize and strike a single chord.

> Men may speak, may be seen by the operations of their members, may be heard speaking together in conversation. But from out of all this exterior detail, whose thought is truly penetrated, whose heart is truly seen into? What he is inwardly engaged on? what he is inwardly capable of? what he is inwardly doing or what purposing? what he is inwardly wishing to happen, or not to happen? – you could watch all the patterns and shapes of the life in front of you and never comprehend these most important things. I think, therefore, that an 'abyss' may not unreasonably be understood of man, of whom it is said elsewhere, 'Man shall come to a deep heart, and God shall be exalted.' [See Ps. 64.6–9][54]

Out of the silence of the 15 years of love that he shared with the mother of his son, Augustine has produced instead a strikingly personal approach to Christian morality. For him, the real gross obscenity that we are always liable to commit is the mistake of thinking on God and the loftiest truths according to the 'trifles and vanities of time'.[55] He really means it when he says that 'all carnal ideas go for nothing; and if the carnality is to be removed, it must first become ashamed of itself'.[56] The ultimate shame, the shame that can put any of us into our proper place before God and history, is not the shame of particular transgressions (which, in any case, is the point on which Christianity has always been most successfully challenged), but the shame of carnal-mindedness itself – the shame of the *litterae superficies*, the 'superficial letter'.[57] 'The Gospel of John exercises our minds, refines and uncarnalizes them, that of God we may think not after a carnal but a spiritual manner.'[58] When the Christian is taught that the Church in his time is supporting a particular moral practice, and that he should too, he should be inspired by this to go (if he can) to the deep heart of the matter. Since the beginning of Christian times, rulers and statesmen have always been trying to have the Church on tap as the highest moral sanction for what they do. But it is the Church that is there to remind them that the conditions of life in this world are perfectly adapted to its fallen character. What the Church supports in its moral practices of choice is their ability to sustain – from across an ocean of difference – a deep (Empedoclean) truth or two about men and women. Augustine explains this by saying that …

> the earth is, in this sense, the end of things; in that it is the last element, in which men labour in a most orderly fashion. And yet, because it is the 'last element', they cannot actually see the deep order of their labours, which specially belongs to the hidden things of the Son.[59]

We can expand Augustine's meaning here by turning now to the philosopher Michael Oakeshott, who had a similar point to make about the distance between the materials that we have to work with in these matters and the real ambitions of virtue.

> Human activity … is always activity with a pattern; not a superimposed pattern, but a pattern inherent in the activity itself. Elements of this pattern occasionally stand out with a relatively firm outline; and we call these elements, customs, traditions, institutions, laws, etc. They are not, properly speaking, *expressions* of the coherence of activity, or expressions of approval and disapproval, or of our knowledge of how to behave – they *are* the coherence, they are the substance of our knowledge of how to behave. We do not first decide that certain behaviour is right or desirable and then express our

approval of it in an institution; our knowledge of how to behave well is, at this point, the institution.[60]

Here is something to really consider about Augustine when he gives us his spiritual autobiography of this time in its form as 'someone like us'. Not the Saint or the Doctor of the Church that he was to become – but the guy with the girl and the dream. What he is not saying is that he was all sinful and unworthy back then: and that if we have been that person that he was, then the same for us. He is not using his life to damn us by association. He is saying only this one thing: 'Have you ever felt like this?' 'Have you ever felt all out of alignment with everything like you had this great big love to give but no one and nothing you could really trust it to?'

> O madness, which does not know how to love men, as men should be loved! O foolish man, who so rebelliously endures man's lot! Such was I at that time.[61]

You are born to a father who cannot understand you at your source and share your anxieties. Is that really just bad luck? And then that father dies, leaving you with the carcass of what you ought to be feeling for him. Here is another deafening silence that Augustine sought to explore.

Fatherhood is one of those institutions, like motherhood and friendship, whose blushes (and failings in the event) are hardly permitted to be seen apart from the esteemed utilities of peace and security that they are said to serve. Such is the way of love when it is said to be unconditional. 'For natural reverence for parents is a bond which the most abandoned cannot ignore.'[62] But from this truth also came another example of the prison that Augustine felt he should never escape. One of the hallmarks of Augustine's writings as a whole is the many ways in which he manages to say that understanding is only ever idiosyncratic to the moment: but that that moment is the rightful place in which we were designed to live by God. It is a hallmark and a standout feature because it is strictly-speaking a *non sequitur*. We can only really look backwards from our birth until we see ourselves in our parents. What striking unconventionalities of thought may then occur in our moments of growing will have to compete with the urge to send them backwards to this home. And so things continue when really they should change. But the change would require the complete miracle of a Father and a Home ahead of time, to which dreams could be sent forwards. This is what is really going on as we get older.

For by things made there cannot be known any but things previously made. I mean, of course, by you, who are a man made in a lower place, and set in a lower place. And yet before that all these things were made, they were known by Him by Whom they were made; so that that which He knew, He made. We say therefore that in that Word by which He made all things (before that they were made) were all things; so that after they have been made, there are all things again – but in one way here, in another there, in the Word. In one way in their own nature by which they have been made, in another in the art by which they have been made. Who could explain this?[63]

In fact this whole fight of Augustine's makes you think of someone like Václav Havel. Because when you try to say the things that Augustine was saying in a Western context, what you invariably end up violating is the calm dispassionate floating head of scientific reasonableness. What we called in Chapter 6 innocence and the 'new ground zero'. Following the account of the fall in Genesis as literally as he could, Augustine would write that the human soul became proud and conspired to have more than it already had in God – which was everything. This left it no route but to isolate that part of the world represented in the carnal and corporeal senses; and then to glorify this materialism and to rule it as though it were a god; and to do this by treating the laws of nature as if they were the *logos* and the *word*. And so it came to pass that, while science could be fascinating, it could never be satisfying – and most importantly of all, it could never be artificially intelligent. This is where Václav Havel has contributed so much. Because he has found a way of writing that illustrates quite beautifully that the basis of human intelligence in society is measured in the values of the personal, subjective, idiosyncratic moments that the modern phenomenologist tries so especially to honour. For when you think about it, nothing that is artificial can be original. And nothing that is original can be thought of by more than one human agent, at one moment in time. And if you are trying to run your people from out of a little book of wisdom (the *saecularem nobilitatem*, the 'distinctions of this world'[64]), that is really a very tiresome problem indeed.

The fault is not one of science as such but of the arrogance of man in the age of science. Man simply is not God, and playing God has cruel consequences. Man has abolished the absolute horizon of his relations, denied his personal 'pre-objective' experience of the lived world, while relegating personal conscience and consciousness to the bathroom, as something so private that it is no one's business. Man rejected his responsibility as a 'subjective illusion' – and in place of it installed what is now proving to be the most dangerous illusion of all: the fiction of objectivity stripped of all that is concretely human, of a rational understanding of the cosmos, and of an abstract schema of a putative 'historical necessity' ... The phenomenon of empathy, after all, belongs with that abolished realm of personal prejudice which had to yield to science, objectivity, historical necessity, technology, system and the '*apparat*' – and those, being impersonal, cannot worry. They are abstract and anonymous, ever utilitarian and thus also ever a priori innocent.[65]

For the soul, loving its own power, slips onwards from the whole, which is a commonweal, to a part, which can belong specially to itself. And this slipping is initiated by that apostatizing pride, which is called the beginning of sin. For of course it might have been most excellently governed by the laws of God, if it had only followed Him as its ruler in the universal creature; but by seeking something more than the whole, and struggling to govern this by a law of its own, it was thrust on into caring for a part (since nothing is more than the whole). And so by learning to lust after something more, it was actually made less; whence also covetousness is called the root of all evil [see 1 Tim. 6.10]. And so we find it in the present state, where it administers that whole, and strives to do something of its own against the laws by which the whole is governed by God. This leaves it to be taken up with its own body, which it possesses only in part; and with the world of bodies in general, so that it fills its vision, and is delighted, by corporeal forms and motions. It has to do this because it can only rule over what is outside it, and inferior to it. And so it becomes wrapped up in this world of corporeal images; and fixes them into the memory in order to extend that world in time; and is altogether foully polluted by the fornication of the fantasy. In addition, because it now refers all its functions to these ends, it can only end up in one of two places. Either it is plunged into a foul whirlpool of carnal pleasure, or it lusts to create a new social order – dominated by the [naturalism] of the senses of the body, and ruled by those who, with swelling arrogance, desire to be superior to other souls who have not yet attained to this level of innocence and objectivity.[66]

What Augustine proves to be so clever at doing – and it really comes across when he has the wet, vivid material of his life to work on – is to make his infallible solidities of thought and expression out of what should not be able to hold up the weight of feathers. You cannot accuse him of anti-intellectualism, as we have said; you can only accuse him of finding his working truths where they are not meant to be found, then actually standing on them. How many of his readers have followed him out – far and high. And then realized what they were doing, and what they were standing on, and lost their nerve and fell? How many times was Augustine aware that he was doing this himself? Testing his nerve against his education, his training, his age. The *saecularem nobilitatem*, 'distinctions of this world'.⁶⁷ He was daring himself to break, not the sound barrier, but the one barrier that is not relative to anything, but which we are still responsible for keeping up:

> There all are righteous and holy, who enjoy the word of God without reading, without letters: for what is written to us through pages, they perceive there through the Face of God. What a country!⁶⁸

Words that make sense only when marked through time. Time that exists only to carry that sense. God Who 'remembers not those many prayers which we pour out unthinkingly, and accepts the one which we can scarcely find.'⁶⁹ Here is how this rhetorician and genius chose eventually to isolate and shame the restlessness of the restless mind: the unquiet of the unquiet heart: the 'unmoved mover' of the fallen human condition.⁷⁰ It is the 'intellectual conscience', our trustiest Lieutenant, which is punctuating and parsing the fleeting character of this fleeting world. In fact Augustine calls is it, 'this grand and wonderful instinct (*vis magna atque mirabilis*) that belongs to men alone of all animals' – 'by its adulterous fondling, our soul, itching in its ears, was corrupted. [Cf. 2 Tim. 4.3]'⁷¹ Incidentally, the term 'intellectual conscience' seems to have first been used in a critical academic sense in 1927 by Olaf Stapledon in his article 'Mr Bertrand Russell's ethical beliefs', in the *International Journal of Ethics*.⁷² There it was used to distinguish the overbearing, philosophical criteria of truth – impositions which are seen to bully, harass and demean the more instinctive insights of the 'moral conscience'. The laws of nature inscribed upon the heart. But it is probably better known through the more impulsive, earlier use of the term by Nietzsche – a use from the other side of its meaning. In his *Die fröhliche Wissenschaft*, he issues this lamentation on the tendency to acquiescence in the masses:

> But what is goodheartedness, refinement, or genius to me, when the person who has these virtues tolerates slack feelings in his faith and judgments and when he does not account the *desire for certainty* as his inmost craving and deepest distress – as that which separates the higher human beings from the lower.⁷³

The Nietzsche example is without question the better known of the two: and it crops up reasonably widely in scholarship and literature when the need is felt to express the primal itch of humankind – that curious preoccupation that we have to be measuring up always to an infallible standard of right. But more to the point, to be doing so also on our own two feet, under our own steam, without outside aid or intervention: in glorious, God-less self-determination. And so it is curious, then, how this simple concept of the intellectual conscience cuts to the quick of so much of what it means to be *human* – both in its best sense and in its worst sense. Aristotle thought that it might even be the concept that categorically separates man from the beasts. In his *Politics*, he would point out how beasts have 'voices': can use them to express pain or pleasure. Speech, on the other hand,

> serves to indicate what is useful and what is harmful, and so also what is right and what is wrong. For the real difference between man and other animals is that humans alone have perception of good and evil, right and wrong, just and unjust.[74]

This is what makes the barrier so difficult to see in order to break through. It only exists while you are prepared to endure the self-knowledge of your own inability to be truly happy on your own resources; and to exist outside the majority on this point. This unquiet heart, this intellectual conscience: it agitates us to all the best achievements of the human race. These achievements are the rungs of the ladder that we climb when we climb above the *status quo*. But this heart wants also to rest in God. So that final step to its true rest has to somehow be the same thing as to throw the ladder away. You cannot climb and rest at the same time.

> Such a one, so acting, and so lamenting, knowledge cannot puff up. And for the simple fact that charity edifies. For such a one has preferred knowledge to *knowledge*. That is to say, he has preferred to know his own weakness, rather than to know the wall of the world.[75]

'All value belongs to possibility,' is how the poet W. H. Auden was to characterize this barrier, this wall, for himself: 'the actual here and now is valueless, or rather the value it has is the feeling of discontent it provokes.'[76] And back again to what Augustine was feeling as he left Thagaste for Carthage:

> There I altogether raged and wept and became distraught – and could experience

neither rest nor reason. For it was I who was still insisting on carrying about my pierced and bloodied soul; though it was rebellious at being carried by me. Yet I could find no place which I thought safe to put it down. Not in pleasant groves, or in games and singing, or in sweet-scented spots, or in rich banquets, or the pleasures of my lover's bed – not even in books and poetry did it find a moment's rest.[77]

To be human means to be equipped with an arsenal of sincere affections that you are forever trying to project onto people and things in the world. But the effort always fails because this arsenal comes from another place; is still vectored on that place; and therefore ricochets back thunder-blasts of unrequited love and holy ambition. The mystery of this is everywhere. But nowhere does it collect and pool more than around the tenderness – otherwise inexplicable, for mere genetic survivalism and the spirit of technical innovation would replace it with eugenics – that a newborn child brings on in the world-weary and the wise. We have already mentioned that Augustine and his lover learnt this firsthand in their unplanned for son, Adeodatus. Now here is the description of that:

> For could it really be a pleasure in itself to lisp shortened and broken words, unless love first invited us? And yet we see that grown men desire to have infants to whom they have to do just this kind of service; and how it is a sweeter thing to a mother to put small morsels of masticated food into her little son's mouth, than to eat up and devour larger pieces herself.[78]

The party-line and response that the punctuation marks of life can be the basis for better and more efficient ways of doing these sorts of things is a three-line whip and a lie. So when Augustine says things like 'Do not run after many things, and strain yourself. The amplitude of the branches may terrify you, but hold by the root, and think not of the greatness of the tree.'[79] Or when he observes that 'custom has very great power either to attract or to shock human feeling.'[80] Or when he exclaims 'Of that sweetness which to you is hidden, the holy Angels drink; you cannot drink and taste that sweetness, captive as you are.'[81] He is not talking in platitudes or chance remarks, he is spooling himself up for an attempt at the barrier and the wall of the world. And in setting himself for this attempt, Augustine is able to say things about the human body and sexuality that would not be possible were he more representative of his age, and its concerns to preserve a frowning dualism of flesh and spirit. Flesh and spirit are different for Augustine. The fact that you can look upon your own body and know that you are doing so proves it. The fact that you can have erotic dreams that move the body in sympathy to the act proves where the sin really lies. Not in the activities themselves, which were created to a good purpose, and the flesh, but in how they preoccupy us and 'itch in our ears' – even into our sleeping states.[82]

But at the same time as they are different, flesh and spirit make up into a single deportment; and Augustine is the early Church Father who went furthest of all in trying to be inspired by this as by a precious muse. What he seems to have understood especially well is that flesh is only completed in the hand that reaches across to it from the other side. To take a drastic example: many people have been inspired to write moving and poignant thoughts up to and around the subject of death. Some may even have been there, so to speak, when the gun went up to the temple. But no one has written back from beyond the grave with real news of the click and roar of their own death. This might mean nothing; but to Augustine it means everything. None but Christ has been across to the other side and back. None but Christ speaks from accurate knowledge of what that place is like.

> Man's body, then, is appropriate for his rational soul, not because of his facial features and the structure of his limbs, but rather because of the fact that he stands erect, able to look up to Heaven and gaze upon the higher regions in the corporeal world. This special deportment (unique in the animal world) betokens that his rational soul should be raised up to spiritual realities, which by their very nature are of far greater excellence. And this should happen so that a man's thoughts may be on Heavenly things, not on the things that are on the earth.[83]

What Augustine was doing here was breaking out of the wisdom that human beauty is a matter of numbers and symmetry, and trying to say instead that it is a matter of choice and willing – a tilt of the soul. No one could be beautiful on a mortuary slab, even if the numbers added up to it. No one could be beautiful as a statue. But in rare and exceptional cases the understanding of what a human body should look like in its relationship of parts can become the consideration secondary to something else. We encounter this, for example, in the sculptures of Michelangelo. For him, beauty was that the body should look upon itself in plastic expectation. More than we can ever look upon the marble, it is looking upon itself. Beauty knows that it hangs on this unresolved quality of the human form. The soul supplies uniqueness and personality, not beauty;

and so it must learn to find itself in the body without coming to reject the body for its difference of materiality. For the bodily form is how the soul makes its shapes of activity in the world. The body obeys, and the body is judged. It is the body that makes the gesture of the finger reaching to God. The soul must learn to speak the body as the language of beauty; and it must not discard it to the fossilization and petrifaction of numbers and symmetry. And, in the opinion of Professor Hans MacKowsky, it was this knowledge which was 'Michelangelo's unique spiritual possession, his soul's monogram so to speak. He paralyzes one with the agony of a self-realization ...'[84]

> Nor does the earthly material out of which men's mortal bodies are created ever perish. Because though it may crumble into dust and ashes, or be dissolved into vapours and exhalations; and though it may be transformed into the substance of other bodies, or dispersed into the elements, and become food for beasts or men, and in this way be changed into their flesh; it will return in a moment of time to that human soul which animated it at the first, and which caused it to become man, and to live and grow.[85]

When Augustine wrote on human sexuality he approached it from this same inspiration. That none of us have had the ultimate experience of it from the other side of consciousness, anticipation, and shame. One thinks of George Santayana's lament, predicated on the whole long history of this difficulty – that 'All this makes the brightest page of many a life, the only bright page in the thin biography of many a human animal.'[86]

If you were to assemble all the historical norms of human sexual life and make them answer for their differences they would tell you not to look at the beguiling diversity that time and season can permit – for this diversity speaks in fact of legalism, and how customs move time on by creating the effect of a clockwork steady justice from quite disparate practices.

> For the difference that separates times causes whatever is the due season to have such great force over the present justice, and doing or not doing of anything, that now a man seems to do better if he chooses against marrying a wife – or at least only marries her if he is quite unable to contain himself. But once upon a time we know that they married even several wives without any blame – and even those who would otherwise have been quite able to keep themselves in check. The lesson is that piety was not absent from these former times, but that it had them under other demands.[87]

Nor will they tell you to set too great store by the social utilities of these norms; and where those might show where progress could lie. For the great problem of sex that is the exceeding shame of the thing itself will not be worked out of men and women by the normally-envisaged exercises in open-mindedness and desensitization. No. For as, say, Michel Foucault has argued, all the loudness of vocalization, all the brazenness of uninhibited sex-talk, is all rather tragicomic; and at the very least an overcompensation – but for what exactly, that is more difficult to say.

> We are often reminded of the countless procedures which Christianity once employed to make us detest the body; but let us ponder all the ruses that were employed for centuries to make us love sex, to make the knowledge of it desirable and everything said about it precious. Let us consider the stratagems by which we were induced to apply all our skills to discovering its secrets, by which we were attached to the obligation to draw out its truth, and made guilty for having failed to recognize it for so long. These devices are what ought to make us wonder today. Moreover, we need to consider the possibility that one day, perhaps, in a different economy of bodies and pleasures, people will no longer quite understand how the ruses of sexuality, and the power that sustains its organization, were able to subject us to that austere monarchy of sex, so that we became dedicated to the endless task of forcing its secret, of exacting the truest of confessions from a shadow.[88]

Augustine comes in at this point by suggesting that what will be truly liberal and progressive will be if the shame of sexual lust is traced to its source in the primal disobedience of man. To him this is the disobedience of Adam and Eve in the Garden of Eden. To him sex (and its role in human relationships) is, intrinsically speaking, no better or worse than anything else. It is simply the particular phenomenon that proves the general rule that, God-like, and therefore doomed to parody God's responsibilities, we are no longer free to incorporate the goodness and pleasure of sexual function into our lives. This is the same thing as to say that the embarrassment and discomposure of sex is really our general, ethical *embarrass de choix*. Sex is something that we must spy from afar, and scheme for; by return, it is the queen-panic whose very pleasure is her mastery of us in an instant. When Augustine ruminates, counterfactually, on the question of how Adam and Eve might have enjoyed sexual intercourse had they not fallen into sin, he is not being a spoilsport. His preferred answer, that they would have enjoyed it untrammelled and unanalyzed, as the greatest

ON THE SINGULAR DEPORTMENT OF DEATH, LOVE AND GRIEF 167

example of human authority over the flesh, is his most serious attempt to isolate and remove the aeons old problem of the partial observer. Of us placed outside ourselves, and looking at ourselves, in flagrante. The aeons old problem of that superior habit of mind. And shame.

> The man, then, would have sown the seed, and the woman received it, as need required, the generative organs being moved by the will, not excited by lust. For we move at will not only those members which are furnished with joints of solid bone, as the hands, feet, and fingers, but we move also at will those which are composed of slack and soft nerves. In fact we can put them in motion, or stretch them out, or bend and twist them, or contract and stiffen them, as we do so unthinkingly with the muscles of the mouth and face.[89]

The traditional complication of sexual love for philosophers and thinkers generally is the fact that it so clearly occupies a unique position on the scale of goodness and pleasure. It is the one ethical commodity in which these two things are said to be fused beyond any need for further qualification. Yet some quality or accident makes it also the magnet and archetype for human perversity.[90] We just cannot seem to handle it with any lasting insouciance. The idea of being sexually liberated is framed always with reference to the idea of 'sex' being somehow dark and taboo; and the gravest inversions of it are criminal and shocking not so much because of the deeds themselves, which have at least an auto-mechanical coherence,[91] but because of the conscious effort to strike a blow to the root of something.

> Human nature is without doubt ashamed of this lust, and justly so; for the insubordination of these members, and their defiance of the will, are the clear testimony of the punishment of man's first sin. Moreover, it was fitting that this should appear specially in those parts by which is generated that nature which has been altered for the worse by that first and great sin. That sin from whose evil connection no one can escape, not even the Cynics [with their shamelessness], however hard they try, unless God's grace expiate in him individually that which was perpetrated to the destruction of all in common, when all were in one man, and which was avenged by God's justice.[92]

Augustine approaches the whole problem from an unusual angle – and from a far more studied distance than he is normally given credit for. What if sexual love is outstanding for being the high and soaring bliss that makes physical sense and sensation of every chased dream of undifferentiated Wholeness – every dream of love actually uniting us to what can never diminish or disappoint? What if all the awkwardness surrounding it, and the long history of its repression and re-description, is the product of the human inability to translate this unconscious realization into the self-conscious modes of the comprehending mind? What if 'sex' is merely the clearest pane through which we see the whole scope and meaning of our dying? It can be unthinking abandon and oblivion when so much of human activity is the mental activity of pacifying time and the piling up of regrets. A blessed relief, or as Augustine describes it, a *humanitatis solacium*, a 'solace of human nature'.[93] And in fact his sole reason for classifying it as the 'greatest of all bodily pleasures' is because, so possessing is it 'that at the moment of time in which it is consummated, all mental activity is suspended.'[94]

Death, love and grief are special categories of feeling. In fact, they are a single category, showing a single deportment; because under them, more than under any other emotions, we actually sense that we are 'performing' beneath a great Onlooker. Even the most unrepentant rationalist would admit to this – would admit that part of the very feeling of these emotions is this onus to do some sort of justice to some sort of primal truth of the human condition. No one wants to disrespect the dead body, even if they have disallowed the possibility of the soul's migration. No one wants the experience of love to be anything other than an invasion and disordering of their whole apparatus for ordered thought. No one can conceive of grief without some dim hope that the memories of which it is made shall mean that some meeting, in some place, will once again be possible. These responses are challenging us to a purer experience of this deportment than we are able. That we are unable is because the purer experience would involve self-abandonment and self-forgetfulness – which seems, for the time being, to be impossible, because these actions would remove what we accept as the very basis of action, perception and experience. So it continues to be a profound problem beneath an unrelenting Son, the problem of what the philosopher H. H. Price was to call the 'unspecified more'.

> No sense-datum, however 'good', can *fully* specify the nature even of the front surface of the accepted thing. There always could be a better one; for instance, we might use a microscope, and then the specification could be pushed further still. Not only so: this imperfection attaches not merely to the single perceptual act but to the whole of our perceptual consciousness. For no series of perceptual acts, however great, could

possibly complete the specification process, although the as yet unspecified margin could be reduced without limit. (Possibly this is what learned men mean when they speak of the 'inexhaustibility of the individual.') Of course if there were what we have called an *omnisentient* being, who could sense simultaneously all the sense-data which belong to a certain thing at a certain time, for him it would be different ... To put it another way, every perceptual act *anticipates its own confirmation* by subsequent acts; or rather the conscious subject in performing the act anticipates its confirmation. And if he did not, his act would not be a perceptual act at all.[95]

When Augustine covers the same ground, he does so by saying that, if we must be precise, all sordidness can trace its parentage to the sordid injunctions of the human mind begun in Adam and Eve. You do not need to actually know this, or bother with it intellectually, to be a good person and to know right from wrong when you see it in any given situation. But if you are less robust in the way that Augustine was less robust, if you have a personality that must always be colliding with this issue, then he has rare words of hope for you, in the promise 'that some of the actions of men [really do] lie in a region between right and wrong, and are to be reckoned, accordingly, neither among good actions nor among the opposite.'[96] There is still, then, the possibility to act in spite of oneself, in sheer humanity, in the state in which the mind comes into its flesh so entirely as to not notice it; though it takes Grace. But the Catholic Church is configured for these unspecifiable acts of glory. It is ready for them. In fact, they are the 'many things, difficult to enumerate, which make up a variety in the robe of the King's daughter, that is to say, of the Church.'[97] And in any case, the language of Grace, redemption and eternity will persist in all walks of life outside the Church because we have no other way to explain why on earth we would have made it that only a thought experiment can prove our individual worth to history. We are proud enough to have wanted to become these self-sufficient and discriminating minds; but the urge to write great books that recover our lost sense of morality is how we pay pilgrimage to a relic that the Church says comes straight from Eden. Where else do we get this notion that it is unfair to stand alone; fairer to stand together; but dubious to compromise the nuclear integrities of our souls? The greatest example of such a great book must surely still be John Rawls's *A Theory of Justice*:

> The perspective of eternity is not a perspective from a certain place beyond the world, nor the point of view of a transcendent being; rather it is a certain form of thought and feeling that rational persons can adopt within the world. And having done so, they can,

whatever their generation, bring together into one scheme all individual perspectives and arrive together at regulative principles that can be affirmed by everyone as he lives by them, each from his own standpoint. Purity of heart, if one could attain it, would be to see clearly and to act with grace and self-command from this point of view.[98]

This is what we love in our friends; but love in such a way that a man's conscience condemns him if he does not love the one who returns his love; if he does not return the love of the one who loved him first, seeking nothing from that person but signs of good will. And so the great mourning and grief, if anyone should die. Those shadows cast by sorrow, that heart drenched in tears, the sweetness turned all bitter, and from the lost life of the dead, a true kind of death for the living ... Do not be foolish, O my soul, and do not deafen your heart's ear with the tumult of your folly. Listen: the Word Himself cries out for you to return: and with Him there is a place of quiet that can never be disturbed, where your love can never be forsaken, if only itself does not forsake that place. Look on how these present things give way so that other things may succeed to them – and all so that this lowest universe may be constituted out of all its parts. But the Word of God asks 'Do I depart in any way?' Establish there your dwelling place. Entrust to it whatever you have, my soul, wearied out by deceptions. Entrust to the truth whatever you have gained from the truth, and you will suffer no loss. All in you that has rotted away will flourish again; all your diseases will be healed [Cf. Ps. 102.3]; all in you that flows and fades away will be restored, and made anew, and bound around you. They will not drag you down to the place to which they descend, but they will stand fast with you and will abide before the God Who stands fast and abides forever. [Cf. 1 Pet. 1.23] So why then are you perverted and still following around after your own flesh? It should follow you who have been converted! For whatever you perceive by means of the flesh exists but in part; and you do not know that whole of which these things are parts; but yet they give you delight. So just think if fleshly sense had been capable of comprehending the whole, and had not, for your punishment, been restricted to but a part of the universe. You would wish that whatever exists at present would pass away, so that all things together might bring you the greater pleasure. For by that same fleshly sense you hear what we speak, and you do not want the syllables to stand steady; you want them to fly away, so that others may succeed to them and you may hear the whole statement. And this is how it always has to be with things out of which some one being is constituted – and the parts out of which it is fashioned do not all exist at once. The truth is that all things together bring us more delight if they can all be sensed at once, in one gulp. Their parts taken singly do not have this effect. But far better than such things is He Who has made all things, and He is our God, and He does not depart: for there is none to succeed to Him.[99]

9

Christian conversion and reflections on the supernatural

Less than the lees of wine,
We that have seen men broken,
We know man is divine.

W. N. Hodgson

The story of Augustine's life when intermingled with his theology and philosophy allows for one insight of his to run clear of all the others. This is his conviction that ordinary human life contains features and qualities that allow it to operate as its own propellant. 'For there is in temporal things a multiplication [*multiplicatio*]', is how he will put it, 'which turns away from the unity of God.'[1]

The final truth of Christianity as far as he is concerned is that it applies itself concertedly to the chief issue of this. Every circumstance contains the possibilities of its own apologetic; it is an itch. And therefore its capacity to command our attention soars in proportion as the irritation of it becomes the reality upon which our next decision will be based. We have seen throughout this book that the paragon of this apologetic is the short intrusion of every mortal life – framed, on one side, by the arbitrary decision of our birth; and on the other side, by the inescapable conclusion of our death. It is the reason why Augustine places such explanatory power on the fact that the supernaturalness of Christ as He came into the world had to exert itself exactly along the lines of the hyper-naturalness of this logic.

> In opportunity of time – exactly when He would – when He knew it to be right: only then was He born. For He was not born without His will. By comparison, none of us is born because he will; and none of us dies when he will. He, however, was born just at the time when He wished that it should happen. And again, when He wished, He died. He was born how He wished it, of a Virgin. He died how He wished it, on the cross.

> Whatever He wished, He did: because He was in such a way Man, that, unseen, He was also God.[2]

If what we call reality has the power to admit the full divinity of Christ in this way, then the natural, even the hyper-natural, cannot then also be the bulwark we demand it to be against everything else that is. For, as we have been noticing throughout this book, Augustinianism comes down not so much on the distinction between faith and reason, but rather on that holding between what he calls the *facientis animus*, the 'revolving mind', and the *articulus occulti temporis*, the 'hidden joints of time'.[3] That cherished rubric in which the Western ideal of enlightenment is set out as the summit of all intellection is anathema to what Augustine is touching here. The wisdom, say, of a Plotinus, who can counsel against any surrender to merely the Good [for, '... to model ourselves upon good men is to produce an image of an image ...'] produces a god who is the sum of all knowledge and wise-prompting. 'We have to fix our gaze above the image [of the Good],' is how he puts it, 'and attain Likeness to the Supreme Exemplar.'[4] And this gives the spiritual and the supernatural (in practice at least) only the power of intervention that our need for certainty and discernment allows it to have. It is there to be the willing receptacle of those objectively existing potentialities that make up the sum of what it is said to be ultimately useful to know in the world. But in these matters, need is a very thin parade indeed; though it is the only parade there is and the ace card that we feel we have the right to play again and again. Augustine says, instead, that we are continuously liable for the centrifugal forces of the revolving mind. These keep us in a motion that bandies the unquiet heart with boasts of the power and portent of the immediate requirements of being. These we take to be our special possession and licence: more real and apparent to us than ever they can be to the gods, for whom to inhabit them as *numa*, as essences, universals and principles, is their highest career and calling.

And so it becomes a curious thing to see how, in all of this, the supernatural is kept more current by our disowning of it than it actually proves expedient to God. Whatever power we give to the substance and credence of our point of view, Augustine chooses instead to call 'need' – and a craven need at that. He says that the hidden joints of time are hidden from us because we *will* not see them, in the active and constantly revolving sinfulness of our condition. And he means that the Christian, born again by Grace, is not asked to believe what is contrary to reason; it is rather that his reason is freed from its squeamishness about what is plain before it. We reach as far as we can, and what we can no longer touch and see we call the supernatural, and into this realm we place the whole stigma of belief.

> And they daily say to me, 'Where is your God?' For of course if a Pagan says this to me, I cannot retaliate by saying, 'Where is yours?' For he might point with his finger to some stone, and say, 'Lo, there is my God!' And when I have finished laughing at the stone, and he has been put to the blush, he can always look up to the heavens, and say, pointing his finger to the Sun, 'Behold there's my God!' See how he has found something to point out to the eyes of the flesh; whereas I, on my part, know that I have a God to show to him, yet cannot show him what he has no eyes to see. For while he could point out to my bodily eyes his God, the Sun, what eyes has he to which I might point out the very Creator of the Sun?[5]

And yet, if this is how we plot our escape into the secular and close the gate behind us, it is a funny kind of escape, and sanity, that leaves so much that should matter to us the wrong side of the gate. Augustine talks of the *cordis vulnera*, the 'wounds of the heart'. He also equates faith directly with *futuram scientiam* or 'future knowledge'.[6] And knowledge, in turn, with 'a kind of life [*vita quaedam est*] in the reason of the knower'.[7] This makes for the irony that, when we are most aloof and assured in the diktats of reasonableness, the coming into view of something wider than our horizon will bring on the spasm that will show how our hyper-natural is entirely dependent upon the very ghost which it lays. Somehow the sheer possibility of being able to say that we have seen the ghost is more comforting to us than the reproving fact, which leaves no space of pause for thought.

> For this He judged expedient for His disciples: that His scars should be kept, so that the wounds of their hearts [*cordis vulnera*] might be healed by them. What wounds? The wounds of unbelief. For He appeared to their eyes, exhibiting real flesh, and they convinced themselves that they saw a spirit. It is no light wound, this wound of the heart. Yes, they have made a whole malignant heresy of it, who have abided in this wound.[8]

The entropy of the human condition comes up to its full meaning and wickedness in the maxim that 'No one loves what he endures, even if he loves to be able to endure it.'[9] For Augustine this always means that God must meet us, and convert us to Him, in the headlong.

It is only logical and fair, when one thinks about it, that the only true point at which any dogma of the mind or principle of interpretation can be given up is when it is held most certainly. These things meet their match as they move towards it. If they fade of their own accord, or can be eroded, piece by piece, they did not mean so much to us anyway. And you cannot be changed by the handing over of something light and trivial. 'For nor is it for anything else that He loves us here but that He may heal and translate [*transferat*] us from everything He loves not.'[10] In this chapter Augustine is wanting us to give him only the fair shake of the hand. And not to underestimate the basic force of his feelings, but to match them to our own, if we can. The compass bearing that he is thinking of for us his readers as we go through this time with him is the plain beautiful ache of ontological goodness and all that actually is – a non-judgemental bearing that the philosopher R. G. Collingwood once gave an excellent description of:

> Aesthetic experiences like hearing music (or again, seeing a play finely acted) involve a kind of pain which is very acute, and cannot be confused with the pain of hearing bad music or music badly played. There seems to be something of this nature – what we might call a tragic element – in all the highest forms of life.[11]

Which is really an addendum to what Immanuel Kant meant when he said that morality is a judging of happiness from the point of view of God – which is unfortunately a point of view which we do not in truth have. So reason must always make its spasmodic leap across the open oculus of the Pantheon.

> Morality, by itself, constitutes a system. Happiness, however, does not do so, save in so far as it is distributed in exact proportion to morality. But this is possible only in the intelligible world, under a wise Author and Ruler. Such a Ruler, together with life in such a world, which we must regard as a future world, reason finds itself constrained to assume.[12]

We left Augustine at Carthage, where he had gone from Thagaste with his lover and son to live and teach. It would be a conventional success. He taught well, and his reputation ensured that he had no trouble in attracting students. However, their antics that had shocked him as a freshman six years ago would now become intolerable to him as a professor. *Eversores* who were not even signed up for his classes would break in on them and cause a ruckus. 'When

I was a student, I refused to have anything to do with these customs; now as a professor I was forced to tolerate them in outsiders who were not my pupils.'[13] But soon fellow Manichees and operators in that religion's network were suggesting a ready solution. Augustine should come to Rome: there he could be looked after by Manichean patrons: and besides, pupils at Rome were known to be far better behaved – and they paid higher fees to boot.[14] And the position promised to Augustine would have an overall higher status and prospects. Augustine's departure for Rome, when it finally came in 383, was to be the occasion for the famous episode in which he deceived his mother about his sailing in order to slip her close control and insistent grief over his soul. She seems to have been living with him and his lover in Carthage.

> Like most mothers and their sons she loved to have me with her, but much more than most mothers; and she did not understand that You were to use my absence as a means of bringing her joy. She just could not see that. So she wept and lamented – and by these very agonies she proved that there survived in her the remnants of Eve, seeking with groaning for the child she had brought forth in sorrow [see Gen. 3.16].[15]

At Rome, Augustine kept very much within the Manichean set to which he owed his chance in the City. But it turned out that the Roman students, though much better behaved, were more sophisticated at evading their fees. 'They are false to their own word, and out of love for money they hold justice in contempt.'[16] But still he taught well and assiduously, and, from outward appearances at least, continued to flourish. 'I began to devote myself busily to the purpose for which I had come to Rome ... I first gathered together in the house some students with whom and through whom I began to gain a reputation.'[17]

As Friedrich Waismann once put it, 'You may confute and kill a scientific theory; a philosophy dies only of old age.'[18] By the end of his first year at Rome, Augustine was in a customary place. Late Antiquity was, intellectually speaking, the nadir of that great age of criticism that had begun in classical Greece on the birth of philosophy. Like the Blue and Green factions in the great circuses, natural philosophy and religion could face the late antique man of letters as shop-shelf choices of lifestyle and personal taste. But choices to be made none the less, even if the old life and death had been run out of them. This was a chattering age, buoyed up on the thought that the great questions had largely been settled. Religion and religious controversy were something to talk about. And everyone was talking. Points might be defended with zeal; and one cause or another might even attract its fanatics; but sincerity of heart and mind, and honour, now looked to many to be the studious retreat from public life altogether. In these respects it was, possibly, an 'information' age, not at all unlike our own, bringing with it the disillusionments, and reactions, that mass information ages tend to bring.

> The thought began to grow in me that those philosophers whom they call the Academics were wiser than the rest. For they were of the opinion that all things are doubtful, and they decreed that no truth can be comprehended by man ... Yet I lived in closer friendship with [the Manichees] than with other men who did not belong to that heresy. However, I had reached a point where I no longer defended it with my former ardour; while regretfully, continued close association with them (Rome concealed many of them) made it awkward for me to seek something different. This was especially so because I despaired, O Lord of heaven and earth, Creator of all things visible and invisible, of finding the truth within Your Church, from which they had averted me.[19]

The ending of Augustine's time at Rome happened suddenly – after a little more than a year. Symmachus, the Prefect of the City, was ordered to locate a new Professor of Rhetoric for the city of Milan – a position of great and obvious prestige, given that the city was an Imperial residence. Augustine tells us that he applied for the position through his Manichean friends; and that he was appointed to it through a successful public discourse – a kind of job interview. And that was that. He was off, to be transported there at public expense in the autumn of 384.[20] Monica had not joined him and his household in Rome, and therefore would not travel with them to Milan. But her time would come. But as to his reference to his private downgrading of Manichaeism: that was to a meeting at Carthage which he had managed to fashion with Faustus – one of the religion's celebrity Elect. They had met a little before Augustine had left for Rome, but Faustus had not even pretended to care to meet Augustine's questions with scientific counterarguments. And so Augustine had been left impressed with the man but unimpressed with his religion.

> He knew that he did not know these subjects, and he was not ashamed to admit it. He was not one of those wordy fellows, from whom I had suffered much, who attempted to instruct me in these matters but said nothing ... He was not completely ignorant of his own ignorance; and he held back from engaging rashly in discussions from which he had no way out or no easy way of retreat. He appeared to me the more for this: for I

declare that more beautiful than all those things I desired to know then was the modest mind that admits its own limitations.[21]

It is with his emphatic declaration of his arrival at Milan in 384 that the mood of his life shows its first real change. But not the logic of it. The underlying logic stays the same. It is just that the hyper-natural begins to be taken over by the supernatural. The logic that had been defeating Augustine all along had been the logic of fatherhood, so tenuous, so open to luck. Now it was to work its goodness on him. 'I came to Milan, and to Ambrose, its bishop, a man famed throughout the world as one of its very best men, and Your devout worshiper.'[22]

From the outside looking in, Ambrose was a good influence upon Augustine; for he could represent the urbane daylight of classical idealism breaking in upon the crude metaphysics of provincial Christianity and its heresies. He could represent spirituality.[23] Augustine was fretting, wondering how Christ could 'be born of the Virgin Mary, without becoming intermingled in the flesh.'[24] But to Ambrose, such things could be scoffed to nothing on the wave of a hand, and an exciting new thought:

> You must not trust wholly to your bodily eyes. For that which is not seen has to be more really seen, if the object of bodily sight is temporal, but the object of the other kind of sight eternal. The kind of sight which proceeds not according to the eye, but to the mind and spirit.[25]

But on the inside, and in addition to this, Ambrose was being adopted into the logic that would save Augustine's life by redeeming his heart's hopes; the logic of hope which says that 'you may receive an inheritance, when you shall not have to carry your father to his grave, but shall have your Father Himself for your inheritance.'[26]

> That man of God received me in fatherly fashion, and as an exemplary bishop he welcomed my pilgrimage. I began to love him, not at first in the manner of a teacher of the truth (which I utterly despaired of finding in Your Church), but only because here was a man who was kindly disposed towards me.[27]

Soon enough, Augustine began to attend Ambrose's sermons in the Basilica. Initially this was as the new Professor of Rhetoric, eager to analyze the techniques of the celebrated preacher of the city. But professional admiration soon gave way to something more profound: 'I had not yet groaned in prayer for You to come to my help, but my mind was intent on questioning and restless for argument.'[28]

Augustine would talk his way around these sermons with the intellectual elite of the city; men who were full of the fashionable doctrines of the Platonists, rediscovered a century earlier. It is now known that Augustine read the writings of Plotinus and other Neo-Platonists in Latin translations by the African professor Manlius Victorinus. This man was eventually to die in Rome as a Christian convert. Augustine divulges only that, 'by means of a certain man puffed up with most unnatural pride, You procured for me certain books of the Platonists that had been translated from the Greek into Latin.'[29] This casualness with facts is telling. For all the scholarly interest that has been generated by the question of what it was that Augustine came categorically and systematically to accept in Christianity – the question of what it was that he was converted to – the man himself would rather redirect us to the detail that mattered most to him at the time. Belief is the finger that God points at us. Of course we instantly assume that it is the finger that we point more effectively at Him. But that is because we are pointing with all the direction and confidence of sin.

> I should have knocked and proposed the question, 'How is this to be believed?' instead of insultingly opposing it, as if it were believed as I thought.[30]

This, then, is the headlong in which God must convert us to Him. Sin is simply its arrow-like purpose and limitless energy. And this means that it is only as we bend our backs against it that we can feel that we have cared far more for everything than this Christian God, with His unremitting looking-on as these dominoes fall.

> Anxiously reflecting on these matters, I was staggered at how much time had passed from my nineteenth year, when I had first been fired with a zeal for wisdom. For then I had determined to abandon all the empty hopes and all the lying follies of my vain desires, if wisdom could be found. But now I was already in my thirtieth year, and still caught fast in the same mire by a greed for enjoying present things that both fled me and debased me. And all the while I had been saying to myself: 'Tomorrow I will find it! It will appear clearly to me, and I will accept it! Behold, Faustus will come, and he will explain everything! Ah, what great men are the Academic philosophers! Nothing certain can be discovered for the conduct of life! But no, we must search more

diligently; we must not fall into despair! See, things in the Church's books that once seemed absurd do not seem absurd to us now ... I will fix my feet on that step where my parents placed me as a child, until the clear truth is discovered ...' But where shall it be sought? And when shall it be sought? For Ambrose has no leisure, and there is no time for reading. Where do we even look for the very books?[31]

These dominoes that fall, and rack up the tension a notch each time; and this God Who has seen it all before, and still says nothing; and the whole plain need to act at once. Yes, Augustinianism has always been about binary coding this place of last resort and no alternative. But now we can go into greater detail than his two vast cities of mankind. For here is Augustine saying that if the material, and what is before our eyes, is a 1; and God, and the spiritual unseen, is a 0; then our foundational realism, our Quantum, is a value-judgement – and our first step in any direction is the Original Sin. In the words of the poet Abraham Cowley, 'We call one Step a Race.'[32]

Augustine is maddeningly adept at remaining in this place where reason and the normal runnings of human thought seem to cannibalize themselves. It is a claustrophobic and increasingly airless strategy in which we seem destined to learn only one thing by consuming everything else. This is that somewhere in the whole atomic structure of Western intellection there is a particle that simply won't divide. It is the vanity of all vanities.

Humanity in Adam and Eve was high-born. These two were gifted intellect and vision to be the special instrument of God's playing. For, without them, there would otherwise have been a kind of non-dynamic powerlessness in the perfection of what God had made. Perhaps 'powerlessness' is too strong a word. At any rate, it is well enough known that perfection on its own magnificent terms is impenetrable and inaccessible – the concept of a rock of adamant. And the philosophers have always feared this. This it is also well enough known. Things may shatter against it, but it will neither feel them nor experience them. It commands our ultimate respect and affection as the pinnacle of virtue and everything: and yet it is irrevocably and undeniably inhuman. And there is the rub – but it usually takes the literature of extremes to really bring it out and take it all the way to the shattering pieces. Aldous Huxley was one who found it out:

> Eschatologists have always found it difficult to reconcile their rationality and their morality with the brute facts of psychological experience. As rationalists and moralists, they feel that good behaviour should be rewarded and that the virtuous deserve to

go to heaven. But as psychologists they know that virtue is not the sole or sufficient condition of blissful visionary experience. They know that works alone are powerless and that it is faith, or loving confidence, which guarantees that visionary experience shall be blissful.[33]

Perfection clearly cannot be self-regarding; but wisdom knows itself to be wise. Loving obedience is the seamlessness that shows the style of God in making man and putting him into the Garden of Eden. 'Inhumanity', when we predicate it of something derogatorily, is a heartfelt look into this logic which becomes also the supreme irony of Philosophy when Philosophy strives to rise above the human to perfection. The irony can be constituted as a question – and John Campbell Shairp was one who asked it:

> Have you ever considered that characteristic of the Hebrew people, that as they attained to a purer, nearer, more intimate thought of God than any other race, so there is in their human affections a home-heartedness, a depth and intensity, elsewhere unapproached?[34]

Love is the image of God that could never otherwise be revealed in a predestined perfection with everything in its place. It is His 'humanity'; it is our 'divinity'. It is His 'risk'; it is our 'insurance'. We must, as James Joyce thought, always be daring to kill 'the priest and the king' within.[35] And this is not blasphemy; it is just to describe the normal, everyday alchemy of what we call the natural and the supernatural, and how they run into each other. What Augustine would eventually call the *rectum temperamentum*, the 'right mean', and *media regio*, 'middle region' of his salvation – 'to remain in Your image, and by serving You to subdue my body.'[36]

Sin, then, is the naturalizing of the supernatural. It is, as we put it above, the binary designating of these things as 1 and 0. And designation spawning designations is the impeccable structure of knowledge and understanding, and the spoken-out-loud of words making sense to us. But Augustine's God does not put His foot down in this way: and that is important: 'For the man who swears, may swear truly or falsely: but He Who does not swear, cannot swear falsely; for He swears not at all.'[37] And this is therefore the point where the cannibalization seems to get going; because truth without falsehood is a picture of a general situation in which we would find it impossible to be ourselves. We have just become so totally habituated to the Cartesian knowing of ourselves as judging heads. So the idea of the holy grail of truth everywhere and not a falsehood in mind or sight would be the same thing as our total capitulation. The fact that we can know all of this in advance and be writing it like this now in this book on Augustine shows what Wittgenstein pronounced: 'What has to be overcome is a difficulty having to do with the will, rather than with the intellect.'[38]

So the universe is not inhuman: and neither is its Creator, God. But of the dispassionate, sexless pretensions of human thought apart from God, there is something most dreadfully inhuman. It is what Augustine calls the 'disorder of our own conversation'.[39] And he will continue into the thought that 'it was not to no purpose that when Christ was crucified the veil of the temple was rent in the midst, but to show that through His Passion the secret things of all mysteries were opened.'[40] What has been underway all this time, then, is a kind of transference. And what we shall see when everything has been put right is what we could have been seeing there all along. As an illustration of this, Augustine tells us that when he was 26 or 27 years old he composed two or three books on the 'Beautiful and the Fitting' – which, incidentally, have not survived.

> I observed with care and saw that in bodies themselves it is one thing to be a whole, as it were, and therefore beautiful because of that wholeness; and another thing to be beautiful because suitable, and well adapted to something else. Just as a bodily part is adapted to the whole body, a shoe to the foot, and the like.[41]

In these books he had been moved, in the first instance, by the thought that the beauty of 'the rational mind, the nature of truth, and the nature of the highest good lay in ... unity.'[42] And at this age he was still just about a Manichee, so 'in my folly I thought, too, that in the division of irrational life there was some kind of substance and nature of the highest evil.'[43] This encouraged him to locate the dynamic of his theory of the 'Beautiful and the Fitting' in an image of a sexless purity of spirit attacked and violated by an evil counterspirit. He decided to 'call the first a monad, as if it were pure, sexless mind. The second [he] called a dyad, like anger in cruel deeds and lust in shameful acts.'[44] This Yin–Yang approach was satisfying to him then and of infinite applicability once you got going with it. But it was also a little obvious – and therefore lacking in the mystery that we would want from a theory of beauty, centred, as all theories of beauty are, in the human form, and how the human form takes into itself all the elements of the world that are not the same on their own.

> In each human being all creation is present – not taken all together, that is, Heaven and earth and all the things in them, but taken in a generic sense. In each human being there is, for a start, a rational creation, which we have proved or believe that the angels possess. There is also, if I may use that term, sensual creation, which even the other animals do not lack. After all, do they not use the senses and sensual movements to seek what is useful and to avoid the opposite? And there is vital creation without sensation, such as can be found in trees. In us bodily growth comes about without our being aware of it, and hairs have no awareness, even when they are cut, and still they grow. And this is how we witness to this vital creation. Bodily creation is even more obviously apparent in us. Though the body has been made and formed from earth, it contains some particles of all the elements of this bodily world for a balanced state of health ... Thus there is no kind of creature that we cannot recognize in a human being: and in that sense all of creation groans and suffers pain in us, awaiting the resurrection of the sons of God [see Rom. 8.22–3].[45]

Here is a theory of beauty in which the human form is beautiful for being the visible obedience of creation. It is the voice that must speak for all other created things which will never have voices. But only on condition that we are resurrected into obedience to have that voice. If we wish instead to be obeyed, we have done the fatal transfer, and committed all beauty to be seen in the static relationships of parts to the whole. And all the while all creation 'groans and suffers pain in us', because it wants to be beautiful in plasticity and movement. What Augustine was able to see that he had got wrong, then, in those first efforts on the 'Beautiful and the Fitting', was that he had not as yet perceived 'that the hinge of this great issue lies in the creative wisdom of You, the Almighty One, "Who only doeth wondrous things." [Ps. 72.18. Cf. Ps. 135.4]'[46]

Human history has always been the history of the antagonisms between the loving intuitions of fellowship and family and the project-management of truth in society. Augustine sets it out by saying that 'Against the violence of love the world can do nothing.'[47] For one reason or other the history of ideas in the West has been particularly receptive to this creative tension, developing distinctive written traditions of criticism and commentary. This has contributed to an anthropology of man in which the teleology of instinct and survival, or materialism, as well as what empiricism makes of the human machine-in-action, has monopolized common sense – and held it over the more occult causes of the moral conscience. In 1969 the philosopher Renford Bambrough summed the whole situation up into this general tendency:

> When [philosophers] speak of our knowledge of the external world they not only do not give reasons for confining their respect for common sense to their treatment of that single topic but assume and imply that their respect for common sense is *in general* justified. When they go on to speak of morality they not only do not give reasons for abandoning the respect for common sense that they showed when they spoke of our knowledge of the external world, but assume and imply that they are still showing the same respect for common sense.[48]

It certainly is curious, when you think about it, that the homogenous structure of the idea of common sense – into which, too, goes all the sacrosanctity and esteem of the truth of sight and touch – should split, in this way, into such a definite 1 and 0. But we now know that Augustine thinks that he has the answer to this in Christian orthodoxy, taken up and aimed at this critical, load-bearing joint. Take, for example, the Christian glorification of the simple humility of the child; which is another way of saying what metaphysics, and for that matter, metaethics and metanarrative, all take to be axiomatic. This is that somewhere, in some farthest recess of time and space, there is a perspective from which everything would be true, because everything would be seen. And from which falsehood would be conceptually impossible because there would be no further going back to any greater perspective. Temporality, and growing out of this naivety, is how we dehumanize God and transfer the blame (of sin) onto Him. And this means, in turn, that only eternity actually exists *because* it is the great fanning out of everything into one complete view. Temporality, like sin, has no positive existence, because it can only be counted out according to the distributive, Boolean effect of falsehood. Our self-consciousness since Paradise has led us into a situation in which materialism and the laws of the natural world have become more real to us than idealism and the single, all-seen anarchic Truth of the supernatural world. This is the 'folly of that scepticism which argues solely on the ground of its own experience, and has no faith in anything beyond.'[49]

> The truth is One, by which holy souls are enlightened. For as much as there are many souls, there may be said in them to be many truths. But really it is as we see it in mirrors: where there are seen many reflections from one face.[50]

We have gone to extraordinary lengths to have civilizations and cities of God on earth. But these triumphs of intellectualism all assumed that we would know what the bad cities of sin would look like so that we could build ours differently. So we have built ideals out of words, all originating from a single value judgement. And then we have had to wonder why we can barely find ourselves in all that fluency. It turns out to be rather neat that it is from a fellow Algerian, Frantz Fanon – a psychiatrist, writing during the Algerian Revolution – that we get one of the most unsentimental descriptions of the modern form of this irony.

> Yes, the European spirit has strange roots ... A permanent dialogue with oneself and an increasingly obscene narcissism never ceased to prepare the way for a half delirious state, where intellectual work became suffering and the reality was not at all that of a living man, working and creating himself, but rather words, different combinations of words, and the tensions springing from the meanings contained in words.[51]

When Augustine is looking at these same 'strange roots' it is not, of course, with quite the same end in view. That is to say, the utopia that this European word-wisdom prevents is not a utopia of socio-economic fulfilment, in which the work of the state is to be made the same thing as the wellbeing of the citizen. A return to what Adam and Eve were first given would be, for him, to have the Soul and its supernatural possessions drop clean through our mortal spans like quicksilver. And he thinks that of all of these possessions it must surely stand to reason that sexual love would be the most astonishing passing-through. For it would in some fantastic way be carrying the whole force of life with it; and without the retarding friction of quantal understanding, it would surely be something other than the erupting mess it is today. For the time being the distance between what we *could* do and what we *want* to do is just too great to be made up on its own terms. 'It is like trying to catch a jelly-fish on a fish hook,' is how the philosopher Gilbert Ryle described the general spirit of defeat.[52]

With the help of Ambrose and his sermons Augustine began to solidify these insights; but only because he had already gone so far himself in introspection and despair. In him at Milan we detect the long sigh, and inhuman longing, for the animalistic carefree of sleep – or even death. That druggy drowsy going about in a fug of recklessness that only the most hardened intellectuals can pull off and sustain. When they are able to see too many things at once, so that the easy decisions become the most dispersed; and the imagined joys of a brute sensory digesting of life become an almost pathological obsession. How ardently did the Russian novelist Gogol write of 'that wonderful sleep which only happy mortals enjoy who know nothing of haemorrhoids, or fleas, or strongly developed intellectual faculties.'[53] Augustine's example of this from Milan concerns a poor drunk beggar, noticed suddenly by him in the street:

> There was no question that he was in high spirits while I was troubled; he was free from care, while I was full of fear. And I tell you this: if anyone had asked me whether I would prefer to be joyful or to suffer from fear, I would have answered at once, 'To be joyful.' But mark this: if anyone had actually pointed to that beggar and asked whether I would prefer to be like him, or such as I then was, so tightly wound about myself, I would unequivocally have said 'myself!' – charged with care and fear as I was.[54]

We know exactly what Augustine means. But this is a ridiculous truth; or a hard truth; at any rate, it is a truth that someone must carry the can for. Because between Augustine and the beggar, who can you find to blame? One man happy for a few coins and a skinful: the other man unable to be happy for every intelligent effort that could conceivably have been made: the only real victim the promise that the effort of the seeking heart will be rewarded, and that the nice guys will come first.

In fact we can pin something down here that Augustine would take through the whole rest of his life. This red mist of righteous anger against God is the first heresy and the last heresy. It is the germ of all the other heresies that take various and complicated names and seem to keep at a safe distance from the daily lives of the rest of us – locked up in the story of the internecine strife of historical Christianity. This righteous anger is how we create the heresy of what he calls the *tota potentia saevientium,* the 'whole power of the rage of men'.[55]

But Augustine takes it deeper than this. If what it means to be human is to be carrying on always with a subterranean rage, then no human has known the contentment of an animal: and by the same token, no animal has known what it is to be leaning always into the force of the disappointment and pointlessness of life. And therefore everything that we call God, and the spiritual, and the supernatural; everything that we look so hard to detect in the visibilities of life but don't; these are all proofs (before they are anything else) of this subterranean rage. And if this is what Augustine means, then you have to say that he is a revolutionary in his subject. Because he is saying that by looking so hard for God we see ourselves as never before, and in the truest light. 'What this sun is to the eyes of the flesh, that is He to the eyes of the heart.'[56] We know ourselves to be existentially in place because of this anger we can feel. But that really does turn the ship around and back to port – so that we are no longer voyaging on the promising winds of the *cogito ergo sum*. God is proving something of us before we are ever proving something of Him; even with all our complicated arguments for or against Him. He is not, as Augustine had thought, 'like a land that would be untilled unless I tilled it.'[57] It is actually all the other way around.

And this turns the table on all those most important objects that we have been appropriating for these complicated arguments of ours. And none more important than 'death'. For of course the 'whole power of the rage of men' – the whole power of Augustine's heresy of all heresies – is death. But now we have the back story (from both his life and the general life of the Western mind) for why he at times sets out to treat this grave matter with such free-wheeling irony:

> [It] takes from you what a fever, or an adder, or a poisonous mushroom can take. Here lies the whole power of the rage of men, to do what a mushroom can! Men eat a poisonous mushroom, and drop dead. Look to this to see what a frail estate the life of man is; which sooner or later you must abandon. Do not let something so obvious organize your thoughts – unless you want to abandon your higher calling and conquer mushrooms![58]

Death is how we stand proud, with hands on hips, saying that we won't go any further. Death caps the materialism of the length of any natural life. The materialism of the length of any natural life then goes on to be the outlook from which we 'insultingly oppose' whatever in Christianity seems beyond death and incredible and 'believed as we thought'. We are referring here to that question which Augustine used to explain his growing receptivity to Ambrose's sermons: 'I should have knocked and proposed the question, 'How is this to be believed?' instead of insultingly opposing it, as if it were believed as I thought.'[59]

Death is the first-born of all the myriad panics of life; lower-grade they may be, and less immediately threatening, but any panic worth the name transmits exactly, and intact, death's adrenal charge to action. And so we see that we have been deceived on the simplest truths, flipped over to their reverse sides like coins. The processes of righteous anger that link us to God are the real currency of value, but we do not see them down our material lines of sight. What we do see down those material lines of sight are the lives of everyone else; and us in them as in a mirror; and all flipped over and become just blood and guts. And a blood-and-guts world is a world that can be held to ransom at the point of a sword.

> Each man recognizes his own life – that life by which he now lives in the body, and which vivifies these earthly members and causes them to grow – by an interior sense, and therefore not by his bodily eye. But as for the lives of other men, though these are invisible, he sees them all with the bodily eye.[60]

It all reminds one of what the French Chancellor Peter Flotte was alleged to have said to Pope Boniface VIII, at the height of the latter's spat with Philip the Fair. 'Your power is in words; ours is real.'[61]

This whole familiar setup in which we feel the earth beneath our feet and the heavens above our heads is not shorthand for the credible and the incredible. The dualism of matter and spirit may really, ontologically, be: but what we mean by this dualism with reference to God is not actually metaphysics, but a rivalry of value judgements. That is to say, it is very difficult to take someone seriously (even God: and even as a concept) when they refuse to be seen or heard or conjure up a noteworthy miracle for this day and age. And the highly unusual thing that Augustine seems to be saying to us today is that all the lines in the sand to do with the natural and the supernatural, time and eternity, we in our fixed place of location and God in His *everywhere* – all these lines of differentiation come *after* the fact of this original sin. God and His oppressive judgements are proving of what our unquiet hearts display to each moment. This is that human rational intelligence is special for requiring the squeeze of its Maker's judgements to set it apart from the infinitely diffusing, impersonal goodness of pure Spirit. It makes you think of what the philosopher Leibniz once worked out: 'Nothing hinders souls, or at least things analogous to souls, from being everywhere, although the dominant, and hence intelligent, souls, like those of men, cannot be everywhere.'[62] Augustine's way of saying this same thing is to return to his metaphor of the honey bee, and the sickly sweet inertia of this life. At the end of Chapter 6 we saw him use it in a pastoral letter to his patron Romanianus. Now we can have it situated in its authentic context at this great turning point of his life:

> It does not matter if one is already, so to speak, honey – in other words, one already disenthralled from the chains of this life, and awaiting the day when he may come up

to God's feast. Or whether, indeed, he is still more like the honey comb, wrapped about with this life as it were with wax – not mixed so as to become one with it, but filling it, needing some pressure of God's hand, not to oppress him, but to express him [*sed exprimentis manus Dei*]. In both cases, there can be no true sweetness until there is the true straining from life temporal into life eternal. To such who desire this above all else, the judgments of God are sweeter than they are to themselves.[63]

And so it was that Ambrose's teachings were able to run imperceptibly into Augustine's recollections of his unhappy state at Milan. And in turn it is these recollections, and the prehistory which we have given them in the earlier chapters, which add the colour and the grandeur and the locality to the Augustinian language of the human will and its permanent opposition to (what would be) its own best interests in God. This makes for something a little different: for normally the lessons of history when they are sought for by Christian realism reach for the overwhelming indictments of human nature in the great wars of civilization and the deeper crimes of perversion. But of course this leaves us only to be appalled at large, yet unshaken in our private conviction that we would do the right thing given the circumstance, and our chance in it. This 'Pelagian moment', nascent in all of us, is the Scepticism that you could say it is really one of the great purposes of Augustine's writings to keep us alert to. In fact, as the novelist Anthony Burgess noticed, 'We tend to Augustinianism when we are disgusted with our own selfishness, to Pelagianism when we seem to have behaved well. ... None of us are sure how free we really are.'[64] And certainly it is true that if you could take every written word of Augustine's and line up a weapon along their sighting, you would indeed find yourself aiming, not at anything abstract, not at grand theory, but rather at this particular moment in this particular man's life.

> I was sure that it was better for me to give myself up to Your love than to give in to my own desires. However, while the one way appealed to me and was gaining mastery, the other still afforded me pleasure and kept me a miserable victim. I had no answer to You when You said to me, 'Awake, thou that sleepest, and arise from the dead, and Christ shall give thee light.' [Eph. 5.14] When on all sides You showed me that Your words were true, and I was overcome by Your truth, I had no answer whatsoever to make, but only those slow and drowsy words like 'Right away. Yes, right away.' 'But just let me be for a little while.' But of course 'Right away, right away' was never 'Right now', and 'Just let me be for a little while' stretched out for a very long time.[65]

Then this poor desperate man would go to Ambrose and hear only the same thing with added authority!

> Why do you put it off till tomorrow? You could gain it all today; and so you should guard against not attaining the one and losing the other. The loss even of one hour is no slight one: for just consider how one hour is a portion of our whole life. There are young persons who desire quickly to attain to old age, so as no longer to be subject to the will of their elders; and there are also old men who would wish if they could to return again to youth. And I approve of neither desire, for the young, disdainful of present things, ungratefully desire a change in their way of living, while the old wish for its lengthening. But the truth is that under the inspiration of God, youth can grow old in character, and old age can grow green with action. For it is discipline as much as age which brings amendment of character. How much the more then ought we to raise our hopes to the kingdom of God, where will be newness of life, and where will be a change of Grace not of age![66]

Monica had not travelled to Milan with her son in 384. A mother's premonition had told her that it should be enough that her sensitive son be left alone with the searing vision of her abandoned by him on the shore at Rome. 'On that shore in the morning she had stood, wild with grief.'[67] And in any case, 'There is nothing in all the dungeons of this world, nay, not even in hell itself, to surpass the dreadful doom of darkness to which a villain is consigned by remorse of conscience.'[68] Monica would return to their family home at Thagaste; return to her central place in that community; and keep up her prayer vigil over her son's soul.

> A chaste and sober widow, most generous in almsgiving, faithful and helpful to Your holy ones, letting no day pass without an offering at Your altar, going without fail to church twice a day, in the morning and at evening, not for empty stories and old wives' tales [*aniles loquacitates*], but that You might hear her in her prayers ... Those same prayers by which she sought from You not gold and silver or any changing fleeting good but the basic salvation of her son's soul.[69]

And you have to take into account how she must have known what complications of thought her brilliant son had to go through just to transact his days. So this must have been a difficult decision for her to stay behind and a real leap of faith. But she seems to have realized her limitations. Augustine must be allowed to go through his own weird process of winding himself tighter around himself. She would wait her turn to act; confident that that time would come. It would be when all his intellectualizing had finally degraded his physical wellbeing; so that he could with a clear conscience and in all seriousness begin the breakdown and cracking up that had been written into his life from the start.

Monica was good to her instinct. She does indeed arrive at just this critical time of make or break for her son. 'By now my mother, strong in her love, had come to me, for she had followed me over land and sea, kept safe by You through all her perils.'[70] This would be in the late spring of 385. Outwardly at least, Augustine could show some signs of positive decision-making and control: he had taken a step beyond simply listening to Ambrose's sermons and actually become a catechumen in the Church. But if Monica knew her son at all, then she knew that he was too original to be following calmly in the wake of any such method. One wonders whether Augustine may have written to her of his distress and brought her out to Milan that way. But if letters had gone across, then they would more likely have originated from one of his close circle of African friends, worried at the signs. For Augustine was, by any conventional reckoning, depressed. He had depression's time-lag response to everything. And he had depression's corresponding hoarding up of regret and guilt at the inability of its host to simply act, and be fluid with it.

> At that time I said many things to my dear friends in this line of thought, and I often pointed out how things went with me in such matters. I found that things went ill with me, and sorrowed over this, and thus only redoubled that very evil. If any good fortune smiled upon me, I found that it was too much trouble to reach out for it, because almost before I could grasp it, it had flown away on my introspection.[71]

It was probably Alypius who wrote. Alypius was one of Augustine's two great friends in Milan. An African like him and from his home town.[72] The other was Nebridius – from Carthage, and a rich country estate; probably a university friend.[73] In his *Confessiones*, Augustine paints a very African picture of the three of them: they were 'the mouths of three men in want, who were sighing out their needs to one another and were waiting for You.'[74] A community of hearts, and a bloodline of spiritual need. Nebridius had journeyed from Carthage to be with Augustine for no other reason than to be with him. Alypius had already been at Rome when Augustine had first arrived there – sent there by his parents to study the law and also make a great career in the Empire. Another brilliant son of Africa, he seems to have travelled with Augustine to Milan. 'He did this so that he might not be separated from me and also that he might to some extent practise the law that he had studied; although he had done so more out of his parents' wishes than his own.'[75] For Alypius' parents were rich like Nebridius'. In fact Augustine tells us that they were among Thagaste's 'leading citizens' [*primatibus municipalibus*].[76] And therefore they would surely have known Augustine's mother – and now they had sons living together at Milan and carrying the town's great hopes. So one suspects that there must have been a good deal of sharing of information between the sets of parents; and that it may well have been through this channel, and Alypius, that Monica first heard of Augustine's ennui and set sail.

Monica had late antiquity's spirit of the Blitz. She had visions: and more to the point, she could inject them into a situation with unswerving confidence. Augustine relates how this happened on her way over to Milan:

> In the midst of storms at sea, she reassured the sailors themselves, whom themselves are more accustomed to being in the position of reassuring and comforting inexperienced travellers upon the deep! She promised them that they would reach port in safety, for You had promised this to her in a vision. And they did.[77]

Incidentally, Augustine would later develop a general way of explaining what he was going through with such personal intensity at the time. It explains something important about his Christology; which in any case is renowned for being relatively unproblematic and straight up and down.[78] We know that he was reading the letters of St Paul at the time.[79] So we should pause and take a brief moment to look at this way of his.

Christology has always been a tough subject for theology, because it is where the perspectives of critical history get their foot in the door. If God had actually walked on earth as His Son did, and if more or less credible witnesses had seen that and recorded it, then He would have been taken up into the same history of the same difficulties. But He didn't do that – and therefore escapes into a different, more rarefied history as the Big Idea. Christ is where Christianity meets the 'Who do you think you are?' and the 'So what?' of critical reasoning. His humanity brings Him into the jurisdictions and quantifications of what C. H. Dodd called 'a real person in action upon a recognizable scene'.[80] But we have now seen enough of Augustine to know that he would see things from the point of view of the other way round. So not, 'What can we prove about Christ?', but 'What does Christ prove about us?' Christ proves that we are not cattle, contentedly grazing, but human lives, beyond despair.

> You are men, so you have got beyond the cattle. You are superior to the cattle; for you are able to understand what great things He has done for you. You have life, you have sensation, you have understanding: you are men! And to this benefit, I ask you, what can be compared? Well then, how about that you are Christians? For just think how things would be had we not received this additional possibility. What then would it profit us that we were men? Would we be more truly happy than the cattle or only more agitated than them? So then we are Christians, we belong to Christ. And for all the world's rage it does not break us, because we belong to Christ. For all the world's caresses, it does not seduce us, because we belong to Christ.[81]

We quoted from Plotinus at the beginning of this chapter; from his *Enneads*, which would have been part of Augustine's staple diet of Neo-Platonism at Milan. We quoted him warning that 'to model ourselves upon good men is to produce an image of an image'.[82] That this does invariably happen, and that this happening is a serious limitation of the human race which produces only circular originalities and nothing new under the sun, is something that has been picked up on, periodically, by certain thinkers. Thinkers like Edmund Burke, who put it that 'Example is the school of mankind, and they will learn at none other.'[83] To Augustine, for men to copy men (even to copy good men) is understandable in a fallen world, but ultimately betraying of what is human. It is how we are 'conformed to the world' when the Scriptures speak about this happening.[84] 'Lust of the world has its beginning from choice of the will, its progress from enjoyableness of pleasure, its confirmation from the chain of custom.'[85] Animals learn from each other in deadpan rote, producing out of it Plotinus' 'image after an image' and the herd – 'For they who mind earthly things are the earth' is Augustine's phrasing of it.[86] So man after man can only be a dimming and blurring after a while that gets more and more disappointing like a set of worn down printing plates.

> For just you mark my brethren what there is in a human soul. It has no light of itself; nor has it any power of itself. Yes, all that is fair in a soul is virtue and wisdom. But not a wisdom that came from itself, nor a strength that came from itself, nor a light that lighted itself, nor a virtue that obeyed itself.[87]

What Christ proves is that mankind needs to be proving God's Will. We need to love and be loved at the highest possible level of the Song of Songs if our own efforts to love are to have any grounding. We need to be judged out of the eternity of an all-conquering seeing if our judging is not simply to fan philosophy's suspicion that its lifeline to the outside world is a double-cross – the double-cross that Spinoza so strongly suspected when he said that 'it is known that the senses sometimes deceive us. But it is only confusedly known, for we do not know in what manner they deceive us.'[88] To be sure of anything, we need, in Augustine's words, the *divina opitulatio*, 'Divine interference'.[89] 'We could think [for all this deception] that Your Word is far from union with men, and we could despair of ourselves, unless He had been "made flesh and dwelt among us." [John 1.14]'[90]

> For everything which can be seen by the bodily eye *must* be in some single place. And nor can what the bodily eye sees be everywhere in its totality; but with a smaller part of itself it has to occupy a smaller space, and with a larger part a larger space. It is not so with God ...[91]
>
> No longer is it to be 'after one's kind,' as though imitating our neighbour who goes on before us, or living according to the example of some better man. You did not say, 'Let man be made according to his kind,' but 'Let us make man in our image, after our likeness,' [Gen. 1.26] so that we may prove what is Your Will [Cf. Rom. 12.2].[92]

Into this deep thinking, Monica arrived, with all her energy and immediate assessment of the situation. When you are chronically depressed you need someone to come in and tap out the rhythm of life for you. This is what Monica did for Augustine; and one suspects that his deep gratitude for this basic service at a touch-and-go time stands behind his enormous veneration of her in his later life. And that veneration does need some explanation of this sort. For it is one thing to say that Monica put Christianity into her son, and that her pursuit of him through it was the rescue of his soul and a lesson for us all in humility and the salt of the earth. But the truth is that her hidebound piety was an immense frustration to his intellectual way of taking joy from life. And leaving her standing on the shore at Rome is a pretty extreme way to say that. Speaking many years later of a simple figure of speech (synecdoche) and how it struck him, he will show how his intelligence and joy was a casting off from the moorings of life into the endless sea. Julian of Norwich wrote that the only place that God can truly be said to occupy on earth is man's soul – 'there He has made

His resting place, and His glorious city'.⁹³ And Augustine seems to have shared this conviction that understanding can leave the page and be as great a thing as Truth actually recognizing a home in our soul – and God-in-us.

> And, indeed, I do not know whether this figure of speech, by which Joseph is put for brothers in general, is one of those laid down in that art which I learned and used to teach. But how very beautiful it is, and how it comes home to the intelligent reader, it is quite useless for me to tell anyone who cannot himself feel it as I do.⁹⁴

We touch also in this quotation something of Augustine's natural charisma and flair for exciting the vision in people. And you have to factor in to this, too – at least from the perspective of those who looked up to him for leadership – antiquity's silent respect for madness. That is, antiquity's silent respect for madness's installation of a temporary but shocking sanity.

Cicero wrote that 'Ajax was always brave – but never so much as in his madness'.⁹⁵

In the actual, frightening climax of Augustine's conversion, Alypius, its only witness, will not intervene, but show this same understanding:

> I turn upon Alypius and cry out to him: 'What is the trouble with us? ... The unlearned rise up and take Heaven by storm, and we, with all our erudition but empty of heart, see how we wallow in flesh and blood ... I said some such words, and my anguish of mind tore me from him, while astounded and dumbfounded he looked at me, and kept silent.⁹⁶

Alypius had been a pupil of Augustine's when he first started teaching at Thagaste; he had then followed him to Carthage and continued his studies under him there. And at about the time that Monica arrives in Milan, we catch Augustine talking also of an ambitious plan for a 'life of quiet apart from the crowd'.⁹⁷ A kind of cooperative 'single household' [*unam familiarem*] devoted to study and the ardour for wisdom: and in which the heat and humidity of 'Augustine's Milan' could hold the day. Augustine mentions that a full 10 men were prepared to follow him into this radical venture – presumably on some country estate. Romanianus, his original patron from Thagaste, was among them. He had bought into Augustine's promise early, as we saw in Chapter 6. Now he was at the imperial court in Milan to settle some business matters and back in company with his protégé. Augustine's description of the founding principle of his idea immediately catches the eye, if only incidentally: for it is curiously close in spirit and wording to Jean-Jacques Rousseau's iconic *Volonté Générale*. For Augustine, 'The whole would belong to each of us individually, and everything would belong to all of us.'[98] While, for Rousseau,

> ... each man, in giving himself to all, gives himself to nobody; and as there is no associate over whom he does not acquire the same right as he yields others over himself, he gains an equivalent for everything he loses, and an increase of force for the preservation of what he has.[99]

But Monica had not come to Milan empty handed. She had carried with her something from Augustine's first days at Thagaste that he had always found confounding. She had carried with her that ambition which he had so often used to lump her and Patricius together into a single object of scorn when it suited his teenage angst. But she knew her son. She knew how he was liable to be 'borne up to You by Your beauty, but soon ... borne down from You by my own weight, and with groaning.'[100] She sensed a real inability in him to achieve a perspective that the rest of us achieve without thinking about it when we say that such intuition is 'all very well', but it needn't make everything else seem black and unpalatable by comparison. And a man has to eat and live, too. Marriage: Monica had had her own experience of taming a husband. Marriage: she had spent her life watching men dip in and out of the cycle of life, and lay their seed, and boast about it afterwards. Marriage: only a woman lengthens the hard, fast burn that carries men into wars, and philosophies, and religious abandon. And it seems that she had allies of her kind in this. For Augustine's community might well have carried off and become a reality before her arrival had it not been that the wives of the men concerned began to register their protest! 'As a result, the whole project, which we had worked out so well, collapsed in our hands; it was completely broken up and thrown aside.'[101]

Monica's work at Milan, once she had got these bearings, became to consolidate the gains already made by Augustine under Ambrose. Time had already slipped into the early spring of 386, and the whole bohemian flapping tent of his lifestyle and his followers, and most especially his lover from Carthage days, must be dealt with. She would nail the tent pegs into the ground. The girl would be sent back to Africa and the son left with her and Augustine in Milan. Augustine's account of how she went about this retains the unmistakable tang of his first feelings about it – and about her undiminished desire for 'grandchildren born of my flesh'.[102] And it is usually like this: that mothers look further down the distance of a relationship than their sons do: and that grandchildren are the mile markers of their depth of vision. And so the general case, as Anthony Trollope put it, is that 'No man likes to be talked out of his marriage by his mother.'[103]

> Steady pressure was put upon me to make a new and more suitable marriage. Soon I asked for a girl's hand, and soon she was promised to me. This was principally through my mother's activity, for she hoped that once I was married the baptism of salvation would wash me clean ... She said that she could distinguish by some sort of savour (which she could never explain in words to me) the difference between Your revelations and her own dreaming soul. Yet the marriage was urged upon me, and the girl was duly asked for. She lacked almost two years of the age of consent, but since she appealed to me, I was willing to wait for her.[104]

The supreme challenge for any biography of Augustine, for scholarship and for the reader, is to make the event of his Christian conversion in the summer of 386 just as much the key to his life story as he was determined to make that life story the key, in turn, to so much of the Western intellectual tradition after him.[105] For when one thinks about it, Augustine already has huge legacies in Roman and ecclesiastical history; as well as theology, philosophy, psychology and letters – legacies that are so firmly established on their own foundations that they would not ordinarily suggest this extra effort that we have been putting out here.[106] The extra effort actually defies the unwritten rule that a great mind is great because it makes these impersonal contributions to the stock cupboards of the world mind. But Augustine challenges this rule that men like him were living posthumous lives – already bound between covers.

As we have expressed it in various ways in this book, Augustine has in all major respects *become* late antiquity to scholarship. He has become, therefore, the paramount example of one religion's rise to precedence of all the others – and his partisan writings still influence how we administer the effects of this today. What is more, conversion events such as his are notoriously hard to document, and not just for the historian: witness the difficulties experienced by the philosophers, psychologists and anthropologists. Generally speaking, and as far as recorded human experience operates, religion must come into the mainstream washings of cause and effect if it is to be respected at all as something that has motivated and modified behaviour.[107] Look, for instance, at how John R. Everett explained the situation:

> However man is conceived, he is clearly a being of many tendencies. He is dependent upon physical nature for his food, drink and shelter; and he is dependent upon other men for friendship, understanding and physical safety. In other words there is no such thing as man except as he is caught up in a network of dependencies. Religion must therefore be considered one restricted area of dependence among many.[108]

Religious conversions, by being registered and understood in this way within the wider cultural developments of which they are a part, end up by becoming only some of the most inevitable of human events. They become the standard interface and regularizing of what is sublime in man (and therefore otherwise difficult to historicize) and what is driven in him and instinctive. Their contents from the personal, subjective point of view might be interesting; but they become practically immaterial if we need simply to be thinking – as is so often the case with Augustine – about the general phenomenon called the Christianization of the Latin West. What we need instead for this are working definitions of Christians and Christianity, so that we can learn to make out the train tracks of the spreading of these concepts demographically and geographically. And so when a pivot-point like Augustine makes what seems to be an inordinate fuss of his conversion in his autobiography, the smooth machinery of all of this shudders and slows.[109] And we are left to deal with what Virginia Woolf called 'that riot and confusion of the passions and emotions which every good biographer detests[!]'[110]

Now there have certainly been analyses of Augustine's conversion different to this – looking at it as a discrete example of its experience-type; but to make it archetypal in the way that he made it archetypal has proved troublesome and a little prosaic.[111] Writing, for instance, in 1902, and surveying the scene of what were then the largely theological biographies of Augustine, the prolific rationalist Joseph McCabe bemoaned what he called their 'perverse *a priori* form'. That is to say,

> Up to the time of his conversion Augustine must be portrayed in uniformly dark colours. Then, of a sudden and with utter contempt of all the laws of the psychologist, the flood-gates of light and grace are opened, and every line must henceforth be written in letters of gold.[112]

Certainly the constituents of Augustine's conversion are not auspicious. And on their own, and at face value, they broadcast nothing to us of the drama of that time. There is his conditioning to some basic tenets of the Christian faith by his mother – but little more than to the name of Christ. There is his difficulty to work these tenets up to anything trustworthy alongside his discovery of the dismaying rusticity of Biblical prose. There is his Gnostic, Manichaean materialism – something which we are liable to see as the blood clot in the ancient mind. There is his worrying, and gnawing, of sexual lust as he experienced it work through his body – and as he satisfied it. This has largely become a closed book to us for two reasons. Either it is that we feel we have moved beyond the ages of prurient fascination; or it is that we feel we should frown upon a man so unable to join our freedom of movement in this thing. And then, finally, there is the great flood of tears from that world-famous scene where he sits under a tree in the garden of his lodgings in Milan and converts, of a sudden, to Christianity. The passion and deluge of this moment has been sending the scruples of textual analysis scurrying for high ground for years.[113] It is written to such a point of dramatic convergence as to seem too good to be true. But it does join Augustine to modern writers such as Isaac Babel, equally displaced, for whom, at a similar moment, 'the world of tears was so huge, so beautiful, that everything save tears vanished from my eyes.'[114]

When it comes to truth we like to wear white lab coats; so such creativity we tend actually to hold against people like Augustine. Tears are wet and messy and they do so quickly wash out the ink of our carefully formed lines.

Why do we have to cry? Why do we have to be wiped clean in the 'world of tears'? Why do we have to be baptized?

Augustine wants us to be thinking (as he so often was) of babies. Of that first gasp for air, newly-born. That first Quantum and value-judgement. That first heedless pitch into the headlong. Viviparous. Because we find that, when he is being most effectively and perceptively criticized, it is because he is being identified as having poured his genius into writing us into what Professor Eugene TeSelle has called the 'ultimate loneliness':

> Despite the brightness of divine light, and the warmth of divine love, with which he felt himself surrounded, he could not affirm, in the last analysis, that God might be

concerned about, affected by, enriched or diminished by, the life of Augustine or any other finite being.[115]

This 'ultimate loneliness' is a criticism of Augustine's brilliance for moving God on a bit, at each time we feel we might finally have got our grip on understanding Him. This is seen to be partly his inheritance from Plotinus, who went further than the middle Platonists in making God the 'Supreme Exemplar'.[116] Plotinus was not so much concerned with the practical side of Platonist philosophy – the side of human flourishing as applied wisdom in the polis. He was too much the mystic. God, to him, was the beautiful painting that explains everything in a second, but that you must not touch.

There is no question that Augustine is relentless in using reason and all the tools of apprehension to kick out the same stool from under them. We earlier used the term 'cannibalistic' to describe his enormous appetite for this. But what does he really mean when he does this? And this question must be answered. For it is one thing to say that God is beyond all human comprehension in His omnipotence. That is merely the most essential orthodoxy – and Augustine has furnished some of the best sound bites for it. But we need a God Whom we can politic with, in the original Greek meaning of that word. And in terms of the development of historical Christianity, we therefore need also a political Augustinianism. For we are so very weary that we imagine the moment of God's final revealing of Himself through the human eyes of extreme fatigue and exhaustion – devoid of all creativity and the heart gone out of us: the 'let us rest for a while' and the differentiation and 'everything in its place' of a conservative European rationalism.

Augustine is very good, in his Protestant moods, at urging us to hope in spite of sin. There is not by any means the precision of the modern formulations of 'justification by faith'; but there is the same pulpit-shaking conviction that a willingness to identify with sin will bring with it the proportional healing of faith in Christ. By the same token he is just as good, in his Catholic moods, at deriving from this existential blessing his final justification for the Church – and for the Church's institutional authority. It is the only solution to human fallibility: it is the only solution to our final inability to know exactly who on earth has been predestined to be saved. But the point is surely a fair one when it is said that, for all of this, he does not produce the God we conceive with our first gasp for air, 'savouring the things of men' [*sapiens tamquam homo*].[117] He does indeed leave us lonely, and ultimately so, if we are trying to see our way to that first gasp through the eyes of materialism, death, and scepticism, if we are trying to use the power of the rage of men to divide the unity of Truth.

However, we have been following the trail of something in this chapter that might address this. And in fact in a sermon of Augustine's on the words of the Gospel, Matt. 17.1, we find a conclusion to what we have been trailing and a making plain of Augustine's reflections on the supernatural. He preaches that there is indeed such a thing as the loneliness of distant perfection – felt like the aloofness of an unapproachable parent. But the ultimate loneliness must surely be something more at home and innate to us. Something that we can be culpable for missing because it was as near as being always there. Our heart's beating, perhaps; or even our own breathing. Or something nearer still: our own Soul.

> Peter sees this, but as a man savouring the things of men says, 'Lord, it is good for us to be here.' [Matt. 17.4; Luke 9.33] He had been wearied along with the multitude, and now he had found the mountain's solitude; and with him there he had Christ the Bread of the soul. What! Should he now depart from this precious place – once again into travail and pains, taking up once again the holy love of the sojourning seeker after God? No, he naturally enough wished well for himself; and so having seen Christ transfigured and speaking with Moses and Elias, he added from a human prudence, 'If Thou wilt, let us make here three tabernacles; one for Thee, and one for Moses, and one for Elias.' [Matt. 17.4; Luke 9.33] To this the Lord made no spoken answer. But notwithstanding this Peter was answered, and emphatically. For while he yet spoke, a bright cloud came, and overshadowed the three. He had desired three tabernacles; and the Heavenly answer showed him that we have One, which human judgment desired to divide. Christ, the Word of God, the Word of God in the Law, the Word in the Prophets. Why, Peter, do you seek to divide them – and dividing them miss your heart's desire? It were more fitting for you to join them. You seek three; understand that they are but One.[118]

We said at the start of this chapter that you cannot be changed by the handing over of something light and trivial. That simply stands to reason. The French sociologist Émile Durkheim said that 'Human passions stop only before a moral power they respect.'[119] Augustine's materialism can certainly be made to seem trivial; even more so can his sexual lust – a peccadillo. Yet in the climax of his Christian conversion which incorporates both these things he is trying very desperately hard to tell us something. Something that the rest of his life's work and biography will be as the footnote to, if we can only find it. What do the tears of a broken-down man tell us? They tell us that we are dry-eyed when we are enduring the world and proud of it. We are a closed fist and a point of reference. A promontory; and Truth and falsehood break either side of us. 'Man is the measure of all things,' said Protagoras. 'Of things that are, that they are; of things that are not; that they are not.'[120] 'But the Lord stretched out His hand,' says Augustine in his sermon, 'and raised them as they lay. And then "They saw no man, save Jesus only." [Matt. 17.7-8]'[121]

> Attached to our lodging at Milan there was a little garden which we had the sole use of. The raging question of whether or not to convert myself to Christ drove me out into it. For there I would be able to thrash about and take on the raging combat I had got going inside myself. I did not as yet know, as You did, that I was entering into a true madness that would bring health. I was in a death agony, but could not as yet see the life that would issue from it. For in those moments I felt myself to be truly the thing of all evil in the world. Alypius had followed me out into the garden, determined to at least be near my side come what may. We took ourselves as far as we could from the house for privacy. But sitting there with him I could not have been more alone. Because we never are more alone when we have taken ourselves down from all apologetic circumstances until we are just the will that we are – and a free choice. And this is all that evil is: the will that won't enter into the covenant with its God. For I tell you that all my bones cried out for me to enter into that covenant, and by their praises they lifted me up to the skies. Indeed it is not by ships, or chariots, or on foot that we enter into it; you do not even have to go into a garden as I had done. You only have to will to do it. To will firmly and finally – and not to twist and turn about, a struggling pathetic will, with one part of it rising, and the other part falling down.[122]

So the dam breaks because the bursting point has become generic, and the shamefulness cosmic. 'Omit not to watch your slightest daily sins: rivers are filled from the smallest drops.'[123] The one man – Augustine – feels himself to be all men in a headlong – and a *Unitatem fecerunt contra unitatem* ['a unity against Unity'].[124] The imbalance is now staggering; but the human inertia is plastic and elastic and will not quite yet snap: 'By an austere mercy You redoubled the scourges of fear and shame, lest that thin little remaining strand should not be broken through but should grow strong again and bind me yet more firmly.'[125] Who could have thought Divinity would be like this? We thought of it always as a sweet word: we wrote it up in books and kept them on hallowed shelves. Now, 'Love is a sweet word, but sweeter the deed.'[126] Humanity lives with its head down, dividing and counting beans – its necessity, a habit; its very certainty, the ultimate loneliness. Ludwig Wittgenstein's experience of it: 'It used to be said that God could create anything except what would be contrary to the laws of logic. The truth is that we could not *say* what an "illogical" world would look like.'[127]

> And so it was that my lovers of old, trifles of trifles and vanities of vanities, were able to hold me back. All they had to do was pluck and pluck away at my fleshly garment and keep my will preoccupied. They kept whispering softly to me: 'Do you cast us off?' and 'From that moment we shall no more be forever and ever!' and again, 'From that moment no longer will this thing and that be allowed to you, forever and ever!'
> But now these voices of my will grew feebler. For from that way in which I had set my face and where I trembled to pass, there appeared to me the chaste dignity of continence, serene and joyous, but in no wanton fashion. She really was virtuously alluring, so that I would come to her and hesitate no longer … And she smiled upon me in that way which women do which is so encouraging – with an enheartening mockery, as if to say: 'Why do you stand on yourself, and thus stand not at all? Cast Yourself on Him. Have no fear. He will not draw back and let you fall.'[128]

So now we come to the end of the story of one man made up to be the story of everyman. God, Augustine's God, defies biography. So the biographer must respect that. The biographer expects to be able to lay out all the millions of pieces of a life like the millions of pieces of a wrecked aircraft – all in a hanger and awaiting investigation and the 'What happened?' and 'Why?' But God is waiting to push all the pieces through the pinprick of a moment.

> But throughout these long years where was my free will? Out of what deep and hidden pit was it called forth in a single moment? A single moment in which to bend my neck to Your mild yoke and my shoulders to Your light burden, O Christ Jesus, 'my helper and my redeemer? [Ps. 18.15]'[129]

We are the remembering race, always looking back to a reality from which to make sense of the moving forwards. But He is the resuscitating God, starting and restarting us afresh in an eternal conservation of emotion.

> If the air of this world is withdrawn, the body dies; there can be no question of it. And if God is withdrawn, the soul dies; and there can be even less of a question of that. For

> when God does resuscitate [*suscitat*] a soul, He has to be in some way continuously resuscitating it thereafter, otherwise it will only die to Him again. So as long as we remain converted to Him, he promises us this eternal resuscitating action.[130]
>
> For the Almighty sets in motion even in the innermost hearts of men the movements of their will, so that He does through their agency whatever He wishes to perform through them – notwithstanding that they may appear to do evil, and it is He Who knows not how to will anything in unrighteousness.[131]

The history of European philosophy is the philosophy of European history in which we have remembered ourselves a thousand years from now. Like the 'Old Soak' in Louis MacNeice's *The Dark Tower*, we have 'never abdicated the life of the womb': 'I wrote this farce before I was born, you know –/This puppet play. In my mother's womb, dear boy.'[132] For a single Anarchic Truth and God's point of view is no future at all that we can be part of. The only energy that we can have of our own creation is the energy to think that there is a Quantum, a Higgs Boson – and that one day there will be one of us to see it, and close our fist around it. That full stop is the same thing as a life worth living. When that goes there will be the great unravelling and mass hysteria and the end of the World.

> For a whirlpool again seizes at me unawares, and whips me round to admit that whatever is true is that which is as it seems. From which it has to result that without a knower, nothing can be true. And so I am left, as it were, to fear a shipwreck on deeply hidden rocks, which may be true, although as yet unknown by a knower. Or, if I shall say that that is true which simply *is*, it follows that there is nothing false anywhere. And out of this I see the same breakers before me again...[133]

10

To write against self-consciousness and its effects

> Man, in becoming more complex,
> becomes less stably organized.
>
> George Santayana

The problem with a Christian conversion is that you have to wake up from it the following morning, much unchanged. 'Lay me down like a stone,' goes the Russian proverb, 'and raise me up like new bread.' The great Italian Augustinian scholar Agostino Trapè called Augustine's conversion *un punto di arrivo e un punto di partenza*, 'a point of arrival and a point of departure'.[1] Tears dry up – after only a short time, in fact. And so then, too, does the world of tears, with all its tangible, salty drama of regeneration. The problem is that a Christian conversion becomes *real* in that moment that it has successfully implicated the 'all of us' in the comparatively dry ice of orthodoxy. A million little details that supported our life in its heat, in its scepticism, and in scepticism's holding off for the next while – these have to now be seen and crossed out as the adjectives for higher-order realities. Now no longer needed. 'Whenever truth is spoken, there is nothing to be said against it.'[2]

After his conversion in the garden of his lodgings at Milan, Augustine only wanted to do one thing. This was to stand stock still. One might call it the instant transfiguration of his 'unquiet heart'. 'A complete will to remain still and see that You are the Lord arose in me.'[3]

Each life is given its chance for a moment of great individual dignity. A moment in which the person of that life summons up a seeing of their own best interests that is so obviously superior to what anyone can any longer do for them. This was that time in Augustine's life; so it was time for Monica to take a back seat and give this new respect to her son. She had done her best for him when he needed her most. He would no longer marry, and there would be no grandchildren of her happy foretelling. But, 'She was filled with exultation and triumph, and yes she blessed You, "Who are able to do above that which we ask or think." [Cf. Eph. 3.20]'[4]

What had everyone got so horribly wrong about Augustine's whole life up to now when he could finally take command and show them what they had been missing, from the boy to the professor? His parents, teachers, friends, everyone. What they had all missed was a thoroughbred creative mind and spirit. Not, admittedly, a type that would be sought for in quite the same way as it would be today; but everyone had been working so hard for his chance that they had missed this basic need reflected in his face. And God only knew how he had bitten the bullet and tried to find himself, too, in the late antique mould of brilliance which would become his profession: eloquence teaching eloquence. But he *had* always sensed a different way. Creativity can never be recognized on the terms on which it wants to know itself:

> So in the speeches of eloquent men, we find rules of eloquence carried out which the speakers did not think of as aids to eloquence at the time moment that they spoke them ... For it is because they are eloquent that they exemplify these rules; it is not that they were the kinds of characters who were using them in order to be eloquent.[5]

Even Ambrose had missed it. When Augustine wrote to him later to ask what books of Scripture he should read to prepare himself for baptism, he recommended the Book of Isaiah. He had chosen a book fit for a philosopher, or a theologian; or at any rate, for a clever clogs convert needing to be reminded of Grace and the historical destiny of Christianity. He had thought too much of his own famous politicking with Emperors and Empresses and missed the writer in the young man before him. But he was not to know; for in this matter Augustine was ahead of his time and drawing already from a deeper well altogether than these 'outward' patterns of victory.

> He recommended the prophet Isaiah: and I believe it was because he is a more manifest prophet of the Gospel and of the calling of the Gentiles than are the other writers. But the truth is that I did not understand the first lesson in this book, and thinking the whole work to be similar, I put it aside to be taken up again when I was better accustomed to the Lord's mode of speech.[6]

Yes, he would stand still, in the growing confidence of his new vocation. He would abdicate his Professorship and *cathedra mendacii*, 'chair of lies'.[7] He would surround himself with 'those things which in my heart are as truly present to me as I am to myself.'[8]

> In Your sight I resolved not to make an immediate and provocative break from the language marts, but gently to withdraw my tongue, so that youths who did not meditate on Your law, or on Your peace, but on foolish lies and court quarrels, would no longer pry from my mouth weapons for their madness.[9]

One of the first things that is forgotten with cases like Augustine is that the genius-insight which knows that it has something to say is not for that reason specially qualified to answer the questions that the rest of us have, and our misunderstandings. What they are seeing all of the time is their normality: not some supercharged version of what we could see. The stunning truths which they can arrive at so casually were not conceived as the answers to any great problems; the great problems for them are all to do with not being able to live out of *their* normality, unthinkingly, in a community of people like them. The genius-mind cannot take the pleasure that we can take in putting them up on the stage.

> I do not claim this perfection for myself even now when I am old; and even less did I claim it when, in early manhood, I had begun to write or to speak to the people. For back then so much authority was already attributed to me that whenever it was necessary for someone to speak to the people and I was present, I was hardly ever allowed to be silent and just listen to others and to be 'swift to hear but slow to speak.' [Cf. Jam. 1.19] I want to judge myself, not on a stage, but before the sole Teacher.[10]

So all of this resolved itself into 'the plan': to see out the final 20 days of teaching before the Vintage vacation (roughly equivalent to the big summer vacation of Italy today), then to set up some kind of interim life outside the City for himself and his household. March 387 would be his first opportunity for baptism at the hands of Ambrose in Milan, and he planned to take it – along with Alypius and his 14-year-old son, Adeodatus.

However, at exactly this moment of Augustine's self-realization, let us not miss the one chance that we have to put to him the classic question of his life:

'What is *Augustinianism*?' What is this thing that hangs over the self-realization of the European mind like a heavy symptom?

Part one: identifying Augustinianism

Augustinianism is Augustine's utter contempt of idols. Not so much the giant efforts in wood and stone that we can titter or gawp at, but the untold idols of the mind.[11] The rules that pop up like tyre spikes after the fact of 'the onward-rushing vision of beauty and order'.[12] 'Do you chase the syllables, and cause them to remain?'[13] 'You ought not to paint in your heart God, as it were, circumscribed with a human form, lest though the temples are shut up, you forge the selfsame images in your hearts.'[14] But as always with Augustine, there are reminders that the fallen human mind is not something that should be stepped out of tomorrow like a torn pair of trousers. The complete remedy for a fallen world would not be a new pair of clothes but the original nakedness of Eden: and that's just not going to happen for all sorts of streetwise reasons: and that doesn't need to happen, either, because Christianity accepts those streetwise reasons for what they say about the need for a Heavenly City apart from this Earthly City, which is now completely configured for its own ends.

> Has not the genius of man invented and applied countless astonishing arts, some the result of necessity, some the result of exuberant invention? And does not this vigour of mind which is so active in the discovery not merely of superfluous but even of dangerous and destructive things, suggest a kind of inexhaustible wealth in the nature which can invent, learn, or employ such arts? For as things are it is the nature of this human mind which adorns this mortal life which we are extolling, and not the faith and the way of truth which lead to immortality.[15]

Obedience to idols is how we become also most perplexing to ourselves, and estranged from ourselves. So it is often only by passing on this perplexity to a man like Augustine, who did not show the same effort and resilience, that we feel that we can reach a conclusion of sorts in the standing enigma of his personality. 'But why linger over a multitude of reasons when the Lord Himself undoes all the windings of human argumentation?'[16] The biographer of Augustine, Gerald Bonner, wrote another book in 2007 to try to make both the visible ends of the personality who could say this meet in Freedom and Necessity:

> It is the twofold aspect of Augustine: the dogmatic predestinarian and the seeker of God, the Doctor of Charity who continually insisted on the necessary damnation of the unbaptized ... which constitutes the enigma of his personality. Not a little of the harshness which has shocked later generations may be ascribed to the Christianity of his age; but we may wonder that so large an intellect did not rise above it.[17]

Augustinianism, if we can imagine Augustine speaking to such a concept at this moment in his life, finds him drawing to an ecstatic deep. He is the writer coming into his gift. He is not seeing the difficulty that we may be in; neither, for that matter, is he seeing the difficulty that his age may be in. What he casually calls an *aenigma similitudinis, a* 'riddle of a similitude',[18] turns out to be how we must so often handle emotions and sentiments becoming the same things to us as reasons and explanations, and the 'windings of human argumentation'.

> As for the moving things in this life, so much the less should they be wept for, the more they are wept over, and all the more must they be wept over, the less we weep when among them ... This I wish to do in my heart, before You in confession, and in my writings before many witnesses.[19]

To be moved and to have found a reason why is not the same thing as to have been stopped dead by it. The reason is something you could step in and out of, but the singular deportment of death, love, and grief – and any heartfelt sadness – should stop the world dead: 'all the more must they be wept over, the less we weep when among them'. What he really means is this: 'Let us not dare to be so proud that we are even lifted up in the evil and sadness of our captivity; but let us sit, and so weep ... For many weep only with the weeping of Babylon, because they rejoice also with the joy of Babylon.'[20]

One person's pain should always be treated as the originality that smashes the 'towers of our most strategic lies'. How the poet Howard Nemerov described them[21]: idols. For idols are wanting to smash our dim sense that the great human pains of love and loss are so unique that they are worth going to pieces over. Are worth going to God over. We must get in first before the idols and their priests, who speak like covering laws, and try to tell us how we are feeling. We must fight back to 'bring out the dimness of shadows into the light of the word.'[22]

Augustine found in himself a joyful skipping deep that is always being remade and never remembered; and never being remembered it meets the writer and his words in new places all the time. It is eternal. It is longed for. It cannot possibly be thought of in terms of ideas, which are human fabrications and the antithesis of originality. Real originality has always to be the very last thing that anyone could have expected: so it is never made with human hands for that straight reason. It comes from somewhere to go to somewhere. The most that we can hope to do is interrupt it. 'After the first death,' wrote Dylan Thomas, 'there is no other'.[23] And Augustine the writer was desperate not to interrupt it. From this time in his life comes his famous 'Vision at Ostia'. His manifesto:

> If for any man the tumult of the flesh fell silent; silent, too, the images of the earth. And of the waters such a silence, and silence on the air. And silent the heavens and the very soul itself; and a silence so that he should pass beyond even himself by not thinking upon himself. And silent his dreams and all imagined appearances, and every tongue, and every sign. And finally, the silence of each and every thing that comes to be through change. If all of these things could happen to a man, and he could still hear, then all these things would say to him, 'We did not make ourselves,' [see Ps. 100.3] but He Who endures forever made us ... if [only] this could be prolonged, and other visions of a far inferior kind could be withdrawn, and this one alone ravish, and absorb, and secret away its beholder within its deepest joys ...[24]

If we take this now with something from the later part of Augustine's life, we can see what he was wanting in his heart all the while which didn't fit with the fort-holding mentality of the *Difensor fidei*. He was wanting to move on, truth to greater truth.

> I am not the sort of person who will not accept correction, especially since blessed Paul commanded that a bishop be in this way docile [see 1 Tim. 3.2]. For one who is docile learns every day and makes progress by teaching what is better; and so I do not reject something better if it is offered me. I am ready for anything, even though we are treated unjustly. Nonetheless, in order not to be an obstacle to the truth, we do not complain of our injuries, but proclaim the glory of God.[25]

Were it not for these insights to follow out it would be very difficult indeed to categorize why Augustine turned out to be so impolitic; why a man with such a cause, and a religious one, was such a poor revolutionary. Where so large an intellect was going if it was making no obvious effort, in Bonner's words, to rise above the harshness of its own conclusions – and its age. The manifesto above certainly provides some insight; and what we have been documenting so far in this book fills in some more. Augustine seems to have thought most comfortably in terms of characters – human characters. The truth that he was inspired to discover was always the truth of some moment's narrative of writing. We called this 'African' at the start of this book and we may as well continue to call it 'African' now. The other way assumes that the laws of logic and historiography are the framework (tight and eternal) within which single human lives are allowed to be marginalized and transfigured into smaller and smaller subsets of systems. Augustine's 'African' way is to assume that single human lives are themselves the proper framework for God's surprising music. That does mean that they are not allowed to be ontologically the most important things: God is: but unless you are reading Augustine and realizing that the language of his words is himself, or you and I, or Adam and Eve, then you are going to find it difficult to follow his effort faithfully.

> Only the strings in harps and other musical instruments actually produce the melodious sounds; but that they may do so, there are other parts of the instrument which are not struck by those who sing, but which are connected with the strings which are struck, and produce musical notes. So also in this prophetic history some things are narrated which have no significance, but are, as it were, the framework to which the significant things are attached.[26]

The opposite nightmare scenario was of course presented by Jean-Paul Sartre, who saw so clearly that the top prize and valedictory for working out what the meta-consciousness of God might look like from this side up was our marginalization to the point of an indestructible totality:

> What men have in common is not a nature, but a metaphysical condition; and by that we mean the combination of constraints which limit them a priori; the necessity to be born, and to die; that of being finite and of dwelling in a world among men. For the rest, they constitute indestructible totalities, whose ideas, moods and acts are secondary and dependent structures, and whose essential character is to be *situated*, and they differ among themselves as their situations differ.[27]

What is very striking, in any case, is that Augustine's 'European' conscience would have its most prominent outing only at the extreme end of his life, when he realized the role that he would play to future generations, and when he tried – in last-minute retrospect – to put the impersonal touch of system and an enterprise into what had been simply one book after the next. This effort was his *Retractiones*, written in 427, three years before his death.

> For a long time I have been thinking over and planning a task, which with the help of the Lord, I am now beginning because I think it should be postponed no longer. This is to review my writings, whether books, letters, or tractates, with a kind of judicial severity, and to indicate, as if with a censor's pen, what may displease me.[28]

His heart may not have been entirely in it, but the effort is dogged and reassuringly modern in a genus, species sort of way. He berates himself for having accepted unquestioningly a conclusion from Pliny's *Natural History*, to the effect that beetles are produced from the little mud balls which they are seen rolling and burying. He now thinks this not to be the case; and few people that he has spoken to recognize it.[29] In another place, and dealing with flying creatures in the book of Genesis, he had missed 'grasshoppers' from his list.[30]

Idol-worship, death, and the whole power of the rage of men: Augustine was against these things so vehemently because they are so rational. La guillotine sèche. There is no escape from their irony. 'If the carpenter could give the idol of his carving a heart, the carpenter would be worshipped by his own idol for his effort.'[31] Or better still is this:

> How much more discriminating than fearful men are mice and serpents, and other animals of such sort, who do not respect the idols of the heathens, when they do not detect in their human forms actual human lives? For this reason, we see them all the time building nests in them; and unless they are deterred by human movements, they can find for themselves no safer habitations! This results in the madness that a man will move himself to frighten off a nesting animal from his god – yes, a service for the selfsame god who cannot perform this basic act of self defence on its own part because it will never move![32]

Love and tears cannot be made to statistics: and hearts cannot be made to methods for another day. The Doctor of Charity seems to have been saying that the corridor of all human hope and feeling is too often portrayed to be society; whereas God works one character, one human life, at a time: 'You are good and all-powerful, caring for each one of us as though the only one in Your care, and yet for all as for each individual.'[33]

> Who was it that gathered the embittered into one society? For all of them, there is one same end of temporal and earthly happiness, because of which they do all their deeds – although we also see them wavering back and forth amid a countless variety of cares.[34]

In fact to categorize Augustine from out of this mood of his you have to go to someone like Victor Serge, stung to the defence of similar thoughts by Stalin's treatment of the free-thinking Russian writers of his day.

For Augustine was certain of one thing: that '[w]ithin me are those lamentable dark areas wherein my own capacities lie hidden from me.'[35] These you cannot even approach by the traditional, forensic processes of unpacking and laying bare. What Augustine calls the *retia carnis*, the 'lattice of the flesh'.[36] For originality bears always God's image; it is humane; and that means also that it has an extempore life story: 'For even what is within [my mind] is for the most part hidden away unless brought to light by some experience.'[37] There is no judgement that we can form over the whole of human society, as from the height of some ultimate right and wrong. There can be no originality in projects of that direction. Augustine thinks that these bear always the suggestion of a kind of nascent Manichaeism – light and darkness, and everything explained from that beginning. Truth, even for the Christian intellectual writing under the banner of Church orthodoxy, is not programmatic; in the sense that 'in this still uncertain state of man's knowledge, it is You alone Who distinguish, "who trieth our hearts" [1 Thess. 2.4] and "call the light day, and the darkness night." [See Gen. 1.5]'[38] He means that we are liable to forget, sometimes, how, in this universe which is non-Manichean, so that every created thing is good and perfect (and so much so that there is really nothing to be said by addition), it is human souls sprung into life which are the only possible truth of the matter. An animal, non-rational, and seamlessly adapted to this surrounding perfection by instinct, would not have the same effect of predication as a human mind, making free-thought's spontaneous approval of its situation. The animals cannot name themselves – and in turn, 'we have *been* Your judgements, which are like a great deep [cf. 35.7; 2 Cor. 5.21].'[39]

And so we come by this, as promised, to Victor Serge, and his insight, as a way to properly understand this intrinsic 'musicality' of Augustine's.

Poets and novelists are not political beings because they are not essentially rational. Political intelligence, based though it is in the revolutionary's case upon a deep idealism, demands a scientific and pragmatic armour, and subordinates itself to the pursuit of strictly defined social ends. The artist, on the contrary, is always delving for his material in the subconscious, in the pre-conscious, in intuition, in a lyrical inner life which is rather hard to define; he does not know with any certainty either where he is going or what he is creating. If the novelist's characters are truly alive, they function by themselves, to a point at which they eventually take their author by surprise; and sometimes he is quite perplexed if he is called upon to classify them in terms of morality or social utility.[40]

In fact music was something that Augustine was never able to be completely comfortable with, and for the reason that it really did indeed seem to run him just too drastically close to his own inner talent. We know that it exercised him a great deal from his many investigations of it; most famously in a work from this time in his life – *De musica*, begun shortly after his baptism in 387.[41] And hymns and the chanting of the Psalms – Church music – was a tradition that was still being established in his day.

> But this sensual pleasure [of hymn-singing], to which the soul must not be delivered so as to be weakened, often leads me astray. My sense will not go with my reason in such wise as to follow patiently after it, but, having won admittance for reason's sake, even tries to run ahead and lead reason on.[42]

However, if we are careful, we can also use this peculiarity of music to Augustine to go deeper still into his personality and the identity of Augustinianism.

The point about music is that it can rise and fall with human emotions; it can accompany them and provoke them. So can the written word when mastered and applied with intelligence. Augustine's *De musica* is, in fact, an investigation into just this common ground from the point of view of technique. It was to be highly regarded and much discussed in the middle ages and beyond, when the discovery of number and order beneath beauty and sensuality was a fascination with endlessly promising results. Its popularity since then has faded somewhat in line with the labelling of this whole line of attack as Scholastic, and a little too dogmatic. There is a well-known painting by Vittore Carpaccio known as *St. Augustine Visited by St. Jerome* (1502). It hangs in the Scuola di San Giorgio degli Schiavoni, in Venice; and it does the due diligence of its day to this aspect of Augustine's importance. Folios of music, secular and sacred, complete the symbolism of objects that Carpaccio has installed around the scene of Augustine sitting at his desk, looking out to his vision of Jerome. The American musicologist Edward Lowinsky was to publish an ingenious reconstruction of the musical scores in this painting in *The Art Bulletin* in 1959. Carpaccio had placed the secular score on the floor – a loose, unattended folio. On the other hand, the sacred score had been bound in a book – and that book placed on a lectern, and the whole arrangement set close to Augustine. 'Significantly,' Lowinsky would conclude,

> ... the sheet and the book of music are followed by the hour glass and the celestial sphere, symbols of higher forms of rhythm regulating Life and the Universe. Is not this order symbolical of St. Augustine's notion of 'the ascent from rhythm in sense to the immortal rhythm which is in truth'?[43]

De musica is the only surviving part of an encyclopaedia-set of books on the liberal arts. What Augustine imagined could be his contribution to God and humanity, before all of that changed and he became a priest. In Chapter 6 we quoted from Cicero's *De officiis*, to the effect that we tend to 'esteem the knowledge of things secret and wonderful as a necessary ingredient of the happy life.'[44] The real occult always has a basis in truth; the essence of magic, when it delights us, is in misattribution. Mere trickery is a spell that we can break by learning to understand it as an illusion with a material foundation. But the liberal arts can become the black arts if the image of God in them is not returned at once to its source. In the closing book of his *De musica*, book VI, Augustine has left us a glimpse of how this was his vision for his encyclopaedia-set: 'These books have been written for those who are addicted to profane letters, incur serious errors and consume their good wits with trifles – and all without knowing what it is that is delighting them in these things.'[45] Had the full set survived, and not just this book, we would have been looking at the Christian happy ending whose absence from his own Roman education had ruined it for him. 'Babylon, then, has persecuted us when we were little; but God has given us when grown up knowledge of ourselves, that we should not follow the errors of our parents.'[46] An alternative, wholesome education, then: but also a gigantic metaphor:

We decided to proceed with this work simply because God has endowed adolescents (or for that matter also individuals of all ages) with intelligence; in order that reason may be the guide that deters them, not all at once but gradually, from literary works pitched to the sensitive medium, for which it is hard not to be attached. Therefore it is possible that by love they can touch the truth of the only God and Lord of all things. The God and Lord Who sustains the human mind without pause of any intermediate sensation.[47]

This side of eternity, we need always to be dragging a sea anchor of sorts: reason. A stabilizing agent. For the sight of our own inner divinity and musicality is fission, barrelling beyond control if pursued for its own sake. The gift of music, of poetry and prose, is a subcutaneous cutting to the quick that God makes use of when He speaks. Augustine's way of explaining this is to say that 'all our spiritual affections, in keeping with their diversity, have corresponding modes of voice and song and are stirred up by a kind of secret propriety [*occulta familiaritate*].'[48] The fission of this place and its danger when turned to for a mere spectacle is that it is 'cloaked over with the title of knowledge and science'. 'Because of it, men proceed to search out the secrets of nature, things beyond our end, to know which profits us nothing, and of which you can desire nothing but the knowing.'[49] Music may lay us open: but the laying open is only the prelude to God speaking into our soul at that moment. Music can prepare us for this event by intercepting and suspending our scepticism of the spiritual; yet we may choose to study only the phenomenon of this beguiling step; and when this happens, 'God is tempted in religion itself, when signs and wonders are demanded of Him ... and are desired only for the experience of them.'[50]

There are those like Augustine who find themselves only as they win admittance to a pristine inner Freedom. It is pristine because it is the original place of all possibilities that was to make that first garden a Paradise. So it is not the freedom that we talk about and recognize today: the freedom of acting now that a thousand million actions have taken place to make up the style of the world of men. We have not entirely forgotten how necessity is the teardrop over each human life. Necessity is what freedom looks like through the eyes of love. And the sum of this is the spirit and the Soul. In a letter to Jerome on the origin of the human soul, written in 415, Augustine will produce this image of the 'sublime Psalm of the vicissitudes of the world'.[51]

Any story of a human life can be reckoned to be true if it is written in sensitivity to this; and any doctrine must respect this, even if it leaves its author short of being able to close up and seal the ends of a system. But we have been led to believe that our Quantum (naked self-determination) is music even before a note has been struck.

Music works its wistful, atavistic effect on us because from a whole hall of listeners it has singled us out for its special treatment. By being able to go to any of us, equally, it goes to each of us, distinctly – and in a style of living in which calculations and rationalism must depend on the exact and impersonal similitude between parts, that is a sudden, brilliant Paradise. For on the whole, our necessities have a way of feeling so much more entrenched in the *real* than God's; but Augustine says that that is because they are of a different order altogether. In his most complete and mature exegesis of the Creation Narrative in Genesis, *De Genesi ad litteram*, completed in 415, he would explain this succinctly: 'The determination was not inherent in the constituent parts of the world but in the decision of the Creator, Whose Will is the necessity of things.'[52] We cannot but notice immediately how this is a different dance altogether to the harmony that is so often attributed to God's interventions in the state, human affairs and our lives. It is music made to the hyper-particular requirements of each of our souls; and such a harmony has to be what necessity looks like when love gives back freely to this Grace. This kind of Harmony and this kind of Grace was always one of the outstanding images of the work of the Victorian novelist George MacDonald:

> Entrancing verses arose within me as of their own accord, chanting themselves to their own melodies, and requiring no addition of music to satisfy the inward sense. But, ever in the pauses of these, when the singing mood was upon me, I seemed to hear something like the distant multitudes of dancers, and felt as if it was the unheard music, moving their rhythmic motion, that within me blossomed in verse and song. I felt, too, that could I but see the dance, I should, from the harmony of complicated movements, not of the dancers in relation to each other merely, but of each dancer individually in the manifested plastic power that moved the consenting harmonious form, understand the whole of the music on the billows of which they floated and swung.[53]

This kind of bare sensuality is the signature of the style of Man. It is the beating heart inside any true character worth the name, in life or literature. It is why one of the most genuine Christian difficulties has been to harmonize the three personalities of the Holy Trinity. What is touching and heart warming, what is familiarity and the home and the hearth, is the dependence of the human seeing on necessity – on God's seeing, inserted into the 'consenting harmonious form' as truth. Truth relevant only to that soul in that moment: truth that cannot survive the trauma of being made into words and communicated to anyone else. This is the same thing as to say that all the emotions of human experience which the Christian recognizes in his God when he thinks of his Face and the narrative of His historical dealings with Man – all these things are to do with the bare sensuality of Possession. 'Let us possess [*possideamus*] Him, and let Him possess us: let Him possess us as Lord; let us possess Him as salvation, let us possess Him as light.'[54] Augustine seems to have felt that he was skirting with blasphemy when he pursued these ideas, but on he would push. Possession, and its unmistakable rhythms of 'one-by-one' [*singula*].[55] Possession, that makes it that things 'have their sequence of morning and evening, hidden in part and in part manifest.'[56] The classical Greeks worked this out, and their genius to have seen it as the life of the mind reflected in the differentiations of excellence and station in the polis.[57] But this is its formal, legalistic side: bureaucratic and satisfying: and Augustine is thinking more of that beautiful madness of Men and Women that has been the suicidal anguish of the poets. The most exemplary form of possession that we have to guide us. Poets such as the South African, Ingrid Jonker, and how we are carved one from the other: *Die god wat jou geskep het uit die wind/sodat my smart in jou volmaaktheid vind* 'The god who crafted you from-out the wind/To fathom your perfection from my heartache's kin'[58]

The Holy Trinity remains a concept to us; and so remaining as a concept it is the mystery that embellishes our humanity by defeating it totally; 'for even our eyes are called lights [*lumina*], and yet when we open them in the dark, they do not see.'[59] As men and women we desire to possess each other on the ready-written script of parts to the whole – and that whole happy ending which is an instinctive sense to us. Yet it is inhuman to possess all things at once in this way. So beauty, love and truth are left to be things on which we can orient as the image of God in us, but only on condition that we preserve the modalities of personalities. Yes we can interpret ourselves, and our romance, from a bird's eye view, adjectivally. But we cannot open these eyes of ours and be hands on heart pleased with that; because such a view from such a height is an 'awful and wonderful excellence.'[60]

> The human shape, the outlines of human limbs, the form of human flesh, the outward senses, stature and motions of the body, the functions of the tongue, the distinctions

of sounds – try not to think of these things when you think of the Trinity. Save, that is, as they pertain to the servant-form, which the only-begotten Son assumed, when the Word was made flesh to dwell among us.[61]

> For a man [ontologically] *is* when not seeing; and when he does see, he is called a man seeing. For him, then, to see is not the same thing as to be a man; for if it were, he would not be man when not seeing. But since he is man when not seeing, and seeks to see what he sees not, he is one who seeks, and who turns to see; and when he has turned and has seen, he becomes a man seeing, who was before a man not seeing. Consequently, to see is to him a thing that comes and goes; it comes to him when he opens his eyes, and leaves him when he closes them. Is it thus with the Son?[62]

The Poet Laureate Cecil Day Lewis saw these 'adjectives of the bird's eye view' as imprints,

> ... preserved in the great memory, of innumerable repetitions of certain modes of experience: like those deep-sunken prehistoric earthworks which are invisible to a man standing upon them, yet whose configurations may be observed from an aircraft flying high above, they are apprehended only by the ecstatic, distanced, impersonal vision of art.[63]

We possess and are possessed by what is straight before us; and it is this tenseless occupation of the present that makes for the tension of everything else, past and future. A tension that is documented poem by poem, and book by book, as we heroically attempt to surmount the inconsolable. And this, too, becomes how Adam was able to sin 'with his eyes open', possessing and possessed by Eve, and vice versa. The serpent knew the potential of all of this; and so by a pinpoint cunning he perverted the original, doctrinal Humanism by making Adam and Eve look across to each other before they looked up to God.

> It was by the drawings of kindred [*sociali necessitudine*] that he yielded to the woman, the husband to the wife, the one human being to the only other human being. For not without significance did the apostle say, 'And Adam was not deceived, but the woman being deceived was in the transgression.' [1 Tim. 2.14] But he speaks thus only because the woman accepted as true what the serpent told her, and the man could not in turn bear to be severed from his only companion, even though this involved a partnership in sin. He was not on this account less culpable, but sinned with his eyes open.[64]

This is Augustinianism. To know that the whole of human life on earth is a passionate affair carried on with the wrong City – and in full view of the tragedy of this fact. *In flagrante*. There is no writing possible but this. To believe that, too, is Augustinianism. 'The devil desires to wear you as an ornament.'[65]

Of course it is not the only position to take. You can think of languages below languages, and logic, until you come out at the tickertapes of ones and zeroes. But the catharsis of this therapy is a placebo. For while Babel may have made it possible to have languages and to create new ones, all languages are not just related to each other in terms of a grammar which makes them possible. Yes, words are signs: and there is an infinite number of ways to express a single thing. But there has never been such a thing as a first language, the pattern of all the others, the cataloguing of the brain. Language is not the key to how we are wired; it is the proof that we are inconsolable lovers. The animals have never spoken because they have never been like this. We speak and write because we blush and are self-conscious. Instinct packs close in around the animals and leaves them no such space, and freedom. The philosophical veneration of language can make it out to be the deepest deep. But the deepest deep is not our skeletal construction from syntax. The deepest deep is that we can be so passionately unfaithful to God.

> As it contemplates supreme wisdom (which, being something unchangeable, cannot be identified with the soul) the soul is also forced to look at its changeable self and in some sense comes into its own mind. The reason is simply that it is distinct from God, and yet is something capable of causing pleasure after God. It would be better if it forgot itself through love of the unchangeable God, or even despised itself utterly in comparison with Him. But if it goes out of its way to produce a false imitation of God, and thus to will to take pleasure in its own power, then the greater it wishes to become the less it becomes in fact. And that is pride.[66]

We speak and write at all because these eyes of ours, 'when we open them in the dark, they do not see'. They are so endearingly wondrously human – and helpless for it. Our eyes are not a sense, as they are to the animals, reporting to their fight or flight. What they see is never that simple 50–50 chance. They see only by retaining, that is by remembering, beauty as form. And of course form is the same thing as the aesthetic argument for necessity; while necessity is the rational argument for Love. And love is simply the highest calling of Freedom.[67] As Mephistopheles expresses it in Goethe's *Faust*: *Ich bin ein Theil des Theils, der anfangs alles war.* 'I am a part of the part, which at the beginning was the whole.'[68]

> The eyes love fair and varies forms and bright and beauteous colours. But let not such things *possess* my soul. May God Who made such things good, indeed, very good – may He *possess* it. He is my Good, not they. Each day they affect me all the while I am awake ... For this queen of colours [*regina colorum lux*], this light which bathes all the things we look upon, drops down in many ways wherever I may be throughout the day; and dropping down it beguiles me while engaged in some task or other and not even observing it. So strongly does it entwine itself about me, that if it is suddenly withdrawn, I seek it with longing, and if it is long absent, it causes mental depression [*contristat animum*].[69]
>
> Bodily delights have their source in all those things with which the bodily sense comes into contact, and which are by some called the objects of sense. But among these the noblest is light, in the common meaning of the word, because among our senses also, which the mind uses in acting through the body, there is nothing more valuable than the eyes. And so in the Holy Scriptures all the objects of sense are spoken of as visible things.[70]

So this is Augustine saying that the whole gift and art of writing, the gift and the art of all human forms of expression, is possible only because we have been so damnably deceived yet continue to perform the sacramental onomastic role of seeing and naming the animals in Eden. We can be *this* passionate about the goodness of the created order; yet by not looking to God first, we love as glowing necessities the cold mechanicals of physics, evolution, and the great turnings of nature. But they do not give back as we have given them: and so we are left always in the great unrequited: forgetting that we are more profound than the eternal lesson that we are seeking in our Academy – with its distinguishing and unpacking of the world as it *is*. 'We are ne'er like angels till our passions die,' wrote the Elizabethan dramatist Thomas Dekker.[71] And Augustine was to put much the same idea like this:

> Therefore we see these things which You have made, because they exist. But of course they only exist because You see them. We see outside ourselves that they are, and within ourselves that they are good. But You saw them as things already made – there, in that place where You saw them as to be made. Now we are moved to do good, after our heart has conceived this out of Your Spirit; whereas at other times, having forsaken You, we

were moved to do evil. There are certain works of ours which are clearly done out of Your gift, but they are not eternal. After such works we hope to find rest in Your great sanctification ... What man will give it to a man to understand this? What angel will give it to an angel? What Angel to man?[72]

We are in a complicating complication. We are, to borrow Heracleitus' expression, 'Immortal mortals, mortal immortals; living [our] death and dying [our] life.'[73] Eternal Rest may well be a profound silence, in which we are unburdened of everything save God's Voice. But for now it continues that we have loved the world. We have even charmed her for a while and she let us do that, infatuated with the qualities that we were able to ascribe to her. But she was none of them and they were all of our noble imagining. As William Somerset Maugham wrote, 'I know nothing more shattering than to love with all your heart, than not to be able however hard you try to break yourself of it, someone who you know is worthless.'[74]

Augustine says that what we are missing is the first step of loving God: 'Your works praise You, to the end that we may love You, and we love You to the end that Your works my praise You.'[75] The only sense that there is to make of the human condition is the sense of this our double-crossing deception. The taking of God out of the equation has set up the devilry of a tautological embrace. The world and all its material magnificence is less than a newborn soul: and yet a newborn soul is more than all its material magnificence as chemicals and atoms.[76] And loving and its painful art of language is the only spirituality that we can cope with. And yet God is the only proof of ourselves that we have – 'what is man, unless because You are mindful of him? [cf. Ps. 8.5]'[77] Though this last is something that we often only realize at the last count, *in extremis*. 'For the truth itself, which is now named the Christian religion, existed and was not missing among the ancients from the beginning of the human race.'[78] Augustine will, for example, speak often of anxious, sometimes wild, mothers, who ran to him with their infants for baptism.[79] For in the tears of mother and child he was left with a lasting image of the sheer appetitive instinct for salvation that the more civilized behaviours can often be a frowning upon.[80] We might say that the world-long reaction against new, analgesic ways to exist has Augustine for one of its champions.

> Away with the reasons of philosophers, who assert that a wise man should not be affected by mental perturbations. God has made foolish the wisdom of this world ... So

we say that a man's mind, like the limbs of his body, is only the more hopelessly diseased when it has lost even the feeling of pain.[81]

'Dumb, then, will he be to God, who forgets Jerusalem.'[82] And this hasn't gone unnoticed. Like this from the literary critic George Steiner:

> It may well be that the forgetting of the question of God will be the nub of cultures now nascent. It may be that the verticalities of reference to 'higher things', to the impalpable and mythical which are still incised in our grammars, which are still the ontological guarantors of the arcs of metaphor, will drain from speech (consider the 'languages' of the computer and the codes in artificial intelligence). Should these mutations of consciousness and expression come into force, the forms of aesthetic making as we have known them will no longer be productive. They will be relegated to historicity. Correspondingly, the modes of response, of hermeneutic encounter as I have outlined them, will become archaeologies. Philology will no longer know a *Logos* for its love ... The humanist, in crucial contrast to the scientist, tends to feel that both dawn and noon are at his back.[83]

Part two: the subtleties of writing about writing

Augustinianism says that you cannot first write and then after that have ideas. Writing is not inanimate like the ink it uses. And ideas can develop only one against the other, in a *phantasia spatii localis*, a 'fantasy of local place'.[84] Each one is a closed fist that closes tighter as it learns to understand itself in distinction from the rest. An alphabet of closed fists is the form of knowledge. And Knowledge shakes a giant fist at the Wisdom of God.[85] This, too, is why the Freudian slips of Augustine always take us to the African beneath the European; for Cicero's wisdom was the quest that he conquered only by learning to speak its name as a foreign, fumigating word: 'Lastly is the seventh, wisdom itself – *i.e.* the contemplation of the truth, tranquillizing [*pacifans*] the whole man ...'[86]

The idea that writing is dipped in and out of, like ink, supports the theory that the biography of a writer like Augustine should choreograph itself principally on what his books and letters and sermons would tell us if they were laid out end to end and read chronologically. Continuities and discontinuities. The opposite, Augustinian, idea suggests that if you took that approach you would eventually find only that the works of his hand end up strangely uninhabited by him. The man you might have looked forward to meeting has gone; and in his place are the harsh and dispiriting contradictions of, for example, Bonner's 'Freedom and Necessity'. Before writing is the second-order activity of writing about something, it is the first-order activity of describing itself. And in any case, we know that Augustine and Augustinianism have a status in the popular imagination that has not been secured on the historicity of his writings and the technicalities of his points-scoring against heresies long gone. Augustine has as many debunkers as he has devotees: and both congregate equally around something that they would say is the residuum that the European mind must isolate and reckon with in itself. This residuum is Augustine's sheer precocity. For this is the man who substantiated a conviction that every twitch and tilt of the human mind, every revolution, was guilt-proof of a dehumanizing idolatry and love of self. We have called it the Whole Power of the Rage of Men; a totalizing and totalitarian conviction, a cannibalizing conviction, balanced against the same in its nemesis. *De civitate Dei contra Paganos*. One love versus another, no middle-ground.[87] And it really is hard not to react to this precocity in one way or another. For a man has produced a diagnosis which he says is interchangeable with every breath of his life – and through his life, with ours. If made down to its basic ideas, those ideas still act like human characters, and Adam and Eve. They anti-Classically animate and take on the dooms of guilt, longing, regret and even lunacy. And once brought out in this way, they posture and prostrate as though there can now be nothing new to be said in addition of them. As far as we are concerned, this might be anti-writing, collapsing in on itself under some enormous single point of mass.

> I think that many teachers arise when there are different and mutually opposed opinions. But when all utter the same words and speak the truth, they do not depart from the teachings of the one true Teacher. They give offense, however, not when they repeat His words at length, but when they add their own; for in this way, they fall from loquacity into falsehood.[88]

In this biography we have followed this as the invitation to a method. We have found his signature at large across all his diverse works; and we have brought these signatures together for a story. The man becomes the writer, not the contradictions of ideas. The contradictions of ideas lead back to the personality, consistent and relentless beneath them. And the personality invites his readers to lay their lives alongside his, at the common points of contact and experience borne out of a shared humanity. A meeting at the most basic level is promised and possible – and that is always slightly thrilling across a distance of 1600 years!

Possidius, his friend, confidant and fellow bishop put it in his biography of him, the first biography of him, that,

> I think that those who gained most from him were those who had been able actually to see and hear him as he spoke in Church, and most of all, those who had some contact with the quality of his life among men.[89]

Augustine could not be so flattering of himself. But he could write like Possidius of all of us – and implore us to value ourselves before God as high as he was determined to value himself:

> I believe that, if I were writing to you, say, about an affair of property, or the settlement of some dispute about money, no one would find fault with me. So precious is this world in the esteem of men, and so small is the value which they set upon themselves![90]

This is the man saying that you admire his writing on peril of being embroiled in it. 'If, brethren, you have understood, your heart also has been spoken to. Intelligence is the gift of God.'[91] There is no possibility – worse, there is no point – in arriving and leaving as a critic, with one's dignity intact. For no one has ever denied that the full appreciation of good writing and ideas – the Critical Faculty – dances with the truth that the critic might, for his very clarity of judgement, have produced the same himself. But it seems that Augustine is the only one to have turned this into a doctrine of a kind of mass autobiography.[92] Every life you encounter is a life that you might just as well have lived yourself if you have encountered it, and you have recognized it, as a human life at all. The possibility is the same thing as the qualification of it. All human communication has Adam looking across to Eve for its logic. 'For I return this fraternal and peaceful word to him [*vocem fraternam et pacificam*].'[93] A sonar ping returning to its source. The information it brings back is of a doctrine of Humanity lamenting God, and the pinpoint accuracy of His Love. 'For there shall be no lust, which is now the cause of confusion.'[94]

> The voice of that people, of that servant, is clearly that voice which you have heard in lamentations in the Psalm, and were moved at hearing, because you are of that people.

> What was sung by one, re-echoed from the hearts of all. Happy are they who recognize themselves in those voices as in a mirror.⁹⁵

By animating all writing in this way and leaving ink for what it is, Augustinianism says finally (and most precociously of all) that there is no originality that is humanly possible. There is only Confession – with Christ as the One interior Teacher of the truth of it all.

> See here now, brethren, see a mighty mystery. The sound of our words strikes the ears, but the Master is within. Do not suppose that any man learns anything from man. We may admonish another by the sound of our voice; but if there is not the One within Who shall teach, any exterior noise we make is in vain. Take the example of this present discourse. Have you not all heard it clearly this morning? Yet how many will go from this place still untaught! I, for my part, have spoken to all of you. But those to whom that Unction within has not spoken, those whom the Holy Ghost does not teach from within: all those go back untaught. The teachings of the master from without are sorts of aids and admonitions. He Who teaches the hearts, has His chair in Heaven.⁹⁶

Real originality only happens when God plays the words for us – when He plays them like notes. 'For which reason music, the science or capacity of correct harmony, has been given also by the kindness of God to mortals having reasonable souls, with a view to keep them in mind of this great truth.'⁹⁷ The high sensitivities that are noticed in Augustine, and sometimes mocked, and which are in either case interpreted to be a famous symptom of the Western experiment with Christian sin (we can now move on), has at least this for its back story and vision. We are led to believe that our Quantum (naked self-determination) is music even before a note has been struck. But the Doctor of Charity is saying here, instead, that by putting itself down so certainly our Quantum actually strikes out the very possibility of all musicality at all. It is a kind of nascent Donatism: 'For the field is the world – not only Africa; and the harvest is the end of the world [see Matt. 13.24–40] – not the era of Donatus.'⁹⁸ As the composer Ned Rorem wrote, 'Music is the sole art which provokes nostalgia.'⁹⁹

> If I were to write anything for the summit of authority, I would prefer to write in such manner that my words would sound forth the portions of truths that each one man

could take from these writings, rather than to put down one true opinion so obviously that it would exclude all others.[100]

Let the Spirit of God speak. Let It speak to us, and let It sing to us. Whether we wish or wish not to dance, let It sing. For as he who dances, moves his limbs to the time, so they who dance according to the commandment of God, obey the sound of His voice in their works. What therefore says the Lord in the Gospel to those who refuse to do this? 'We have piped unto you, and ye have not danced; we have mourned unto you, and ye have not lamented. [Matt. 11.17]'[101]

The creeping, careful accuracy of scholarship has a side-effect on Augustine which a book like this can to some extent overcome as it takes in everything in one gulp. Augustine does not fare well played at that slow speed. That precocity of his that has all of our lives spinning together, and together to him, and from him to Adam and Eve – well, that only comes together into sense at a speed that overcomes the intervening detail. At any slower speed he does not really make it across the ages to here – a scratchy record and a warbling voice. The endless sea of specialist literature on him is also, in this respect, a cruel sea; thought it does not set out to be so. Because it can make it seem that he is only for the initiated; whereas the truth is that he was the writer bursting to be the writer. As that man he is agelessly meeting all writers everywhere, in that special place of theirs which is entered always at something else's chance. Nostalgia is real, a home, and a future – and, as go those final lines from William Stafford's poem, 'And then one small snowflake slit the air–/He heard all linked things cry, "Augustine."'[102]

It is therefore something to be seriously noted that it is only once, in all his writings, that Augustine lets slip the mask. That it is only once, for six brief lines, that he takes us voluntarily into his own experience of this place. What we might call the place of his extreme vocational insecurity as a writer before God. His life as he lived it in perpetual vivisection; on the table, learning at his source, as best he could, the linked-up biology of universal Man. 'For cutting and healing his heart's wound, he made a lancet of his tongue.'[103]

To reach a scalpel of expression; to reference always an exposed and compelling heart; and having done that, to leave the rest for something else's chance. The Reader. Who may feel, at Music's thrill, the touch of an unimagined portion of truth, worked free and floating up from plain, passed-by materialism – but if left at that, ordinary biology, and no hope. The twentieth-century

Italian novelist Riccardo Bacchelli, writing on the centenary of another great Italian novelist, Antonio Fogazzaro, thought that this was a magnificent but underappreciated spectacle going on all the time, but seldom seen for what it is. He meant the ability of naive realism (Fogazzaro was a romantic, drawing mysticism from the simple rounds of life) to start off a riot and a fission. But never the other way round.

> [Writing] justly, out of respect for humanity – but more than that, out of respect for the torment of one who suffers humanity with their whole soul, and passionately. In fact, writing for all which we might be obliged to consider weak, or even non-existent, if it had invaded lines of logic. And yet, in spite of that last barb, we say that these are truly the trademarks of Fogazzaro's writing that flourish *because* of the very empirical precision of his narration. This is a phenomenon that is today made old-fashioned and trite because it is [too much] portrayed as the dichotomy between science and faith, Darwin and St. Augustine; the positivistic evolution of Spencer and the theological concept of creation; Pithecanthropus and the clay of Adam. For in truth the great things ricochet from the simple honest things; and we admit at once that it is only natural that they should.[104]

We might say this by saying that the continuing war of ideas between Science and the Supernatural is being fought over the atomic shadows of real flesh, in some intermediate place, with experimental knowledge.[105] Matter is all the time recognizing itself in Spirit; but only through Humanity appointed to the task, in the traditional eternal questions of the meaning of life, and the Olympus of idols that answer them until God does.

> It is, for instance, by signs corporeally expressed that we understand the [Biblical] generations of the waters, on account of the swelling deeps of the flesh. By things mentally conceived we understand, rather, human generations, on account of the fecundity of reason ... And so it is that to human offspring has been appointed the task of replenishing the earth, the dryness of which appears in its longing for You ...[106]

Good writing can be Spirit's detail on the page. It can trigger the full effects of this kind of recollection from something as scientific (and as unpromising) as an accurate narration of the plod of a life. But in making this, its ping of appeal, one human to another, Adam to Eve, it stops tragically short of the true originality. Who is God.

> For it is only the mind that causes whatever it is that you love in the body that you love. When the mind has left it, it is a corpse at which you have a horror; and how much you may have loved its beautiful limbs, you make haste to bury it. We say, then, that the ornament of the body is the mind: and the ornament of the mind is God.[107]
>
> And consider, finally, how we distinguish otherwise between living and dead bodies, except by seeing at once both the body and the life, which we cannot see save by the eye? But isn't it telling that a life without a body we cannot see thus.[108]

But what of these six brief lines that have gone nearly unnoticed and un-cited, but for their apparent obscurity of meaning (which is sometimes alluded to in a footnote)? It is his fabled clarion call *interior intimo meo*, 'more inward than my inmost self',[109] that has been drowning their delicate moment and washing out their sound. This Christian inward turn for self-knowledge, and God, that has become one of the standards against modernity – and, some would say, even postmodernity's best ally when it is in retro mood.[110] And yet writing dipped in and out of, like ink, supports a personality who is confident in the Classical mould – a detachment of reason spiralling outwards to its same in the heavens. While it was by being under-confident in all these things and spiralling inwards that Augustine leapt ahead of his peers and masters.[111] Ambrose represents a true Christian Platonism and the ageless pretensions of the written page. For him, 'a book has no feeling of modesty'.[112] Whereas Augustine brings Classicism across to Christian Romanticism and the broken-hearted: 'The sacrifice of God is a troubled spirit: a broken and a contrite heart, O God, You shall never despise.'[113]

Self-consciousness has built eternal cities against the sky; and civilization has brought grid-pattern order; but 'the oil strains out secretly into the vat, the lees run openly down the streets.'[114] Self-knowledge, and the *interior intimo meo*, have always been alchemized with true knowledge, an alternative City, and the grand Christian response to the Secular and its Academy. And Augustine has always been maddeningly impolitic, and short of this goal, and in need of so much coaxing and teasing out. And now we see why. Self-knowledge at the extreme depth of the tunnel that he sought it at is not an Academy, or a building, but an endless field of emotions – ventricles moving like grass in the directionless winds. For those who reach this place it may be possible to write any tale and have it be compelling because it will tell of this sight; and, telling of this sight, it will set humanity

TO WRITE AGAINST SELF-CONSCIOUSNESS AND ITS EFFECTS 229

and its natural against the rigid straight-backed otherness of the angels and the supernatural. But all of this is only the prelude; beautiful wet earth; and God must speak.

'At length I breathed You in, as far as breath may enter into this house of grass.'[115]

The six lines that we have been after appear in Augustine's *Confessiones*, breaking the surface narrative at just the point where he marks the effect that music has on him when it shows him his genius for seeing to the beautiful within himself that isn't really a place at all until God makes it solid with his Word. Perhaps we are so used to accepting or rejecting the great minds of antiquity for their arched and pointed determination of purpose that this one note in a million – so deeply, deeply personal – hasn't truly registered. But it cracks the mould in which Augustine is cast, and shows, not Patristics loosing bolts, but creative soul impaling on Creator God.

'He vomits up his soul of blood'[116]

> See how I stand! Weep with me, and weep for me, you who can also bring about within yourselves this place. But for you who cannot, be glad: these problems do not affect you. But You, O Lord my God, please, please hear me, and return Your gaze to me, and see me, and have mercy on me, and heal me. For in Your sight of this place I become a riddle to myself, and that is my infirmity.[117]

We can add something to what we have been saying by pointing out that the composer Beethoven was another creative soul whose work brought Classicism across to Romanticism – for his age, of course, from the eighteenth to the nineteenth centuries. For it is striking indeed how his composing can be interpreted to summit on this same feature that we have picked out from Augustine's writing. It was Nietzsche who noticed it. Beethoven's music is always teaching itself to itself. If it were a language, it would not be a language that we could have invented from scratch.

> Beethoven's music often seems like a deeply affected *meditation* on unexpectedly hearing again a piece, 'Innocence in Sound', long believed to have been lost: it is music *about* music. In the songs of beggars and children in the streets, in the monotonous tunes of travelling Italians, at the dances in the village inn or on carnival nights – that is where he discovers his 'melodies': he collects them together like a bee, by seizing a

sound here, a brief resolution there. To him they are recollections of a better world, in much the same way as Plato conceived of ideas.[118]

Likewise we might say that Augustine's writing is 'writing about writing'. It is not writing for the sake of communication: it is writing for the sake of loving God. It is not invented, but taught by an interior Teacher. This is why it can be borne in by any class of person, from any distant place. It is not for creating new ideas; it is for rebuking us. And it does this always by leaving us short of the real, surmounting words; so that we remain mired in the famous questions of 'meaning' that philosophers of language know so well. If language were a truly 'meaningless' occupation, to be turned this way and that to different things, then we should drive it on before us like a slave. But that is not what happens with it. It does not merely show us the world as it is – as holiday pictures that we can talk about because we were there. Augustine says that all *conceivable* places are places that you could have been to once upon a time. And if it is possible to talk and write in that way, then what does it mean to do it? It means that even in our Gadarene intensities of light, language has its curious way of making us feel that we are describing something else. Talking our way through Someone Else's pictures. 'Truth, therefore, is not in mortal things. But Truth is, and is not nowhere.'[119] The meaning of language is 'God, who is loved, wittingly or unwittingly, by everything that is capable of loving.'[120]

> How many farms and desert places now come in to us? No one can tell how numerously they come in; and they come in because they would believe. We say to them, 'What will you?' They answer, 'To know the glory of God.' Believe me when I tell you that we wonder and rejoice at such a claim of these rustic people. They come I know not whither, roused up by I know not whom. But I shouldn't truly say, 'I know not by whom', because of course I know exactly by whom it is. I know because He says, 'No one can come to me, except the Father which hath sent me draw him.' [John 6.44] They come suddenly from the woods, the desert, the most distant and lofty mountains: all to the Church. And many of them, no, nearly all of them hold this language, so that we see it is true that God teaches them within.[121]
>
> 'In the languages there is diversity; gold in the thoughts.'[122]

Perhaps, however, it is not quite entirely true to say that our six brief lines and what they say of Augustine's personality have just their single showing. There is one final and more formal setting in which their same sense can be made out.

His *Retractiones*. In a brief section in which he returns to his *De musica*, written approximately 40 years earlier.

We cannot handle Possession, our doctrinal Humanity, without Grace and its little cold showers of truths. Because everything is so clearly numbers, smaller numbers and the patterns between numbers in a Unitary Science, we find that we have nearly ceased to ask quite how it is that we get from this across to ourselves anymore – and quite how it is that we have anything left to write about now that our superheroes are presented to us as the super-efficiencies (we'll get there) of nature and technology; which are super only because they do not have the hold-ups of the human eye. So here is Augustine to say that the end of language as we know it – the blessed Quiet – will be when all these brave antagonisms end.

> A statement I made in this book – 'For bodies are the better to the extent that they are harmonious by reason of numbers. But the soul is made better through lack of these numbers it receives through the body, as when it turns away from the carnal senses and is changed by the divine numbers of wisdom.' [*De mus.*, VI, 4, 7] – should not be interpreted to mean that there will not be corporeal numbers in incorruptible and spiritual bodies when they will be more beautiful and more lovely. Or indeed that the soul, when perfect, will no longer be sensible to these numbers because it is made better here below by being deprived of them. For here there is need to turn itself away from carnal senses to grasp the intelligible things because it is weak and less capable of devoting its attention to both at the same time. The soul should certainly shun enticements to these corporeal things as long as it can be attracted to shameful pleasures. However, when it will be firm and perfect, it will not be turned from the contemplation of wisdom by corporeal numbers; and so it will perceive them in such a way that it will not be enticed by them, nor be made better by lacking them. Rather, it will be so good and righteous that [these numbers] can neither lie hidden nor take possession of it.[123]

Part three: his soul of blood

We must now return to where we left the narrative of Augustine's life, but in light of everything that we have been saying. To the beginning of the rest of his life which he will so disarmingly call the *modicum*, a 'little while'.[124]

First there is Cassiciacum, the place where he eventually chooses to take his household in preparation for baptism. We know it now to be almost certainly modern-day Cassiago di Brianza, situated about 20 miles to the northeast of Milan, in the Province of Lecco. Augustine made use of the rural retreat of Verecundus, a prominent Milanese grammarian and a colleague of his. It seems to have been a substantial villa with baths for their use when the weather turned really cold. With him there were Monica, Adeodatus – and close friends Alypius, Licentius, Lastidianus, Rusticus and Trygentius. They arrived some time in September 386 and would stay until Easter the following year; Augustine being baptized by Ambrose at Milan on the night of the 24–25 April, along with Adeodatus and Alypius. This was a time in which Augustine wrote his first books – philosophical dialogues arising out of the conversations and intellectual activities of everyone present. Augustine led the way, poking and questioning like a Socrates during the day, then reasoning with himself and praying at night. It is the work of his nights, his *Soliloquiorum*, which remains the showpiece from this time. It is the first of its kind in which a man keeps up a dialogue with his own thoughts (the title was an invention), and Augustine's proudest achievement from this period. Its engaging humanism puts it with the *Confessiones* and all those other passages in his works where we hear the writer's voice.[125]

The total of books produced from this eight-month period is impressive. In addition to the *Soliloquiorum* there are three others: *Contra Academicos*, *De beata vita*, and *De ordine*. However, altogether (though not the *Soliloquiorum*) they are a disappointment to Augustine. 'Is it that chain of reasoning which I am wont so to caress as if it were my sole treasure, and in which perhaps I take too much delight?'[126] The true joy of Cassiciacum will prove to have been the physical and geographical break with Milan and its 'chair of lies'; because the kind of writing he produces there – books of philosophical understanding – will turn out to be more of the 'long while' than the 'little while'. For when you think about it, these books that solve problems of knowledge can be considered good books only as they form up like centipedes – each premiss anticipating its conclusion along a length. And the disappointment then becomes that a centipede you can image all as one design to write it out as the book need not be written out at all if it already exists like that. So the writing it out is done for the sake of something else; which turns out to have been a kind of pseudo-originality; and really just the cutting up of the centipede into an infinite number of pieces for study – as many as you can imagine, stretching to infinity like seconds and nanoseconds. 'It would seem that our grand edifice, fortified by its great length of discourse, has crumbled to the cuts made to a centipede.'[127] This horror spectacle of a human intelligence which can only touch things by cutting them and making them smaller and smaller becomes one of the main images of this time and is never, in fact, forgotten.[128] In letters to his friend Nebridius, who could not join them at Cassiciacum, Augustine will speak of it repeatedly:

> For what is poorer than to be susceptible of endless diminution? And what more truly rich than to increase as much as you will, to go where you will, to return when you will and as far as you will, and to have as the object of your love that which is large and cannot be made less?[129]

This will be a setback, but also his first great lesson in the metaphysics of writing and what is possible by it.

> The Lord is not slack concerning His promise: just a little while [*modicum*], and we shall see Him, where we shall have no more any requests to make, or any questions to put; for nothing shall remain to be desired, nothing lie hidden to be inquired about. This little while appears long to us because it is still in continuance; when it is over, we shall then feel what a little while it was.[130]

If Cassiciacum had been a different kind of success and Augustine had gone on from it as the Christian philosopher and conspired and plotted great encyclopaedia sets of (centipedes of) wisdom, then he might have found himself returned, through a hidden back door, to everything that he was anxious to leave behind.[131] As it was, this way was blocked to him: and he became, by chance, a Churchman. A writer – but saved from a kind of writing that would have replaced all of this personality of his with straight up and down lines of longitude and exactitude. A man preserved by lines like this becomes a Mind: made tight and round by these same lines of understanding that bind up the universe, but not properly speaking passionate and sensual. This, as Hegel's philosophy was later to show, is the certain consequence of Thought. What begins as personal mental activity in the individual becomes its perfection of achievement in disembodiment. The eradication of personality guarantees the essential truth that truth itself is something that is being written by all of us, all of the time.[132] Understanding becomes the pen that is writing the book it is reading in ever more inanimate inks of the summaries of its ideas. But as the writer John Buchan complained, there is no 'sexuality' in this – 'nothing even of that implicit sympathy with which one human being explores the existence of another.' Readers and writers beneath such a higher power become used and vanquished things; like 'a chattel, a thing infinitely removed from intimacy.'[133] So many books of knowledge tend to be criticized and ranked as though God Himself had passed through school and university.

> During a certain discussion in this book [*De immortalitate animae*], thinking only of the souls of men, I said: 'Science does not exist in one who learns nothing.' [I, 1] Likewise in another place, I said: 'Science does not include anything that does not pertain to some branch of knowledge.' [I, 1] It did not occur to me that God does not learn the branches of knowledge, and yet, of course, He has a knowledge of all things including also a foreknowledge of future events.[134]

What secures Augustine's personality in the end is the swift chain of events that take him back to Africa, into the episcopal see of Hippo Regius, and into a strange reunion with the past that he left behind him as a dream. All children etch powerful dreams in reflection of their surroundings; and then drift away from them like flotsam on the various tides of age. They have the monopoly on hope in the world. But because it so often comes out as romantic suspicion of their descent, it is ignored or turned over for fun. If it persists, it becomes the longest cruelty that there can be. In some cases, though, the original strength of feeling *does* persist and meets, at the critical time, the career that allows its expression. In the defence and the positioning of Christianity Augustine found something that came easily to him from his years of training. In the religion and its writings he found there esteemed exactly what wrings the hearts of children. What had wrung *his* heart. A melancholy – but not for men, which comes later, in a backwards look: but for what men do.

> Who would not rejoice if suddenly, while he was wandering abroad, ignorant of his descent, suffering want, and in a state of misery and toil, it were announced: 'You are the son of a senator! Your father enjoys an ample patrimony on your family estate! I bid you return to your father at once!' How hugely would he rejoice if this were seriously said to him by someone whose promise he could trust? But just such a one whom we can trust, an Apostle of Christ, has come and said to us, 'You have a father! You have a country! You have an inheritance!'[135]

After baptism at Milan the desire to return to this inheritance seems to have become the mood that united Augustine and his community. There was still his portion of the family estate at Thagaste to provide a home and an income: so now it was simply a case of organizing and retracing steps – from Milan to Rome and the port of Ostia; and then from Ostia to Carthage by ship; and finally from Carthage overland to home. Driven on by an instinct, rather than a clearly formed future, the momentum is composed of things which Augustine can and can't know. He can know himself better than ever; and that he does not fear the institution of death. Only the things of this world that smooth and stretch and iron the 'little while'. And conquer its trust.

> I am now thirty three years of age: so for almost these last fourteen years I have been ceasing to desire them. Nor have I sought anything from them, if by chance they should be offered, beyond the necessities of life and such a use of them as agrees with the state of a freeman. A single book of Cicero has thoroughly persuaded me, that riches are in no wise to be craved – but that if they come our way, they are only to be with the utmost wisdom and caution administered.[136]

At Ostia, Monica will die suddenly from a fever at the age of 56. Her death is lovingly remembered in the *Confessiones* as a Catholic model death.

> 'Son, for my part I cannot now find any delight in this life. What I can still do here, and why I am here, I cannot now know. For now I find that all my hopes in this world have been accomplished. One thing there was, for which I desired to linger a little while in this life: this was that I might see you a Catholic Christian before I died. God has granted this to me in more than abundance, for I see you his servant, with even earthly happiness held in contempt. What am I doing here?'[137]

But it will be the death of Adeodatus within two years of Monica, at around the age of only 18, which will finally move Augustine on from the intensities of that whole time when his lover and son were accelerating him into mystery after mystery. Like his mother – not dead, as we know, but departed – Adeodatus will draw the greatest salute that it is possible for the Rhetor to give his son. The salute of silence. He is not entirely lost to us, though. We have something of his personality and abilities recorded in the dialogue *De magistro*, written out as a philosophical discussion between Augustine and him. Who might he have been had he lived into his manhood? His father rated him exceptionally highly; and it is difficult to think of comparable examples of such intensive home-schooling and what they produce. You have also to include the revolutionary content of the education. John Stuart Mill emerging from his father John Mill and the philosophy of utilitarianism is probably the famous example of the type.

> There is one of our books which is called *De magistro*, and in it he speaks with me. You know that his are all the ideas which are inserted there, in the form of the person of the one talking with me. He was in his sixteenth year. I had experience of many still more wonderful things in him. To me his power of mind was a source of awe. Who except You is the worker of such marvels?[138]

Adeodatus died at Thagaste; it is thought he died in 389, while Augustine was establishing a small monastic community on his estate. He was hoping to follow the example of St Anthony of Egypt, whose life had made a big impression on him in a chance discussion with his fellow African Ponticianus at Milan. 'His name was famous among your servants, but up to that very hour it had been unknown to us.'

> His discourse turned to the flocks within the monasteries and to their way of life, which is like a sweet-smelling odour to You, and to the fruitful deserts in the wilderness – and all of which we had known nothing. There was a monastery at Milan, filled with good brothers, situated outside the walls, under the fostering care of Ambrose – but we had not even known about that.[139]

But such a quiet ascetic life was always going to be a stretch when Africa was welcoming home her famous son. In those days, there was no strict priestly formation or the serving of titles. It was the time when orthodoxies were everywhere being created. Expectations and the form of things had often to look to the already existing institutions of Roman life. So Church congregations tended to admire celebrities who brought something credible with them from the world. And they wielded the power of popular acclaim: you could literally be shoehorned and roughhoused into your next job. It could be a frenzy; like when a hungry tribe corners a big animal that will feed them for months.

> I feared the office of bishop to such an extent that, as soon as my reputation came to matter among 'servants of God', I would not go to any place where I knew there was no bishop. I was on my guard for this: and I did what I could to seek salvation in a humble position rather than be in danger in high office. But, as I said, a slave may not

contradict his Lord. So it was that I came to this city to see a friend, whom I thought I might gain for God, that he might live with us in the monastery. I felt secure, for the place already had a bishop. But I was grabbed. I was made a priest … and from there, I became your bishop.[140]

The bishop at Hippo Regius where Augustine was 'grabbed' was Valerius. The date of Augustine's ordination there was 391. He was to be a priestly assistant to the elderly Valerius, taking over from him in time. That time would come in 395, at the age of 40. In a letter to Valerius written in 391, we see Augustine's explanation of what had happened to bring him so forcefully into the Church. It is the miracle that happens when God is allowed to take up the reins of a personality and show that He knows best. For we have to see everything adrift, from the deck of a ship, under the 'riddle of a similitude'[141] – thirsty because we want to drink, hungry because we want to eat, lusting for the land to come in sight. Like in the Akkadian saying – 'Their insight changes like day and night: when starving they become like corpses, when replete they vie with the gods.'[142] We cannot in this sense surprise ourselves; but this does not stop us from forming arrogant theories about conditions on the ship that cannot, in truth, be surpassed. For if the deck of the ship is our only point of reference then the additions of wisdom literature are there to make only a proverbial contribution going along.

> But I think that it was the purpose of my Lord to rebuke me [in my ordination], because I presumed, as if entitled by superior knowledge and excellence, to reprove the faults of many sailors before I had learned by experience the nature of their work. Therefore, once I had been sent in among them to share their labours, I began to feel the rashness of my censures; even though before that time I judged this office to be beset with many dangers. And hence the tears which some of my brethren perceived me shedding in the city at the time of my ordination, and because of which they did their utmost with the best intentions to console me, but with words which did not reach my case at all, because they could not see the real cause of my sorrow. But my experience has made me realize these things much more now than when I merely thought about them. Not, that is, because I have now had experience of new waves or storms which I could not previously have known by mere observation, or report, or reading, or meditation. But because I had been so naive in my high estimation of my own skill and strength for avoiding them. The Lord, however, laughed at me, and was pleased to show me by actual experience what I am.[143]

What Augustine begged from Valerius in light of this was time apart to read the Scriptures afresh, especially St Paul. These, he had decided, would prepare him for the priesthood. And in any case, something which he had gone through since Milan had changed them for him. In just six years time he would begin his *Confessiones* (397), the work of his Christian literary maturity, completing them in 400. What had happened to allow this to happen? The answer is that the ink of the Scriptures had come alive and run before his eyes. No other ink is prepared to do this; for it wishes to attain deathlessness on the page if it has been written by men. But Christianity is writing about writing that surpasses and surmounts what deathlessness demands in dry, inanimate ink. Only it takes Christ to show it to us.

It used to be that people read only aloud, never quietly to themselves. Strange to think. It is often said that Augustine's description of Ambrose doing just this at Milan is the first recorded instance of it in Western history.[144] It left a big impression on him; and it has since become famous as the start of something that we can now take for granted. 'When he read, his eyes moved down the pages and his heart sought out their meaning, while his voice and tongue remained silent.'[145] There is nothing wrong with reading silently; it is a practical necessity of modern life. But for the same way that Socrates felt books indulged free thought and the memory, we must wonder why words mean such prowess to us as we carry them off to seclusion.[146] And why, as with Plato, the end of the Dialogue and the 'intellectual word' brings us back to mythology – and to the poetic descriptions of gods and heavens that comfort us now because once we tried to better them.[147] They are nostalgia, in the sense that we have forgotten how this adventure of ideas, and of the distinctions between ideas, began with thinkers like Empedocles – stretching and reaching for the meaning contained in the realization that human blood is not something *in rerum natura*. '[The heart] dwelling in the sea of blood which surges back and forth, where especially is what is called thought by men; for the blood around men's hearts is their thought.'[148] And back to Augustine for what we really mean:

> Our intelligence is better pleased and more thoroughly arrested by what we are able to perceive wordlessly in the mind; for words fall short of an attention that wants to pool around these things; whereas words call us off from that with their noise and inability to shed their individual meanings and flow round things.[149]

Blood and thought are not in opposition; though they coagulate and dry one without the other. And language is the exceptional union of the two; with the purpose that all writing is to some extent or other the multiplication of this primal number. But whether these multiplications come out as fictions or non-fictions, there is a kind of blood-thought which trumps their advantages because it is not diminished by extension. It is a kind of guts, the specially-human that spirits can only dream of. It turns out that there really is a kind of understanding – and to Augustine it is the superior kind – in which you simply hold onto something for all you're worth. And it turns out that this is the blood-thought we want most of all, and even began with, in more honest, vital sounds. 'For to confess is this, to utter the thing that you have in your heart. For if you have one thing in your heart, and another thing on your tongue, you are speaking, not confessing.'[150]

We are educated to grow up into the belief that Reality is something that makes God ridiculous as we endure it. All the tilts and turnings of our self-understanding and all the balancing points of our literature extol this endurance. But only one literature takes endurance and its damaging self-congratulations and delivers, instead, incongruity – the incongruity of a human life, its secret descent from somewhere, which we have always suspected to be the more compelling narrative for all of this that we are in. 'For this heaven which we look up to with these eyes of ours, is not very precious before God. Holy souls are the heaven of God.'[151]

So this is what Augustine's Bible (we should properly say his rediscovery of the Bible) is about. And this is how it is that from a snap ordination and Valerius, comes into its sudden and complete sense the whole unasked for glory of his Rhetor's Life. From Africa to the giddy heart of Empire; and then back again; because everything that is human and trying can be met with just one question: 'How can a guileful [*dolosus*] man follow Simplicity?'[152]

> The tongue has done what it could, has sounded the words: now let the rest be thought by the heart. For what has even John himself said in comparison of He Who Is? Or what can be said by us men, who are so far from being equal to John's merits? Let us return, then, to that unction of Him. Let us return to that unction which inwardly teaches us what we cannot speak. And because we cannot at present see what is to be taught, let our part and duty be in desire. The whole life of a good Christian is holy desire. What you at present long for, you do not yet see: by longing, though, you are made capable: so that when that has come which you may see, you can be filled. For just as, if you would

fill a bag, and also know how great the thing is to fill it, you stretch the opening of the sack or the skin, or whatever else it be, to make it capable of holding more: so God, by deferring our hope, stretches our desire. And by that desiring, actually stretches the mind. And by that stretching, actually makes it more capacious.[153]

11

Last days and reflections on the style of man

Many a man has been willing
to go to the world below
animated by the hope of seeing there
an earthly love,
or wife, or son,
and conversing with them.[1]

Socrates

That we cannot inhabit our good works because we should be attributing them wholesale to the prevenient action of Grace is one of the serious complications of Christian orthodoxy – it sits fully at odds with the laws of ownership and responsibility, and how we use these laws to trace virtue and good character in the world. Not to mention how we explain ourselves into a human history that we expect to be able to explain us back.[1] A textbook classic leap of faith if we must make it: 'For the question we labour to solve is this: that we call ourselves sinners. For if any man shall say that he is without sin, he is a liar.'[2] An important part of the work of Hannah Arendt was to show precisely that …

> It is not knowledge and truth which is at stake, but rather judgements and decisions, the judicious exchange of opinion about the sphere of public life and the common world, and the decision what manner of action is to be taken in it, as well as to how it is to look henceforth, what kinds of things are to appear in it.[3]

That it is actually so serious that we cannot inhabit our good works on any logical or physical reckoning is Augustine's staggering uprating of this situation. Salvation history is something that God switches on and off for each soul like a light. Time and mortality and the constant shelving and re-referencing of ourselves in memory is the real predestination which He is crying out to save us from. For the supernatural knows no such thing; though it esteems the special qualities of human eyes; and it likes to be able to see through them to what it has made for itself. God loves man as his special predicate, and is intent on saving him, and restoring this brilliant arrangement.[4] At the very least we should know better from the giant clue contained in our free will:

> So you would put Christ under fate? Where are the fates? In heaven, you probably say, in the order and changes of the stars. But how then can fate rule Him by whom the same heavens and the stars were made; while even your own will, if you consider it rightly, transcends even the stars?[5]

> With a mighty voice You speak to your servant in his interior ear, and break through my deafness, and cry out: O man, true it is that what my Scripture says I do myself say. Yet that Scripture speaks in time, but does not affect my Word: because that Word exists along with me in equal eternity. So the things that you see through my Spirit I *am* seeing, just as those things which you speak by my Spirit I *am* saying. So it is also that when you see those things in time, I do not see them thus in time; and the same as when you say those things in time, I do not say them in time.[6]

In the previous chapter we rolled this whole situation up into Augustine's 'precocity'. Because if one is honest it catches in the throat. It shows what there has always been to fear in the traditional conception of the master and commander God and His lieutenant, the universe, all ordered up in ranks and keeping step. In the words of Professor Frederick Sontag:

> Such a view of the world may properly be called 'aristocratic.' Those who are intellectually oriented and well educated, with a certain amount of the world's fortune, are less likely to find any fault with the natural structure as it is given, whereas the unfortunate who suffer more are not so likely to see it in Augustine's enthusiastic terms.[7]

We cannot commit true originality, which requires Eternity for its seeing and conception.[8] We cannot truly see beyond the present of our own noses. Therefore we can only inhabit the future by remembering ourselves to have been there. In the same way, we can only inhabit the past by having it foretold to us. When Augustine describes how God did this for him, he uses an outstandingly singular expression: 'You drew Your own outlines upon my memory of what I should afterwards turn back to investigate for myself' [*quid ipse postea per me ipsum quaererum, in memoria me deliniasti*].⁹ So we are the Remembering Race. And we have taken this for our Style.

> Our time is very near to each one of us, seeing that we are mortal. We walk in the midst of chances. If we were made of glass, we should have to fear chances less than we do now. For what is more fragile than a vessel of glass? And yet it is kept, and lasts for ages. For though the chances of a fall and a smash are feared for it, yet there is no fear of fever or old age [which cannot be warded off].¹⁰

This means too that biography and autobiography from the Christian point of view (we might say 'spiritual' biography and autobiography) become something that must summit on the event of conversion, then move to a consideration of this style of man and its implications. This is what Augustine's *Confessiones* famously does, ending in books on Memory, Time and Eternity, Form and Matter, and the Creation of the World. What literary reason might have caused him to do this has long interested scholars; and it remains an up-to-the-minute and wide-open question of scholarship. The Pullitzer prize-winning historian Gary Wills has been the latest to take it on in his rich and rewarding *Augustine's "Confessions": A Biography*.¹¹ What in this book we have been saying about the personality of the man as a writer might now be able to supply its own reason.

A life to the summit of God's sudden intervention can be climbed, it can be written, and it can be read. But as for what should follow it, we find that there is no more rock: only an impassable distance of open sky to Heaven. Fyodor Dostoyevsky's *Crime and Punishment* was a novel that sought to respect this in its aspiration to be a narrative passing literally from one world into the next:

> But now a new history commences: a story of the gradual renewing of a man, of his slow progressive regeneration, and change from one world to another – an introduction to the hitherto unknown realities of life. This may well form the theme of a new tale; the one we wished to offer the reader is ended.¹²

Augustine will even instruct his parishioners in a sermon how the real ancients used to mix this ever-present possibility into their correspondences as a matter of course. Where we now 'salute', and offer good wishes, they distinctly wished each other the possibility of salvation: 'He that salutes, wishes salvation. For so the ancients in their letters wrote thus, "Such a one sends salvation to another." [*ille illi salute*] Salutation derives its name from this salvation."[13]

But how seriously should we be expected to take Augustine's image of the Remembering Race? It is a powerful and poetic image, but it is also a negative image that leaves us in the dark by its very design. It acknowledges that our business as rational creatures in a fallen world is to be dealing with the ethical considerations of the future. But it is in the first instance only a deftly-sketched description of this. How does it offer us more and become a description of how things could move on – a positive vision of hope?

We must, as we said at the start of this book, be thinking *aesthetically* to answer this question. We must, because the idea of predestination has never, in truth, been something that offended us *intellectually*. The idea of predestination was there all along if we chose to notice it; its role was to make other ideas possible. Other ideas that would seem to be opposed to it, such as freedom.

> The thronging [*frenisque*] course of circling ages is ever recalled anew to the image of immovable quiet: for by whose laws the choice of the soul is a free choice: so that to the good come rewards and to the evil come pains – and these distributed by necessities settled throughout the nature of everything.[14]

But we notice that this is always the way in a love story involving God. That is to say, the outbursts from our side are emotional and unreasonable, and so their covering over as the opposite puts us into these strange contortions. Predestination should be as reasonable a conjecture as gravity, given what we know about the logics of historical explanation. Predestination might just as well be our chosen word for the future dream of a science that will leave nothing to chance and all things known.

So it is we who are at fault, we who are at sin: and predestination has been our intellectual creation from the start. In what sense, then, does it offend against us aesthetically? And how does Augustine's God offer us what we really need in beauty and truth? We need to recap a little; let us do so by considering the following:

> And so also has He prepared those mansions, and is still preparing them and He who has already made the things which are yet to be, is now preparing, not different ones, but the very mansions He has already prepared. In other words, what He *has* prepared

in predestination, He *is* preparing by actual working [*praeparat operando*]. These mansions of ours already *are*, as respects predestination. If it were not so, He would have said, 'I will go and prepare,' that is, 'I will predestinate.' But because they are not yet in a state of practical preparedness, He says, 'And if I go and prepare a place for you, I will come again, and receive you unto myself.'[15]

This passage is Augustine's way of ridding us once and for all of the unhelpfulness of the geometries of 'good works'. The unhelpfulness of good works in religious arguments has always been that they function like angles in geometrical proofs. You only need one or two to be able to work out what the rest should be with total precision. And history shows that everyone, over the course of a normal life, has scored at least 'one or two'; so might from them deduce, most reasonably, that if they did the maths and completed the proof they would find that high sinfulness is a fright, but nothing more. And that a religion of frightening must have cynicism somewhere in it, and a profiting high priest, and best to be avoided. So good works should go the way of the idea of predestination. They are similarly 'included' in reality. By focusing on them we only reinforce reality and how we appear individually in the human condition. We do not change reality. What is wrong, and therefore what is sinful, is what is impulsively, aesthetically dissatisfying in this *modus operandi*.

The Western mind has always itched to be the first-born of reason. So much so that we can say that the happy endings of its sciences and its ethics are pursued because they are assumed to be the happy endings of all men everywhere. They have retained their Platonic, necessary conceptual element. But on the other hand, this is a democratic approach that calls on each of us to abdicate something of our individuality in order that we might become, together, the consecrated proofs of universal truths – and societies. Here Augustine displays his genius for the argument drawn from the outside place. We have gone along with him in calling this his African eye. The eye that came back at his education after he had concluded it, in his own way, at Cassiciacum – and made good the instincts of his boyhood.[16] We want to love and be loved – us to God. In fact it is only by reverse engineering from this need that we can support and justify what has actually happened to the human race in languages and literatures, arts and sciences. These things are altogether how we love ourselves in compensation. They are pride disguised as our intellectual conscience.

This leaves it for Augustine to point out that God may be offering us the chance to disengage from this machine and leave mechanical, bloodless thought behind for good. For He does not require us to do what we habitually do then complain about to Him. He does not require us to terrify ourselves with necessity and the fates – which is reality seen full-face. He has a face, too: and as Augustine emphasizes in the passage above, He is 'actually working' for our chance. Just like it is said that He was originally working for Adam and Eve's chance before they fell. God can speak a single truth into a single life, at a single moment of time: and this truth cannot be known until it is heard. Here is a doctrine of humanity conceived as a pinpoint accuracy of love.

> For it is not in space that any one is far from God, but in affections. You love God, you are near unto Him. You hate God, you are far off. You are standing in the same place, both while you are near and far off.[17]

> If you love one thing, and loved another thing before, you are not now where you were.[18]

Salvation history involves a departure from human history; but this departure becomes how we in fact draw near to the closeness of nothing with nature – and with everything else of life that we have tried to understand. So salvation history is the true wisdom of the philosophers, in every age-long dream of it. 'Let the ancient, the perpetual, the eternal, to you the new, call off your understanding from time to this.'[19]

In this book we have used the previous three chapters in particular to show how Augustine works up to this conclusion in his treatment of three sets of traditionally 'kept-apart' ideas. Man and woman; the natural and the supernatural; and self-consciousness and what we might call naive realism. His unifying treatment of man and woman is arguably the most surprising to encounter in a Patristic mind; but yet his language is authentically, philosophically romantic: 'For men are born of the bloods [*sanguinibus*] of male and female.'[20] In all three cases we know that there is a definite counter-history of where the kudos should lie. But in Augustine we encounter a thinker; from the perspective of Christianity we encounter an apologetic; that singles out kudos itself for the brunt of its attack. It is a brilliant new tactic, or instinct, or both. For of course kudos and the intellectual conscience are what we have referred to as the quantum-like security of our whole strategy (against God). So Augustine is dismissing these steps as the instrumental first steps of self-harming self-love. And for proof of this, he is then introducing those very truths of human experience which are usually discarded in these discussions which keep things apart. We mean those naive realisms of the heart that can make it so successfully into the artistic forms of expression as a lamentation, but nowhere else. With kudos thus removed altogether, his project is complete where it started – and indeed where we started in the opening Chapter.

> I know you want to keep on living. You do not want to die. And you want to pass from this life to another in such a way that you will not rise again, as a dead man, but fully alive and transformed. This is what you desire. This is the deepest human feeling: because mysteriously, the soul itself wishes it, and instinctively desires it.[21]

Here he is saying that the only ideas that need to be kept apart in the reckoning of anything from the point of view of 'the deepest human feeling' are love-of-self and love-of-God. And this leads directly into that other, unmistakable feature of Augustinianism. The idea of the human being as the gold standard of this. Augustine says that we are all taught to occupy the exact same historical space called the 'present' by a worldwide conspiracy of essentially well-meaning people. Parents, siblings, teachers, and on. Not by absolutely everyone, of course; but this is not his point. And from this, as the simplest conclusion, emerged the biggest decision of his life and ministry. Without doubt the biggest decision for a discreet man to make. Without doubt an unheard of decision for an ancient man to make. He chooses to give us his life as guilt-proof of the whole of this in an autobiography that ends more or less where we now find ourselves here.

> For as a substitute for this life the soul is put, respecting which it is said in that passage that if a man hate not his own soul also, he cannot be my disciple [see Luke 14.26].[22]

We must now ask him: 'What happens when a human being dislocates from ordinary history into salvation history?'

> 'Love itself is new and eternal; therefore is it ever new, because it never grows old.'[23]

The future is the one thing we encounter on a daily basis that cannot be touched or grasped at all – and so we remember it as like the past. 'It is necessary that the words of the Book of Wisdom be illustrated in us: "The thoughts of mortal men are timid, and our fore-castings uncertain." [Wis. 9.14]'[24] Nothing quite touches the irony of what we are about as this boastful vision of something that no human eye has ever seen. The same science that debunks ghosts needs this one giant ghost for the place of all its experiments to come real in. The future belongs to God like the farthest undiscovered galaxies belong to Him – though we are more inclined to grant Him ownership of those.

> If we are ignorant not only of the time in which an event is to be, but even whether it shall be at all, we say, 'It will happen if God wills' – not because God will then have a new will which He had not before, but because that event, which from eternity has been prepared in His unchangeable will, shall then come to pass.[25]

The future is urgent business, our every waking breath. And Augustine takes the sweeping point of view that, if we begin with the future, say in just the way that we currently begin with the past, we may experience our first real sighting of something the opposite to the 'arrow of time'. Instead of the onward plough and everything that guarantees it, only a love that is 'ever new' and 'eternal'; 'never growing old'. He means not so much motion in the opposite direction, but an endlessly recurring creation. It is the sense in which Adam and Eve were always dying to something in the Garden of Eden as they remained in God's Will. They had not yet sinned and founded the Remembering Race: their past meant nothing to them that it does to us now. They were always dying to it and being brought on in the future. 'We exist under Grace,' is how Augustine puts it, 'which, making us to love what is enjoined of us, really holds sway over the free.'[26]

Today, after the Second Adam has visited us, it is more the case that we are always dying and being resurrected anew. For we have been born fighting for survival; and because we are not God, or even gods, we have no natural foresight to make use of and must rely instead on the faculty of memory. This is what is so aesthetically displeasing about the whole arrangement. Memory is something that is now being used out of place – for what it was not intended. To Augustine, a great deal is explained out of this basic gaucheness.

In the first place, it means that the ongoing processes of Christian reform should give ultimate respect to what cannot be altered in this arrangement. They should give ultimate respect to what Christ the Saviour is accomplishing all the time in the lives of His pilgrims: what He is doing for them that they physically and logically cannot. Maturity and old age have a way of not faring well when the eye is on brighter things to come. They can easily be seen as obstacles to new forms of thinking, as they so tragically have been in times of accelerated social revolution – 'Sharper is the fight of the young; we know it well, we have passed through it.'²⁷ To Augustine, however, what we become in our old age is a true lesson. With the years passed by, we are that much more our experiences and our loves, our regrets and our losses: we are that much closer to realizing how such a collection is a unique quality of *mortal* rationality. Memory allows us to be sociable and empathetic, as well as to have the genuine experiences of freedom. To be something above plain life, and the plain sensation of it. Living our narratives, but also becoming parts of other people's, too. What memory does not do well is prediction and certainty. Christian reformers should beware what Professor Oliver O'Donovan has called:

> ... the secret guilt which infects every culture's thoughts about its ancestors, and which in ours has fuelled the famous 'quarrel' of the moderns with the ancients – and now (good Lord!) produces 'post'-modernity – must be overcome. The resurrection of the dead makes equal and reciprocal sharing.²⁸

Memory does not do prediction and certainty well because, when called upon for these things, it can only bring the letter up to what the Spirit should be taking care of. And this has allowed the question of 'time' to become one of the classic problems of thought – but only because it is how we chase our tails. That is to say, we 'see' the ghost of the future by making value judgements in the present; which means that the question of time is irresolvable so long as these value judgements continue to be our quantum and kudos. If there were no future, we should have no reason to continue to make them. And if our quantum and kudos produce time as one of their chief effects, we can hardly expect them to turn around and investigate themselves with much success! By the same reasoning, Augustine seems to be leaving it open that a kind of 'time travel' is possible if time is seen in this, its moral aspect. His famous language of how we 'change our loves' seems really to include this possibility that, by a choice of will, we obliterate our historical space and become bound to salvation history and its eternity.

> There is no physical movement that registers in the sensation of it without some intervening passage of time. By the same token, we cannot spontaneously move through time without the intervening help of memory. By this reasoning the writers (of medicine) have shown that there are three species of ventricles in the brain. The first is to be found close to the face; from it branch off all the sensory nerves. The second is located to the rear, at the base of the brain; it governs all physical movements. As for

the third, it is located between these two; and so situated, it is reasoned to be the seat of memory. For it happens that there has always to be some time lag [however infinitesimally small] between the physical movement and the sensation of it. If we were not constantly remembering the physical movement during the space of this time lag, we should experience only sensations: we should have no cognizance of the movements that caused them: and we should have therefore no basis whatsoever for our characteristic concern with what ought to be done and the next moment's movement.[29]

So you think that you can comprehend a body by the eye, but really you cannot at all! For whatever you look at, you do not see the whole of it. If, say, you see a man's face, you do not see his back at the time you see the face; and when you see the back, you do not at that time see the face. You do not then comprehend a body by seeing it all at once; but when you see another part which you had not seen before, memory aids you to remember other parts of the body which you have already seen. With this aid, you could never say that you had comprehended anything – even on the surface. So you find that you tend to handle what you see, turning it about on this side and that. Or you may actually walk yourself round it to see the whole. But all at once in one view you cannot see the whole. And as long as you turn it about to see it, you are seeing the parts; and by putting together those parts, you are fancying that you are seeing the whole. But this must not be understood as the sight of the eyes, but the activity of the memory.[30]

When I began this book I took care to highlight Augustine's creative genius as one prevailing reason for the urgency, and impatience of form, of many of his ideas and stretches of writing. I tried to pick this up in its development in his youth – one mind against a disappointing world. And I showed that enlightenment came as a series of false dawns until everything was finally settled with God at Hippo; and words and writing were able to settle on themselves and become his treasured metaphor for how we must give things up to God; and how God will then return them to us in the arrangement we recognize as having always wanted. 'Before you felt God, you thought that you could express *God*. But then you began actually to feel Him: and in feeling Him, you felt what you cannot actually express.'[31]

Augustine never wanted to be creative in words but to be honest. When speaking of the Septuagint translation, he will mark this distinction by calling by the name of 'human bondage' what the translators 'owed to the words'. The truth of those words was something altogether different. It was alive – it was 'divine power, which filled and ruled the mind of the translator'.[32] And I have pointed out repeatedly that, in the case of a born writer like Augustine, these discoveries issue in a special challenge and a potential stalemate between the wishes of a creative man and *the* Creator God. However, it also allows it that when pride can miraculously be removed, and the Bible returned to, what follows can be, intellectually-speaking, the pinnacle and end of the story.

> Not for nothing have You willed that these dark secrets be written on so many pages. Nor are those forests to lack their harts, who will retire to them, and regain their strength, walk about and feed, and lie down and ruminate. [Cf. Ps. 28.9] Lord, perfect me, and open these pages to me. Behold, Your voice is my joy, Your voice is above a flood of pleasures. [Cf. Ps. 118.72] Grant me what I love, for I love in honesty – and this too have You given to me! Do not forsake Your gifts, and do not despise this Your plant which thirsts for You. Let me confess to You whatever I shall find in Your books; and let me 'hear the voice of praise,' [see Ps. 26.7] and drink You in, and consider 'the wonderful things of Your law,' [see Ps. 119.18] – from that beginning when You made heaven and earth, even to an everlasting kingdom together with You in Your holy city.[33]
>
> The poverty of man's understanding is spendthrift of words, because searching speaks more than does finding, pleading takes longer than acceptance, and the hand that knocks is busier than the hand that receives. We hold the promise: who shall destroy it?[34]

Once established in this routine and more willing to look around him, Augustine was able to sight his novelist's eye on the marathon tussle between the past, which we have lived and seems real, and the future, which is about to be created and is at that moment of its dawn more metaphysically real than anything else. They are like two halves of the mould into which you could pour any conceivable human life in a seamless fit. This also came to be the same thing to him as the mood of his age. Late antiquity, and especially in border provinces like North Africa, was the age of anxious faces. Every day, Augustine looked out on this in the faces of his parishioners. Tales would come in from outlying towns of vicious raids and atrocities. The barbarians were everywhere becoming bolder and realizing what they could get away with. In such tense times, Christianity historically prospers as the help of last resort; but it can just as easily suffer once cruelty and pain begin to speak badly of God, and the power of the future seems to rest with the strong-armed invader. 'Fear not, therefore, lest any mighty man should corrupt the promises of God. He does not corrupt, because He is truthful; He has no one more mighty by whom His promise may be corrupted.'[35]

To help his flock, Augustine began to go inside himself more and more to learn there what truly helps a distressed and fearful people – and what reasonable point of contact there can be between the written-out wisdom of the Unseen God and this flesh-blood race, toiling to preserve the force and beauty of life. He studied himself: a man lying in bed at night remembering a lost lover and a lost son. And he started to learn to see this activity as the wonderful thing, the crowning thing. The moment when humanity stops negating itself, stops disdaining the emotions, learns to feel what feeling them means, and hands them up to God for the furnishing of His kingdom. Of course it was not always like this. For a time these seemed the memories to get away from – the threats to a more serene and impassive contemplation.[36] But the key realization in the end – and what becomes the recurring homily of Augustine to his dying days – is that men and women should not lust to 'exceed the bounds of mankind'. In the case of his parishioners, and the upward aspirations of Roman society, this could often mean encouraging them to strive to see the human, crouched, as it so often was, beneath the misfortune, the squalor and the disease.

> Although a marbled house does contain you, although fretted ceilings cover you, you and the poor man together have for covering that roof of the universe, the sky ... In the bowels of your mothers you were both naked.[37]

But there was another sense to this homily. The mysterious sense. Perhaps it marks also where we should end. We know, at any rate, that it was what pleased his old bones most at the close of his life – this mysterious sense.

He fell fatally ill in August 430 with a fever and took to his bed, understanding that he was to die. Possidius records in his *Vita* that, in the final 10 days of his illness, Augustine remained in a continuous penance.[38] He had ordered that the four Psalms of David dealing with this subject be copied out and fixed to his walls in a way that he could read them aloud over and over. Outside, the Vandal invaders had nearly totally conquered North Africa. Hippo Regius happened to be a fortified town and one of the last stands against their onslaught. But it was holding out against the inevitable; and when Augustine died there on 28 August, it was amidst a scene of citizens and refugees, terrified and besieged.

So it was penance that Augustine set about as his last stand. 'The world does not let up: it does not still its persecutions, its temptations ... Even in bed you must be an athlete. Racked with fever you can fight and win.'[39] But not penance to do with bad works – or even with good works performed badly. Because these are the subsets of a larger neglect. And it is this larger neglect that must be fought against if we are not to leave the world as we entered it – in wholehearted self-consciousness.

Once we were held by parents, and loved by them, and remembered by them. It took us time to learn to love them back from our oblivion of infant self-absorption. And then, having grown up and loved, and lost a son, and said goodbye, forever, to a lover (as Augustine did), we are found at the other end, on a bed. And the world has not let up. By cunning parabolic inevitability, it has not. And so we dare not forget now, when the world is daring us to. We dare not let pain, and fear, and death, and the whole power of the rage of men cause us to forget now. This is penance. Not to forget that when we elevated the mind above the body, and looked down upon ourselves, and saw that we were naked and afraid, we committed our self-understanding to the data and metadata that can only take us deeper beneath nakedness and fear, down to our *interius nostrum tenebrosum et fluvidum*, our 'dark and fluid inner being'.[40] And the real problem is that no dualism will ever succeed as a description of this, for, as Augustine puts it, we are always wanting 'to cut short one side so as to make room for evil'.[41] The infinite regress of self-consciousness is the same thing as the truth that we can only feel ourselves alive in the soul, yet only recognize ourselves unique in the body. 'Transition gives them being, and the death of what they give birth to gives them individuality'.[42]

So there is this great wrong called self-consciousness, which makes for the parabola of our lives. And mankind is fallen from start to finish because of it; unless God intervenes. But though that may be true, it also makes self-consciousness only as much as a default – a condition of this kind of life we live. So a Christianity that would boom sinfulness against it turns out not to be Augustine's last will and testament. This is instead his wish to draw our wonder to this race of ours that propagates generations in straight lines. For there are no such lines in eternity, where things are coeval: and this makes it that mothers lifting children to their arms and all the bonds of true friendship are also the precise scintillating acts of will that true evil truly fears.

> Fire, for example, engenders a coeval brightness. But among men you only find sons younger, fathers older; you do not find them coeval. But as I have said, in this example I have shown you a brightness coeval with its parent fire. For fire begets brightness, yet is it never without brightness.[43]

> Indeed, that fire will shine as long as it exists: so that if you could somehow imagine to 'take its light from it', you would also at the same time extinguish it. For without the light it could not be fire. But Christ is light inextinguishable and co-eternal with the Father, always bright, always shining, always burning.[44]

Perhaps Augustine meant that the human race is God's originality. Our un-predestined willingness an image of His character: our rationality the thing to be taken for granted, and left alone. Rationality stirred up is self-consciousness: 'Yet, when these works are referred to the praise and adoration of the Creator Himself, it is as if morning has dawned in the minds of those who contemplate them.'[45] Perhaps that is why he came in the end to believe so strongly in another parabola, and another parabolic inevitability. Not books to save us that talk of the flesh and how we must leave it behind, but Christ delivering the most natural and beautiful of messages in the person of His own body – *ex ore veritatis*, 'from the mouth of truth'.[46]

> How great the difference, when two are in a prison, between the criminal and him that visits him! For a person comes to visit his friend, and enters in, and both seem to be in prison; but they differ by a wide distinction. The one is pressed down by his cause: the other has been brought there by the cause of *humanity*. So it is that in this our mortal state, we were held fast by our guiltiness, and He in mercy came down to us. He entered in to the captive's prison, a Redeemer not an oppressor. The Lord shed His blood for us, redeemed us, and changed our hope. As yet we bear the mortality of the flesh, and take the future immortality upon trust. On the sea we are tossed by the waves, but we have the anchor of hope already fixed upon the land.[47]

We may be congenital materialists, but how we get it so wrong so much of the time is by self-love. No longer looking to God, and made Godless, we miss His originality – His humanity. The future confronts us; and we fall back on the resources of mind; and our hearts are made unquiet. Because, though we *are* human, we cannot create ourselves in the present. We cannot light up our souls *ex nihilo*.

> For we know full well that all eye-salves and medicines are derived from the earth alone. By dust it was that you were blinded, and so by dust it will be that you are healed. Once it was flesh that wounded you: now let it be flesh that heals you.[48]

Abbreviations of Augustine's writings

Contra Fort.	*Acta seu Disputatio contra Fortunatem Manichaeum*	Debate with Fortunatus, a Manichee
Contra Crescon.	*Ad Cresconium grammaticum partis Donati lib. 4*	To Cresconius, a Donatist Grammarian
Ad Emeritum	*Ad Emeritum Donatistarum episcopum, post collationem Lib. 1*	To Emeritus the Donatist Bishop, after a Meeting
Ad inquis. Ian.	*Ad inquisitiones Ianuarii*	Responses to Januarius (Letters 54–5)
Adn. in Iob	*Adnotationes in Iob lib. 1*	Comments on Job
Adv. Iud.	*Adversus Iudaeos tractatus*	Against the Jews
Brev. coll. cum Don.	*Breviculus conlationis cum Donatistas lib. 3*	A Summary of a Meeting with the Donatists
Coll. cum Maxim.	*Conlatio cum Maximus*	Debate with Maximus
Confess.	*Confessiones*	Confessions
Contra Acad.	*Contra Academicos lib. 3 (De Academicis)*	Against the Sceptics
Contra Adim.	*Contra Adimantum Manichei discipulum lib. 1*	Against Adimantus, a Disciple of Mani
Contra adv. L. et P.	*Contra adversarium Legis et Prophetarum lib. 2*	Against the Adversaries of the Law and the Prophets
Contra duas ep. Pelag.	*Contra duas epistolas Pelagianorum lib. 4*	Against Two Letters of the Pelagians
Contra ep. Don.	*Contra epistolam Donati*	Against the Letter of the Donatists
Contra ep. Man.	*Contra epistolam Manichaei quam vocant fundamenti lib. 1*	Against the 'Foundation Letter' of the Manichees

Contra ep. Parm.	*Contra epistolam Parmeniani lib. 3*	Against the Letter of Parmenian
Contra Faustum	*Contra Faustum Manichaeum lib. 33*	Against Faustus, a Manichee
Contra Felicem	*Contra Felicem Manichaeum lib. 2*	Against Felix, a Manichee
Contra Gaud.	*Contra Gaudentium Donatistarum episcopum lib. 2*	Against Gaudentius, a bishop of the Donatists
Contra Hilarum	*Contra Hilarum lib. 1*	Against Hilarus
Contra Iul.	*Contra Iulianum lib. 6*	Against Julian
Opus imp. c. Iul.	*Contra Iulianum opus imperfectum*	Against Julian, an Unfinished Work
Contra litt. Petil.	*Contra litteras Petiliani lib. 3*	Against the Letter of Petilian
Contra Maxim.	*Contra Maximinum Arianum lib. 2*	Against Maximus, an Arian
Contra mend.	*Contra mendacium lib. 1*	Against Lying
Contra Prisc. et Orig.	*Contra Priscillianistas et Origenistas*	Against the Priscillianists and The Origenists
Contra Secund.	*Contra Secundinem Manichaeum lib. 1*	Against Secundius, a Manichee
Contra Arian.	*Contra sermonem Arianorum lib. 1*	Against an Arian Sermon
De ag. Christ.	*De agone Christiano lib. 1*	On the Christian Struggle
De an. et eius or.	*De anima et eius origine lib. 4 (De natura et origine animae)*	On the Soul and its Origin
De bapt.	*De baptismo contra Donatistas lib. 7*	On Baptism against the Donatists
De b. vita	*De beata vita lib. 1*	On the Happy Life
De bono con.	*De bono coniugali lib. 1*	On the Good of Marriage
De bono vid.	*De bono viduitatis*	On the Good of Widowhood
De cath. rud.	*De cathechizandis rudibus lib. 1*	On the Instruction of Beginners
De civ. Dei	*De civitate Dei*	The City of God
De con. adult.	*De coniugiis adulterinis lib. 2*	On Adulterous Marriages

De cons. Evang.	*De consensu Evangelistarum lib. 4*	On Agreement among the Evangelists
De cont.	*De continentia*	On Continence
De corr. Donat.	*De correctione Donatistarum lib. 1*	On the Correction of the Donatists (Letter 185)
De corrept. et gr.	*De correptione et gratia lib. 1*	On Admonition and Grace
De cura pro mort.	*De cura pro mortuis gerenda lib. 1*	On the Care of the Dead
De div. qq. 83	*De diversis quaestionibus 83 lib. 1*	On Eighty-Three Varied Questions
De div. qq. ad Simpl.	*De diversis quaestionibus ad Simplicianum lib. 2*	To Simplicianus, on Various Questions
De div. daem.	*De divinatione daemonum lib. 1*	On the Divination of Demons
De doctr. Christ.	*De doctrina Christiana lib. 4*	On Christian Doctrine
De dono pers.	*De dono perseverantiae*	On the Gift of Perseverance
De d. anim.	*De duabus animabus lib. 1*	On the Two Souls
De fide et op.	*De fide et operibus lib. 1*	On Faith and Works
De fide et s.	*De fide et symbolo lib. 1*	On Faith and the Creed
De fide r. quae n. v.	*De fide rerum quae non videntur*	On Faith in Things Unseen
De Gen. ad litt.	*De Genesi ad litteram lib. 12*	On the Literal Interpretation of Genesis
De Gen. ad litt. l. imp.	*De Genesi ad litteram liber imperfectus*	On the Literal Interpretation of Genesis, an Unfinished Book
De Gen. c. Man.	*De Genesi contra Manichaeos lib. 2*	On Genesis against the Manichees
De gestis cum Em.	*De gestis cum Emerito Lib. 1*	On the Proceedings with Emeritus
De gestis Pel.	*De gestis Pelagii lib. 1*	On the Deeds of Pelagius
De gr. Chr.	*De gratia Christi et de peccato originali lib. 2*	On the Grace of Christ and Original Sin
De gr. et l. arb.	*De gratia et libero arbitrio lib. 1*	On Grace and Free Will

De gr. N. T.	*De gratia Novi Testamenti lib. 1*	On the Grace of the New Testament (Letter 140)
De haer.	*De haeresibus*	On Heresies (Letters 221–4)
De immort. an.	*De immortalitate animae lib. 1*	On the Immortality of the Soul
De lib. arb.	*De libero arbitrio lib. 3*	On Free Will
De Mag.	*De Magistro lib. 1*	The Teacher
De mend.	*De mendacio lib. 1*	On Lying
De mor. Eccl. cath.	*De moribus ecclesiae catholicae et de moribus Manichaeorum*	On the Morals of the Catholic Church and the Morals of the Manichees
De mus.	*De musica lib. 6*	On Music
De nat. boni	*De natura boni lib. 1*	On the Nature of the Good
De nat. et gr.	*De natura et gratia lib. 1*	On Nature and Grace
De nupt. et conc.	*De nuptiis et concupiscentia lib. 2*	On Marriage and Concupiscence
De 8 qq. Dulc.	*De 8 Dulcitii quaestionibus lib. 1*	On Eight Questions from Dulcitius
De 8 qq. V. T.	*De 8 quaestionibus ex Veteri Testamento*	Eight Questions on the Old Testament
De op. mon.	*De opere monachorum lib. 1*	The Works of Monks
De ord.	*De ordine lib. 2*	On Order
De o. an. et de sent. Iac.	*De origine animae et de sententia Iacobi lib. 2*	On the Origins of the Soul, and Some Thoughts on a Verse in James (Letters 166–7)
De pat.	*De patientia*	On Patience
De pecc. mer. et rem.	*De peccatorum meritis et remissione lib. 3*	On the Merits and Forgiveness of Sins
De perf. iust. hom.	*De perfectione iustitiae hominis*	On the Perfection of Man's Righteousness
De praed. sanct.	*De praedestinatione sanctorum*	On the Predestination of the Saints
De praes. Dei	*De praesentia Dei lib. 1*	On the Presence of God (Letter 187)

De quant. an.	De quantitate animae lib. 1	On the Greatness of the Soul
De s. virg.	De sancta virginitate lib. 1	On Holy Virginity
De serm. Dom. in m.	De sermone Domini in monte lib. 2	Discourse on the Sermon on the Mount
De sp. et litt.	De Spiritu et littera lib. 1	On the Spirit and the Letter
De Trin.	De Trinitate lib. 15	On the Trinity
De un. bapt. c. Petil.	De unico baptismo contra Petilianum lib. 1	On the One Baptism against Petilian
De un. Eccl.	De unitate Ecclesiae lib. 1	On the Unity of the Church
De util. cred.	De utilitate credendi lib. 1	On the Utility of Belief
De vera rel.	De vera religione lib. 1	On the True Religion
De vid. Deo	De videndo Deo lib. 1	On the Vision of God (Letters 147–8)
En. in Ps.	Enarrationes in Psalmos	Commentaries on the Psalms
Ench.	Enchiridion ad Laurentium lib. 1	A Manual on Faith, Hope, and Charity
Ep.	Epistolae	Letters
Exp. i. ep. ad Rom.	Epistolae ad Romanos inchoata expositio lib. 1	Unfinished Commentary on the Letter to the Romans
Exp. ep. ad Gal.	Expositio epistolae ad Galatas	Commentary on the Letter to The Galatians
Exp. ep. Iac. ad d. t.	Expositio epistolae Iacobi ad duodecim tribus	Commentary on James's Letter to the Twelve Tribes
Exp. q. p. ep. ad Rom.	Expositio quarumdam propositionum ex epistola ad Romanos	Statements in the Letter to the Romans
Loc. in Hept.	Locutionem in Heptateuchum lib. 7	Sayings in the Heptateuch
Post coll. c. Don.	Post collationem contra Donatistas lib. 1	After the Meeting with the Donatists
Pr. et test. c. Don.	Probationum et testimoniorum contra Donatistas lib. 1	Proofs and Testimonials against the Donatists

Ps. c. p. Don.	Psalmus contra partem Donati	Psalm against the Donatist Sect
Quaest. Evang.	Quaestiones Evangiolorum lib. 2	Questions on the Gospels
Quaest. c. pagani	Quaestiones expositae contra Paganos numero sex	Six Questions against the Pagans (Letter 102)
Quaest. in Hept.	Quaestiones in Heptateuchum	Questions on the Heptateuch
Quaest in Mt.	Quaestiones sedecim in Evangelium secundum Matthaeum lib. 1	Sixteen Questions on the Gospel according to Matthew
Regula	Regula ad servos Dei	Rule of the Servants of God
Retract.	Retractiones	Retractions
Ad Caes. eccl.	Sermo ad Caesariensis Ecclesiae Plebem	A Sermon to the People of the Church of Caesariensis
Ad cat. de symb.	Sermo ad catechumenos de symbolo	On the Creed, to the Catechumens
De disc. Chr.	Sermo de disciplina Christiana	On Christian Discipline
De urbis exc.	Sermo de urbis excidio	Sermon on the Sack of Rome
De util. ieiunii	Sermo de utilitate ieiunii	Sermon on the Utility of Fasting
Serm.	Sermones	Sermons
Solil.	Soliloquiorum lib. 2	Soliloquies
De s. Script.	Speculum de sacra Scriptura	The Mirror of Scripture
In Io. ev. tr.	Tractatus in Ioannis Evangelium	Tractates on the Gospel of John
Ep. Io.	In epistulam Ioannis ad Parthos Tractatus	Tractates on the First Letter of John

Notes

Chapter 1

1   Comfortably occupying the first place of these historians is Peter Brown. See especially his *The Rise of Western Christendom: Triumph and Diversity, A.D. 200–1000*, 2nd edn (Oxford: Blackwell Publishing, 2008). Brown is a particularly convincing exponent of the view that Christianity's simple universalism furnished the foundations for the early medieval world. Previous attempts to refer the unity of early Europe to some resilient centralizing force, whether the Mediterranean economy (see H. Pirenne, *Mohammed and Charlemagne*, trans. Bernard Miall (London: Unwin, 1939)) or Roman Catholicism (see Christopher Dawson, *The Making of Europe: An Introduction to the History of European Unity* (London: Sheed and Ward, 1932)), misinterpreted the ubiquitous but suprisingly disconnected character of early Christianity. For Brown, this institution was '… a remarkably universal religion, endowed with common codes which could spring up in many different environments.' However, '… its principal feature … resided in its very diversity' (Brown, *The Rise of Western Christendom*, 14–17).

2   See P. F. Strawson, *Individuals: An Essay in Descriptive Metaphysics* (London: Methuen, 1964), 10: '… there is a massive central core of human thinking which has no history – or none recorded in histories of thought; there are categories and concepts which, in their most fundamental character, change not at all. Obviously these are not the specialities of the most refined thinking. They are the commonplaces of the least refined thinking; and are yet the indispensable core of the conceptual equipment of the most sophisticated human beings.'

3   Germaine de Staël, 'Essay on fictions', in *Major Writings of Germain de Staël*, trans. Vivian Folkenflik (New York: Columbia University Press, 1987), 72–3.

4   Like it did another African thinker, closer to our time – James Baldwin, writing in 1960s America. 'The word "sensual" is not intended to bring to mind quivering dusky maidens or priapic black studs. I am referring to something much simpler and less fanciful. To be sensual, I think, is to respect and rejoice in the force of life, of life itself, and to be *present* in all that one does, from the effort of loving to the breaking of bread … Something very sinister happens to the people of a country when they begin to distrust their own reactions as deeply as they do here, and become as joyless as they have become. It is this individual uncertainty … this inability to renew themselves at the fountain of their own lives, that makes the discussion, let alone elucidation, of any conundrum – that is, any reality – so supremely difficult. The person who distrusts himself has no touchstone for

reality – for this touchstone can be only himself' (James Baldwin, *The Fire Next Time* (Harmondsworth: Penguin, 1969), 43.
5   Charles Morgan, 'The glow of living, or *liberty in time*', in *Liberties of the Mind* (London: Macmillan, 1951), 147.
6   Pierre Simon Laplace, *Essai philosophique sur les probabilités*, trans. John Stuart Mill (Paris: Courcier, 1814), 7 – quoted in John Stuart Mill, *A System of Logic* (London: Longmans Green, 1875), 350–1.
7   Cf. Sir Arthur Eddington's psychological presentation of these conclusions: 'I conclude therefore that our ingrained form of thought is such that we shall not rest satisfied until we are able to represent all physical phenomena as an interplay of a vast number of structural units intrinsically alike. All the diversity of phenomena will be then seen to correspond to different forms of relatedness of these units or, as we should usually say, different configurations' (Sir Arthur Eddington, *The Philosophy of Physical Science* (Cambridge: Cambridge University Press, 1949), 125.
8   Augustine shows his alertness to these proprieities at *Contra Acad.*, I, 1, 1: 'For it may be that what is commonly referred to as fortune is governed by a certain hidden order; and in events, we do not term anything "chance" unless its reason and cause are unknown.'
9   Virgil (trans. H. R. Fairclough), *Eclogae*, IV, 4–7.
10 Peter Brown, *Augustine of Hippo: A Biography* (Los Angeles: University of California Press, 2000), 512. The quotation from Prosper of Aquitaine is referenced as S. Muhlberger, *The Fifth Century Chroniclers*, ARCA Monographs 27 (Leeds: F. Cairns, 1990), 131.
11 See *En. in Ps.*, XCV, 15: 'For Adam himself signifies in Greek the whole world; that is to say, there are four letters, A, D, A, and M. And we notice also that in Greek, the four corners of the world have these initial letters, Ανατολὴ, they call the East; Δύσις, the West: Adam. As such we say that Adam has been scattered over the world. He was in one place [Eden]; he fell; and was shattered into small pieces. As small pieces he filled the whole world. But thanks to the mercy of God, these fragments were gathered together from every side, and forged together again by the fire of love. One was made of what had been broken. That Artist knew well how to do this; so let no one despair now. Yes, it is a great thing, but reflect Who that Artist was.'
12 Right up to the hands on pleasure of late antiquity's 'creosoting the fence'! – that is, *dealbatione lutei parietis* 'whitening the mud wall'. See *En. in Ps.*, LXX, 9: 'Why do they think me a monster and insult me? Because I believe in what I cannot see. They are happy in those things they can see. They exult in drink, in wantonness, in chamberings, in covetousness, in riches, in robberies, in secular dignities, in the whitening of a mud wall. Yes, in these things they exult. But I walk in a different way, contemning those things which are present, and fearing the prosperous things of the world. I walk secure in no other thing than the promises of God.'
13 This is different to the idea of ancient wisdom literature being a resource for archetypes of the common stock of human consciousness. In other words, of this resource being intrinsically superior to modern techniques of introspection. That attitude is a form of sentimentality. What we are suggesting here is simply that ancient wisdom literature is (circumstantially) better at articulating the idea that our deathless outpourings of spirit must marry to vanishing corporeality. For an ingenious dismantling of the former

sentimentality, see Jean Starobinski and Frederick Brown, 'The inside and the outside', *The Hudson Review* 28, no. 3 (1975): 333–51. His main argument is that 'Making the most remote past coefficient to our most intimate depth is a way of refusing loss and separation, of preserving, in the crammed plenum we imagine history to be, every moment spent along the way' (p. 334).

14 *Confess.*, IV, 1, 1.
15 Cf. Stephen Toulmin and June Goodfield, *The Discovery of Time* (London: Hutchinson, 1965), 271: 'The World of Ideas is self-contained, cogent and certain, just because we fashion it deliberately so that our minds can move freely and confidently within it.'
16 The famous incantation of his *Confessiones*: 'Lord, You have made us for yourself so that our heart is unquiet until it rests in You' (*Confess.*, I, 1, 1). Cf. Inge's expression of this idea: '[T]he spirit of man does not live only on tradition; it can draw direct from the fountainhead' (W. R. Inge, 'Religion', in R. W. Livingstone (ed.), *The Legacy of Greece* (Oxford: The Clarendon Press, 1923), 28).
17 A useful reference point at this early stage is Professor Paul Tillich's idea of the 'absent God' or the 'God above God': 'The absent God, the source of the question and the doubt about himself is neither the God of theism nor of pantheism; he is neither the God of the Christians nor of the Hindus; he is neither the God of the naturalists nor of the idealists. All these forms of the divine image have been swallowed by the waves of radical doubt. What is left is only the inner necessity of a man to ask the ultimate question with complete seriousness. He himself may not call the source of this inner necessity God. He probably will not. But those who have had a glimpse of the working of the divine Presence, know that one could even ask the ultimate question without this Presence, even if it makes itself felt only as the absence of God. The God above God is a name for God who appears in the radicalism and the seriousness of the ultimate question, even without an answer' (Paul Tillich, in *The Listener*, 3 August 1961 (London: BBC), 169).
18 *Confess.*, X, 8, 15.
19 Cf. *En. in Ps.*, XLVII, 2: '"Out of the North come clouds," and not black clouds, not dark clouds, not lowering, but of "golden colour". Whence but by grace illumined through Christ? See, "the sides of the North are the city of the great King" [see Job 37.22].' Also *Confess.*, X, 36, 59.
20 *De civ. Dei*, XIV, 28 (trans. R. W. Dyson). On the evidence, F. C. Copleston might have been right to call them 'camps' (see his *A History of Philosophy*, vol. 2 (New York: Doubleday, 1962), 100). See also D. J. MacQueen's comment that 'For Augustine the beginnings of the *civitas*, as an organised expression of man's social and political life, antedate the earliest records of secular history. Nevertheless this institution stems from a unity itself prior even to the most ancient forms of communal existence. The unity here in question is actually one of "racial stock" (*genus*) or origin, and the fellowship to which it has given rise precedes and in a sense transcends the entire human domain of the social and of the secular politics.' (D. J. MacQueen, 'The origin and dynamics of society and the state according to Saint Augustine: part I', *Augustinian Studies*, vol. IV (1973), 78–9).
21 See how Augustine handles this insight at *In Io. ev. tr.*, VII, 8: 'A father beats a boy, and in another place a boy-stealer caresses. If you were simply to name the two things: blows and caresses: who would not choose the caresses over the blows? Yet if you consider the

matter in terms of the acting subjects, it is charity that beats, and iniquity that caresses. Now see what we are insisting upon. The deeds of men are only discerned by the root of charity.'

22 Evelyn Waugh, *Brideshead Revisited* (Harmondsworth: Penguin, 2000), 324.
23 See *De civ. Dei*, XIV, 10: 'Their love of God was unclouded, and their mutual affection was that of faithful and sincere marriage. From this love there flowed a wonderful delight, because their enjoyment was to love what only there was to love. Their avoidance of sin was in this sense tranquil; and so long as it was maintained, no other ill at all could invade them and bring sorrow.'
24 *En. in Ps.*, LXX, 20.
25 *In Io. ev. tr.*, XLI, 10.
26 *Ibid.*, VII, 2.
27 Cf. C. G. Jung, *Answer to Job*, trans. R. F. C. Hull (London: Routledge and Kegan Paul, 1954), 178: 'Faith is certainly right when it impresses on man's mind and heart how infinitely far away and inaccessible God is; but it also teaches his nearness, his immediate presence, and it is just this nearness which has to be empirically real if it is not to lose all significance. Only that which acts upon me do I recognize as real and actual. But that which has no effect upon me might as well not exist. The religious need longs for wholeness, and therefore lays hold of the images of wholeness offered by the unconscious, which, independently of the conscious mind, rise up from the depths of our psychic nature.'
28 Cf. at this point Professor Sidgwick's venerable conclusion that '[the question whether] ... the movements in the particles of organized matter which we suppose to be inseparable concomitants of our ever-varying conscious states ... should be continued for a longer rather than a shorter period, is in itself quite indifferent to us ... [In fact] one's individual happiness is, in many respects, an unsatisfactory mark for one's supreme aim ... It does not possess the characteristics which, as Aristotle says, we "divine" to belong to Ultimate Good: being (so far, at least, as it can be empirically foreseen) so narrow and limited, of such necessarily brief duration, and so shifting and insecure while it lasts. But Universal Happiness, desirable consciousness or feeling for innumerable multitude of living beings, present and to come, seems an End that satisfies our imagination by its vastness, and sustains our resolution by its comparative security' (Henry Sidgwick, *The Methods of Ethics* (London: Macmillan, 1884), 395–401).
29 Friedrich Schleiermacher, *Monologen* (Leipzig: Verlag von Felix Meiner, 1914), 28.
30 *En. in Ps.*, CIX, 20.
31 *Ibid.*, LXX, 14.
32 Leo Tolstoy, *War and Peace*, trans. Rosemary Edmonds (Harmondsworth: Penguin, 1974), 1444.
33 *En. in Ps.*, XLVII, 2.
34 Benjamin Jowett, *Select Passages from the Introductions to Plato* (London: John Murray, 1904), 151.
35 *Serm.*, XCVIII, 6.
36 Peter S. Hawkins, 'Divide and conquer: Augustine in the Divine Comedy', *Proceedings of the Modern Language Association* 106, no. 3 (1991): 479–80.

Chapter 2

1. As Raymond H. Gettell explained it: 'In Roman thought the state did not absorb the individual, as in the theory of Plato, nor was the state considered non-essential, as in the teachings of the Epicureans. The Romans separated state and individual, each having definite rights and duties. The state was a necessary and natural framework for social existence; but the individual, rather than the state, was made the center of legal thought, and the protection of the rights of the individual was the main purpose for which the state existed.' (Raymond G. Gettell, *History of Political Thought* (London: George Allen & Unwin, 1932), 67).
2. John Burnet, 'Law and nature in Greek ethics', *International Journal of Ethics* 7, no. 3 (1897): 332.
3. See Polybius, *Histories*, XXXVI, 17.
4. Still the most stimulating and accessible introduction this idea is Numa Denis Fustel de Coulanges (with Forewords by Arnaldo Momigliano and S. C. Humphreys), *The Ancient City: A Study on the Religions, Laws, and Institutions of Greece and Rome* (Baltimore, MD: Johns Hopkins University Press, 1980).
5. Eusebius, 'Oration in honour of Constantine on the thirtieth anniversary of his reign', in Maurice Wiles and Mark Santer (eds), *Documents in Early Christian Thought* (Cambridge: Cambridge University Press, 1975), 231–4.
6. *En. in Ps.*, XLI, 1.
7. *De Trin.*, XIV, 12, 16.
8. A brief, rigorous and critical introduction to the theory of historicism is Karl R. Popper, *The Poverty of Historicism* (London: Routledge & Kegan Paul, 1961). See also the discussion in E. H. Carr, *What is History?* (Harmondsworth: Penguin, 1968), 87–108.
9. *Ep.*, CIV, 3, 11.
10. C. S. Lewis, *The Great Divorce* (London: HarperCollins, 2002), 141.
11. See Friedrich Nietzsche, *Twilight of the Idols/The Anti-Christ*, trans. R. J. Hollingdale (London: Penguin Books, 1990), 117.
12. For a short but detailed overview see G. W. H. Lampe, 'Christian theology in the Patristic period', in Hubert Cunliffe-Jones (ed.), *A History of Christian Doctrine* (London and New York: T&T Clark, 2006), 21–180. On the question of Augustine's use of Platonism see A. H. Armstrong, *Augustine and Christian Platonism* (Villanova: Villanova University Press, 1967); Gerard O'Daly, *Platonism Pagan and Christian: Studies in Plotinus and Augustine* (Aldershot: Ashgate, 2001); and Carol Harrison, *Beauty and Revelation in the Thought of St. Augustine* (London and New York: Oxford University Press, 2002).
13. See Numenius, Fragment 8.
14. Bertrand Russell, *The Problems of Philosophy* (London and New York: Oxford University Press, 1970), 75.
15. For more on the fascinating subject of intellectual speculation in the age before philosophy see F. M. Cornford, *From Religion to Philosophy: A Study in the Origins of Western Speculation* (Princeton, NJ: Princeton University Press, 1991). Cf. Henri Frankfort et al., *Before Philosophy: The Intellectual Adventure of Ancient Man* (Harmondsworth: Penguin, 1961).

16 Thomas More, *Utopia*, trans Paul Turner (Harmondsworth: Penguin, 1984), 126.
17 A. N. Whitehead, *Religion in the Making* (Cambridge: Cambridge University Press, 1927), 31.
18 G. S. Kirk and J. E. Raven, *The Presocratic Philosophers: A Critical History with a Selection of Texts* (London: Cambridge University Press, 1962), 203, fragment 229.
19 See, for instance, Bernard Bosanquet's remark that '[t]he [Greek] mind which can recognise itself practically in the order of the commonwealth, can recognise itself theoretically in the order of nature' (Bernard Bosanquet, *The Philosophical Theory of the State* (London: Macmillan, 1925), 5).
20 Lucretius, *De rerum natura*, III.
21 J. W. Dunne, *The Serial Universe* (London: Faber & Faber, 1934), 13.
22 G. S. Kirk and J. E. Raven, *The Presocratic Philosophers*, 95–6, fragment 95.
23 Hume's problem is set out in Part III of his *A Treatise of Human Nature*. Isaiah Berlin offers an excellent summary of it: 'When events of type A have been constantly observed without fail to be conjoined with events of type B, a habitual association is set up in the imagination so that whenever we observe a new A, the idea of B arises in the mind with an overwhelming force, this force being itself an introspectively observable feeling. This feeling of force we now illegitimately project into the external world, and imagine a "force" or "power" as pushing and pulling events or objects in the world' (Isaiah Berlin, *The Age of Enlightenment: The 18th Century Philosophers* (New York: Mentor Books, 1963), 188). Hume's point is that it is impossible to prove logical necessity between events in time. For another excellent summary of the problem see Karl Popper, *Objective Knowledge, An Evolutionary Approach* (Oxford: Oxford University Press, 1972), 3–4.
24 Julian Huxley, *Essays of a Biologist* (London: Chatto & Windus, 1923), 173.
25 Aristotle (tr. Richard Hope), *Metaphysics* (New York, Columbia University Press, 1983), 983*b*.
26 As the pre-Socratic philosopher Parmenides would make the case: 'Nor shall I allow thee to say or to think, "from that which is not" … Nor will the force of true belief allow that, beside what is, there could also arise anything from what is not; wherefore Justice looseth not her fetters to allow it to come into being or perish, but holdeth it fast' (G. S. Kirk and J. E. Raven, *The Presocratic Philosophers*, 273, fragment 347).
27 L. S. Stebbing, *A Modern Introduction to Logic* (London: Methuen, 1930), 404.
28 Some well-known modern thinkers who have come out in identifying this inclination as the prototype of all knowledge are Herbert Spencer, William James and R. G. Collingwood. From Spencer: 'intelligence progresses by acts of discrimination; and it continues so to progress among men, from the ignorant to the most cultured. To class rightly – to put in the same group things which are of essentially the same natures, and in other groups things of natures essentially different – is the fundamental condition to right guidance of actions' (Herbert Spencer, 'The new Toryism' in *The Man Versus the State, With Six Essays on Government, Society, and Freedom* (Indianapolis: Liberty Fund Inc., 1982), 11). James simply says that '[t]he first thing the intellect does with any object is to class it along with something else' (William James, *The Varieties of Religious Experience: A Study in Human Nature* (London: Longmans, Green & Co., 1913), 9). And Collingwood advances the idea by pointing out how, '[i]n studying the world of nature, we begin by

getting acquainted with the particular things and particular events that exist and go on there; then we proceed to understand them, by seeing how they fall into general types and how these general types are interrelated. These interrelations we call laws of nature; and it is by ascertaining such laws that we understand the things and events to which they apply' (R. G. Collingwood, *The Idea of History* (Oxford: The Clarendon Press, 1951), 205-6).
29 Kirk and Raven, *The Presocratic Philosophers*, 105-7, fragment 103.
30 G. K. Chesterton, *The Everlasting Man* (San Francisco: Ignatius Press, 1993), 38-9.
31 Alfred Tarski, 'Truth and proof' in Oswald Hanfling (ed.), *Fundamental Problems in Philosophy* (Oxford: Basil Blackwell, 1972), 287.
32 Plato, *Republic*, trans. Richard W. Sterling and William C. Scott (New York and London, W. W. Norton & Company, 1985), 344c. This argument is put forward by the protagonist Thrasymachus.
33 Plato, *Euthyphro*, trans. Benjamin Jowett (Oxford: The Clarendon Press, 1903), 17-18.
34 Aristotle could already state this confidently, as an item of common sense: 'Language serves to declare what is advantageous and what is the reverse, and it therefore serves to declare what is just and what is unjust. It is the peculiarity of man ... that he alone possesses a perception of good and evil, of the just and the unjust, and of other similar qualities; and it is association in [a common perception of these things] which makes a family and a polis' (Aristotle, *The Politics of Aristotle*, trans. Ernest Barker (Oxford: The Clarendon Press, 1960), 1253a).
35 See Plato's dialogue *Apology* for an account of his trial and execution.
36 W. E. H. Lecky, *History of the Rise and Spirit of Rationalism in Europe* (London: Longmans, Green & Co., 1910), xi.
37 Plato, *Laws*, trans. A. E. Taylor, X, 897.
38 Ibid., *Epistles*, VII, 341c.
39 Ibid., *Laws*, X, 903.
40 Ernst Troeltsch, 'Empiricism and Platonism in the philosophy of religion: to the memory of William James', *The Harvard Theological Review* 5, no. 4 (1912): 404.
41 Plato, *Republic*, 519e-520d.
42 Karl Popper is the most convincing exponent of the view that Plato is the first in the line of grand enemies of the 'open society'. See his *The Open Society and its Enemies* (London, Routledge & Kegan Paul, 1966).
43 Plotinus, *Enneads*, trans. E. R. Dodds, I, 2, 6.
44 Rom. 7: 18-19.
45 Ernest Barker, in his Introduction to John Healey's translation of the City of God (London: J. M. Dent & Sons, Ltd., 1931), xx.
46 In the words of Eduard Zeller: 'Stoic apathy, Epicurean self-contentment, and Sceptic imperturbability, were the doctrines which suited the political helplessness of the age' (Eduard Zeller, *The Stoics*, trans. Rev. Oswald J. Reichel, *Epicureans and Sceptics* (London: Longmans, Green & Co., 1880), 17).
47 It was Isaiah Berlin (1909-97) who first described the freedom of the ancients as 'positive'. In his famous paper 'Two concepts of Liberty', given as the inaugural lecture for the Chichele Chair of Social and Political theory at the University of Oxford,on 31 March 1958, he argued that the history of ideas has furnished two main conceptualizations of

'freedom' or 'liberty'. The first, 'positive liberty', is the more ancient. It is, Berlin explains, '... involved in the answer to the question "What, or who, is the source of control or interference that can determine someone to do, or be, this rather than that?"' The second, 'negative liberty', is more modern: for '... it is involved in the answer to the question "What is the area within which the subject – a person or group of persons – is or should be left to do or be what he is able to do or be, without interference by other persons?"' (Isaiah Berlin, 'Two concepts of liberty', in *Four Essays on Liberty* (London: Oxford University Press, 1969), 171).

48 Indicative of this change in the Graeco-Roman world was the enormous popularity of the 'associations'. These were voluntary members-only institutions, typically centred on a local god or common interest – or sometimes on both, as in the case of the wine-loving Dionysiasts. Their symbolic rôle, to the scholar, is analogous to that of the single-interest group in today's large Western states. For more on the ancient phenomenon see John S. Kloppenborg and Stephen G. Wilson (eds), *Voluntary Associations in the Graeco-Roman World* (London: Routledge, 1996).

49 See B. Hoellen and J. Laux, 'Antike Seelenführung und Kognitive Verhaltenstherapie im Vergleich', *Zeitschrift für Klinische Psychologie, Psychopathologie und Psychotherapie*, 38 (1988): 255–67.

50 Gilbert Murray, *Five Stages of Greek Religion* (Oxford: The Clarendon Press, 1925), 155.

51 Probably the outstanding example of this was the process by which the ancient Greek tendency to divinize human beings of exceptional merit passed into the Roman imperial cult. For more see S. R. F. Price, 'Gods and emperors: the Greek language of the Roman imperial cult', *Journal of Historical Studies*, 104 (1984): 79–95.

52 See, for instance, G. J. Szemler, 'Priesthoods and priestly careers in ancient Rome', *Aufstieg und Niedergang der Römischen Welt*, II/16.3 (1986): 2314–31. See also Mary Beard and John North (eds), *Pagan Priests: Religion and Power in the Ancient World* (London: Duckworth, 1990).

53 At *Confess.*, I, 16, 25–6. Augustine quotes Cicero's lamentation: 'Homer invented these things and assigned human attributes to the gods. I wish that he had rather given divine attributes to us' (Cicero, *Tusculan Disputations*, I, 26, 65). Cf. *De civ. Dei*, IV, 32. Juvenal was another who picked up on this detail: 'Fortune has no divinity, could we but see it: it's we,/We ourselves, who make her a goddess, and set her in the heavens' (Juvenal, *The Sixteen Satires*, trans. Peter Green (Harmondsworth: Penguin, 1967), X, 364–6, 217).

54 Symmachus, *Prefect and Emperor: The Relationes of Symmachus, A.D. 384*, trans. R. H. Barrow (Oxford: The Clarendon Press, 1973), 39.

55 The Edict of Milan, which was mentioned by us above as a formative document of Roman religious tolerance and equality, uses the language of the *Summa Divinitas* 'Supreme Godhead' – an indiscriminate reference to the type of Neoplatonic deity then popular in educated circles. There is an English translation of this edict with a brief commentary in Sidney Z. Ehler and John B. Morrall (eds), *Church and State through the Centuries* (London: Burns & Oates, 1954), 4–6.

56 Acts 17. 22–8.

57 T. R. Glover, *Paul of Tarsus* (London: Student Christian Movement, 1925), 22. Some general aspects of the difference in approach to the concept of 'god' in religion and

philosophy are covered in Charles Hartshorne, 'The god of religion and the god of philosophy', in G. N. A. Vesey (ed.), *Talk of God* (London: Macmillan & Co., 1970), 152–67.
58 This text in J. von Arnim, *Stoicorum Veterum Fragmenta* (New York: Irvington Publishers, 1986), vol. I, no. 537.
59 See Philo, *De Opificio Mundi*, L, 143.
60 Henry Drummond, *Natural Law in the Spiritual World* (London: Hodder & Stoughton, 1884), 6.
61 Marcus Aurelius, *The Meditations*, trans. G. M. A. Grube (New York: The Bobbs-Merrill Co. Inc., 1963), 84, n. 52.
62 *En. in ps.*, LVII:1.
63 *Ep.*, CCXLVI, 2. Cf. *In Io. ev. tr.*, 49:12; *Confess.*, III, 7 and 8; *Solil.*, II, 34 and 35.
64 His exact expression is 'the love of knowledge is a kind of madness' (C. S. Lewis, *Out of the Silent Planet* (London: HarperCollins, 2000), 53).
65 Seneca, *Epistulae Morales ad Lucilium*, trans. Robin Campbell (Harmondsworth: Penguin, 1969), LXV, 7, 120.
66 *De gr. Chr.*, XXIV, 28. Cf. *De corrept. et gr.*, XLI.
67 *Confess.*, IX, 10, 24.
68 *Ep.*, CXVIII, 3, 17. This letter, written to the young aspiring philosopher Dioscorus in 410, is an excellent summary of Augustine's thinking on the Western intellectual tradition. See also *Ep.*, CCXXXII, 6.

Chapter 3

1 See *Confess.*, XIII, 34, 49.
2 See *ibid.*, I, 8, 13.
3 *En. in Ps.*, XLIV, 23.
4 *Ep.*, X, 2.
5 *Serm.*, CXLV, 2.
6 See his study *Salvation in History*, trans. Sidney G. Sowers (London: SCM Press, 1967).
7 *De civ. Dei*, IV, 33. Cf. V, 21.
8 See R. A. Markus, *Saeculum: History and Society in the Theology of St. Augustine* (Cambridge: Cambridge University Press, 1988), 231.
9 *De mor. Eccl. cath.*, VII, 12.
10 *Confess.*, IV, 11, 16.
11 *De Cat. rud.*, VI, 10.
12 See *De civ. Dei*, XIV, 1: 'Now the kingdom of death so held men that all would have deserved to be driven headlong into that second death to which there is no end had God's unmerited Grace not redeemed some of them. Thus it is that all the many nations of the earth can be arranged under just two so-called orders of human society – this notwithstanding their different rites and customs, and their different forms of language, arms, and dress. What is more, if we follow our Scriptures, we may properly speak of these as two cities [Cf. Eph. 2.19; Phil. 3.20].' Cf. also his comments on Christian dress and manners

at ibid., XIX, 19: 'The Heavenly City is not disturbed by the dress or manner of those who hold to the faith that arrives at God; but only if these things do not contravene the Divine precepts. It is in this sense that philosophers who become Christians are required to change their false doctrines, though not their dress or customary mode of life ...'

13 *En. in ps.*, XXV, 5
14 *Serm.*, LII, 16. Cf. CVII, 5.
15 Charles G. Herbermann *et al.* (eds), *The Catholic Encyclopedia* (New York: The Encyclopedia Press, 1913), 94.
16 *Serm.*, LX, 2.
17 *Serm.*, X, 7, 10.
18 *De gr. et l. arb.*, XVII, 33.
19 See *Confess.*, X, 28, 39: 'Is not the life of man upon earth a trial, without any relief whatsoever?' Cf. *En in ps.*, CXIX, 17–20; *Serm.*, XLVII, 1; *Serm.*, XXIII(B), 12; *En. in ps.*, CXLVI, 4–5; *De civ. Dei*, XIX, 27.
20 See, for example, *In Io. ev. tr.*, X, 4: 'Love me, says God to you: favour with me is not had by making interest with some other, like with a patron: your love itself makes me present to you.'
21 *In Io. ev. tr.*, X, 40, 65.
22 *Confess.*, X, 26, 37.
23 *De fide r. quae n. v.*, II, 4.
24 *Ep.*, XLVII, 2.
25 *In Io. ev. tr.*, VIII, 2.
26 *En. in Ps.*, XLI, 7.
27 *Confess.*, XIII, 23, 34.
28 *Serm.*, CXIX, 3.
29 *En. in Ps.*, V, 6.
30 Michel de Montaigne, *Essays*, trans. Donald M. Frame (Stanford, CA: Stanford University Press, 1995), Bk. III, No. 4, 'Of diversion', 636.
31 See, for instance, E. R. Dodds, 'Augustine's Confessions: a study of spiritual maladjustment', *Hibbert Journal* no. 26 (1927–8): 459–73; and C. Klegemann, 'A Psychoanalytic study of the Confessions of St. Augustine', *Journal of the American Psychoanalytic Association* no. v (1957): 469–84.
32 At *Confess.*, II, 3, 5.
33 Augustine's father was a pagan by birth, but he seems to have tolerated his wife's Christianity very well and certainly allowed her to bring up their children as Christians. As he grew older he wavered, eventually making a full confession on his deathbed, as was then common.
34 These included a dream which convinced her to give up her boycott of her Manichee son and share his table (*Confess.*, III, 11, 19-20) and the prophecy of a bishop in the African Church (*Confess.*, III, 12, 21).
35 *Confess.*, I, 11, 17.
36 On the physical remains of Augustine's Africa see S. Gsell, *Les monuments antiques de l'Algerie* (Paris: A. Fontemoing, 1901). For more general information on the cities and province of Roman North Africa see C. Lepelley, *Les Cités de l'Afrique romaine au*

Bas-Empire, 2 vols (Paris: Études Augustiniennes, 1979 and 1981); and B. H. Warmington, *The North African Provinces from Diocletian to the Vandal Conquest* (Cambridge: Cambridge University Press, 1954).

37 *Serm.*, XXIIIB, 13.
38 See *Confess.*, VII, 7, 17.
39 See *Confess.*, VI, 11, 19. Cf. *Serm.*, CXXVIII, 8: 'Adultery has its pleasure. I confess that it has its pleasure.' And LXXX, 7: 'Temporal blessings include health, substance, honour, friends, a home, children, a wife, and all the other things of this life in which we are sojourners. We should put ourselves up in the "hostelry of this life" as travellers passing on, not as owners intending to remain.'
40 *En in Ps.*, LXX, 17.
41 Gen. 1.31.
42 *Confess.*, X, 34, 53.
43 *En. in Ps.*, XLI, 8.
44 This phrasing is from Percy Bysshe Shelley and his poem 'Ode to a skylark'. It would later be incorporated by George MacDonald into his own verse: 'The bliss of the animals lies in this, that, on their lower level, they shadow the bliss of those – few at any moment on earth – who do not "look before and after, and pine for what is not" but live in the holy carelessness of the eternal *now*' (quoted in C. S. Lewis (ed.), *George MacDonald: An Anthology: 365 Readings* (New York: Touchstone, 1990), reading 314, 130.
45 *De cath. rud.*, XVIII, 30. See also *De cont.*, VI, 16: 'God did not want to import to man the power not be able to sin, but chose rather to make him such that it should lie in his power to sin, if he would; not to sin, if he would not. The one forbidden, the other, enjoined. The reason being that it might be to him in his initial state a good and continuing desert not to sin. Then, when taken up into eternal life, a just reward not to be able to sin. For this, after all, is how He makes His Saints: as to be without all power to sin.'
46 The language of 'formation' is Augustine's. See, for example, *De Gen. ad litt.*, I, 9, 17. See also *Serm.*, LXVII, 8: 'Acknowledge then that you are not to yourself a light. At best you are but an eye, you are not the light. And what good is even an open and a sound eye, if the light is wanting?'
47 *Ad cat. de symb.*, I, 2. Cf. *Serm.*, LV, 3: 'You are stronger than the lion, in that which you were made after the image of God. What! Shall the image of God tame a wild beast; and shall not God tame His own image?'
48 For a general account of family life in late antiquity with particular reference to Augustine, see B. Shaw, 'The family in late antiquity: the experience of Augustine of Hippo', *Past and Present* no. 115 (1987): 3–51.
49 Augustine will describe his father as an '… inconsiderable burgher …' (*Confess.*, II, 3, 5); and elsewhere himself as '… a poor man, born of poor parents' (*Serm.*, CCCLVI, 13). Augustine's first biographer, his fellow bishop, Possidius, confirms that the family were *de numero curialium* 'of the ruling class' (Possidius, *Vita Sancta Augustini*, I). Augustine gives his own brief account of the term at *En. in Ps.*, CXXI, 7: 'For if we use the word *curies* in its proper sense, we understand nothing, save the *curies* which exist in each particular city, whence the terms *curiales* and *decuriones*, that is, the citizens of a *curia* or a *decuria*; and you know that each city has such *curies*. But there are, or were at one time, *curies* of

the people in those cities, and one city has many *curies*, as Rome has thirty-five *curies* of the people. These are called tribes.'
50 For a contemporary view on the rôle and duties of this class see Cicero, *Oratio pro Sestio*, IV, 10.
51 The *Codex Theodosianus* contains a number of decrees relating to African *Decuriones* and their creative attempts to escape their duties. Many were to flee into the desert to take up the monastic life.
52 As Brown points out in his *Poverty and Leadership in the Later Roman Empire* (Hanover: Brandeis University Press, 2002), 15: 'Impoverishment was what most ancient persons feared most for themselves. And with good reason. Impoverishment could come at any time, from any number of misfortunes … [Late Antique society] was a world of persons who considered themselves, and often with good reason, to be vulnerable to impoverishment.' Cf. *Serm.*, LXI, 11: 'How many are they who were rich yesterday, and are poor today? How many go to sleep rich, and through robbers coming and taking all away, wake up poor?'
53 *Ep.*, XXXIII, 5.
54 *Confess.*, II, 3, 6.
55 James E. Dittes, 'Continuities between the life and thought of Augustine', *Journal for the Scientific Study of Religion* 5, no. 1 (1965): 138.
56 Monica's devotion to the cause of her son's Christianity (and of course his recording of it) was to lead to her own sainthood as a paragon of Catholic womanhood. See, for example, Ian Holgate, 'The Cult of Saint Monica in Quattrocento Italy: Her Place in Augustinian Iconography, Devotion and Legend', *Papers of the British School at Rome* 71 (2003): 181–206.
57 H. I. Marrou thought that '[b]y a calculation of probabilities we are permitted to infer that Augustine was, without doubt, of pure Berber stock' (H. I. Marrou, *Saint Augustin et l'augustinisme* (Paris: Seuil, 1956), 11). Bonner's opinion was that '[i]t seems likely indeed that Augustine came of Berber stock, though his culture and outlook were thoroughly Roman' (Gerald Bonner, *St. Augustine of Hippo, Life and Controversies* (Norwich: The Canterbury Press, 1986), 21). See also Vernon J. Bourke's comments in his review article, 'Perler's Contribution to Augustine Biography', *Augustinian Studies*, vol. II (1971), 224–7. For Augustine's remark that his family spoke only Latin at home, see *Confess.*, I, 14, 23. For further discussion of Augustine's ethnic background see W. H. C. Frend, 'A Note on the Berber Background in the Life of Saint Augustine', *Journal of Theological Studies* xliii (1942): 188–91; Chr. Courtois, 'S. Augustin et la survivance de la punique', *RAf* 94 (1950), 239–82; M. Simon, 'Punique ou berbère?', *Annuaire de l'Inst. de Philol. et d'Histoire Orientales et Slaves* xiii (1955), 613–29 (*Recherches d'Histoire Judéo-Chrétienne*, 1962, 88–100); G. Charles-Picard, *La civilization de l'Afrique romaine* (Paris: Librairie Plon, 1959), 393–5; F. Vattioni, 'S. Agostino e la civiltà punica', *Aug* 8 (1968): 434–67.
58 John K. Ryan, 'Introduction', in his *The Confessions of St. Augustine* (New York: Doubleday, 1960), 18.
59 *Ep.*, CXXXVIII, 19.
60 *Confess.*, VIII, 6, 14.
61 *Ep.*, XVII, 2.

62 *Contra Faustum*, I, 1.
63 *Op. imp. c. Iul.*, II, 33.
64 Ibid., 1, 7; 6, 18.
65 *De ord.*, II, 17, 45.
66 Quintilian, *Institutio Oratoria*, trans. The Rev'd John Selby Watson (New York: The Bobbs-Merrill Co., 1965), Preface, 12. See also Laurie's comment that '... in all things – even in the study of Greek – there was a Roman practical aim, while in all subjects, save literature and what bore directly on the full understanding of the poets, the Roman was superficial and utilitarian. Might we not say, superficial *because* utilitarian?' (S. S. Laurie, *Historical Survey of Pre-Christian Education* (New York: Longmans, Green & Co., 1895), 340).
67 Augustine's experience of corporal punishment and his later coming to terms with it as a resident evil are well-known and noteworthy. For a situating of the general issues that it brings about from the theological and psychological points of view see Jaco Hamman, 'The rod of discipline: masochism, sadism, and the Judeo-Christian religion', *Journal of Religion and Health* 39, no. 4 (2000): 319–27.
68 See *Serm.*, LXXVIII, 1.
69 *Confess.*, III, 4, 7.
70 *Serm.*, LX, 3.
71 At *De civ. Dei*, XI, 27.
72 See Clifford Ando, *Imperial Ideology and Provincial Loyalty in the Roman Empire* (Berkeley, CA: University of California Press, 2000).
73 *En. in Ps.*, CXLVIII, 2.
74 See *De civitate Dei*, IV, 4. See also *Confess.*, X, 36, 59, where Augustine describes this combination of emotions as intrinsic to the intoxicating effect of power, and therefore to be regarded as one of the great temptations of life.
75 *De cons. Evang.*, IV, 10, 15.
76 Juvenal, *Sat.*, VII, 147-149.
77 *De doctr. Christ.*, IV, 3, 5.
78 Johann Gottfried Herder, 'Letters for the advancement of humanity', trans. David Williams, in David Williams (ed.) *The Enlightenment* (Cambridge: Cambridge University Press, 1999), 213.
79 *Ep.*, XVII, 2.
80 Peter Brown, *Augustine of Hippo* (Berkeley: University of California Press), 10. See also the observation of S. S. Laurie, that '... nothing is more certain than this in education, that the moment the vesture of thought becomes an object of worship – whether in the shape of word-cunning, elegance of style, or rules of rhetorical construction and rhythmical effect – the result must be decline and decay' (Laurie, *Historical Survey*, 392).
81 Robert Graves, *Count Belisarius* (Harmondsworth: Penguin, 1975).
82 *Serm.*, LXX, 2.

Chapter 4

1 See *Serm.*, LX, 2.

2   See Vladimir Nabokov, 'Scenes from the life of a double monster', in *Nabokov's Dozen* (Harmondsworth: Penguin, 1960), 124.
3   Sigmund Freud, 'The origin and development of psychoanalysis', *The American Journal of Psychology* XXI, no. 2 (1910): 181–218. Cf. Gordon W. Allport, *Personality: A Psychological Interpretation* (London: Constable & Co. Ltd., 1962), 493: 'Behind the manifestations of an individual's style stretches a whole life history, back to the cradle and his first departures from the schedule prepared for him and all other infants.'
4   Augustine gives his own comprehensive overview of Donatism in a letter to Count Boniface (*Ep.*, CLXXXV), written in 417. He also gives a short synopsis of his understanding of the cardinal error of the heresy at *Contra litt. Petil.*, I, 6, 7: 'It has to be that if man receive the sacrament of baptism from a faithful or a faithless minister, he puts his whole hope in Christ. If not, then he rightly falls under the condemnation that "Cursed be the man that trusteth in man." [Jer. 17.5]'
5   See *Serm.*, CXLVI, 2.
6   See *ibid.*, LXI, 2.
7   *De sp. et litt.*, XXV, 42.
8   Alexander Solzhenitsyn, *Cancer Ward* (Harmondsworth: Penguin, 1972), 476.
9   *De bapt.*, I, 15, 23.
10 *Confess.*, I, 6, 7.
11 *Solil.*, II, 20, 36.
12 *De civ. Dei*, XXI, 14.
13 *Confess.*, I, 6, 10.
14 *De Trin.*, XI, 1, 1.
15 *Confess.*, I, 6, 10.
16 Cf. *En. in Ps.*, LXV, 10: 'Every one that is born must give place to one going to be born: and all this order of things rolling along is a kind of river.' It is worth also reproducing A. J. Carlyle's historical summary of the situation: 'The regulations of society ought to be just, and yet we are constantly compelled to amend them. Their claim to the obedience of man is founded upon the fact that they represent justice, and yet they are never in the complete sense of the word just. The perplexity with regard to the past found a solution for many centuries in the theory of a change in the condition of human nature, in the judgement that principles of perfect justice which were adapted to a condition of perfect innocence cannot well be adapted to a condition of vice and perfection. In the eighteenth century, when many thinkers understood very imperfectly the social significance of the faultiness of human nature, the difficulty resulted in the revolutionary bias given to the conception of the return to nature. Gradually men have turned back to the conception of perfect justice as belonging to the future, as being the ideal towards which the institutions of society tend, the principle which governs their development; but the difficulties of the actual condition have not therefore been completely solved.' (Sir R. W. and A. J. Carlyle, *A History of Mediaeval Political Theory in the West*, vol. I (Edinburgh and London: William Blackwood & Sons, 1962), 61–2).
17 *In. Io. ev. tr.*, VI, 25.
18 *De civ. Dei*, I, 11.
19 Cicero, *De off.*, I, 4.

20 *Serm.*, CXXIV, 2.
21 *Ibid.*, CVIII, 3.
22 See Bertrand Russell, *A History of Western Philosophy* (London: George Allen & Unwin, 1946), 374: 'I do not myself agree with this theory, in so far as it makes time something mental. But it is clearly a very able theory, deserving to be seriously considered. I should go further, and say that it is a great advance on anything to be found on the subject in Greek philosophy. It contains a better and clearer statement than Kant's of the subjective theory of time – a theory which, since Kant, has been widely accepted among philosophers.'
23 *De civ. Dei*, XI, 6; cf. XII, 16.
24 *De civ. Dei*, XI, 6.
25 *Confess.*, IV, 10, 15.
26 *Ibid.*, XI, 11, 13.
27 *Confess.*, XI, 14, 17.
28 *Ibid.*, 15, 19.
29 *Serm.*, IV, 8, 13.
30 William James, *The Principles of Psychology*, vol. 1 (New York: Cosimo, 2007), 609.
31 *Confess.*, XI, 15, 20.
32 *Ibid.*, 19, 25.
33 The phrase 'I am here' was suggested to me by the title of Christopher Potter's excellent short history of the universe – Christopher Potter, *You are Here: A Portable History of the Universe* (London and New York: Windmill Books, 2010).
34 *Confess.*, XI, 27, 36.
35 *De civ. Dei*, XI, 21. Cf. *En. in Ps.*, LXXXIX, 15.
36 R. W. Dyson was the first to notice that, in this sense, all Augustine's remarks on time can be arranged for study under two heads. On the one hand, there is the dogmatic realism of his insistence that time is a legitimate creation of God. Then on the other, there is his analysis of time as (no more than) an extension of the priorities of the human mind. See R. W. Dyson, 'St. Augustine's Remarks on Time', *The Downside Review* (July 1982): 221–31. It is also possible to bring out this feature of Augustine's thought by seeing four, rather than two, idioms at work in his remarks on time. See, for example, J. M. Quinn, 'Four faces of time in St. Augustine', *Recherches Augustiniennes* 26 (1992): 181–231; and supplement this with J. F. Callahan, *Four Views of Time in Ancient Philosophy* (Cambridge, MA: Harvard University Press, 1948). For additional perspectives see L. Boros, 'Les categories de la temporalité chez saint Augustin', *Archives de Philosophie* 35 (1958): 323–85; R. J. Teske, 'The world-soul and time in Saint Augustine', *Augustinian Studies* 14 (1983): 75–92; K. Flasch, *Was ist Zeit? Augustinus von Hippo. Das XI. Buch der Confessiones: Text, Ubersetzung, Kommentar* (Frankfurt am Main: Vittorio Klostermann, 1993); and Catherine Rau, 'Theories of time in ancient philosophy', *The Philosophical Review* 4 (1953): 514–25.
37 *En. in Ps.*, CXLIII, 11.
38 *Confess.*, I, 6, 10.
39 *Ibid.*, I, 6, 7.
40 See *ibid.*: 'For all my salvation comes from You, my God. This was something I afterwards

observed when once You had cried out to me by means of those many things which You bestowed on me both inwardly and outwardly.'

41 *Confess.*, I, 16, 26. Cf. *En. in Ps.*, CIV, 26, where Augustine describes the 'variety of speech' as *medentem fastidio*, 'remedy for weariness'. One of his most considered statements of his position in this matter comes at *De doctr. Christ.*, IV. As Joseph Anthony Mazzeo explained it, '… that book not only brought rhetoric back to its ancient concern for truth by recreating a platonic view of rhetoric in the midst of IVth-century sophistic, but it also became the final statement of St. Augustine's view of the relations of rhetoric to Christianity by expressing a profound adaption of the language of rhetoric to his metaphysics and theology. The nature and uses of signs became strictly related to the realities to be sought (discovery) and to their formulation (statement), so that the use of the arts of language is utterly dependent on the structure of reality, a relationship with which no other classical rhetorician other than Plato had been concerned' (Joseph Anthony Mazzeo, 'St. Augustine's rhetoric of silence', *Journal of the History of Ideas* 23, no. 2 (1962): 176. For a more recent discussion of the cultural legacy of Book IV see John D. Schaeffer, 'The dialectic of orality and literacy: the case of book 4 of Augustine's De doctrina christiana', *Publications of the Modern Languages Association* 111, no. 5 (1996): 1133–45.

42 *De fide et s.*, II, 4. Cf. *De Trin.*, VIII, 6: 'And when indeed I wish to speak of Carthage, I refer myself internally to the image of what I wish to speak; but of course, this is an image that I have received through the body, that is, through the perception of the body, since I have been present in that city in the body, and saw and perceived it, and retained it in my memory. For its word is the image it has made in my memory – not just the sound of its two syllables when Carthage is named, or even when that name is thought of silently, but what I actually discern in my mind when I utter that dissyllable with my voice. What I apprehend even before I utter it.'

43 Ludwig Wittgenstein, *The Blue and Brown Books: Preliminary Studies for Philosophical Investigations* (Oxford: Blackwell, 1978), Brown Book, I, 77. For a recent elaboration of this aspect of Wittgenstein's criticism of Augustine see Keith Dromm, 'Wittgenstein on language-learning', *History of Philosophy Quarterly* 23, no. 1 (2006): 79–94.

44 *Confess.*, I, 8, 13.

45 *De util. cred.*, I, 1, 1.

46 *Serm.*, CVII, 3.

47 Gerard Watson picks up on this in his article, 'St. Augustine's theory of language', *The Maynooth Review* 6, no. 2 (1982): 4-20. He cities Eugenio Coseriu as mentioning this in his history of the philosophy of language (Eugenio Coseriu, *Die Geschichte der Sprachphilosophie von der Antike bis zur Gegenwart*, vol. 1 (Tübingen: Tübinger Beitrage zur Linguistik, 1975), 123); and goes on to list the omission of Augustine from Steinthal (H. Steinthal, *Geschichte der Sprachwissenschaft bei den Griechen und Römern*, 2 vols (Berlin: F. Dümmler, 1890–1)), Lersch (L. Lersch, *Die Sprachphilosophie der Alten*, 3 vols (Bonn: H. B. König, 1838) and Bochenski (J. M. Bochenski, *Ancient Formal Logic* (Amsterdam: North Holland, 1951).

48 *Serm.*, CVII, 17.

49 *De cont.*, VII, 17.

50 *Serm.*, LXXV, 1, 1.
51 *Ibid.*, XCII, 7, 9.
52 *De lib. arb.*, III, 24. Cf. *De pecc. mer. et rem.*, II, 35, 21: 'They therefore served God, because that dutiful obedience was committed to them by which God can alone be worshipped.'
53 *De pecc. mer. et rem.*, I, 25, 37.
54 Cf. *In Io. ev. tr.*, XII, 14.
55 Cf. *Serm.*, CXLI, 4: 'And so you will find men who live well but are not Christians. However, though they run well, they do not actually in the Way. And in fact, the more they run, the more they go astray; because they are out of the Way. But if such men as these come to the Way, and hold on to the Way, how great will be their security, because they will both walk well, and not go astray!'
56 Richard Roberts, 'The war and the doctrine of sin', *The Biblical World* 52, no. 3 (1918): 283–4.
57 *Serm.*, CXXXVI, 1.
58 *En. in Ps.*, L, 10.
59 As Augustine concedes at *Ep.*, CLXXX, 2: 'The really difficult question is this: If it is true that a new soul created out of nothing is imparted to each child at birth, how can it be that the innumerable souls of those little ones (in regard to whom God knew with certainty that before attaining the age of reason, and before being able to know or understand what is right or wrong, were to leave the body without being baptized) are justly given over to eternal death by Him with whom there is no unrighteousness! [Cf. Rom. 9.14]'
60 At *De serm. Dom. in m.*, XXIII, 78, Augustine reinforces his conviction that the prerequisites of true freedom and eternal life are a return to the presence of God: 'And hence the apostolic teaching gives the name of adoption to the process by which we are called to an eternal inheritance, that we may be joint-heirs with Christ [see Rom. 8.17]. We are made sons by a spiritual regeneration; and therefore we are adopted into the kingdom of God, not as aliens, but as being made and created by Him. As such, it is one thing that He brought us into being through His omnipotence, when before we were nothing. It is quite another that He now offers to adopt us, so that, as being sons, we might enjoy along with Him eternal life for our participation. In effect, then, He does not say, "Do those things because you are sons;" but, "Do those things, that you may be sons."'
61 *De pecc. mer. et rem.*, I, 17, 22.
62 *Confess.*, I, 7, 11.
63 *In Io. ev. tr.*, VII, 23.
64 *De Trin.*, XIV, 5, 7.
65 *Confess.*, I, 8, 13.
66 Christopher Kirwan, *Augustine: The Arguments of the Philosophers* (London and New York: Routledge, 2009), 35.
67 Therese Fuhrer, 'Augustinus: Ein Autor im interdisziplinären Focus. Zur Rolle der Klassischen Philologie im Dialog mit Philosophie und Theologie', in J. P. Schwindt (ed.), *Klassische Philologie inter disciplinas. Aktuelle Konzepte zu Gegenstand und Methode* eines *Grundlagenfachs* (Heidelberg: Walter de Gruyter, 2002), 169–85.
68 This work has been published as Karla Pollmann, Willemien Otten *et al.* (eds), *The Oxford Guide to the Historical Reception of Augustine* (London and New York: Oxford University

Press, forthcoming), in 4 volumes. It should be consulted as a superb resource for many of the subjects covered in this book. As Editor-in-Chief, Pollmann has brought together 400 international scholars, writing the 600 contextualized articles that form the core of its contribution.

69 The idea to use the concept of 'vacuum' in this way came to me in a conversation with Dr Ernesto Paparazzo, of the Istituto di Struttura della Materia del CNR, Area della Ricerca di Roma. I am grateful to him for forwarding me his paper on this subject, in which he corrects some longstanding assumptions about the ancient philosophers' understanding of vacuum. See Ernesto Paparazzo, 'Vacuum: a void full of questions', *Surface and Interface Analysis* 40 (2008): 450–3.
70 *In Io. Ev. tr.*, XXXIX, 4.
71 See *De civ. Dei*, II, 7: 'The philosophies are not the commandments of the gods, but the discoveries of men, who, at the prompting of their own speculative ability, made efforts to discover the hidden laws of nature, and the right and wrong in ethics. And in dialectic what was consequent according to the rules of logic, and what was inconsequent and erroneous. And some of them, by God's help, were to make great discoveries; but when left to themselves they were betrayed, in the end, by human infirmity, and fell into mistakes. And this was ordered by divine providence, that their pride might be restrained, and that by their example it might be pointed out that it is humility alone which has access to the highest regions.'
72 *Serm.*, LXXV, 2, 2.
73 *Ep.*, CXXXVII, 2, 8. Cf. *De cura pro mort.*, XVI, 19: 'The limits of human things are one matter, the signs of divine virtue another. In the same way is there a difference between things done naturally and those done miraculously. And yet it is truly said that nature is continuously sustained by God, and miracles are themselves only a special arrangement of nature.'

Chapter 5

1 *Confess.*, II, 3, 6.
2 *Ibid.*
3 *Confess.*, II, 6, 13.
4 *De gr. Chr.*, II, 38, 43.
5 *Confess.*, II, 6, 14.
6 *En. in Ps.*, CXXXIX, 13.
7 *Ibid.*, LXXXII, 11.
8 *Confess.*, II, 2, 2.
9 *Ibid.*, II, 1, 1.
10 *Ibid.*, II, 2, 4.
11 *Serm.*, IX, 12.
12 *Confess.*, II, 3, 6.
13 *De doctr. Christ.*, IV, 3, 4.
14 *Confess.*, II, 3, 5.

15 *Confess.*, I, 9, 14.
16 *Ibid.*, I, 12, 19.
17 *Ibid.*, I, 14, 23.
18 See, for example, *In Io. ev. tr.* LXXVII, 5: 'But when the Lord proceeded to say, "Not as the world giveth, give I unto you, [John 14.27]" what else does He mean but, "Not as those give who love the world, give I unto you?" For in the earthly city, peace is referred always to the exemption from the annoyance of lawsuits and wars; it is devised for the enjoyment, not of God, but of the friendship of the world. And although this arrangement works within its own terms of reference, and the righteous peace are no longer persecuted, there can be no true peace where there is no real harmony. And in such a city, however outwardly fine, there is no real harmony when all hearts are privately and variance and the proof of this is that each goes as far as possible to do what he will.'
19 Cf. *Serm.*, CXLI, 4: 'Far better is it to halt in the way, than to walk on confidently outside the way.'
20 *En. in Ps.*, LXIV, 6.
21 *Confess.*, I, 18, 29.
22 See, for example, how Augustine expresses this thought in the following metaphor, used to comfort a Christian mother, Italica, during the Visigoth siege of Rome in 409: '... they discern even in their present tender age how dangerous and baneful is the love of this world. God grant that the plants which are small and still flexible may be bent in the right direction in a time in which the great and hardy are being shaken' (*Ep.*, XCIX, 3).
23 F. Scott Fitzgerald, *The Beautiful and Damned* (Harmondsworth: Penguin Books, 1983), 335–6.
24 *De civ. Dei*, III, 14.
25 *Confess.*, I, 9, 14.
26 *Ibid.*, I, 18, 28.
27 *Ibid.*, I, 18, 29. Cf. *En. in Ps.*, XXX, 16: 'In Your power are my lots. For I see no desert for which out of the universal ungodliness of the human race You have elected me particularly to salvation. And though there be with You some just and secret order in my election, yet I, from whom this is hid, have attained by lot unto my Lord's vesture [see John 19.24].'
28 See especially *De praed. sanct.*, III, 7: 'It was ... thus that that pious and humble teacher thought – I speak of the most blessed Cyprian – when he said that, 'we must boast in nothing, since nothing is our own' [*Testimonia ad Quirinum*, III, 4]. And in order to show this, he appealed to the apostle as a witness, where he said, 'For who maketh thee to differ *from another*? And what hast thou that thou didst not receive?' [1 Cor. 4.7]. And it was chiefly by this testimony that I myself also was convinced when I was in a similar error; when I thought that the faith whereby we believe in God is not God's gift, but rather something in us, and from us; and that it is by this thing innate that we go on to obtain the gifts of God – the gifts by which we may live temperately and righteously and piously in this world. For I did not think that the plain act of faith [for all its bareness and decision] was such that it could be preceded by God's Grace ... And this my error is sufficiently indicated in some small works of mine written before my episcopate.'
29 This thesis has a particular association with the striking *Time* magazine cover of April 8,

1966, which boldly emblazoned the question 'Is God Dead?' in stark red lettering over a plain black background. It was prompted by the work of radical Protestant theologians such as Thomas J. J. Altizer, William Hamilton and Paul M. Van Buren, and their assertions that modern theology must bite the bullet and embrace the fact that in so far as God seems wholly dependent upon the human belief in Him for His existence, He must accept the basic human right to recast Him and bring Him up to date. See Thomas J. J. Altizer and William Hamilton, *Radical Theology and the Death of God* (Harmondsworth: Penguin, 1968); and Paul M. Van Buren, *Theological Explorations* (London: SCM Press, 1968). See also the poignant article by Clarence Augustine Beckwith, written in 1911, on the outlook for theology in light of developments in psychology. It ends with this statement: 'One wonders at times whether psychology will eliminate religion altogether – to say nothing of God.' (Clarence Augustine Beckwith, 'The influence of psychology upon theology', *The American Journal of Theology* 15, no. 2 (1911): 204).
30 *Solil.*, I, 5.
31 *Confess.*, II, 3, 7.
32 *Ibid.*, II, 2, 4.
33 *Ibid.*, I, 12, 19. Cf. *De civ. Dei*, XXI, 12: 'But eternal punishment seems hard and unjust to human perceptions, because in the weakness of our mortal condition there is wanting that highest and purest wisdom by which it can be perceived how great a wickedness was committed in that first transgression.'
34 *De mor. Eccl. cath.*, I, 7, 11.
35 Gen. 3.1.
36 *Serm.*, LXXV, 7, 8.
37 *F. invis.*, I, 1.
38 *Serm.*, XCI, 3, 3.
39 These quotations are from *Serm.*, XCI, 4, 4. Cf. Also what he has to say at *Ep.*, XXII, 2, 8: '... the man who has not declared war against this enemy has no idea of its power.' And *En in Ps.*, IX, 23: 'For the mind conscious of evil, but suffering itself no immediate punishment for that evil, believes that God does not judge. And so are God's judgments taken away from its face.'
40 *Contra litt. Petil.*, I, 29, 31.
41 Goulven Madec has coined the phrase 'evil genius of Europe' to describe how Augustine is often resorted to when an explanation for the enduring complex about sin is sought. He writes in his defence at G. Madec, 'Saint Augustin est-il le malin génie de L'Europe?' *Petites Études augustiniennes* (Paris: Institut D'Études Augustiniennes, 1994), 319–30.
42 *Ep.*, XIX, 1.
43 *Confess.*, II, 4, 9.
44 *Ibid.*, II, 6, 14.
45 *Ibid.*, II, 8, 16.
46 *Ibid.*, II, 9, 17.
47 See *ibid.*, II, 10, 18.
48 On his battles with the Greek language see *Confess.*, I, 13, 20; 14, 23.
49 *De fide et s.*, V, 19.
50 Juvenal, *Saturae*, XV.

51 At *Confess.*, I, 16, 26, Augustine distinguishes between the instrument of language – a noble and splendid thing, perfectly adapted to the sociable nature of man – and the attitude of his teachers who treated it as '… that wine of error which through them was offered to us … Unless we drank it, we were flogged, and we had no freedom of appeal to any sober judge. Yet, O God, in Whose sight I now safely recall this, in my wretchedness I willingly learned these things and took delight in them. For this I was called a boy of great promise.'
52 Tacitus, *dial.*, XXX.
53 *Confess.*, IV, 12, 18. See also *De civ. Dei*, XVIII, 47.
54 *Ep.*, CI, 2.
55 *Ibid.*, XXVII, 2.
56 *In Io. ev. tr.*, VIII, 1.
57 *En. in Ps.*, XXX, 8.
58 *In Io. ev. tr.*, XIV, 6.
59 C. S. Lewis, *The Abolition of Man* (New York: HarperCollins, 2001), 43–4.
60 Karl Popper, *The Open Society and its Enemies*, vol. 2 (London: Routledge & Kegan Paul, 1963), 270.
61 *Ibid.*, 272.
62 *De nat. et gr.*, I, 6, 6.
63 *En. in Ps.*, LXXXV, 24.
64 See Sigmund Freud, 'Difficulties and first approaches,' in *Introductory Lectures on Psychoanalysis*, vol. 1 (Harmondsworth: Penguin, 1976), 117: 'I put myself to sleep by withdrawing from the external world and keeping its stimuli away from me. I also go to sleep when I am fatigued by it … The biological purpose of sleep seems therefore to be rehabilitation, and its psychological characteristics suspense of interest in the world. Our relation to the world, into which we have come so unwillingly, seems to involve our not being able to tolerate it uninterruptedly. Thus from time to time we withdraw into the premundane state, into existence in the womb. At any rate, we arrange conditions for ourselves very like what they were then: warm, dark and free from stimuli … The world, it seems, does not possess even those of us who are adults completely, but only up to two-thirds; one-third of us is still quite unborn.'
65 See *Confess.*, VII, 5, 12 for Augustine's own use of this metaphor: 'Thus by the burdens of this world I was sweetly weighed down, just as a man often is in sleep. Thoughts wherein I meditated upon You were like the efforts of those who want to arouse themselves but, still overcome by deep drowsiness, sink back again.' Augustine will go on to use this metaphor on a number of occasions. See *Contra Acad.*, I, I, 3: 'That part of you, then … which has somehow been lulled to sleep in you by the drowsy lethargy of this life, providence, working in secret, has decided to rouse in secret by means of the several harsh buffetings which you have suffered.' Then cf. also *De b. vita*, 35; *Solil.*, I, 2; and *Ep.*, I, 2. It is probable that Augustine first encountered this metaphor in the Bible. See 1 Cor. 15.34; 1 Thess. 5.6; 1 Pet. 5.8.
66 *Confess.*, I, 19, 30.

Chapter 6

1. See *Confess.*, V, 13, 23.
2. See *ibid.*
3. The New Academy, or Third Academy as it was officially known, was one of three main post-Aristotelian schools to emerge during the Hellenistic period. The other two were Stoicism and Epicureanism. Archesilaus (b. c. 315 BC) is taken to be the originator of the school, which was recognized to be in the line of the Platonism of the original Academy – most especially, of course, its scepticism of sense impression and the material world. However, it is Carneades (b. c. 213 BC) a century later who did most to systemize the school's doctrines. Consequently, he is often credited by the ancients with being the founder of the school (see, for example, Sextus Empiricus, *Pyrrh.*, I, 220; Lucian, *Macrob.*, XX; Eusebius, *Pr. Ev.*, XIV, 7, 12). Augustine seems to have known this school of thought mainly through Cicero and his dialogue *Academica*. Scepticism's historical stand seems always to have been against the philosopher's reliance on the device of special illumination, or moral imperative. The wise man should consider the arbitrary and historically determinate character of all human principles of right, and guard his assent accordingly.
4. *C. Acad.*, I, 1, 2.
5. Historians of ideas often talk in terms of the following distinction between the ancient and the medieval–modern rationalization of knowledge. Ancient thinkers tended to respect a dichotomy of 'things' and the words that attach to them and carry their essence into the comprehending mind as ideas. From Anselm and Abelard onwards (late eleventh century), a trichotomy emerged. Things still translated into words, but now was added the category of 'meanings'. Words have, and create, meaning – and it is this meaning that the mind actually comprehends. See, for example, F. Edward Cranz, 'Quintilian as ancient thinker', *Rhetorica: A Journal of the History of Rhetoric* 13, no. 3 (1995): 219–30.
6. See especially Peter Brown, *Augustine of Hippo* (Berkeley: University of California Press), 54–61.
7. *En. in Ps.*, XLIV, 17.
8. *De mor. Eccl. cath.*, I, 3, 4.
9. *Ep.*, CXVIII, 3, 13.
10. Cf. *En. in Ps.*, LXXXV, 7.
11. *En. in Ps.*, LXXXV, 7.
12. *Ep.*, CXLV, 2.
13. *Serm.*, LXXV, 5, 6.
14. *De civ. Dei*, XIV, 7.
15. There is inevitably a question as to whether Augustine had homosexual relations during these pre-Christian days. It is a legitimate question to ask, given the mores of his times and the sincerities of his personality. But it seems that on the balance of evidence he did not. For the full argument that reaches this conclusion see Alan G. Soble, 'Correcting some misconceptions about Augustine's sex life', *Journal of the History of Sexuality* 11, no. 4 (2002): 545–69.
16. *Confess.*, III, 1, 1.

17 Apuleius, *Florida*, XX.
18 *Confess.*, III, 1, 1.
19 *De Trin.*, IX, 2, 2.
20 *Confess.*, III, 8, 16.
21 *Ibid.*, III, 1, 1.
22 *Ibid.*, III, 8, 16.
23 Evelyn Waugh, *Brideshead Revisited* (Harmondsworth: Penguin, 2000), 77.
24 *Confess.*, III, 3, 5.
25 Jaroslav Pelikan and Helmut T. Lehman (eds), *Luther's Works: American Edition* (Philadelphia: Fortress Press, 1957–75), 336–8.
26 *Ep.*, CCX, 2.
27 *Ibid.*, XXXVIII, 2.
28 *Confess.*, III, 3, 5.
29 G. A. Studdert Kennedy, from his poem 'Dead and buried'.
30 *Confess.*, III, 2, 4.
31 *Ep.*, XXIII, 2.
32 See, for instance, *De mon.*, XX: 'For who knows not that each does the more quickly profit when he reads good things, the quicker he is in doing what he reads?'
33 *De un. bapt. c. Petil.*, I, 14, 15.
34 A. E. Housman, 'The stars have not dealt me the worst they could do', in *The Collected Poems of A. E. Housman* (London: Jonathan Cape, 1967), 152.
35 Both these quotations from *Confess.*, III, 3, 6.
36 See *ibid.*, III, 3, 6.
37 *De civ. Dei*, III, 1.
38 *En in Ps.*, LVII, 16.
39 Augustine gives a succinct definition of his 'negative' or 'privation' theory of evil at *De Gen. ad litt.*, VIII, 14, 31: 'Evil is not a substance: the loss of the good is what we call evil. God is the unchangeable Good; man, in what belongs to the nature in which God has created him, is indeed a good, but not unchangeable good as God is. A changeable good, which is inferior to the unchangeable Good, becomes a greater good when it adheres to the unchangeable Good, loving and serving Him with a rational and free response of the will.' See also *De lib. arb.*, III, 1, 1.
40 Erich Fromm, *The Fear of Freedom* (London: Kegan Paul, Trench, Trubner & Co., 1945), 27–8.
41 Ernst Cassirer, *The Myth of the State* (New Haven and London: Yale University Press, 1963), 288.
42 *De Trin.*, X, 1, 3.
43 *Confess.*, III, 11, 19.
44 *De civ. Dei*, XIV, 4.
45 See, for example, *En in Ps.*, CXXXVI, 4: 'But then other citizens of the holy Jerusalem ... observe how the natural wishes and the various lusts of men hurry and drag them hither and thither, and drive them into the sea. This they see – but seeing it they do not throw themselves into the waters of Babylon, but sit down and weep ...' And *Ep.*, XLVIII, 2: 'As men must keep the way carefully in walking

between fire and water, so as to be neither burned nor drowned, so must we order our steps between the pinnacle of pride and the whirlpool of indolence ...' Augustine will actually use this imagery of Scylla and Charybdis against the Sabellians at *In Io. ev. tr.*, XXXVI, 9.

46 *Confess.*, III, 3, 6. Cf. *En in Ps.*, V, 12: '... with lying and blind flattery men draw to themselves those whom they entice to sin; and in this sense they devour them, when they turn them to their own way of living. And when this happens to them (since by sin they are devoured), those by whom they are led along are rightly called open sepulchres: for they are themselves in a manner, lifeless, being destitute of the life of truth; and they take in to themselves dead men, whom they have slain by lying words and a vain heart.' And LXXII, 18: 'They desire to play a fraud upon mankind in all their naughtiness. Yet they themselves are victims of the first fraud: for they have chosen earthly good things, and forsaken the eternal.'
47 *De pat.*, IV, 4.
48 *Confess.*, X, 36, 59.
49 *Ibid.*, II, 5, 11.
50 Fyodor Dostoyevsky, *The Idiot*, trans. David Magarshack (Harmondsworth: Penguin, 1967), 47–8.
51 John McTaggart, *Some Dogmas of Religion* (London: Edward Arnold, 1906), 292.
52 *En. In Ps.*, VII, 1. Cf. *De Cat. rud.*, XIV.
53 For more on this dialogue see M. Ruch, *L'Hortensius de Cicéron: Histoire et reconstitution* (Paris: Les Belles Lettres, 1958); L. Straume-Zimmermann, F. Broemser and O. Gignon (eds and trans), *Marcus Tullius Cicero: Hortensius, Lucullus, Academici libri*, Sammlung Tusculum (Munich: Artemis, 1990); and M. Testard, *Saint Augustin at Cicéron*, 2 vols (Paris: Études Augustiniennes, 1958).
54 *Confess.*, III, 4, 7.
55 A thorough examination of how the immediate effects of the *Hortensius* might have run out into Augustine's life is still John Hammond Taylor, 'St. Augustine and the "Hortensius" of Cicero', *Studies in Philology* 60, no. 3 (1963): 487–98.
56 *Ep.*, XXIII, 4.
57 *Ibid.*, CXVIII, 4, 26.
58 Democritus, Fragment 593, in Kirk and Raven, *The Presocratic Philosophers*, p. 424.
59 *Serm.*, XVI (A), 11.
60 *In Io. ev. tr.*, X, 5.
61 *Ep.*, CCLXIII, 4.
62 *Confess.*, III, 5, 9.
63 Greek manuscripts of the full Biblical canon would have been available in Augustine's day, but we have already noted his difficulties in acquiring the Greek language as a schoolboy. In any case, he has left no suggestion that he ever had access to one of these complete sets. A systematic and critical attempt to reconstruct the 'Bible' that Augustine worked from is A.-M. La Bonnardière, *Biblia Augustiniana* (Turnhout: Brepols, 1967–75). See also La Bonnardière's *Saint Augustin et la Bible* (Paris: Editions Beauchesne, 1986).
64 *De cath. rud.*, II, 3.
65 Cicero, *De officiis*, I, 4.

66 See, for example, *De cath. rud.*, II, 4; *De Trin.*, VIII, 16; *En. in Ps.*, XC(B), 13; XXXV, 14; and *Confess.*, XII, 13, 16.
67 Edmund Husserl, *Ideas: General Introduction to Pure Phenomenology*, trans. W. R. Boyce Bibson (London: George Allen & Unwin, 1931), 183.
68 *Confess.*, XI, 11, 13.
69 The phenomenologist's manifesto, as expressed by Husserl, is that '[g]enuine science, and the genuine absence of bias which inwardly distinguishes it, demands as the foundation of all proofs judgements which as such are immediately valid, drawing their validity directly from *primordial data intuitions*' (Husserl, *Ideas*, p. 83).
70 *Ep.*, XIX, 1.
71 *Ibid.*, XV, 2. Cf. *Ep.*, I, 2: 'Now, however, such is the indisposition to strenuous exertion, and the indifference to the liberal arts, that so soon as it is noised abroad that, in the opinion of the most acute philosophers, truth is unattainable, men send their minds to sleep, and cover them up for ever.'

Chapter 7

1 Peter Brown, *Augustine of Hippo* (Berkeley: University of California Press), 35.
2 Gerald Bonner, *St. Augustine of Hippo, Life and Controversies* (Norwich: The Canterbury Press, 1986), 157.
3 David Hume, *Dialogues Concerning Natural Religion* (Harmondsworth: Penguin, 1990), 121.
4 *Confess.*, III, 6, 10.
5 *Ibid.*, III, 6, 10.
6 See, for example, *Confess.*, V, 3, 3–6: 'As I had already read many doctrines of the philosophers and retained them in my memory, I compared some of them with the long fables of the Manichees. And I found much more probable the words of the philosophers ... These words said by these philosophers concerning the truths of Your material creation, I checked over and found proofs of – whether by mathematical calculations, the orderly succession of the seasons, or the visible testimony of the stars. Certainly, when I compared them with Mani, who in the course of his ravings had written prodigiously about these things, I found no explanations of solstices, equinoxes, or the eclipse of the greater lights. Nothing, in fact, as I had learnt with such profit from those books of natural philosophy.
7 See *Confess.*, V, 3, 3.
8 *Contra ep. Man.*, XXII, 15 – XXVIII, 31. Augustine confirms that this *Letter of the Foundation* was addressed by Mani to a man called Patticus (a transliteration of Pattik), a fellow believer, who needed to be assured on the precise nature of the generation of Adam and Eve according to his religion (see *Contra ep. Man.*, XII, 14). The most accessible introduction to the fundamentals of Manichaeism is probably that given by Bonner in his biography of Augustine (Bonner, *St. Augustine of Hippo*, pp. 157–92). See also Peter Brown, *Religion and Society in the Age of Augustine* (London: Faber, 1972), 94–118. There is now an extensive literature on this religion, which is garnering greater appreciation as

scholarship moves away from its negative image of old. John Kevin Coyle, *Manichaeism and its Legacy* (Leiden: Brill, 2009); L. J. R. Ort, *Mani: A Religio-Historical Description of his Personality* (Leiden: Brill, 1967; Nicholas J. Baker-Brian, *Manichaeism: An Ancient Faith Rediscovered* (London and New York: T&T Clark, 2011); G. Widengren, *Mani and Manichaeism* (New York: Rinehart & Winston, 1965); R. Cameron and A. J. Dewey, *The Cologne Mani Codex* (P. Colon. inv. nr. 4780) *'Concerning the Origin of his Body'*, Texts and Translations 15; Early Christian Literature 3 (Missuola: Scholars Press, 1979); Iain Gardner and N. C. Lieu (eds), *Manichaean Texts from the Roman Empire* (Cambridge: Cambridge University Press, 2004); F. Decret, *Aspects du manichéisme dans l'Afrique romaine. Les controverses de Fortunatus, Faustus et Félix avec saint Augustin* (Paris: Études Augustiniennes, 1970) and *Mani et la tradition manichéenne*, Maîtres Spirituels 40 (Paris: Éditions du Seuil, 1974); S. Giversen, 'Recent studies in Manichaeism: a general view,' in M. Rassart-Debergh and J. Ries (eds), *Actes du IVe Congrès Copte, Louvain-la-Neuve, 5-10 septembre 1988*, Publications de l'Institut Orientaliste de Louvain 41 (Louvain-la-Neuve: Institut Orientaliste de l'Université Catholique de Louvain, 1992), 265–76; H.-C. Puech, *Le manichéisme, son fondateur, sa doctrine*, Bibliotèque de Diffusion 56 (Paris: Musée Guimet, 1949); F. C. Burkitt, *The Religion of the Manichees: Donnellan Lectures for 1924* (Cambridge: The University Press, 1925); Jason David BeDuhn (ed.), *New Light on Manichaeism: Papers from the Sixth International Congress on Manichaeism* (Leiden: Brill, 2009); Johannes van Oort, Otto Wermelinger and Gregor Wurst (eds), *Augustine and Manichaeism in the Latin West: Proceedings of the Fribourg-Utrecht International Symposium of the International Association of Manichaean Studies* (Leiden and Boston: Brill, 2001).

9 *In Io. ev. tr.*, I, 14.
10 *Contra ep. Man.*, XI, 12.
11 *De util. cred.*, XIII.
12 J. W. Dunne, *The Serial Universe* (London: Faber & Faber, 1934), 235–6.
13 *En. in Ps.*, V, 11.
14 *Serm.*, LXVIII, 7.
15 *Confess.*, V, 5, 8.
16 *Ibid.*, IV, 28-30.
17 *De civ. Dei*, II, 1.
18 *Confess.*, III, 6, 10.
19 Aristotle (trans Gerald F. Else), *Poetics*, 60a1.
20 Karl R. Popper, *Conjectures and Refutations: The Growth of Scientific Knowledge* (London: Routledge & Kegan Paul, 1969), 34–5. A more nuanced view begins with A. A. Derksen's point that, '… like a pseudo-czar pretends to be a czar, the pseudo-scientist often pretends to be, and often aims to be, a scientist. Small wonder that at least at the surface … attempts to distinguish science from pseudo-science by means of such … features as respect for empirical evidence and falsifiability failed.' See his paper, 'The seven sins of pseudo-science', *Journal for General Philosophy of Science/Zeitschrift für allgemeine Wissenschaftstheorie* 24, no. 1 (1993): 17–42. This quotation occurs on p. 19. For a direct and illuminating refutation of Popper on the case of Psychoanalysis see Adolf Grünbaum, 'Is Psychoanalysis a pseudo-science? Karl Popper versus Sigmund Freud', *Zeitschrift für*

philosophische Forschung 31, no. 3 (1977): 333–53; and, 'Is psychoanalysis a pseudo-science? (II)', *Zeitschrift für philosophische Forschung* 32, no. 1 (1978): 46–69.
21 *Confess.*, III, 10, 18.
22 *Ibid.*, VIII, 10, 24.
23 *En. in Ps.*, XXX, 14.
24 Blaise Pascal, *Pensées*, VI, 393.
25 *Nat. b.*, XIV.
26 *Confess.*, IV, 1, 1.

Chapter 8

1   *Serm.*, LXVIII, 2.
2   See, for instance, *De nat. boni*, XLVI and *De haer.*, XLVI. Augustine will always claim that he did not witness anything of this nature while a Manichee. On this, see *Contra Fort.*, III.
3   For the account of Monica's dream and this quotation see *Confess.*, III, 11–12.
4   *Ibid.*, IV, 4, 7.
5   *Ibid.*, IV, 4, 8.
6   *Ibid.*, IV, 2, 2.
7   *Ibid.*, VI, 15, 25.
8   Jostein Gaarder, *Vita Brevis: Floria Aemilia's Letter to Aurel Augustine* (London: Phoenix, 1998).
9   Edith Wharton, *The House of Mirth*, Elizabeth Ammons (ed.) (New York: W. W. Norton & Company, 1990), 126.
10 *Ep.*, XCV, 2.
11 See *Solil.*, I, 4.
12 *Confess.*, IV, 1, 1.
13 *Ibid.*, IV, 12, 19.
14 *En. in Ps.*, XXXV, 3.
15 *Ep.*, CII, 14.
16 *In Io. ev. tr.*, XXXIII, 8. See also *En. in Ps.*, LXX, 1: 'Every sinner and unjust man, who is already despairing of himself, and thus already having the mind of a gladiator, so as to do whatsoever he wills, because he must needs be condemned. Well, every such man may yet observe the Apostle Paul, to whom so much was forgiven by God.'
17 *En. in Ps.*, CXLV, 9.
18 *Ibid.*, LXXXV, 8.
19 *Confess.*, IV, 7, 12.
20 *Ibid.*, IV, 8, 13.
21 See, for instance, *De util. cred.*, III, 9: 'There is nothing more deadly than that whatever is there be understood to the letter, that is, to the word: and nothing more healthful than that it be unveiled in the Spirit.'
22 *De lib. arb.*, III, 69.
23 Cf. *In Io. ep.*, IX, 1: 'We like not the sluggish [pigros], because for the languid [languentibus] ones we are afraid.' And also *En. in Ps.*, LXXXV, 24: 'Now we fight against ourselves

... we carry about a house of sleep, this flesh of ours [*geramus domum somni carnem istam*].'
24 *Confess.*, III, 8, 16.
25 *De Trin.*, XX, 7, 10.
26 *Ep.*, XVIII, 2.
27 *De bon. con.*, XVII, 20.
28 Cf. the following from Thomas Aquinas' *Summa Theologica* (trans. Fathers of the English Dominican Province; rev. Daniel J. Sullivan), I, qq. 20, art. 2: 'A lover is placed outside himself and made to pass into the object of his love in so far as he wills good to the beloved, and works for that good by his forethought even as he works for his own.'
29 William Styron, *Sophie's Choice* (New York: Random House, 1979), 426.
30 *De Gen. ad litt.*, IX, 18, 34.
31 See *De ord.*, II, 4, 12: 'What is more terrible than the hangman? What is more cruel and fearsome than his mind? Yet he holds a necessary place among the laws themselves, and he is always inserted into the order of the well-governed city. He may well think himself hurtful in his mind; yet, by the appointment of another, he is the penalty of evildoers.'
32 See *De civ. Dei*, XIX, 6: 'But though we may acquit the judge of any personal malice, we must none the less condemn human life as miserable. And if he is compelled to torture the innocent because his office and his ignorance constrain him, is he a happy as well as a guiltless man? It would surely be a more balanced judgement, and more in keeping with human dignity, if he were to admit at once that the necessity of acting thus is a wretched one for him.'
33 *De op. mon.*, XL.
34 Mary Wollstonecraft, 'The wrongs of woman, vol. 2,' in Gary Kelly (ed.) *Mary and the Wrongs of Woman* (Oxford and New York: Oxford University Press, 1980), 172.
35 *Serm.*, CXXXII, 3.
36 *De gr. et l. arb.*, XL, 19.
37 *En. in Ps.*, XVIII, 11.
38 *Ibid.*, CXIII(II), 11.
39 D. H. Lawrence, *Women in Love* (Harmondsworth: Penguin, 1981), 538–9.
40 *En. in Ps.*, LXXXIII, 8.
41 See *De civ. Dei*, XX, 30.
42 *De Trin.*, XIII, 1, 3.
43 *De civ. Dei*, XX, 21.
44 *In Io. ev. tr.*, III, 2.
45 Kirk & Raven, *The Presocratic Philosophers*, Fragment 288.
46 *Div. qq. ad Simpl.*, II, 3. Cf. Steven Goldberg, *The Inevitability of Patriarchy* (London: Temple Smith, 1977), 193–4: 'Nature has bestowed on women the biological abilities and psychophysiological propensities that enable the species to sustain itself. Men must forever stand at the periphery, questing after the surrogate powers, creativity, and meaning that nature has not seen fit to make innate functions of *their* physiology ... What is lacking in the male is an acceptance that radiates from all women save those few who are driven to deny their greatest source of strength. Perhaps this female wisdom comes from resignation to the reality of male dominance; more likely it is a harmonic of the

woman's knowledge that ultimately she is the one who matters. As a result, while there are more brilliant men than brilliant women and more powerful men than powerful women, there are more good women than good men. Women are not dependent on male brilliance for their deepest sources of strength, but men are dependent on female strength. Few women have been ruined by men; female endurance survives. Many men, however, have been destroyed by women who did not understand, or did not care to understand, male fragility."

47 *Ep.*, CCXI, 10.
48 *Confess.*, II, 5, 10.
49 *De s. virg.*, XXX, 30. Augustine's formal works on this subject are *De bono coniugali* (401); *De sancta virginitate* (401); *De bono viduitatis* (413); *De coniugis adulterinis* (419); *De nuptiis et concupiscentia* (419). For more on the main issues arising out of the question of Christian marriage in Augustine's day see G. H. Joyce, *Christian Marriage: An Historical and Doctrinal Study*, 2nd edn (London: Sheed & Ward, 1948); P. L. Reynolds, *Marriage in the Western Church: The Christianization of Marriage during the Patristic and Early Medieval Periods* (Leiden: Brill, 1994); A. H. Curtis, 'Marriage in the Bible and the early Christian Church', *Expository Times* 59 (1947): 12–79; É. Schmitt, *Le marriage chrétien dans l'oeuvre de saint Augustin* (Paris, Études Augustiniennes, 1983); David G. Hunter (ed.), *Marriage in the Early Church* (Eugene, OR: Wipf & Stock Publishers, 2001); *Marriage, Celibacy, and Heresy in Ancient Christianity: The Jovinianist Controversy* (Oxford: Oxford University Press, 2009); P. Brown, 'Sexuality and society in the fifth-century A.D.', in E. Gabba (ed.) *Tria corda: Scritti in onore di Arnaldo Momigliano* (Como: Edizioni New Press, 1983), 49–70; *The Body and Society: Men, Women and Sexual Renunciation in Early Christianity* (New York: Columbia University Press, 1988). The secondary literature on Augustine's treatment of these issues is very comprehensive. See especially M.-F. Berrouard, 'Saint Augustin et l'indissolubilité du marriage. Evolution de sa pensée', *Recherches Augustiniennes* 5 (1968): 139–55; G. Bonner, '*Libido* and *Concupiscentia* in St. Augustine', *Studia Patristica* 6/*Texte und Untersuchungen zur Geschichte der altchristliche Literatur* (1962), 303–14; N. Cipriani, 'Una teoria neoplatonica alla base dell'etica sessuale di S. Agostino,' *Augustinianum* 14 (1974): 351–61; E. Clark, '"Adam's only companion": Augustine and the early Christian debate on marriage', *Recherches Augustiniennes* 21 (1986): 139–62; 'Vitiated seeds and holy vessels: Augustine's Manichean past' and 'Heresy, asceticism, Adam and Eve: interpretations of Genesis 1–3 in the later Latin fathers', in *Ascetic Piety and Women's Faith: Essays in Late Ancient Christianity* (Lewiston/Queennston: Edwin Mellen Press, 1986), 291–349 and 353–85; *St. Augustine on Marriage and Sexuality* (Washington, D.C.: Catholic University of America Press, 1996); D. G. Hunter, 'Augustinian pessimism? A new look at Augustine's teaching on sex, marriage and celibacy', *AS* 25 (1994): 153–77; D. F. Kelly, 'Sexuality and concupiscence in Augustine', in *Annual of the Society of Christian Ethics* (Dallas: Society of Christian Ethics, 1983): 81–116; E. Scalco, 'Sacramentum connubii et institution nuptial. Une lecture du *De bono coniugali* et du *De sancta virginitate* de saint Augustin', *Ephemerides Theologicae Lovanienses* 69 (1993): 27–47; F.-J. Thonnard, 'La morale conjugale selon saint Augustin', *Revue des Études Augustiniennes* 15 (1969): 113–31.
50 *De fide r. quae n. v.*, VIII, 11.

51 *De Trin.*, II, 8, 14.
52 A. Martin and O. Primavesi, *L'empédocle de Strasbourg* (P. Strasb. Gr. Inv. 1665-6). *Introduction, Édition, Commentaire* (Berlin and New York: Walter de Gruyter, 1998), *a*(ii) 18-30.
53 Thomas Hobbes, *Leviathan* (Harmondsworth, Penguin, 1968), IV, 46.
54 *En. in Ps.*, XLI, 13.
55 *Ep.*, CIV, 3.
56 *Contra Faustum*, XXV, 2.
57 See *De civ. Dei*, XX, 21.
58 *Serm.*, CXL, 6.
59 *En. in Ps.*, IX, 29.
60 Michael Oakeshott, 'Rational conduct', in *Rationalism in Politics and Other Essays* (London: Methuen & Co., Ltd., 1967), 105.
61 *Confess.*, IV, 7, 12.
62 *De civ. Dei*, II, 4.
63 *En. in Ps.*, LXI, 17.
64 See *Ep.*, CCXII, 1.
65 Václav Havel, 'Politics and conscience', in Jan Vladislav (ed.) *Václav Havel: or Living in Truth* (London: Faber & Faber, 1990), 142.
66 *De Trin.*, XII, 9, 14.
67 See *Ep.*, CCXII, 1.
68 *En. in Ps.*, CXIX, 6.
69 *Ibid.*, LXXXV, 7.
70 The reference to the 'unmoved mover' is to Aristotle, and his conclusion that time and change are derivatives, presupposing an eternal primary being itself un-acted upon, but enacting time and change in a way that shows that its very nature as a principle, 'is to be in act.' (Aristotle, *Metaphysics*, trans. Richard Hope, 1071*b*).
71 *Confess.*, IV, 8, 13.
72 Olaf Stapledon, 'Mr Bertrand Russell's ethical beliefs', *International Journal of Ethics* 37, no. 4 (1927): 390–402.
73 Friedrich Nietzsche, *The Gay Science*, trans. Walter Arnold Kaufmann (New York: Vantage Books, 1974), Aph. 2.
74 Aristotle, *Politics*, trans. Sir Ernest Barker, 1253*a*.
75 *De Trin.*, IV, 1.
76 W. H. Auden, 'Balaam and his ass', in *The Dyer's Hand and other Essays* (London: Faber & Faber, 1987), 116.
77 *Confess.*, IV, 7, 12.
78 *De Cat. rud.*, X, 15.
79 *En. in Ps.*, LXXIX, 2.
80 *De civ. Dei*, XV, 16.
81 *Serm.*, CXLV, 3.
82 See *De Gen. ad litt.*, XII, 15, 31: 'For who, when he speaks about the subject of carnal intercourse in even the most scholarly and studious manner is able to refrain from thinking and twitching about the subject? And of course this gets taken to another degree

in sleep. For when the image that arises in the thoughts of the speaker becomes so vivid in the dream of the sleeper that it is indistinguishable from actual intercourse, it immediately moves the flesh and the natural result follows. But the essential point to grasp is that this happens without sin; just as when the matter is spoken of without sin by a man wide awake, who doubtless thinks about it in order to speak of it.'

83 *De Gen. ad litt.*, VI, 12, 22.
84 Hans MacKowsky, 'Michelangelo's first sculpture', *The Burlington Magazine for Connoisseurs* 53, no. 307 (1928): 170.
85 *Ench.*, LXXXVIII.
86 George Santayana, *The Life of Reason* (London: Constable & Co., Ltd., 1954), 93.
87 *De bono con.*, XV, 17.
88 Michel Foucault, *The History of Sexuality*, trans. Robert Hurley. Vol. 1 (Harmondsworth: Penguin, 1990), 159.
89 *De civ. Dei*, XIV, 24.
90 As in the case of what Augustine calls 'criminal and sordid loves' [*flagitiosis et sordidis amoribus*] at *De Cat. rud.*, IV, 7: 'We see how those who desire to be loved in return make it their special and absorbing business, by whatever means they find to be within their power, to advertise the strength of the love which they themselves bear. And they go worse than this. They affect to put forward an appearance of justice in whatever it is they are offering; and this leads to the situation where they can actually believe that their demands are being made in all fairness to those souls whom they are laboring to beguile.'
91 See, for example, *De civ. Dei*, I, 25: 'If that lustful disobedience, which still dwells in our mortal members, follows its own law irrespective of our will, then surely its motions in the body of one who rebels against them are as blameless as its motions in the body of one who sleeps.'
92 *De civ. Dei*, XIV, 20.
93 *De bono vid.*, VIII, 11.
94 *De civ. Dei*, XIV, 16.
95 H. H. Price, *Perception* (London: Methuen & Co. Ltd., 1950), 178–80.
96 *Ep.*, LXXXII, 13.
97 *Ibid.*, XXXVI, 14, 32.
98 John Rawls, *A Theory of Justice* (London: Oxford University Press, 1973), 587.
99 *Confess.*, IV, 9, 14 and 11, 16–17.

Chapter 9

1 *En. in Ps.*, XI, 9, 9.
2 *De cat. ad symb.*, VIII. Cf. *Serm.*, CXL, 1; *In Io. ev. tr.*, VIII, 10.
3 *Confess.*, III, 9, 17. See also *En. in Ps.*, XI, 9, 9: '"The ungodly walk in a circle round about," [see Ps. 12.8] that is, in their desire of things temporal, which revolves as a wheel in a repeated circle of seven days; and therefore they do not arrive at the eighth, that is, at eternity.' And *De mon.*, XL: 'With cunning craftiness and machinations the enemy both whirl themselves round and in their whirling strive to make the minds of the weak whirl.

For the weak cohere to them, so (in a manner) spin round with them – and so join them in the mad not knowing of where they are.'

4   Plotinus (tr. Stephen MacKenna and B. S. Page), *Enneads*, I, 2, 7.
5   *En. in Ps.*, XLI, 6.
6   *Ibid.*, XVIII, 3.
7   *De Trin.*, IX, 4, 4.
8   *Serm.*, CXVI, 1.
9   *Confess.*, X, 28, 39.
10 *In. Io. ev. tr.*, CXXIV, 5.
11 R. G. Collingwood, *Religion and Philosophy* (London: Macmillan & Co., Ltd., 1916), 126.
12 Immanuel Kant, *Immanuel Kant's Critique of Pure Reason*, trans. Norman Kemp Smith (London: Macmillan & Co., 1964), 639.
13 *Confess.*, V, 8, 14.
14 *Ibid.*
15 *Ibid.*, V, 8, 15.
16 *Ibid.*, V, 12, 22.
17 *Ibid.*
18 D. M. Mackinnon, F. Waismann and W. C. Kneale, 'Symposium: verifiability', *Proceedings of the Aristotelian Society, Supplementary Volumes* 19, Analysis and Metaphysics (1945): 150.
19 *Confess.*, V, 10, 19.
20 *Ibid.*, V, 13, 23.
21 *Ibid.*, V, 7, 12.
22 *Ibid.*, V, 13, 23.
23 For the wider historical background to this see Roland J. Teske, 'Spirituality: a key concept in Augustine's thought', *Revista Portuguesa de Filosophia* 64, Fasc. 1, Filosofia e Espiritualidade: O Contributo da Idade Média/Philosophy and Spirituality in the Middle Ages (2008): 53–71.
24 *Confess.*, V, 10, 20.
25 Ambrose, *De mysteriis*, XV.
26 *Serm.*, LV, 5.
27 *Confess.*, V, 13, 23.
28 *Ibid.*, VI, 3, 3.
29 *Ibid.*, VII, 9, 13.
30 *Ibid.*, VI, 4, 5.
31 *Ibid.*, VI, 11, 18.
32 Abraham Cowley, from his poem 'Life'.
33 Aldous Huxley, 'Heaven and Hell', in *The Doors of Perception and Heaven and Hell* (Harmondsworth: Penguin, 1971), 110.
34 John Campbell Shairp, 'Friendship in ancient poetry', *The North American Review* 139, no. 336 (1884): 455.
35 See James Joyce, *Ulysses*, 574.
36 *Confess.*, VII, 7, 11.
37 *En. in Ps.*, CIX, 17.

38 This quotation from his *Culture and Value*, eds H. G. Von Wright and H. Nyman; trans. P. Winch (Oxford: Blackwell, 1980), 17.
39 *En. in Ps.*, XIII, 4.
40 *Ibid.*, LXX(II), 9.
41 *Confess.*, IV, 13, 20.
42 *Ibid.*, IV, 15, 24.
43 *Ibid.*
44 *Ibid.*
45 *Contra Prisc. et Orig.*, VIII, 9, 11.
46 *Confess.*, IV, 15, 24.
47 *En. in Ps.*, XLVII, 14.
48 Renford Bambrough, 'A proof of the objectivity of morals,' *The American Journal of Jurisprudence* 14 (1969): 39.
49 *De civ. Dei*, XIV, 23.
50 *En in Ps.*, XII, 2. On the way that this 'anarchic Truth' is interpreted in literary theory, according to Mikhail Bakhtin's concept of the 'monological', see Eugene Vance, 'The functions and limits of autobiography in Augustine's "Confessions"', *Poetics Today* 5, no. 2 *The Construction of Reality in Fiction* (1984): 399–409.
51 Frantz Fanon, *The Wretched of the Earth*, trans. Constance Farrington (Harmondsworth: Penguin Books, 1961), 253.
52 Gilbert Ryle, 'Feelings', in William Elton (ed.), *Aesthetics and Language* (Oxford: Basil Blackwell, 1967), 70.
53 Nikolai Gogol, *Dead Souls*, trans. David Magarshack (Harmondsworth: Penguin, 1987), 141. Incidentally, Augustine suffered terribly from haemorrhoids during his life. See his *Ep.*, XXXVIII, 1.
54 *Confess.*, VI, 6, 9.
55 *Serm.*, LXII, 15.
56 *Ibid.*, LXXVIII, 2.
57 *Confess.*, XIII, 1, 1.
58 *Serm.*, LXII, 15. Cf. *De lib. arb.*, III, 10, 29: 'Timid, as a result of his consciousness of his mortality, fearing sufferings and death from the vilest, most abject, even the most minute of beasts, and uncertain of the future …'
59 *Confess.*, IV, 13, 20.
60 *De civ. Dei*, XXII, 29.
61 Flotte's statement is recorded by C. Raymond Beazley, in his *A Notebook of Mediaeval History* (Oxford: The Clarendon Press, 1917), 159.
62 Gottfried Wilhelm Leibniz, *Die philosophischen Schriften*, 7 vols, C. I. Gerhardt (ed.), trans. Bertrand Russell (Berlin: Weidmannsche Buchhandlung, 1875–90), IV, 512.
63 *En. in. Ps.*, XVIII, 11.
64 Anthony Burgess, *1985* (London: Arrow Books, 1985), 57.
65 *Confess.*, VIII, 5, 12.
66 Ambrose, *Ep.*, LXIII, 97–8.
67 *Confess.*, V, 8, 15.
68 *Ep.*, CLI, 10.

69 *Confess.*, V, 9, 17.
70 *Ibid.*, VI, 1, 1.
71 *Ibid.*, VI, 6, 10.
72 A good deal is known about Alypius, though entirely through Augustine's writings. For full references see A. Sizoo, 'The year of Alypius' birth', *Vigiliae Christianae* 2, no. 2 (1948): 106–8.
73 A detailed study of this man exists; see John V. Gavigan, 'St. Augustine's friend Nebridius', *The Catholic Historical Review* 32, no. 1 (1946): 47–58.
74 *Confess.*, VI, 10, 17.
75 *Ibid.*, VI, 10, 16.
76 *Ibid.*, VI, 7, 11.
77 *Ibid.*, VI, 1, 1.
78 Relatively, in the sense that Christology in the fourth century took in every twist and turn of the pressing question of what to do with the Kingdom of Christ in a world in which religion had long served the ambition of politics. For a thorough overview see George Huntston Williams, 'Christology and church-state relations in the fourth century', *Church History* 20, no. 3 (1951): 3–33 (part 1); and 'Christology and church-state relations in the fourth century', *Church History* 20, no. 4 (1951): 3–26 (part 2). See also the landmark new critical edition of Augustine's *De Trinitate* by Giovanni Catapano & Beatrice Cillerai: which attests to the increasing attention now turning to how and why Augustine can handle the mystery of the Trinity so fluently (Giovanni Catapano & Beatrice Cillerai, *Agostino: La Trinità* (Milan: Bompiani, 2012).
79 See *Confess.*, VIII, 6, 14.
80 C. H. Dodd, *The Founder of Christianity* (London: Collins, 1971), 36.
81 *Serm.*, CXXX, 4.
82 Plotinus, *Enneads*, (trans Stephen MacKenna and B. S. Page), I, 2, 7.
83 Edmund Burke, *Thoughts on the Prospect of a Regicide Peace: In a Series of Letters* (London: J. Owen, 1796), no. 1, vol. 5: 331.
84 See Rom. 12.2.
85 *De pat.*, XIV.
86 *De civ. Dei*, XX, 29.
87 *En. in Ps.*, LVIII, 18.
88 Baruch Spinoza, *Tractatus de intellectus emendation*, trans. R. H. M. Elwes, X, 77.
89 *De civ. Dei*, XIII, 7.
90 *Confess.*, X, 43, 69.
91 *Ep.*, XCII, 3.
92 *Confess.*, XIII, 22, 32.
93 Julian of Norwich, *Revelations of Divine Love*, trans. Clifton Wolters (Harmondsworth: Penguin, 1978), 206.
94 *De doctr. Christ.*, IV, 20.
95 Cicero, *Tusculanae quaestiones*, IV, 23.
96 *Confess.*, VIII, 8, 19.
97 *Ibid.*, VI, 14, 24.
98 *Ibid.*

99 Jean-Jacques Rousseau, *Du contrat social, ou principes du droit politique* (Paris: Éditions Garnier Frères, 1962), 244.
100 *Confess.*, VII, 17, 23.
101 *Ibid.*, VI, 14, 24.
102 *Ibid.*, VIII, 12, 30.
103 Anthony Trollope, *The Belton Estate* (Harmondsworth: Penguin, 1993), 368.
104 *Confess.*, VI, 13, 23.
105 This challenge seems to be enjoying renewed recognition today as the West is forced to defend its favourite but problematic concept of 'selfhood' – a concept that, to other traditions, can appear indulgent and needlessly prurient. On this challenge and its definition in these terms see especially the 2011 special edition of the *Journal of Religion* 1, no. 91, entitled: 'Special issue: the Augustinian moment'. From the Preface by Editor, Willemien Otten: 'Augustine has been at the center of a host of recent studies and developments, all of which show that despite the secularization of Western culture, there is a significant expansion, rather than reduction, of his role. From a major Latin church father he has developed into an enduring intellectual patriarch and epistemological mainstay of the West. As a result, his works and reception have a different fate than other patristic writings, as they remain actively and widely discussed in a variety of scholarly fields, both inside and outside the sphere of Christianity' (p. 1). See also Dom David Knowles's classic assessment: '[He] is that marvellous personality ... at once a type and yet intensely individual, that illuminates every page and seems so often to be as it were our own mind and soul alone with God ...' (Dom David Knowles, *The Evolution of Medieval Thought*, 2nd edn (London and New York: Longman, 1988), 31).
106 As Margaret R. Miles has stated it: '... Augustine was not just any fourth-century person; *his* compelling insights, more than those of any other leader of the early centuries of the Christian Church, have formulated the ideas of self and world, God and the Church, that structure Western consciousness, whether our relation to this inherited worldview is one of acceptance or resistance' (Margaret R. Miles, 'Infancy, parenting, and nourishment in Augustine's "Confessions"', *Journal of the American Academy of Religion* 50, no. 3 (1982): 351.
107 See how Paul B. Maves put out the call for research on this subject in his 1963 paper, 'Conversion: a behavioural category', *Review of Religious Research* 5, no. 1 (1963): 41–8. These 'mainstream washings' are described by Wendy Doniger O'Flaherty towards the end of her exploration of the power of mythic thought to make sense to us in spite of the standard coordinates of reality: 'So we are stripped down to our naked myths, the bare bones of human experience. They are ... a means of flying so low, so close to the ground of the human heart, that they can scuttle underneath the devastating radar of the physical and social sciences ... For now that we have been challenged to relax our stranglehold on inherited Enlightenment maps of reality on this side of the mouth of God, we may be able to make use of mythic maps that chart a very different kind of enlightenment on the other side' (Wendy Doniger O'Flaherty, 'Inside and outside the mouth of God: the boundary between myth and reality', *Daedalus* 109, no. 2, Intellect and Imagination: The Limits and Presuppositions of Intellectual Inquiry (1980): 121.

108 John R. Everett, *Religion in Human Experience: An Introduction* (London: George Allen & Unwin, 1952), 42–3.
109 This effect is now generally conceived as the 'prominence of Augustine's own person' in his accounts of his life – and by extension therefore also of his theology. The imputation is of a mild cult of personality that he did little to discourage. The offence is against the ambition of a more sanitized Western tradition. See Lyell Asher, 'The dangerous fruit of Augustine's "Confessions"', *Journal of the American Academy of Religion* 66, no. 2 (1998): 227–55.
110 Virginia Woolf, *Orlando* (London: Penguin, 1942), 10.
111 See, for example, Rein Nauta, 'The prodigal son: some psychological aspects of Augustine's conversion to Christianity', *Journal of Religion and Health* 47, no. 1 (2008): 75–87; F. Bolgiani, *La Conversion de S. Agostino e l'VIII libro delle Confessioni* (Turin: 1956); T. J. van Bavel, 'De la Raison à la Foi: La Conversion d'Augustin', *Augustiniana*, 36 (1986): 5–27; L. C. Ferrari, *The Conversions of Saint Augustine* (Villanova: Villanova University Press, 1984); 'Truth and Augustine's conversion scene', *Collectanea Augustiniana* (New York: Peter Lang, 1990), 9–19; C. Starnes, *Augustine's Conversion: A Guide to the Argument of the 'Confessions' 1-9* (Waterloo, Ont.: 1990); G. Bonner, 'Augustine's "conversion": historical fact or literary device?', *Augustinus*, 37 (1993): 103–19; R. Guardini, *The Conversion of Saint Augustine* (Chicago: 1960); L. Daly, 'Psychohistory and St. Augustine's conversion process', *Augustiniana*, 28 (1978): 231–54; J. M. Le Blond, *Les conversions de saint Augustin* (Paris: 1950); P. Muñoz, 'Psicologia de la conversión en san Agustín', *Gregorianum*, 22 (1941): 324–52; Robert J. O'Connell, *Images of Conversion in St. Augustine's Confessions* (Bronx, New York: Fordham University Press, 1996); W. J. Sparrow Simpson, D. D., *St. Augustine's Conversion: An Outline to the time of his Ordination* (New York: The Macmillan Co., 1930); Arthur Little, 'The conversion of Saint Augustine', *The Irish Monthly* 74, no. 872 (1946): 59–67; James Wetzel, 'Life in unlikeness: the materiality of Augustine's conversion', *The Journal of Religion* 91, no. 1 (2011): 43–63.
112 Joseph McCabe, 'The conversion of St. Augustine', *International Journal of Ethics* 12, no. 4 (1902): 450–1.
113 See, for instance, Lawrence Rothfield's response to this situation in his article, 'Autobiography and Perspective in the Confessions of St. Augustine', *Comparative Literature* 33, no. 3 (1981): 209–23.
114 Isaac Babel, 'In the basement,' in *Collected Stories*, trans. Walter Morison (Harmondsworth: Penguin, 1961), 266.
115 Eugene TeSelle, 'Augustine as client and as theorist', *Journal for the Scientific Study of Religion* 25, no. 1 (1986): 100.
116 Plotinus, *Enneads*, trans Stephen MacKenna and B. S. Page, I, 2, 7.
117 *Serm.*, LXXVIII, 3.
118 *Ibid.*, LXXVIII, 3.
119 Emile Durkheim, *The Divisions of Labor in Society*, trans. G. Simpson (New York: The Free Press, 1964), 3.
120 See Plato, *Theaetetus*, 160e–165e.
121 *Serm.*, LXXVIII, 5.

122 *Confess.*, VIII, 8, 19.
123 *En. in Ps.*, XCIII, 9.
124 *Serm.*, LXII, 18.
125 *Confess.*, VIII, 11, 25.
126 *In Io. ev. tr.*, VIII, 1.
127 Ludwig Wittgenstein, *Tractatus Logico-Philosophicus*, trans. D. F. Pears and B. F. McGuinness (London: Routledge & Kegan Paul, Ltd., 1974), 3.031, p. 11.
128 *Confess.*, VIII, 11, 26-27.
129 *Ibid.*, IX, 1, 1.
130 *En. in Ps.*, LXX (II), 3.
131 *De gr. et l. arb.*, XLII, 21.
132 Lois MacNeice, *The Dark Tower* (London and Boston, Faber & Faber, 1979), 40.
133 *Solil.*, II, 15. Cf. *De Trin.*, XV, 10, 17: 'For no one knows what is false, except when he knows it to be false; and if he knows this, then he knows what is true: for it is true that that is false.'

Chapter 10

1 Agostino Trapè, *Agostino: l'uomo, il pastore, il mistico* (Roma: Città Nuova Editrice, 2001), 128.
2 *En. in Ps.*, LXX, 17.
3 *Confess.*, IX, 2, 4.
4 *Ibid.*, VIII, 12, 30.
5 *De doctr. Christ.*, IV, 3, 4.
6 *Confess.*, IX, 5, 13.
7 *Ibid.*, IX, 2, 4.
8 *Ep.*, IV, 2.
9 *Confess.*, IX, 2, 2.
10 *Retract.*, Prologus, 2.
11 Cf. *In Io. ev. tr.*, XIX, 1: 'And if now at length idols have been cast down from their own temples, how much more ought they to be cast down from Christian minds!'
12 See p. 152 above.
13 *In Io. ev. tr.*, XX, 10.
14 *En. in Ps.*, LXXV, 11.
15 *De civ. Dei*, XXII, 24.
16 *In Io. Ev. tr.*, LXVI, 2.
17 Gerald Bonner, *Freedom and Necessity: St. Augustine's Teaching on Divine Power and Human Freedom* (Washington, DC: Catholic University of America Press, 2007), 15.
18 *Confess.*, IX, 10, 25.
19 *Ibid.*, X, 1, 1.
20 *En. in Ps.*, CXXXVI, 4.
21 Howard Nemerov, from the poem, 'Sigmund Freud', in *Poetry* 62, no. 5 (1943): 261.
22 *En. in Ps.*, LIX, 1.

23 Dylan Thomas, from his poem 'A refusal to mourn the death, by fire, of a child in London'.
24 *Confess.*, IX, 10, 25.
25 *Coll. Cum Maxim.*, XV, 14.
26 *De civ. Dei*, XVI, 2.
27 Jean-Paul Sartre, 'What is literature?', in *"What is Literature?" And Other Essays*, trans. Bernard Frechtman (Cambridge, MA: Harvard University Press, 1988), 261.
28 *Retract.*, Prologus, 1.
29 See *ibid.*, I, 6, 9. The work is *De mor. Eccl. cath.*, II, 17, 63; the Pliny reference can be found at *Naturalis Historiae*, XI, 28, 34.
30 See *Retract.*, II, 41, 3.
31 *Serm.*, CXLI, 3.
32 *En. in Ps.*, CXV, 5.
33 *Confess.*, III, 11, 19.
34 *Ibid.*, XIII, 17, 20.
35 *Ibid.*, X, 32, 48.
36 *Ibid.*, XIII, 15, 18.
37 *Ibid.*, X, 32, 48.
38 *Ibid.*, XIII, 14, 15.
39 *Ibid.*, XIII, 2, 3.
40 Victor Serge, *Memoirs of a Revolutionary, 1901–1941*, trans. Peter Sedgwick (London and New York: Oxford University Press, 1967), 265.
41 The other notable investigations are in his philosophical dialogue *De ordine* and periodically throughout his *Enarrationes in Psalmos*.
42 *Confess.*, X, 33, 49.
43 Edward E. Lowinsky, 'Epilogue: the music in "St. Jerome's Study"', *The Art Bulletin* 41, no. 4 (1959): 301.
44 See p. 125 above.
45 *De mus.*, VI, 1, 1.
46 *En. in Ps.*, CXXXVI, 21.
47 *De mus.*, VI, 1, 1.
48 *Confess.*, X, 33, 49.
49 *Ibid.*, X, 35, 54–5.
50 *Ibid.*, X, 35, 55.
51 *Ep.*, CLXVI, 13.
52 *De Gen. ad litt.*, VI, 15, 26.
53 George MacDonald, *Phantastes: A Faerie Romance for Men and Women* (London: Paternoster Press, 2008), 175.
54 *In Io. ev. tr.*, II, 13.
55 *Confess.*, XIII, 34, 49.
56 *Ibid.*, XIII, 33, 48.
57 See *De civ. Dei*, XVII, 14: 'For the rational and well-ordered concord of diverse sounds in harmonious variety suggests the compact unity of the well-ordered city.'
58 Ingrid Jonker, from her poem, 'Ontvlugting'.

59 *In Io. ev. tr.*, XIV, 1.
60 *De Trin.*, XV, 6, 10.
61 *In Io. ev. tr.*, XL, 4.
62 *Ibid.*, XXI, 4.
63 C. Day Lewis, 'The eternal spirit's eternal pastime', in *The Poetic Image* (London: Jonathan Cape, 1947), 142.
64 *De civ. Dei*, XIV, 11.
65 *Ep.*, XXVI, 6.
66 *De lib. arb.*, III, 76.
67 See *De nat. boni*, III: 'We Catholics worship God, the principle of all good, great or little. The principle of all beauty, great or little. The principle of all order, great or little. The more measure, beauty and order shine out in created things, the more we say they are good. The less the shining out of measure, beauty and order, the less we say they are good. Measure, beauty and order are the three general goods that we find in all created things, whether spiritual or material.'
68 Johann Wolfgang von Goethe, *Faust: Eine Tragödie*, kapitel VI.
69 *Confess.*, X, 34, 51.
70 *De mor. Eccl. cath.*, XX, 37.
71 Thomas Dekker, *The Honest Whore*, Pt. 2, Act. 1, Sc. 2.
72 *Confess.*, XIII, 38, 53.
73 Heraclitus, fragment 242, in G. S. Kirk and J. E. Raven (eds), *The Presocratic Philosophers* (Cambridge: Cambridge University Press, 1962), 210.
74 William Somerset Maugham, 'A casual affair', in Anthony Burgess (ed.), *Maugham's Malaysian Stories* (Hong Kong, Singapore and Kuala Lumpar: Heinemann Asia, 1978), 185. Cf. *Confess.*, X, 34, 52: 'But that corporeal light of which I spoke seasons for its blind lovers this world's life with an alluring and perilous sweetness.'
75 *Confess.*, XIII, 33, 48.
76 See *Ep.*, XXVI, 6: 'Now, if you found in the earth a golden chalice, you would give it to the Church of God without quibble. But you have received from God talents that are spiritually as valuable as gold; and these you devote to the service of your lusts, and surrender yourself to Satan. Do it not, I entreat you.'
77 *Confess.*, XII, 26, 36.
78 *Retract.*, I, 12, 3.
79 See *De pecc. mer. et rem.*, I, 18, 23; *De gr. et l. arb.*, XXII, 44; *Serm.*, CCXCIII, 10.
80 It was in dealing with heresies that he would remember this most – and especially in dealing with the Donatists, whose terrorism and violence encouraged the return of coercion and all the questions of Christian conduct that that brought. See *Ep.*, LXXXIX, 6: 'What remedies, then, must the Church apply when seeking with a mother's anxiety the salvation of them all; and distracted by the frenzy of some and the lethargy of others? Is it right, is it possible, for her to despise or give up any means which may promote their recovery? She must necessarily be esteemed burdensome by both, but only because she is the enemy of neither. For men in frenzy do not like to be bound, and men in lethargy do not like to be stirred up. Nevertheless, the diligence of charity perseveres in restraining the one and stimulating the other – and out of love to both. Both are provoked, but

both are loved; both, while they continue under their infirmity, resent the treatment as vexatious; but both will express their thankfulness for it when they are cured.'
81 *In Io. ev. tr.*, LX, 3.
82 *En. in Ps.*, CXXXVI, 17.
83 George Steiner, *Real Presences: Is there anything in what we say?* (London and Boston: Faber & Faber, 1990), 230–1.
84 *De Trin.*, XII, 14, 23.
85 See *ibid.*: 'When a discourse relates to these things, I hold it to be a discourse belonging to knowledge, and to be distinguished from a discourse belonging to wisdom [cf. 1 Cor. 12.8], to which those things only belong, which neither have been, nor shall be, but *are* – and on account of that eternity in which they *are*, are said in addition to have been, and to be, and to be about to be, without any changeableness of times. For neither have they been in such a way that they should cease to be, nor are they about to be in such way as if they were not now; but they have always had, and always will have, that very absolute being. And they abide, but not as if fixed in some place as are bodies, but as intelligible things in incorporeal nature. In other words, they are at hand to the glance of the mind as things visible or tangible in place are said to be so to the sense of the body.'
86 *De serm. Dom. in m.*, I, 3, 10.
87 In his *Retract.*, I, 9, 6 Augustine bears out what we have been doing by treating the heresies of his day as 'nascent' – as branching out from a single 'unconscionable' theme of Christianity. As combated by aiming at this same torso each time. This is the mystery of why the free will should ennoble us philosophically but then also relegate us psychologically: 'Observe how long before the Pelagian heresy had come into existence we spoke as though we were already speaking against them … Then, the question was taken up in this form: "From what misery, justly imposed on sinners, is man freed by the Grace of God because man could fall by his own will, that is, by free choice, but could not also rise?" [He is referring to his early work *De libero arbitrio* (387); see especially, II, 19, 50 & II, 20, 54]'
88 *Retract.*, Prologus, 2.
89 Possidius, *Vita Sancta Augustini*, XXXI, 9.
90 *Ep.*, XLIII, 1, 2.
91 *In Io. ev. tr.*, XL, 5.
92 See *Confess.*, XII, 26, 36: 'I cannot believe that to Moses, Your most faithful servant, You would grant a lesser gift than the one I would will and desire from You for myself, had I been born in the same time as he, and had You established me in his office, so that by ministry of my heart and tongue there might be produced those books of Yours which for so long after were to profit all nations.'
93 *Ibid.*, XII, 25, 35.
94 *De civ. Dei*, XXII, 17.
95 *In Io. ev. tr.*, X, 7.
96 *Ep. Io.*, III, 13.
97 *Ep.*, CLXVI, 13.
98 *Contra litt. Petil.*, III, 2, 3.
99 Ned Rorem, *Edition Peters Contemporary Music Catalogue, 1975* (New York: C. F. Peters, 1975), v.

100 *Confess.*, XII, 31, 42. Cf. The opening lines to his first, unfinished, attempt at literally interpreting Genesis, *De Gen. ad litt. l. imp.*, I, 1: 'With regard to the obscurities of natural things which we know were made by the omnipotent God, the Creator, we should make an investigation, not by affirming, but by inquiring.'
101 *En. in Ps.*, CXXVIII, 1.
102 William Stafford, 'Augustine', *Poetry* 91, no. 4 (1958): 251.
103 *En. in Ps.*, L, 8.
104 Riccardo Bacchelli, *Saggi critici* (Milano: Mondadori, 1962), 196. Cf. how Augustine makes the same suggestion at *En. in Ps.*, XLIX, 5: 'Hidden then was the God of gods, both when He walked among men, and when He hungered, and when He thirsted, and when fatigued He sat, and when with wearied body He slept, and when taken, and when scourged, and when standing before the judge …'
105 See *De Trin.*, XII, 11, 16: 'For when he neglects the love of wisdom, which remains always after the same fashion, and lusts after knowledge by experiment upon things temporal and mutable, that knowledge puffs up, it does not edify [see 1 Cor. 8.1].'
106 *Confess.*, XIII, 24, 37.
107 *In Io. Ev. tr.*, XXXII, 3.
108 *De civ. Dei*, XXII, 29.
109 See *Confess.*, III, 6, 11.
110 For a full introduction to, and treatment of, it in light of both these possibilities see James Wetzel, 'Augustinian anthropology: Interior intimo meo', *The Journal of Religious Ethics* 27, no. 2 (1999): 195–221. Also Lieven Boeve, Mathijs Lamberigts and Maarten Wisse (eds), *Augustine and Postmodern Thought: A New Alliance against Modernity?* (Leuven: Peeters, 2009).
111 See *Retract.*, VII, 3: '… for I am responsible to myself more than to all other men, although to God more than to myself.'
112 Ambrose, *De virg.*, I, 1.
113 *En. in Ps.*, CXXX, 4.
114 *Ibid.*, LXXX, 1, 1.
115 *Confess.*, IX, 7, 16.
116 This is an adaptation on the sense of an original quotation from Virgil's *Aeneid* – by Michel de Montaigne. The original can be found at *Aeneid*, IX, 349 as *Purpuream vomit ille animam et cum sanguine mixta/Vina refert moriens*. Montaigne's adaption at *Essays*, II, 12 – coming out as *Sanguineam vomit ille animam*.
117 *Confess.*, X, 33, 50.
118 Friedrich Nietzsche, *Human, All Too Human: A Book for Free Spirits*, trans. R. J. Hollingdale (Cambridge: Cambridge University Press, 1996), 345.
119 *Solil.*, I, 29.
120 *Ibid.*, I, 2.
121 *En. in Ps.*, CXXXIV, 22.
122 *Ibid.*, XLIV, 24.
123 *Retract.*, X, 2.
124 See *In Io. Ev. tr.*, CI, 6.
125 See *Ep.*, III, 1: 'I read your letter beside my lamp after supper: immediately after which I

lay down, but not at once to sleep; for on my bed I meditated long, and talked there with myself – Augustine addressing and answering Augustine.'

126 *Ep.*, III, 3.
127 *De quant. an.*, XXXI, 63. The full example of the centipede being cut occurs across XXXI, 62–3. The incident happened at Cassiciacum. Two of Augustine's young cousins had segmented the animal, and then presented to him and Alypius the philosophical challenge of its parts – each now moving independently in different directions. Can the immaterial soul of the Platonists and Christians be cut with a knife like butter?
128 As this example much later at *De civ. Dei*, II, 19, of truths 'which strike the ear, not with the uncertain sound [*concertationibus strepere*] of a philosophical discussion, but with the thunder of God's own oracle pealing from the clouds.'
129 *Ep.*, III, 2.
130 *In Io. Ev. tr.*, CI, 6.
131 He explains what was his envisaged schedule of this work at *Retract.*, I, 6, 6.
132 See, for instance, G. W. F. Hegel, *Early Theological Writings*, trans. T. M. Knox (Chicago: University of Chicago Press, 1948), 310: 'The concept of individuality includes opposition to infinite manifoldness and juncture with it; a man is an individual life, inasmuch as he is distinct from all elements, and from the infinity of individual lives external to him, but he is only an individual life inasmuch as he is one with all elements, with all the infinity of lives external to him; *he* is only inasmuch as the totality of life is divided, he being one part and everything else the other part; he *is* only inasmuch as he is no part, and nothing is sundered from him.'
133 John Buchan, *Greenmantle* (Harmondsworth: Penguin, 1956), p. 168.
134 *Retract.*, I, 5, 2.
135 *En. in Ps.*, LXXXIV, 9.
136 *Solil.*, I, 17.
137 *Confess.*, IX, 10, 26.
138 *Ibid.*, IX, 6, 14.
139 *Ibid.*, VIII, 6, 15.
140 *Serm.*, CCCLV, 2.
141 *Confess.*, IX, 10, 25.
142 See W. G. Lambert, *Babylonian Wisdom Literature* (Oxford: The Clarendon Press, 1960), 40 f., 43.
143 *Ep.*, XXI, 2.
144 Though it has been challenged by Michael Slusser. In a scholarly note he has drawn attention to the fact that Cyril of Jerusalem, in his *Procatechesis*, 14, issues an instruction that women should read silently over devotional material while awaiting their prebaptismal exorcisms. This puts a dating of around 350 to the expectation in the Greek-speaking world that people should at least be able to read in this way. See Michael Slusser, 'Reading silently in antiquity', *Journal of Biblical Literature* 111, no. 3 (1992): 499.
145 *Confess.*, VI, 3, 3.
146 See, for instance, how Socrates mocks himself at *Phaedo*, 102: 'He added, laughing, I am speaking like a book, but I believe that what I am saying is true.'
147 See Plato, *Republic*, VII, 532*b*.

148 Empedocles, Fragment 458, in Kirk and Raven (eds), *The Presocratic Philosophers*, p. 344.
149 *De Cat. rud.*, XIV.
150 *In Io. Ev. tr.*, XXVI, 2.
151 *En. in Ps.*, XCVIII, 3.
152 *Serm.*, C, 1.
153 *Ep. Io.*, IV, 6.

Chapter 11

1 See how Augustine puts this at *De civ. Dei*, IX, 5: 'In our ethics, we do not so much inquire *whether* a pious soul is angry, as *why* he is angry; not whether he is sad, but what is the cause of his sadness; not whether he fears, but what he fears.'
2 *Ep. Io.*, IV, 12.
3 Hannah Arendt, *Between Past and Future* (New York: Penguin Books, 1961), 223.
4 See *Serm.*, LXVII, 8: 'Acknowledge that you are not to yourself a light. At best you are but an eye, you are not the light. And what good is even an open and a sound eye, if the light is absent?'
5 *In Io. ev. tr.*, XXXVII, 8.
6 *Confess.*, XIII, 29, 44.
7 Frederick Sontag, 'Augustine's metaphysics and free will', *The Harvard Theological Review* 60, no. 3 (1967): 301.
8 See how Augustine explains this at *De civ. Dei*, XXII, 14, levering on the philosophical understanding of principal ideas: 'All the members of the body are potentially in the seed, though, even after the child is born, some of them – the teeth for example – may be wanting. In this seminal principle of every substance, there seems to be, as it were, the beginning of everything which does not yet exist; or rather does not appear to exist; but which in the process of time will come into being, or rather into sight. In this, therefore, the child who is to be tall or short is already tall or short.'
9 *Confess.*, IV, 3, 6.
10 *Serm.*, CIX, 1. The image of the glass vessel suited Augustine. He would use it again at *De civ. Dei*, IV, 3 to depict, this time, the tense vigilance of the man made happy by *libido dominandi*: 'Their joy may be compared to glass in its fragile splendour, of which one is horribly afraid lest it should be suddenly broken in pieces.'
11 See Gary Wills, *Augustine's "Confessions": A Biography (Lives of Great Religious Books)* (Princeton and Oxford: Princeton University Press, 2011).
12 Fyodor Dostoyevsky, *Crime and Punishment*, trans. David McDuff (Harmondsworth, Penguin, 1997), 434.
13 *Serm.*, CI, 9.
14 *Solil.*, I, 4.
15 *In Io. Ev. tr.*, LXVIII, 1.
16 A reminder of those instincts at *De civ. Dei*, XXII, 22: 'O the punishments of childhood: without which there would be no learning of what the parents wish: and the parents, who rarely wish anything useful to be taught …'

17 *En. in Ps.* LXXXIV, 11.
18 *In Io. Ev. tr.*, XXXII, 1.
19 *Ibid.*, XXI, 17.
20 *Ibid.*, II, 14.
21 *Serm.*, CCCXLIV, 4.
22 *De serm. Dom. in m.*, XV, 42.
23 *En. in Ps.*, CXLIX, 1.
24 *De civ. Dei*, XXII, 29.
25 *Ibid.*, XXII, 2.
26 *De cont.*, III, 8.
27 *Serm.*, CXXVIII, 11.
28 Oliver O'Donovan, *The Desire of the Nations: Rediscovering the Roots of Political Theology* (Cambridge: Cambridge University Press, 1999), 288.
29 *De Gen. ad litt.*, VII, 18, 24. Now cf. how A. A. Grib brings this logic up to the theoretical language of modern science: 'We can observe the quantum universe only by "moving in time" since we cannot measure two non-commuting (complementary) observables at one and the same moment. One must "move" in time in order to observe at this moment this complementary observable and at another moment that one. This is connected with the difference in the logical structure of human consciousness which is Boolean (distributive) and the non-Boolean, non-distributive structure of the quantum Universe. So "movement in time" and the irreversibility of time arising from quantum measurements are purely human in their origin.' (A. A. Grib, 'Time and eternity', *Studies in Science and Theology* 1 (1993): 108.
30 *Serm.*, CXVII, 5.
31 *En. in Ps.*, XCIX, 6.
32 *De civ. Dei*, XVIII, 43.
33 *Confess.*, XI, 2, 3.
34 *Ibid.*, XII, 1, 1.
35 *En. in Ps.*, LXXV, 1.
36 See, for example, how differently he treated the memory of his lover during the nights of Cassiciacum: 'Remember, for example, how securely yesterday we had pronounced that we were no longer detained by any evil thing, and loved nothing except Wisdom; and sought or wished other things only for her sake? To you how low, how foul, how execrable those female embraces seemed when we discoursed concerning the desire of a wife! Yet just now, in the watches of this very night, when we had again been discoursing together of the same things, you were tickled by the thoughts of them and unable to hold your determination of overcoming them – far, far less, we admit, than you were wont, but also far otherwise than you had thought possible' (*Solil.*, I, 25).
37 *En. in Ps.*, LXXII, 13.
38 Possidius, *Vita*, XXXI, 1–3.
39 *Serm.*, CCCVI/E.
40 *Confess.*, XIII, 14, 15.
41 *C. Ep. Man.*, XLIII, 49.

42 *Ibid.*, XLI, 47.
43 *Serm.*, CXVIII, 2.
44 *In Io. Ev. tr.*, XXII, 10.
45 *De civ. Dei*, XI, 29.
46 *Confess.*, VIII, 1, 2.
47 *Ep. Io.*, II, 10.
48 *In Io. Ev. tr.*, II, 16.

Index

Adeodatus xv–xviii, 58, 145, 163, 206, 232, 235–6
   death of xviii
Adler, Alfred 138–9
aesthetic experience 174
Ajax 194
Alcmaeon 154
Alypius xvii–xviii, 190–1, 194, 206, 232
Ambrose, Bishop of Milan xvi–xvii, 108, 177, 179, 184–8, 205–6, 228, 232, 238
anamnesis 15, 36
Anaximander 20
Anthony of Egypt, St 236
anti-intellectualism 82–4
apeiron 20
Apuleius 52, 89, 111
Aquinas, St Thomas 10
Arendt, Hannah 241
Arianism xix
Aristotle 9–10, 18, 33
   Categories xv
   Poetics 138
   Protrepticus 121
'artificial intelligence' 34–5
The Athenaeum, Rome 106
atonement 128
Auden, W.H. 162
Augustine
   African heritage 52, 210
   birth xv
   and Christian morality 94–7, 110, 156
   contemporary influence and continuing legacy 1–6, 34, 107
   conversion to Christianity xvi–xviii, 14, 108, 122–5, 193–8, 204–5, 232
   death xix, 252
   education xv, 52–3, 88–90, 98–9, 105–8, 112, 115
   and love 108–11, 144–5, 149
   as a Manichee 21, 146, 198
   as a member of the Church xviii, 137, 190, 234–9
   parentage *see* Monica; Patricius
   personality 110, 190, 194
   pragmatism 98
   precocity 223, 226, 242
   as Professor of Rhetoric at Milan xvi–xvii, 52, 105–6, 176–7, 184, 191, 194–5, 206
   return to Carthage 148, 174
   return to Thagaste 142–3, 148
   son *see* Adeodatus
   stay in Cassiciacum 231–3
   teaching in Rome 175–6
   teenage years and thinking on the psychology of adolescence 94, 113
   theological positions xix, 6, 9, 54
   thinking on marriage and virginity 154
   use of polemics and political language 97, 99
   Works:
      autobiography 53–4, 86, 93, 97, 110, 197
      De beata vita xviii, 232
      De civitate Dei xix, 5, 12, 55, 62, 110
      Confessiones xix, 5, 45–7, 51, 58, 63, 66, 70, 90, 97, 135–6, 143, 148, 156, 190, 229, 232, 234, 238, 243
      Contra Acadamicos xviii, 106, 232

Contra epistulam Manichaei vocant fundamenti 130
Enarrationes in Psalmos xix
De Genesi ad litteram xix, 216
De grammatica xviii
De immortalitate animae xviii
In Iohannis Evangelium Tractatus xix
De libero arbitrio xviii, 78
De magistro 235–6
De musica xviii, 213–14, 231
De ordine xviii, 232
De praedestinatione 93–4
De pulchro et apto xvi
De quantitate animae xviii
Retractiones 211, 230–1
Soliloquiorum xviii, 62, 232
De Trinitate xix, 63, 117
De utilitate credenti 133–4
Augustinianism 7, 14, 179, 207–8, 219, 222–5, 247

Babel, Isaac 198
babies 198; *see also* infancy
Bacchelli, Riccardo 226–7
Bahram I, King 128
Bambrough, Renford 182–3
Barker, Ernest 28
beauty, theory of 181–2
Beethoven, Ludwig van 229–30
belief 133–4; *see also* religious belief
Boniface VIII, Pope 187
Bonner, Gerald 127, 207–10, 223
Brown, Peter 5–6, 56, 107, 127, 233
Buddha 129
Burgess, Anthony 188
Burke, Edmund 192
Burnett, John 11

Calvinism 29
Campbell Sharp, John 180
Carpaccio, Vittore 213–14
Carthage 105–14
Cassiago di Brianza 232
Cassian, John 93–4

Cassiciacum xvii, 231–2
Cassiodorus 125
Cassirer, Ernst 117–18
Catholic Church 169
Chesterton, G.K. 21
Christian reform 248–9
Christianity 5–6, 12–15, 29–30, 33–9, 42, 54, 58–60, 67, 79, 82, 96, 114–15, 118, 126, 128–9, 134–5, 156–7, 171, 197–9, 221, 241, 251
Christology 25, 191
Cicero 65, 124–5, 194, 222, 235
    Hortensius xv, 53, 121, 125, 136
    De officiis 125, 214
    De re publica 55
Clare, John 105
Cleanthes 32
Collingwood, R.G. 174
Confession 44, 225
Constantine, Emperor 12–13, 39
corporal punishment 90–1
cosmopolitanism 31
creation, intrinsic goodness of 35
creativity, human 77–8
Cullmann, Oscar 39
Cyprian 2, 52

Dante Alighieri 10, 37
Day Lewis, Cecil 218
death, thinking on 143–4, 147, 186
Decurions 50
Dekker, Thomas 220
Democritus 123–4
Dittes, James E. 51
Dodd, C.H. 191
Donatism xix, 41, 60–1, 225
Dostoyevsky, Fyodor 121, 243
Drummond, Henry 32–3
Dryden, John 142
Dunne, John William 134
Durkheim, Emile 200

Elchasaites 129
Empedocles 155, 238

Enlightenment thinking 3
The Enyclopédie 138
Epicureanism 31
eschatology 179–80
eternal law 94–5
eternity, concept of 67–9, 126, 140
ethics 22, 24; *see also* morality
eugenics 27, 163
Eusebius 13, 39
Everett, John R. 197
eversores 115–16, 174–5
evil 116–17, 128

faith, definitions of 122
Fanon, Frantz 1, 184
fatherhood 158
Faustus of Milevis xvi, 52, 108, 176–7
fear as the work ethic of history 100
fictional works 6
Fitzgerald, F. Scott 92
Flotte, Peter 187
Fogazzaro, Antonio 227
Foucault, Michel 166
free will 58, 96–9
freedom, concepts of 7–8, 24, 36, 100, 118, 215
Freud, Sigmund 59, 103, 138–9
Fromm, Erich 116, 118
future projections of present reasoning 71–2

Gaarder, Jostein 146
genius-insight 206
Glover, T.R. 32
Gnosticism 21, 131–3
God
 belief in 4
 righteous anger against 185
 understanding of and love for 7–8, 14, 199
God's creation 35, 40, 66–7
God's looking-on 178–9
God's omnipotence 199
God's omniscience 84
God's revealing of Himself 199
God's silence or death 93–4, 121

God's Will 193
Goethe, J.W. von 219–20
Gogol, Nikolai Vasilevich 184–5
good works 244
Grace, doctrine of 93, 101, 241
Graves, Robert 56
'Great Comfort' 123
Greek thought 12, 15, 17, 22, 28, 39
grief 147

Hadrian, Emperor 106
harmony of parts 17
Havel, Václav 159
Hawkins, Peter S. 10
Hegel, G.W.F. 14, 233
Hellenism 29
Heracleitus 17, 221
Herder, Johann Gottfried 56
Hippo Regius 252
historicism 14
Hobbes, Thomas 155–6
Hodgson, W.N. 171
Holy Trinity 216–17
Housman, A.E. 115
human nature 82, 188
Hume, David 18, 127
Husserl, Edmund 126
Huxley, Aldous 179–80
Huxley, Julian 18

idealist thinking 75, 108
imagined knowledge 117
impassability 67
induction, problem of 18
infancy 58–9, 62–6, 72–6, 80–3
innocence 58–9, 62–3, 80–1, 112, 116–17
'intellectual conscience' 161
Isaiah, Book of 205

James, William 70
Jesus Christ 12, 55, 129, 133, 191–3, 201, 248, 254
 supernatural nature of 171–2
Jonker, Ingrid 217

Jowett, Benjamin 9
Joyce, James 180
Julian of Eclanum 52
Julian of Norwich 193–4
Juvenal 56, 98

Kant, Immanuel 174
Karter 128
Kirwan, Christopher 81–2
kudos 246–9

Lactantius 2
language
  human acquisition of 75, 81
  philosophical veneration of 219
  theories of 75–7, 81–2
  see also Latin language; Punic language
Laplace, Pierre Simon 3–4
Latin culture 52, 56
Latin language, use of 56
Lawrence, D.H. 152
Lecky, W.E.H. 24
Leibniz, Gottfried 187
Lérins, Vincent 93–4
Lewis, C.S. 14, 34, 101
love
  nature of 111
  see also self-love; sexual desire
Lowinsky, Edward 214
Lucretius 17
lust 86, 166, 198, 200
Luther, Martin 112

MacDonald, George 216
Machiavellian thinking 102
MacKowsky, Hans 165
MacNeice, Louis 203
Madauros xv, 89
Mani 132–8
  Letter of the Foundation 130–1, 133
Manichaeism xv–xix, 21, 35, 108, 127–34, 137–40, 143–4, 175–6, 212
  five commandments of 139
  'Hearers' in 139

Manlius Victorinus xvi, 178
Marcus Aurelius, Emperor 33
Markus, R.A. 40
marriage 195–6
Marx, Karl 14, 138–9
materialism 186, 200
Matthew's Gospel 194
Maugham, William Somerset 221
Maximianus 97
Maximinian of Madaura 52
Maximus of Madauros 56
McCabe, Joseph 197
McTaggart, John 121 metaphysics 120
Michelangelo 164–5
Milan, Edict of (313) 12
Mill, John Stuart 236
modernity 228
Monica xv–xviii, 46–7, 50–1, 94, 99, 142–5, 175–6, 189–98, 204–5, 232, 235
  Augustine's deceiving of 175
  death of xviii
Montaigne, Michel de 46
morality 22, 174; see also ethics
More, Thomas 16
Morgan, Charles 3
multiculturalism 3
Murray, Gilbert 29
music and musicality 213–16, 225, 229

Nabokov, Vladimir 58
nationalism 41
natural order 28
Navigius 143
Nebridius 190–1, 233
Nemerov, Howard 208
Neoplatonism 25, 66–7, 111, 178, 192
Nietzsche, Friedrich 14–15, 161–2, 229–30
Numenius 15

Oakeshott, Michael 157–8
O'Donovan, Oliver 249
original sin 121, 187
Oxford Guide to the Historical Reception of Augustine 82

Pascal, Blaise 141
Patricius xv, 46–7, 50–1, 55–6, 85, 87, 90, 99, 105–6, 113, 195
  death of 142
patronage 107
Paul, St 27–8, 31–2, 98–9, 126, 191, 238
'pear tree' story 97
Pelagianism xix, 59, 188; *see also* semi-Pelagians
Peter, St 135
Petilian, Bishop 114
phenomenology 126
Philip the Fair 187
Philo 32
philosophy, history of 120
Plato 14–17, 22–7, 35, 82, 103, 135, 230, 238
  Euthyphro 23
  The Laws 25
  The Republic 22, 26–7
Platonism 9, 14–15, 25–6, 66–7, 178. 199, 245; *see also* Neoplatonism
Pliny 211
Plotinus 27, 172, 178, 192, 199
pluralism 11–12, 102
Pollmann, Karla 82
Polybius 12
Ponticianus xvii, 52, 236
Popper, Karl 101–2, 120, 138–9
Portalié, Eugène 42
possession 217
Possidius 224, 252
post-Aristotelian philosophers 28, 31
postmodernity 228
predestination, doctrine of 14, 41–2, 241–4
pre-Socratic philosophers 17–25
Price, H.H. 168–9
professors, public 106
Prosper of Aquitaine 5
Protagoras 201
Protestant work ethic 29
pseudo-science 138
puberty 85–9
Punic language 56

quantum 225, 249
Quintilian 52–3

rationalism 2, 26, 168
rationality 17, 118, 187, 244, 254
  mortal 249
Rawls, John 169–70
realism 22, 41, 102
relativism 17, 36
religion
  impulse to 134
  in the service of the state 16
religious belief 122–3; *see also* God, belief in
religious conversions 197; *see also* Augustine: conversion to Christianity
Remembering Race image 243–4, 248
rhetoricians 106
Roberts, Richard 79–80
Roman Empire 11–12, 16, 28, 30, 39, 128–9
Romanianus xv, 106–8, 126, 143, 187, 194
Rorem, Ned 225
Rousseau, Jean-Jacques 195
Russell, Bertrand 15–16, 66, 69, 161
Russell, George William 85
Ryan, John K. 52
Ryle, Gilbert 184

'sacred history' (Markus) 40
salvation history 39, 246–9
Santayana, George 165, 204
Sartre, Jean-Paul 210
Schleiermacher, Friedrich 8
self-consciousness 253–4
self-love 37, 254
semi-Pelagians 93
Seneca 35
Serge, Victor 212–13
sexual desire 86, 111, 150–1, 154–5, 163–8, 184, 198, 200
Shapur I, King 128
Simplicius 20
sin 180, 199; *see also* original sin
sleep and sleepfulness 103
Socrates 6, 17, 22–4, 101, 238, 241

Solzhenitsyn, Alexander 61
Sontag, Frederick 242
Sophists 17
soul, human 165–7, 187, 193–4, 200
Spinoza, B. 193
Staël, Germaine de 2
Stafford, William 226
Stalin, Joseph 212
Stapledon, Olaf 161
Stebbing, L.S. 19
Steiner, George 222
Stoicism 28, 31, 33, 35
Strawson, P.F. 1–2
Studdert Kennedy, G.A. 114
Styron, William 150
subjectivism 20–1
supernatural realm 171–3
Symmachus xvi, 31, 176

Tacitus 99
Tarski, Alfred 21
Tennyson, Alfred 11
Tertullian 2
TeSelle, Eugene 198
Thales of Miletus 17–20
Thomas, Dylan 209
time, theories of 66, 69, 71, 74
Tolstoy, Leo 8–9, 54
Trapè, Agostino 204
Troeltsch, Ernst 26

Trollope, Anthony 196
'two cities' doctrine 7, 9, 41

'unquiet heart' image 6

Valerius, Bishop of Hippo xviii, 237–9
Verecundus xvii, 232
Virgil 4, 10, 58
Virgin birth 177
virginity, consecrated 154
Volusianus 84

Waismann, Friedrich 175
Waugh, Evelyn 7, 112
Wharton, Edith 146
Whitehead, A.N. 16
Wills, Gary 243
wisdom 77–8, 84
    classical pursuit of 124
    different conceptions of 52
Wisdom, Book of 247
Wittgenstein, Ludwig 75–6, 202
Wollstonecraft, Mary 151
woman
    creation of 154
    equality of 151
Woolf, Virginia 197
Wordsworth, William 38

Zoroaster and Zoroastrianism 128–9